Tera, My Journey H

Presented by the Healing Arts Series
by Kathleen Milner

Chapter Outline

Release

Cover Art

Acknowledgements

Introduction

Tera-Mai™

Audio and Video Tapes

Readers' Comments

Release

Kathleen Milner is not a medical specialist capable of diagnosing or prescribing. She works with symptoms and healing energies, and she is a channel of healing energy, which facilitates self-healing. She can neither be responsible for, nor can she guarantee the form the healing may or may not take. Reiki & Other Rays of Touch Healing is not a substitute for conventional medical treatment.

While the Constitution of the United States of America and the Supreme Court's Roe vs. Wade decision guarantees that each individual has the right to choose how to heal and maintain the physical body, individual discernment and discrimination is mandatory in selecting any kind of traditional or alternative therapist or treatment. It is advisable to witness healing demonstrations by those stating that they are channeling healing energy. Furthermore, questioning and observing firsthand the long-term and short-term effects of any kind of treatment is also advisable. Tera-Mai™ is trademarked as a healing system with standardized initiations. Even so, I would advise people to check out anybody, including myself, who is teaching healing. **"If the proof of the pudding lies in the eating, than the Truth of the energy lies in the healing."** Kathryne O'Connell, Killarney, Ireland.

In 1990, a student of one of my students, Beth Sanders, had the Zen monk, whom Takata had initiated, flown to California to experience the Reiki initiations and attend his Reiki Mastership class. He wanted to know if what I had taught Beth Sanders and Beth had taught him were the same as what Takata had taught the Zen monk. He appealed to the monk's consciousness of getting to the Truth, and that fraud should not be a part of Reiki. After the Mastership class, the monk said that it was identical with the following differences: 1) Kathleen's class format was clearer. (I am a former first grade teacher). 2) Takata taught the breathing but it was never emphasized. 3) Takata never allowed questions.

In 1996, I facilitated a healing session for Naomi White Bear (the widow of White Bear of Frank Water's Book of the Hopi). Naomi told me and the women who were watching, that the techniques I was using on her were the same as those used by the Hopi medicine men (these same methods and others are described herein and visually demonstrated on the video, Healing Hands.) Naomi went on to say that the difference was that the medicine men did everything 4 times (once for each of the 4 directions); while I typically repeat processes 3 times (3 being the number of creation). Either system works because both ideas are based upon thought constructs that work. Reiki means energy; specifically, energy that comes from God. Techniques or symbols (there are many healing techniques and symbols) can be tools that are used with healing energy. Healers and healees all have their preferences and the more the healee becomes involved in the healing process, the better the results.

There are two stories that are told about the healing power of Reiki that have helped 'sell' people on the powers of Reiki. One is that after a woman lost the tip of her finger, the severed tip was wrapped and she was taken to a hospital. On the way to the hospital Reiki was administered and by the time the woman reached the hospital, the wound had healed and the surgeon was unable to reattach the tip of her finger. A second story involves an individual who suffered a broken limb, and like the first individual, had Reiki administered while on route to the hospital. By the time they reached the hospital, the bone had knit together, however, since the bone had not been set, the doctor had to re-break the bone. Personally, I do not believe either one of these stories. In the first place, nobody's name is ever mention – neither that of the victim, the healer, witnesses nor medical personnel. Secondly, there is no medical documentation period! Third, the Almighty is Intelligent as well as Loving and so are the angels and other spiritual forces that work with healing energies that emanate from Source. In all of my years of experience in working with people and supervising my students in the classroom, I have always observed that the healing energy from Source runs through my students and myself and that the higher spiritual forces (Holy Spirit) that work through my students and myself make wise choices. When people simply make up stories they lose their credibility and reputation in the end, but before that happens they institute manmade restrictions on how and when healings can happen. For example, the idea that absentee healing cannot be sent to somebody while they are in surgery because they might wake up is ludicrous! The doctors and nurses who have taken my classes and are thus actually channeling healing energy during an operation have NEVER had this experience! The same people who narrowly define healing are often the same individuals who freely alter initiations that they have received. While there are many excellent metaphysical options available, there is also deception, ego, politics and self-delusion. There are three systems of healing and empowerment that were available for price tags of well over $10,000 that are no longer popular because they neither empowered nor healed. Other people have taken initiations because they are free or inexpensive or offered by somebody with an impressive title and later found that the initial "friendly" energy transfer was malevolent and the healings they facilitated decreased in occurrence and impact and then stopped entirely. An author is only an author after his/her work is published, a swimmer is only a swimmer if s/he is willing to get into the water and float, and a healer is only a healer if miracles occur regularly and consistently.

Cover Art

In 1989, I painted a series of five oil-on-canvas paintings of Holy Hill, which is located in the scenic rolling hills of Wisconsin's countryside. The entire experience was incredibly self-healing for me. The monastery in the background, like many other Catholic churches, was built over an energy vortex where Native Americans performed ceremonies. Within the vortex are high-vibrational, healing qualities, which an individual channeling elemental healing rays is able to tune into and use to amplify his/her own natural healing abilities. In one of the chapels off to the side of the altar on the second story can be found a statue of Mary and the Baby Jesus, which sits in the center of the energy vortex. Outside of the chapel and down the corridor hang countless crutches, wheelchairs and canes that were left in grateful thanks by those who had been healed.

Exorcisms are no longer performed by the Roman Catholic Church and healings are no longer performed by the monks in this sacred space, but the healing energy remains. Of the five paintings, this one appeals the most to viewers, who seem to be drawn into the magic and memories that this painting invokes. Spirits of shamans and ancient ones can be seen behind the tree in the foreground to the left. Nature spirits and angels play on the hillside as the sun sets between the steeples of the monastery. The last rays of the sun paint the landscape in hues of gold and orange, the first healing color on Mother Earth.

I almost sold this painting several times to individuals who loved it. When the painting went unpurchased time and time again, I was impressed that perhaps Holy Spirit had another purpose for this piece of art. My writing process has been completely backwards. Before I wrote my first book, I spoke and did workshops at holistic expos. Two companion videos to my first book, Reiki & Other Rays of Touch Healing (first edition October 31, 1994), came out before the book and were reviewed by Body Mind Spirit magazine in August of 1994. I took a class through the University of Wisconsin Extension called "How to Publish Your Book" before I wrote it - needless to say, I was the only one in the class who hadn't yet written one. And before I begin writing, I see a vision of which piece of art Holy Spirit wants me to use for the cover art.

In the first edition, the cover turned out much darker than the original painting and thus, many of the subtler colors were lost. Blue is a difficult color to print. Doug Dickson (Print Source One) has corrected the film so that the cover looks more like the oil painting.

The foreword to this book was written by one of my students. He did such a wonderful job that I chose to put it on the back cover. I believe that the relationship that he describes between Reiki and Buddhism can be applicable to other religions as well.

May you enjoy reading this book as much as I enjoyed writing it.

Acknowledgements

Within this book, I have given credit to my students and others whose knowledge has contributed to the writing of these pages. In addition, I would like to thank all of my students, who have also served as my teachers; my children, Lee and Jennifer Owrey; my parents, Joseph and Marian Milner; and my spirit horse, Abez. I will also be eternally grateful to Lynn Marie Driessen for her proofreading skills; a friend in spirit, Jackie, who helped me edit; and Doug Dickson (Print Source One) for helping me design and put together the cover and color inserts.

In <u>Reiki & Other Rays of Touch Healing</u>, I made a conscious effort to give credit where credit was due. Apparently, I was too conscientious, because in January of 1997, Marcy called to tell me that she would like her name removed from all Reiki teaching materials. She went on to say that the Reiki wars and the high costs of many Reiki initiations appalled her. She said that while the experience we had in the Siddha ashram was magical, she neither smelled Vabute nor did she see Sai Baba, and she now feels that she should not accept responsibility for the Reiki symbols, empowerment or missing initiation procedure. I felt that my first book was written honestly and from my heart using the facts as I understood them to be true at the time, but I did tell her that I would include the above statement in <u>Tera, My Journey Home</u>.

Another interesting occurrence happened in the summer of 1995 when I was in Holland. A Dutch devotee of Sai Baba had just returned from India with the news that Sai Baba had spoken before a large gathering of people and said, "I have meditated upon this matter. It was not me who worked with Kathleen and Marcy, but another higher being." In the past, whenever the astral projection or spirit of the man with an Afro and dressed in orange appeared, I would ask three times, "In the name of my Lord Jesus Christ, you are Sai Baba ! ?" The astral projection or spirit would remain. Immediately after I heard this news, the being in orange appeared in Jane Rijgersberg's living room. I had also been told that "Sai Baba" has been a term of endearment that many Indian sages, gurus and yogis have been called for thousands of years. So, this time I asked, "In Divine Truth, in Divine Truth, in Divine Truth, you are Shri Satya Sai Baba ?! ?" The figure remained, but immediately changed to a thin man with considerably less hair and wearing golden robes.

Why did I believe that the astral projection or spirit who came to me was Sai Baba? Well, in the books written about Sai Baba, he is quoted as saying, "When you see me, it is me!" There were no qualifiers such as, "Except when you see me around Kathleen or her students." In addition, I was not aware of all of the questions that I needed to ask.

There are people who believe that Sai Baba was referring to his own higher self. What I have come to believe is that many higher forces were involved in bringing back the full healing energy to the initiations. That I was involved in a consciousness-raising experience at the time was evidenced to me by the fact that the walls and ceiling of the Siddha ashram, which was a small house in Los Angeles, expanded to cathedral size. It is further evidenced by the healing work that my students and their students are able to do when they have been initiated into and follow the initiation procedure as has been laid down by Holy Spirit.

Tera-Mai™ establishes standards for healing initiations. Personally, I have no problems with the existence of other Reiki systems. If other people are living out their truth, then they should go for it. Like most people, I do have a problem with people who use my name, claim to be doing what I am doing, but change the initiations without telling their students. I was once sued on a business tort because after I exposed someone's fraud, their income went down. Is this the world turned upside down? Needless to say, the individual did not win.

As for the cost of initiations, my prices come from Holy Spirit who expects me to honor myself, my time and the work that I am contributing and furthermore, I believe that this is true for each and every one of us. To enter the Golden Age, we all need to come into balance and resolve and integrate our love with our power. Money is one expression of our personal power. If we give ourselves permission to have support and/or money, we can live decently and do the things that we want to do and need to do in order to be self-realized. Money gives each of us the possibility of expressing our lives creatively, as well as leaving this planet in far better condition than when we came in. Greed is the opposite of poverty and if greed is a sin, then so, too, is poverty. In actuality, greed and poverty are both extreme conditions of an unconscious mind.

Buddha instructed his followers not to 'buy into' everything he told them. Replacing one dogma with yet another dogma keeps us from our own connection to Mother-Father God and the self-empowerment that comes in the living of that reality. Buddha said, question! Meditate on the possibilities! Live it and see what works for you! Ask God for confirmation of the Truth so that you might know it for yourself! This is what I invite you to do with my book, for I realize that there will be passages and concepts that will be a stretch to your consciousness. When you find things herein that do work for you and it feels right to do so, use them in your own healing process.

Introduction

After I wrote <u>Reiki & Other Rays of Touch Healing</u>, a friend of mine offered to proofread it. Charlotte is a former schoolteacher and has a wonderful command of the proper use of the English language. Charlotte did catch things that my eyes did not see; however, I think Charlotte got too caught up in reading my book, and I do take that as a compliment. Over a year ago, I gave the book to a woman from Canada to proofread, but she never got back to me. Finally, Lynn Driessen not only proofread my first book, but the manuscript for <u>Tera, My Journey Home</u> as well.

Before I wrote <u>Reiki & Other Rays of Touch Healing</u>, I was not much of a writer. The gift of writing came to me quite unexpectedly. I had a friend-client whose father had died. As a child, her mother had abused her severely. Perhaps the rest of her family felt guilty for not stopping it, because they treated her miserably. Two of her therapists had called me because they felt that she should not be going to the funeral alone, and neither of them could attend. So, I called my friend-client and asked her if she would like me to go with her, and she accepted my offer. The funeral service followed the wake in the funeral home. When we arrived, we got lost in the building and ended up entering the room through a side door. The casket was immediately in front of us. Her family took one look at her and walked to the other side of the room. Later, when everyone was eating dinner, one of the family members came over and fetched my friend-client's own son and his family, who were sitting next to us, but did not invite her to sit with them.

When an individual makes his/her final transition, s/he leaves gifts behind for those whom s/he has loved. During the funeral, I was aware that my friend-client's father was unable get through the attitudes of his other children; they received nothing from him. When I felt his presence in front of me, it was like fine angel dust was blown over me and I experienced an opening inside my brain. While I had not known him, he was grateful to me for helping his daughter. The next time I sat down to type and each time after that, I noticed my writing was different. People who own all four editions of <u>Reiki & Other Rays of Touch Healing</u> often comment on the change.

With this second edition of <u>Tera, My Journey Home</u> we have tried to correct any remaining glitches. The story of "Stormsfury's Last Son - *The Reality of Good and Evil*", was not completed when I sent my manuscript off to the printer. I apologize for the abrupt ending to the first chapter. Because of the demand for the material within <u>Tera, My Journey Home</u>, I opted to release <u>Tera, My Journey Home</u> as a limited first edition with the first chapter in its semi-finished state. ISBN 1-88690389-1 will not be printed again.

In "Stormsfury's Last Son", I found myself in the midst of people working out their issues in plots that I thought only belonged in the movies. I have changed all of the names of Hilda's horses and the characters with the exception of those who wanted their real names included in my book. Hilda had told me on several occasions that she wanted to write her autobiography so that other women could learn from her mistakes but she felt that she was not up to the task. Once, she looked at me out of the corner of her eye and said, "Perhaps, you will be the one to write my story?" I learned much from Hilda and all of the master teachers in her life; hopefully, you will also.

While I was finishing and expanding "Stormsfury's Last Son", I found myself working on other chapters as well with the result being that this is a much larger book; 120 pages longer to be precise. "Holland and Rembrandt's Daughter - *Reincarnation & the Spiraling Dance of Life*" gives examples of how past life experiences can influence and also heal our current lives. "England and Anne Boleyn - *The Dance Continues*" has been added to this second edition. When I do past life regressions for people I sometimes give them examples from my own experiences. Oftentimes, this gives them the courage to look at and heal their own issues that have been pushed down and buried in a lead box deeply in their subconscious but are still causing problems in their current lifetime.

"Ama Deus - *Shamanic Healing from the Jungles of Central Brazil*" was brought to the United States by the late Alberto Aguas. Ama Deus means, "I love God". I give this system to my students in the beginning Shamanic class that I teach. It is one way for them to use their healing and divination abilities. Ama Deus is in this book because I have found out during my travels that some people have altered these symbols and in doing so, the symbols and Ama Deus no longer work. Other individuals took the symbols found within Ama Deus and turned it into a multi-level healing class costing thousands and thousands of dollars.

For similar reasons, I have chosen to include "Tera-Mai™ Seichem I - *Using Healing Energy Without Outside Aids*" and "Tera-Mai™ Seichem II - *Using All Four Elemental Healing Rays to Energize Symbols*", which are the handouts that I give to my students. If you are a healer, you will be able to use many of these techniques. If you are considering taking a healing class, this will give you an understanding of what you will be able to do after receiving a Universal initiation into a healing energy or healing energies. Initiations come from God and are

Universal by nature. Initiations that are personal (designed by mankind) either do not last the test of time, close the crown chakra (the healer is left giving of him/herself rather than having healing energy from Source flow through him/her), or they set up a negative vibration. This is the reason why many teachers, myself included, urge individuals to do their own investigation. There are some people who are doing initiations first, foremost and exclusively; they never give public healing demonstrations or even do any kind of healing work. If the teacher/initiator is not doing healings on a regular and consistent basis, the likelihood of the initiate doing healings on a regular and consistent basis is nil to none.

"Healing Process - *Ancient Art of Hands-On Healing as It Is Practiced Today*" documents a variety of witnessed accounts of healings as facilitated by some of my students. The chapter, "Symbols - *Abstract Vehicles for Practical Means*", has some symbols that people have given to me which have proven successful. Much research has gone into "Iridology and Herbs - *Healing the Body with Herbs & the Iris as a Diagnostic Tool*". It includes a method for taking herbs that I have found works for me. "Moving Qi – *With Movement, Sound & Visualization*" has also been added to this second edition. In this chapter there are practical metaphysical exercises that have been used for centuries to heal the body and increase psychic abilities.

"Hawaiian Shamanism and the Goddess - *The Other Side of the Veil*" discusses the direct link between the spirituality and metaphysics of Hinduism and that of the indigenous Hawaiians. How ceremonies, healing and magic work and what is accomplished are also discussed. I have included additional aspects on healing rays and the initiation process in the chapter, "Initiation - *All Healing Energy Comes from Mother-Father God*". "Meditation - *Creating Health & Developing Psychic Abilities*" includes the first guided meditation that the angels gave to me in 1990, <u>Journey to Sacred Mountain</u>. You may record it for your own personal use. Meditation can be a way to develop psychic abilities, clear psychic channels that are already open, clear the mind and heal the body.

"Holy Kabbalah - *A Look at Ourselves & Our Relationship to God as Seen Through Oil Paintings*" was written ten years ago. I had intended to include it in my first book, <u>Reiki & Other Rays of Touch Healing</u>, but the cost of having color separations and then printing the eight paintings was beyond my reach. In this second edition of <u>Tera, My Journey Home</u>, Doug Dickson has retaken pictures of the paintings and created new color film so that the photographs herein look more like the original paintings. You may or may not agree with me, but I think that you will find the chapter interesting.

Stormsfury's Last Son

The Reality of Good and Evil

Leaving Wisconsin with my two cats, Ziggy and Janis, for Arizona, I had no intention of buying another horse. Abez, my horse of nine years, had been dead for only ten months and Arizona was just too hot. My friend, Susan Kramer, knew that I missed riding and working with horses. Susan had a friend, Sylvia, who had a horse that she could no longer ride because of her heart condition and ill health. When Susan introduced us to one another, Sylvia told me that her horse needed to be exercised and that she had been praying for somebody like me to come along. I began to ride Silver in September 1995. Susan left me with a warning; "Sometimes people don't fully realize the consequences of their prayers and become resentful later when their wish has been granted."

Silver had never been trained properly. While Sylvia had taken a class on barn management and horse care at the local community college, she said that she had not been impressed to take the second part of the class where 'how to ride the horse' was taught. Thus, I began from scratch training Silver. First, we worked on the ground and he learned to listen to my voice and move away from the pressure of my hand. Then we walked only and did exercises to increase the strength in his hindquarters, and it wasn't long before we were trotting. Silver had improved so much by October that I included him in the video I produced, <u>Healing Animals</u>. At the end of the video, Silver and I demonstrate some fundamental riding principles and techniques.

I continued to ride Silver, but by December, Sylvia started to act very strangely. She began fussing at me and her horse for meaningless things. As I was not charging her for training her horse, I wanted to resolve the situation or simply step out of the picture. It turned out that Sylvia was jealous of me because I was able to do things with her horse that she had never been able to do, and she told me that she was afraid that she was losing her horse. Rather than looking at me as an opportunity for the horse to grow, Sylvia's own jealousy was pushing her horse away from her.

I have always practiced the ancient art of hands-on healing on a donations-are-accepted basis. One day, I had two women, Rosemarie Sherman and Cynthia Kyle, both of whom were quite psychic, come to me for healings. I am only a facilitator or a channel for God's healing energy, and I never know what to expect. I do try to get my clients as involved in the healing process as I

1

can by asking them to visualize themselves, their angels helping them or their issues, pains or fears. At some point during each of their individual healing sessions, they each saw a horse who said that he belonged to me. When Rosemarie first gave me the message, I thought that Abez was telling me through Rosemarie that he was still watching out for me, but Rosemarie had seen a bay horse, not a chestnut. An hour later, Cynthia saw the same horse who gave her the same message. I wondered who this horse was.

When we use patience, skill and love to help a horse move through its fear and teach it new skills, it grows spiritually as well as emotionally and physically. Horses learn to become more conscious of their bodies as the riding cues become softer and softer. When the rider's seat is relaxed, allowing the horse's body to move the rider's hips and legs, the horse feels like he is receiving a back massage. If the rider tunes into the energy and essence of the horse rather than bullying the horse, then they both enjoy the ride, and they consciously become a team. Whenever any of us learn a better way of doing something, it is difficult, if not impossible, to return to the old way of doing things. Silver could not go back to the unconscious riding efforts of Sylvia and her friends. Before I left Silver and Sylvia, she asked me if I would check out a stable for her. For the horse's best interest, I drove over to the ranch to find out the conditions and the cost of board.

When I arrived, I found that the horses were kept in stalls rather than large, open, partially covered pens and they were not turned out. As Sylvia was not able to exercise Silver herself (her health was so bad that she could hardly open or close the gate to the ranch where she boarded Silver), this stable was not a viable option. I explained this to the stable owner, and she sent me to the ranch across the street. There I met Lydia, the owner's horse trainer, who lived on the owner's second ranch with a former horse show judge, Peter Sikes. Later, Hilda told me that Peter had awarded her many ribbons. Lydia cared for all and rode some of the owner's horses. She made extra money by giving lesson on Hilda's ridable horses. Lydia showed me the stalls with runs, but they were way out of Sylvia's price range. Before I left, Lydia introduced me to two of the owner's horses that she could not do anything with, Hassle Free and Baskabas. When Baskabas saw me, he got excited. He seemed to be saying, "Here I am! Don't you recognize me?" He literally claimed me for his own. Lydia then told me that if I would be willing to work with Baskabas without being paid, as I had done with Silver, I could take Baskabas on as a project.

One of the most important things I learned from Abez was to pay attention. The first day I went out to work with Baskabas, I got him out of his run and put him in crossties in the showbarn, which Lydia referred to as her barn. Lydia walked in while I was brushing Baskabas, stopped in front of him, reached up to pet his head, and he responded by trying to bite her. She walked to the

2

side of his head, cradled his head in one arm and then punched him in his head with her fist. This type of punishment is cruel and produces short-term results and long-term problems. In addition, in the time it took Lydia to punch him in the head, the seven seconds had already elapsed whereby she could have reprimanded him in a much more effective and kinder manner. Baskabas' attempt to bite Lydia was not normal. Something was very wrong. When I searched within to ask what I should say to her, the answer I received was "Nothing!" When I asked if I should walk out of the entire situation, the answer was, "No! Stay and work with the horse. Keep this incident to yourself." I reasoned to myself that perhaps if she could see how I could bring Baskabas back to being a ridable animal, she might alter her own training methods. Maybe this was what the horse was trying to tell Rosemarie and Cynthia?

I continued brushing Baskabas and noticed that his second vertebra was sticking out. It was not difficult to miss! When I asked Lydia about it, she said that it was from an old injury. I placed my right hand on the touch point for the neck, which is between the 7th cervical and the 1st thoracic vertebrae, and my left hand on the 2nd vertebra. After about ten minutes, it gently moved back into place on its own accord and stayed there; however, the swelling of the tissue all around the second vertebra remained. His body was telling me that this was not an old injury!

It was obvious that Baskabas was close to 200 pounds underweight; his hipbones were clearly visible, and I could also see between the tops of his legs. Lydia had told me that she had been riding him the month before. Now, there are trainers who think that if they half-feed a spirited horse, the horse will not have enough energy to buck them off. I also had to ask myself the question, "If she can't do anything with him now and she was riding him in December, what happened?"

The first week I worked with Baskabas, I spent a lot of time brushing him and talking to him. I also walked him around the property, occasionally asking him to stop or move away from the pressure of my hand. I could not use pieces of carrots for rewards; he was so hungry that he became too excited if he knew that I had food in my pockets. Every day, he became more attached to me. Not owning him placed limitations on what I was able to do, such as increasing his allotment of alfalfa and hay. Lydia was easy enough to read. It was obvious that if there were changes, she would have to think that they were her ideas, not mine.

Lydia was in charge of Hilda Hood's sixteen horses. There were Arabs, National Show Horses (half Arab and half Saddlebred) and Hackney Ponies. Six of the horses were retired from national show competition and they were kept in two large, dirt turnout areas. Except for being

3

fed and watered, they were utterly ignored. They had not been trimmed in over a year, which caused their feet to spread out so that they looked less like hoofs and more like platypus feet. One of the horses was so thin that every bone in his body was visible, and so arthritic that he leaned to one side when he walked. It was hard to look at him without crying. Oftentimes when I brought Baskabas back to the showbarn, Lydia would be grooming or saddling one of Hilda's horses for the purpose of riding it herself or getting it ready for one of her riding students. Repeatedly, I witnessed her punching horses in the head; it appeared to be her standard method of discipline. As a consequence, every one of Hilda's horses was head shy. Like Baskabas, they had been ruined to the point that they could never be shown again successfully in national competition.

Attached to the showbarn was an apartment that the farm manager, Jerry, shared with a local cowboy-horse trainer, Gus. The tension between Lydia and Jerry was bone chilling. The ranch had been allowed to fall into a state of disrepair; the only work I ever witnessed Jerry doing was ordering hay and collecting boarders' checks. Occasionally, Jerry's daughter would come over and work with one of her father's horses. Neither she nor Jerry ever cleaned up after themselves. Lydia refused to do it and I cannot say that I blamed her. I refused to work in filth, so I was the one who cleaned up after not only Baskabas, but Jerry's horses as well.

In addition to Jerry, Gus and Lydia, Victor boarded six Arabian horses in another barn and another trainer, Beth, gave lessons to most of Hilda's other boarders, who kept their horses in two additional barns and fifty or so small, covered, open pens. Both Beth and Lydia acted as if they owned the ranch and each one of them had their territory staked out. The ranch hands were all Mexican men who lived in small, humble apartments on the ranch. Most of them had families in Mexico to whom they sent money each week. I felt as if I had been dropped into a soap opera that might have been appropriately called "As the Barn Turns".

Lydia had told me that Baskabas had been winning as a carthorse in national competitions until he refused to do it any longer. Just like people, animals avoid painful situations. Lydia said that Baskabas' trainers continued to try to show him until they unloaded him from a horse trailer at a show and he obliged them by taking out a car in the parking lot. He totaled it! By that time, the ranch hands could not even enter his stall without Baskabas trying to bite or kick them. Lydia said that she had talked Hilda into having him gelded because he was too dangerous.

After working with Baskabas for a week, I thought that it was time to saddle him up and ride him for a walk around the farm so I could see what was going on with him. Lydia intently watched me as Baskabas dropped his head into the bit when I bridled him. However, when I tried to mount him, he kept moving away from me. Gus was close by, so I asked him if he wouldn't mind holding Baskabas for me while I got on. Once I was in the saddle, the horse's body became so stiff, I felt as though I was sitting on a marble statue rather than a living animal. He stood motionless for a long time while I gently talked to him and softly patted and scratched his neck. When he finally moved forward, with every other step he took, Baskabas would alternately rear and then buck. Even though I remained relaxed and had my heels down (that keeps the rider secure on the horse's back) I could feel his power; if Baskabas really wanted to dump me, he was fully capable of doing just that. He was not in physical discomfort. This unnatural, learned behavior was the aftereffect of severe abuse. Either Lydia had lied to me about riding Baskabas in December or her training methods left more to be desired than I originally had thought. I wanted to finish riding Baskabas on a good note, so I asked a woman who was standing nearby if she wouldn't mind leading us around for a few minutes. I instructed her not to let his head go down or up (preventing him from bucking or rearing). I then dismounted, loosened the girth (part of the reward system), patted him and told him he was a good boy. Victor and his wife had been watching the entire time. I led Baskabas back into the barn, unsaddled him, fed him carrots, groomed him, and he at last breathed a sigh of relief.

I started going to the stable in the afternoon, at a time when Lydia was not usually around, and began from scratch with Baskabas, using completely unorthodox training. The crossties in the showbarn had safety latches, which means that if the horse panics, the latches give, rather than the horse flipping over and breaking his neck. After brushing Baskabas, I saddled him and then mounted him while he was in the crossties. Immediately after getting on him, I reached over and gave him a piece of carrot. I patted him, told him he was a good boy, got off and gave him another carrot. I did this over and over again every day for about a week. In addition, I placed my hands on the touch points for the emotions and mental processes, and he would respond to this by yawning (a form of release). When Baskabas got to the point that he looked forward to having me on his back and was relaxed and breathing when I was on him, I saddled and bridled him and took him outside to see what changes my efforts had brought about. When I tried to mount Baskabas, he again moved away from me and again Gus was around to help hold him. Once I was on Baskabas, he stiffened, but this time I did not have the sensation that I was on a pinless grenade. He stood motionless for ten minutes or so while I talked to him and rubbed his neck. Then he took one step forward, I told him that he was a good boy, and then we stood still for another ten minutes. I stayed on him for thirty or so minutes while he did his step-pause routine. He had mastered resistance to get out of working when he was abused as a carthorse, and now he was using the same technique to avoid being ridden. I relaxed by breathing into my whole body, remained watchful that his head neither went too far down nor too high up, and tuned in psychically to what was going on by asking, "Should I ride through this?" The answer I received was, "Yes!"

We continued in this way for several weeks, each day taking more steps and less pauses, fewer bucks and rears. I had to remain ever watchful when I was on him; sometimes he would turn his head around to the side and open his mouth as if he were considering taking a bite out of my leg. When he tried this tactic, I never gave him enough rein to find out whether or not he would actually follow through. On the other hand, I would sometimes give him his head and let him stretch his neck to the ground; it seemed to help him relax and give him a sense of confidence and comfort knowing that he was not totally confined. I overheard several people say that they thought that I was crazy. Crazy or not, what I was doing seemed to be working. If Baskabas was having a bad day, I would either find something that we could do successfully and end on a good note, or dismount and handwalk him through whatever it was that I had asked him to do that he was incapable of doing. When Baskabas 'messed up,' I would simply say, "Let's try that again."

As a former schoolteacher, I was aware that the learning process is not a straight road lined with only green go-ahead lights. When we acquire any new skills, we all take two steps forward and one step backward. This is natural! Real problems develop when parents, teachers or trainers overreact or take it personally when the child or animal fails to correctly perform a procedure that the child or animal did correctly the day before. The child or animal is not insulting the adult's intelligence; the child or animal is involved in a learning process and what is required from the adult is understanding and patience. In Baskabas' case, he was unlearning fear response conditioning, as well as relearning new behavioral patterns.

One day, Lydia asked me if I was going to start trotting him soon. I looked at my window of opportunity and answered carefully and kindly, "There is not enough flesh around his backbone. I am afraid that my weight is going to hurt his spine if we trot." She decided to increase his feed.

The next day, while I was saddling Baskabas, Lydia asked me if I would like to go out and ride on the shoulder of the road with her and Legend, Baskabas' half brother. I asked her if she really thought that that was a good idea, and she responded that Baskabas' behavior was better outside of the ring and away from the riding arenas on the farm where he had been abused. I could understand her reasoning, but I was really getting the impression that she was rushing both Baskabas and myself. As she was in charge, I agreed.

6

We started walking off of the ranch with Lydia riding Legend in front of us. When we reached the road, Lydia was having problems with Legend, so Baskabas and I led the way across the street. Once on the other side of the street, Lydia went in front again. Baskabas was actually doing very well, even when a garbage truck backfired as it drove by us. However, Legend spun around, ran into Baskabas and then ran down the road. Baskabas spun around, taking off in hot pursuit after them. Galloping back to the barn in a panic down a busy road is dangerous! The automatic pilot inside of me, who knows how to ride, sat my physical body tall, my hips froze so that I was no longer allowing his back to move my hips and legs, I held the reins firmly and called out, "Whoa". Baskabas stopped in his tracks and it was at that moment that I knew that he trusted me. Because Baskabas stopped, Legend also stopped. Lydia decided that we should continue with our ride. When we got back onto the ranch, suddenly Baskabas froze. His brain was fried; he had had enough. I got off, loosened the girth, told him he was a good boy, walked him back to the barn and gave him carrots. I then turned him out so that he could buck and run off his mental and emotional frenzy.

It is dangerous for horses to be turned out with ponies. If a pony should kick a horse in the leg, the pony could break the horse's leg; if a pony should kick a horse in the belly, the pony could kill the horse. Lydia turned out one of Hilda's Hackney Ponies, Topside, with Hilda's three geldings and two mares. One afternoon, I went out to the turnout to get Baskabas. For some reason, Topside was having a bad day. Before I could stop her, she kicked Baskabas in his left rear leg. The crack was deafening. I chased her off and turned to look at Baskabas. He was holding his left rear leg in the air. I asked the angels what to do. The answer I got was that it would not be possible to work on him in the turnout area with the other horses. They asked me to lead him back to the barn and they said that they would manage his leg while I did this.

When I got Baskabas into the crossties, I worked through his aura, drained the pain and laid my hands on the injury. Then I went up to the touch points for the bones. (Right hand between the 7th cervical and 1st thoracic vertebrae. Left hand on the inside of the humerus of the left front leg. As the horse's humerus is inside of his body, I willed my etheric hand inside of his body.) I worked back and forth until Baskabas finally breathed a sigh of relief and put his weight back on it. I looked at him and asked, "You're feeling better, aren't you?" He nodded, yes. (Animals are a lot more intelligent than most people realize.) I asked myself, "Why did this have to happen?" The answer I received was point-blank; "It was the horse's way out if you hadn't come along. Because you are here in his life, we are able to release the trauma and heal the leg through you. He'll be fine." I rode Baskabas the next day.

Lydia knew about my book, Reiki & Other Rays of Touch Healing. Sometimes, she would stop to talk to me about magic and healing. She didn't tell me much about her magic spells and I had a gut feeling that she was using magic to make Jerry quit his job. What Lydia did tell me was about the interesting manner in which she did healings on horses. It might seem strange that someone who abuses horses also heals them; perhaps it was God's way of trying to get through to her. God also works through each one of us. While she was caught up in telling her story, I could see that she had been abused as a young girl. The awareness came to me that if I stayed out of judgement with Lydia, then I would not get caught up in her stuff and her magic would have no effect on me. Lydia told me that on several occasions she had been confronted with horses who had serious injuries. As she stood before the animal, the horse's pain would come into her and she would know exactly which bone, tendon, joint or muscle, or combination thereof, was involved. Sometimes when this occurred, she would literally have to be carried to bed. As her body healed over the next 24 to 48 hours, the horse would heal also. East Indian gurus have healed in this same manner, taking on the pain, disease and karma of an individual. Healers in the past have often had to be careful not to take on what they were healing their client of and the old books on healing speak of this fact.

Shortly thereafter, I was in the midst of cleaning Baskabas' left rear hoof when Lydia walked up and started to talk to me. She must have tried to pet Baskabas' head and he responded by trying to bite her; or perhaps she was simply trying to get me out of the picture, because while I was holding Baskabas' left hind leg, she punched him in the head. I could feel his body react against the left side of my body, but he remained standing on three legs and his left leg did not kick out at me in response to the blow. I put his hoof down and turned to face her. She actually finished her sentence and walked off. I finished cleaning his feet and then began brushing him. In the past, when I brushed his neck, sometimes he would reach around with his mouth wide open as though he were going to take a bite out of my arm. It was a response condition from having his head and neck pulled too far back when his trainers hitched him up to a cart. I had boarded Abez at barns where Saddlebreds were also stabled. I would see these horses standing in their high show shoes in the aisle or in their stalls for hours, rigged up with their necks pulled tightly back and tails jacked up. One of Hilda's Hackney Ponies, Asaph, had only a stub for a tail because one of Hilda's trainers had broken his tailbone by pulling his tail too far up. As I brushed Baskabas' neck this time, he continually turned around with his mouth open as though he wanted to bite my arm. Baskabas hadn't been abused; he'd been brutalized by one trainer after the other.

Baskabas was coming along slowly and sometime in the beginning of March, Lydia announced to me that she was thinking about using Baskabas as a lesson horse. Besides his neck injury and being highly spirited and still not 'normally ridable', Baskabas had been a stallion for six of his seven years. I could hardly believe what I was hearing, but I didn't say one word to Lydia. Her idea was so dangerous that I decided that it was time I met Hilda Hood.

Hilda's home was on the ranch, and I picked a time to call on her when Lydia was not around. I had no idea how I was going to approach her. I rang the doorbell and stood in front of the double oak doors for some time while a small black dog barked as she ran back and forth in front of the long window next to the door. A wheelchair passed by the long window next to the double doors. The lock turned, the door opened, and there sat a vulnerable, depressed, sickly woman who looked to be in her late eighties. The finer quality of her soul reached out to me as I stood in her doorway. She quickly sized me up, decided that she liked me and invited me in. We moved to a dimly lit room off of the kitchen and sat around an octagonal table that was piled high with papers and unpaid bills.

My heart went out to Hilda and I introduced myself to her simply as Kathleen. I told Hilda that I was the one whom Lydia had found to ride Baskabas and that I was being very careful when I rode him not to reinjure his neck. She was surprised that not only had Lydia not told her about me, but that nobody had told her about Baskabas' neck injury. She told me that Baskabas was Stormsfury's last son. Because Lydia had talked Hilda into gelding Baskabas, his bloodlines would never be passed down. The conversation changed; Hilda asked me what I did and when she found out that I was an author, she showed me an article in a horse magazine that she had written. She told me that she had been an opera singer and had studied at the Juilliard School in New York under a scholarship. After graduating, she had gotten married and moved to Arizona. She sang in Mexico City and Los Angeles because her first husband did not approve of her singing career and he did not want her to travel. I love the opera and found her stories interesting. She also told me that she had had a series of barn managers, including her current managers, Jerry and Daisy at Skylark, who had stolen large sums of money from her. At that point, Hilda's driver, Fernando, came into the house and asked in Spanish if Hilda needed him for anything. Before I left that day, Hilda expressed to me her concern about her failing memory.

Before I went over to visit with Hilda again, I stopped at Country Health and picked up some herbs, including Ginkgo Biloba and Gotu Kola, as well as a multimineral. Hilda was delighted that I had thought to remember her. She wanted to pay me, but something told me that she would be resentful paying over $70. I said, "Let me do this for you. After all, I am riding your horse." She kept insisting and I kept saying no. All of a sudden, she blurted out, "All right for you, Kathleen, I am willing Baskabas to you." I was shocked. Even though I had known Hilda for only

9

a short time, I knew that this was completely out of character for her. I asked her, "When was the last time that you saw Baskabas?" When she told me that she hadn't seen him since he was a colt, I asked her if she would like me to bring him over. So, I helped her wheel out to her backyard and I went to get Baskabas. She did not notice how underweight he still was. What caught her attention and what she talked about for months later was how Baskabas kept putting his head on my shoulder. She had heard the stories about how unmanageable he still was. Hilda said, "This is the first time in Baskabas' life that he is happy." I wondered if Hilda realized that it was her own trainers who had ruined the horse through their abusive training methods. When I asked her about it later, she said that the stall cleaners were the ones who had abused him. I wondered if she had actually talked herself into believing what she was saying. When I asked her another time, she said, "Trainers have to do things to horses. This is a business." As she said this, I watched, as her eyes became slits and her soul and body contracted. What Hilda and her trainers were never taught is that when a horse misbehaves, it is always the rider's fault. Even when I watched the dressage riders at the Olympics, it was not the horse's fault if he was not ready and was being shown anyway.

I continued to check in on Hilda and listened to her tell and retell her stories. Her first husband had divorced her and she received a small percentage of their joint property. Her second husband, Bob, was schizophrenic and had on many occasions beaten her. The last time he beat her, he had put her into the hospital for six months. She left the hospital in a wheelchair, where she remained for almost a year. It was when her trainers began lifting her from her wheelchair and into a horse cart so that she could drive her horses that she regained her sense of balance so that she could walk again. Hilda and Bob were then divorced and separated for a number of years. Hilda's brother-in-law, Fred Hood, called Hilda after his mother died and asked Hilda if she would take Bob back. Hilda and Bob saw each other again and got back together. This time Bob stayed on his medication, but Fred immediately started court procedures to get guardianship over his brother, Bob. Fred tried no less than six times to get legal guardianship of Bob. Each time, an attorney represented Hilda in court and each time, Fred lost. The last time Fred took Hilda to court (four years prior to our conversation), Hilda had cancer and could not attend any of the legal proceedings. The six-hour cancer surgery she went through put her into a nursing home to recover for three months, and also upset her balance again so that she was back in a wheelchair. Her lawyer, Potter, failed to show up for the guardianship trial and then failed to file an appeal to the guardianship. Fred then had Hilda and Bob divorced against their wishes. There was fear in her eyes and severe agitation in her voice when she almost shouted, "Fred even had his lawyer get a copy of my mother's will. What would they want with that old thing?" Hilda and Bob had sole and separate property, but Fred was awarded a monetary sum and he seized the money out of three of Hilda's bank accounts. Potter had represented Hilda at the divorce trial and did a very poor job, as Hilda was the one who should have been compensated when the marriage ended. I wondered why hadn't she gotten another attorney the day after Potter failed to show up for the guardianship trial? When one abusive situation ended for her, she attracted another that was even worse. When she wasn't being physically beaten anymore, Fred started using the legal system to take revenge on Hilda by getting guardianship of her husband and then having them divorced. When those trials were over, she attracted manager after manager who robbed her blind. Rather than firing them or calling the police, she complained about them and accepted people's pity. Whenever Hilda spoke about Fred, her body tightened as her soul contracted with hatred; when Hilda's dark shadow side came to the surface, it was obvious. Hilda enjoyed hating Fred so much that she had not wanted to pay attention to what was going on around her. If she took time to take care of her business, then that was time spent that she couldn't be hating Fred.

At the time of her divorce, Hilda owned three horse ranches free and clear. She sold one of them to a man named Delanti in order to pay her taxes that year. Delanti had been paying Hilda off over the past four years as he sold the homes he had built on her former ranch. When he came over to her house, Delanti would bring home-cooked meals and homemade wine and do little repair jobs around Hilda's home. Just about the same time I had met Hilda, Delanti had left an offer of $1,800,000 with Hilda to buy Skylark Ranch, which was adjacent to the housing development he had constructed on Hilda's former property. Hilda thought his offer was a joke. She had had several offers of well over $3,000,000 for the same ranch, and she told me that she would only consider selling Skylark for $5,000,000. The first week in April, Hilda told me that Delanti was coming over to give her the final payment on the original property that he had purchased from her. Something didn't seem right, but I had no clue as to what it could be!

I continued working with Baskabas and he continued to improve; however, he was still not normally ridable. One day, Lydia announced that she was ready to start using Baskabas as a lesson horse to teach little children how to ride. I responded, "I met Hilda and she is willing him to me. As I am the only one who is allowed to ride him, I do not want him used as a lesson horse and I do not think that Hilda would approve either." Lydia was shocked and obviously upset. She said, "We'll see about that. I'm going over to speak to Hilda." As I watched her literally march off to Hilda's house, I really wanted to go along, but something inside of me said to leave her be.

I didn't get over to see Hilda until three or four days later. I wanted to ask her what had transpired between her and Lydia, but I thought that that was Hilda's business. Hilda, on the other hand, could hardly wait to tell her story. Lydia had found Hilda at home that day, and she told Hilda that she didn't think that I should be riding Baskabas any longer. Hilda then told her, "Leave Kathleen and Baskabas alone!" Lydia responded by saying, "But Baskabas and I love one another." Hilda remained adamant and Lydia left. Lydia showed up the next morning with pictures of herself and Baskabas, hoping to convince Hilda to change her mind. Hilda looked through the pictures and said, "Love you? My horse doesn't even like you. His ears are back flat against his head in every one of these pictures." Hilda then repeated to Lydia, "Leave Kathleen and Baskabas alone! This is the first time in that horse's life that he is happy."

Baskabas and I were doing turns on the forehand (the horse moves his back legs only in a circle while keeping his front legs relatively stationary) and turns on the haunches (the horse moves his front legs only in a circle while keeping his back legs relatively stationary). Both of these exercises strengthen the horse's rear end so that he powers off of his haunches when he carries a rider on his back. (Good trainers and riders start off with these kinds of exercises after they have walked the horse for a while.) Furthermore, these kinds of exercises strengthen the horse's back so that he does not become a swaybacked teenager. We were doing other lateral movements as well and I was just beginning to safely trot him a little. If Baskabas became frightened or acted strangely when I was riding him, I would tune in and ask, "Should I ride through this?" Every time, I heard the answer, "Yes!" If I felt his brain was becoming too stressed, I would dismount, always leaving the horse with good feelings about himself and our ride together.

One day, I went out to ride Baskabas and I knew something was wrong; I could see it in his eyes. When he was in the crossties, he kept stretching his neck out and yawning. As always, he dropped his mouth into the bit when I bridled him. The vets all told me that if his neck bothered him while I rode him, he would not be as cooperative as he was when I tacked him up (saddled and bridled him). When I walked him out of the barn, he kept bobbing his head into my arm. I mounted him and as we rode to the riding arena, he spooked at everything and anything that he saw. Once in the ring, I almost fell off twice when he bolted and skirted around. I tuned in and asked if I should ride through this. I heard, "Get the hell off of that horse!"

I dismounted and walked him back to the barn, all the while his head kept bobbing into my arm. I put him into the crossties. On every exhale, he stretched his neck and yawned as though he was trying to release something caught in his throat. His compulsive-obsessive behavior was a signal that he had been abused again; as Lydia and I were the only ones who had the opportunity, it had to be one of us. I walked him to a large turnout area and let him run and buck out his mental and emotional tension for over an hour. When Victor and his wife came over to see what was going on, Baskabas came over to the fence. When they tried to pet him on his head, he jerked his head back and then tried to bite them. They knew something was wrong! I was in tears! I was too close to the horse to objectively find out what had happened. Psychics and animal communicators, including Cynthia Kyle, all came up with the same scenario. Each one saw Lydia trying to bridle Baskabas for perhaps an hour. He refused to let her, and she responded repeatedly by punching him in the head. One psychic said that the reason she stopped was because her hand had become too sore and bruised.

So, I started working all over again with Baskabas. I led him around and periodically asked him to halt or move away from the pressure of my hand. By the end of two weeks, my right arm was black and blue from him bobbing his head into it. Lydia, in the meantime, had gone to Hilda and told her that I was the one who had abused Baskabas. Lydia then turned around and accused me of saying bad things about her to Hilda. Victor and his wife had heard what Lydia had done, and they went to Hilda. They told Hilda that they had watched me working with Baskabas from the start, and while they had never personally seen Lydia punch a horse in the head, they also told Hilda that they knew that I was always kind and patient with Baskabas and would never abuse him.

Hilda had found out other things about Lydia. It disturbed Hilda that Lydia would often come over and visit with her for over an hour, leaving Hilda's horses on a broken walker. One of the young girls who boarded a pony on Hilda's ranch had started collecting money for the purpose of paying a farrier (blacksmith) to trim the hoofs of Hilda's retired horses. When the young girl had gone over to get Hilda's permission to have this done, Hilda said that she would give Lydia the money to have her retired horses trimmed. Even though Lydia was given the money, the six horses remained untrimmed! When Hilda told me this, I asked her why she kept Lydia on. Hilda responded by saying that she only had to pay Lydia $500 a month and that she would have to pay a good horse trainer $3,000 a month. It was clear why Hilda was having problems! If we are not willing to pay good help good money, in the end we pay a much dearer price. If Hilda had hired and paid a good and patient trainer from the start, Baskabas had the ability, beauty and dazzle to be a champion. Because of her greed, she lost both the prestige of owning another champion, as well as the stallion fees she could have collected.

Jerry, the manager, quit and took Hilda's 2-horse trailer with him. A man named Jacob had approached Hilda for the purpose of having her hire him as her ranch manager. She turned him down because he wanted $1,200 a week to start. When he reapproached her and agreed to work for less, Hilda hired him to run both ranches since Daisy had quit managing Skylark. There is a not-so-funny joke in Ireland that when the British left Southern Ireland, they took everything but the picks and shovels with them when they left. When Daisy left Skylark Ranch, she took anything she could get her hands on including the picks and shovels. The hunter/jumper trainer at Skylark told me that they thought the only reason Daisy hadn't taken the tractor was because she didn't have room for it in her moving van.

Hilda liked Jacob; she even trusted him with the checkbooks from both ranches. Every Friday, Jacob would go to Hilda's home and go over the bills with her. He would make out the checks and Hilda would sign them. Hilda became upset when Jacob asked her if she would go into partnership with him - her money, his expertise. As Hilda told me this, psychically I saw an agreement, which read, "In the event of either partner's death, the remaining partner shall inherit the business." From that time on, she became distrustful of him, but he remained on as her manager and controlled her checkbooks, even after she found out that Jacob and Daisy were friends. I thought that this was an incredible coincidence, but I did not interfere by giving Hilda unsolicited advice; it is unwelcome and seldom, if ever, acted upon. When I asked her attorney if there was anything that he could do, he responded by saying, "It's her money, her doctor says that she is competent, and if she refuses to get the police or myself involved, there is nothing that I can do." I treated Hilda as though she was my own grandmother, listening attentively to her stories and her complaints, while I watched the theater evolve and revolve around her.

When I rode Baskabas, if Jacob was around, he would call out to me, "Be careful, Kathleen, that horse is dangerous." On May 4, Jacob walked over to me while I was riding, put his hands on my saddle and said, "The horse is yours now, Kathleen." He then proceeded to tell Lydia and other people on the ranch. When I was through riding, I went over to see Hilda and she told me the same thing, "The horse is yours now, Kathleen." She also added that I should be careful, but if something should happen to me, I was responsible. I knew that Hilda was not giving me Baskabas out of the goodness of her heart; rather, it was probably Jacob who had told her to either tell me that I couldn't ride Baskabas any longer or give him to me. This realization took much of the joy out of receiving Baskabas. Hilda did not have either his registration papers or his yellow hauling tags, which is a certification of registration through the Department of Agriculture, to give me. I simply assumed that they were lost or stolen along with so many of Hilda's other things.

Shortly after I was gifted with Baskabas, the shoe on his right front foot came off for the third time. The first time Baskabas had lost the shoe, Lydia had the farrier build his hoof up before putting the shoe on. That shoe came off when I turned him out one day. When the shoe came off, it took the rest of the hard hoof wall with it. Lydia decided to have him shod for a second time. I did not own him and I couldn't stop it. So, while the farrier pounded the nails into the soft hoof, I stood in front of Baskabas and extended my left arm and hand towards his right hoof; my right hand and fingers pointed straight down. In this way, I drained his pain. As the farrier worked, Baskabas slowly dropped his head until it rested between my left arm and the left side of my body; I could feel the weight of it resting on me. The farrier couldn't believe that Baskabas had remained quiet. I couldn't believe that he and Lydia had actually pounded nails into soft flesh. When the shoe came off the third time, I called Todd Howell, a farrier who had come highly recommended.

Attached to the barn that had stalls with runs were two partially covered open pens. There was room enough to trot, but not canter. I had moved Baskabas to one of these pens. After Baskabas lost his shoe for the third time, I filled the open pen with a thick layer of sawdust. Todd trimmed Baskabas' other three hoofs quite short so that he would not throw his bone or muscle structure out of alignment. Throughout the summer, I came out periodically during the day and evening to make certain that his run was clean because he was at serious risk of dying should an infection enter and come up through the right front hoof. Because he had been half-starved for so long, none of his hoofs were strong. So I gave him minerals soaked in apple juice every day and put Vaseline on all of the hoofs at the top of the hoof and slightly into the hairline to help them grow.

A man named Troy had moved into the apartment in the showbarn after Jerry and Gus left. Jacob had asked Hilda about him, but Hilda kept telling Jacob, "Leave Troy alone. He works directly for me." Apparently, Jacob wanted a better answer, so he asked Troy to his face, "What are you doing here?" For whatever Troy's reasons were, he answered "I'm Hilda's new manager." Jacob responded by marching over to Hilda's house, throwing her checkbooks on her table and announcing, "I quit!"

Hilda called me. She was hysterical. She asked me if I would come over and help her. She didn't even know how Jacob was collecting her boarders' checks. So, sometime in the middle of May, I became Hilda's unpaid ranch manager until she could hire another manager. We went to Skylark, and in going through the papers, I found out that Jacob had instructed all of Hilda's boarders to send their checks to his own private mailbox. When I went over to see if there was any mail for her, the owners of the mail service said that they wouldn't let anyone other than Jacob have the mail unless the FBI directed them to do otherwise. The police department, the district attorney's office and the postal inspector all told Hilda that they were not going to do her bookkeeping for her. She got her mail and when she got her records in order, she was supposed to call them back.

I delegated a lot of responsibility for running the two ranches to other people and concentrated on getting her financial affairs in order. In going through Hilda's returned checks, bank statements and records, it was obvious that she had had a whole string of managers and employees who had stolen conservatively a half million dollars from her. All of the canceled checks from the ranch Jerry managed while he managed it were missing; Hilda told me that she thought Jerry had been stealing her monthly bank statements out of her mailbox. She told me that once Jerry had gone to the bank and cashed a check in the amount of $10,000 that he had signed her name to. I wondered why she had kept him on. In going over the checks from both ranches since Jacob had taken over, I found that there were checks made out to the same people for the same services from both of her accounts, and gross overpayments, such as $30,000 for hay in one month. Jacob had paid himself $1,200 a week through June and written himself $40,000 worth of additional checks for the month of April alone. Lydia had changed farriers without telling Hilda. His bill for trimming and shoeing five horses and four ponies and just trimming one other horse was $1,250, which meant that the farrier and Lydia were probably splitting at the very least an extra $500. When I helped Hilda go through her files, she discovered that some were missing. It quickly became obvious that Hilda needed an accountant.

Hilda had become distrustful of her attorney, Mr. Maroney. In her mind, she connected him with Jacob because they had come to her house together on one occasion. I asked her if she would like me to ask my attorney, Ira Schwartz, to come out and try to straighten things out. She responded positively; so, Ira and his associate spent almost the entire day with her. At Skylark Ranch, we found horses that had never paid board. Butch and Peter Sikes, Lydia's partner, were trying to follow us without being seen. Even the various plots in Hilda's bad movie had subplots, and most of the characters had their own unique schemes whereby they were stealing from her. A few days later, when Hilda refused to pay Ira his fee, he quit, kept the retainer and wrote the rest of her bill off as a loss. It was becoming more and more difficult to stay out of judgement with Hilda as well as those who were stealing from her.

Hilda's situation was becoming desperate! In quizzing her further, I found that she did like the accountant who had done her income taxes for her in the past and that he had suggested to her that he would like the job of billing her boarders. She agreed to have Frank come over to talk about the position. Frank said that he would like to be paid $1,000 to $1,500 a month for doing the billing, and I helped convince Hilda to hire Frank and pay him the full amount he requested.

Hilda was reluctant, but she did hire Frank. In the meantime, someone else had found a new manager, Charles. Hilda's nightmare was finally over.

It turned out to be only a short coffee break; the games were about to continue with new players. The first week in June, Hilda called me to say, "Do you remember when I told you that Delanti was coming over to give me the last $20,000 payment on Skylark?" I responded that I did remember. Hilda breathed a sigh of relief and continued, "After Delanti left, I wheeled over to rest in my recliner. When I put my head back, it suddenly occurred to me that the receipt I had signed was different from the other receipts that Delanti had me sign. I got back in my wheelchair and went over to my table. Delanti's offer of $1,800,000 for Skylark Ranch was gone. I knew that he had tricked me." Back in April, it had never even entered my mind that Delanti would resort to fraud in order to get Hilda to sell the property that he coveted for $2,000,000 under market value. I was wondering how Hilda could so clearly describe an event that happened two months ago. Hilda started crying and she asked me if I would come over and talk to her. She was distraught when I arrived. I tried to calm her down. She repeated the same story. I thought her disorientation was due to the fact that she was so upset. I told her that she couldn't ignore this matter and that she was going to have to call Mr. Maroney and have him deal with Mr. Delanti, which she did. When Mr. Maroney called me, I told him what Hilda had said to me, and he responded, "She is just confused. Hilda probably called you after she received the escrow instructions in the mail."

I stopped by later that week to see how Hilda was doing. She looked considerably better; however, she announced that she was going to rehire one of her old managers, Ken, who had been convicted of dealing drugs when he worked for her several years ago. Ken had occupied the apartment in the showbarn and after he went to prison, somebody broke into the apartment and stole everything of value, including Hilda's trophies that she had won over the years for showing her horses. I could see by the look in her eye that she was considering firing Frank and Charles, thinking that she would save money by just having Ken. I knew that she resented paying Frank $1,500 a month. I didn't think it would be a good idea to have Ken doing both the billing and the collecting of her boarders' checks. I simply reminded her that the police said that they would not do her accounting work for her. If she was going to try to get her money and things back from her old managers, then she was going to have to keep Frank on. To my surprise, she kept Charles on to manage Skylark, Ken managed the ranch where Hilda and my horse lived, and Frank continued his efforts to straighten out Hilda's accounting mess and do the billing. As all of the homes and apartments were occupied on the ranch, Ken moved in with Hilda. Besides having full access to the house, Ken's bedroom also had sliding glass doors that led to a private porch. The porch had its own half-hidden gate, which allowed Ken to come and go without going through the house.

The day Ken started working for Hilda was the day Hilda's papers and financial records began to mysteriously shuffle around. He bad-mouthed all of us - Frank, Charles, Mr. Maroney, Maria the maid and myself. He wanted us all out of the way. Hilda was blind to what was going on. I never said anything to her, even when Ken completely messed up Frank's accounting system by going to Hilda's mailbox and getting the boarders' checks himself for Hilda to deposit, without keeping a record for Frank. However, I did speak up for Frank and Mr. Maroney whenever she criticized them. Three of Hilda's old sweaters disappeared in July, and Ken talked Hilda into believing that Maria had taken them. When Hilda asked me what I thought, I reminded her that Maria was a size 18 and that she was a size 6. Hilda responded, "You can do a lot with a needle and thread, you know." From that point in time, Hilda's mental and physical health went drastically downhill.

Whenever I saw Ken on the ranch, I was polite to him and never interfered with his work. One day I noticed that the old retired horse, who had all of his bones showing, kept lying down as though he were trying to die. I asked Ken if he was calling a vet to have the horse humanely put down. Ken replied that he didn't think Hilda would go for that. Later that week, they had to call the vet when the horse went down and couldn't get back up again. Shortly afterwards, I went out to the barn and saw a horse running loose and then realized that it was the spirit of the horse who had been put down. I called for the angels and the Light and told the spirit horse to go to a better place. Later, I heard Hilda tell a friend that she had to put one of her valuable Arabs down. The horse who had all of his bones showing was not an Arab! I didn't say anything; Hilda would only have argued with me. If the events that transpired in Hilda's life were in a soap opera, nobody would believe it. Everyone would think that the writers had gone too far.

Lydia was still working as Hilda's trainer. The kids on the ranch told me that whenever she walked by Baskabas' pen, he would pin his ears back against his head, turn around and put his rear end in her face and walk to the other side of his pen to get a drink of water. That is a horse insult! The only other person who was around Lydia and had seen Lydia punching horses in the face wasn't talking. Then one day Hilda called Maria's daughters to her home. The girls told her that they had seen Lydia teaching people to punch their horses in the face when they were riding by shortening one rein in order to bring the horse's head within striking distance. When I heard that story, I received a visual impression of Lydia riding Baskabas and trying the same form of punishment on him. Baskabas freaked out and went down, injuring both Lydia's knee and his neck. Hilda said that Lydia teaching people to punch horses in the face while they were on board was the last straw and that she was going to fire Lydia. I had heard that before! When I was leaving Hilda's home, Hilda's driver, Fernando, was walking in front of me and a friend whom I had brought along. I thought that I would test out my theory that Fernando could speak and understand English very well and that Lydia was paying him for information. I said to my friend, "Won't Lydia be surprised when she finds out she is being fired." The next day Lydia quit.

I ended up being Hilda's trainer for three weeks. The first time I went to Legend's stall to let him out, he startled and put his head in the corner of his stall. His body was shaking. That was a sure sign of abuse. Lydia had underfed him and he was close to 200 pounds underweight. Maria's daughters told me that the last time Lydia tried to ride Legend, she had asked the girls to hold him for her while she tacked him up. I talked calmly to Legend. Perhaps because he had seen me being kind and gentle with Baskabas, he chose to walk over to me. I was able to put his halter on and turn him out. Like all of Hilda's horses, he needed a kind, loving person of his own.

In August, Hilda began repeating sentences only seconds after stating them the first time. I never knew where she was going to stand on any particular issue. One day she liked Maria, the next day Hilda was accusing her of stealing the dog's bones, soap, brownies, old clothes that were too small for Maria or thread and then telling Maria never to come back to her home again to clean or cook for her. One day, I went to see Hilda and found her sitting in her recliner looking half-dead. I found out that she had thrown Maria out of her house, and since Ken did not cook for her, Hilda had not eaten for three days. She did not want me to call her doctor. I ran to a nearby deli and bought some soup. I stayed while she ate, and she seemed to get better. From then on, whenever Maria was banished, either I would bring her soup or Frank's wife would cook for her.

Hilda even began going back and forth about having given me Baskabas and then telling me that she was willing him to me. I felt like a yoyo on a string. Frank asked me if I thought she was on drugs. I didn't know what the problem was; Hilda's subconscious was hiding it from me. One day when I went over to visit Hilda, she told me how the lights in her house had gone out Saturday night shortly after Ken had left to go out for the evening. She was frightened. She also had a bladder infection. Ken had taken her to her doctor on Friday and her doctor had given her some medication. When she had tried to get up to go to the bathroom in the middle of the dark night, she had fallen out of her wheelchair. She managed to get back into the wheelchair, but she could not find the toilet. When she couldn't hold it any longer, she urinated and sat frightened in her cold, wet clothes until daylight. None of Hilda's neighbors had lost their electricity, and the electricity on the rest of Hilda's ranch had remained on. The next time I saw Ken, it was in

Hilda's house and he said to me, "I returned to my bedroom early Sunday morning. I used my own entrance because I didn't want to disturb Hilda. I knew that the electricity had gone out while I was gone because my digital alarm was blinking. I crashed on my bed and went to sleep without taking my clothes off." Anyone else would have checked to see if Hilda was all right. He had not checked on Hilda because he already knew that she was in trouble. I simply knew that he was the one who had flipped the switch on the fuse box Saturday night. I also suspected that just as Delanti had tricked Hilda into signing the agreement to sell him Skylark, Ken had gotten Hilda to sign a will leaving him her inheritance. I discovered that Victor and his wife and others suspected Ken. Nobody could understand why she kept him on. There were other near-fatal accidents.

Baskabas would cringe when he heard his name. He had had it yelled at him too many times. When I asked the angels what his real name was, I saw the cover of A Dictionary of Angels by Gustav Davidson. One day, I sat down with the book in my lap, got into a slight meditative state and asked, "All right, if his name is in here, please show it to me." I opened the book and there, highlighted in pink, was the name Merod, one of Solomon's angels of magic. I closed the book and asked for confirmation. The book fell off of my lap and onto the floor. It opened to the same page, which is not a page that the book would typically open to. What a beautiful name for such a beautiful horse, I thought. One evening, my daughter, Jennifer, and I stopped to check on Merod before going out to dinner. I was watching my horse when she called out, "Marauder". He came to attention and both of his ears twitched. He liked the name. The Mexican workers still called him "Loco."

In August, Hilda asked me if I would go with her and support her at a trial where she was being sued by Potter. He wanted $40,000 for not attending the guardianship trial, not filing an appeal to the guardianship and messing up the divorce. She fell completely apart before the trial. On several occasions, she looked as if she were going to die. Once, I even called her personal physician and his office got Hilda to come in for an exam. He gave her additional medication for her round-the-clock pain, which varied in severity. He told her that her body parts were wearing out. While Hilda was in denial of the fact that she was dying, she did ask me about the dying process. I explained that after the soul leaves the body, it has three days to go to the Light that holds unconditional love and joy, much like the movie Ghost. The things that prevent the soul from leaving are trauma or dark thoughts or heavy emotions. She told me that she was afraid to die; that she didn't think that she would make it to the Light I described. I suggested that she might consider letting go of her hatred for Fred. She came to attention, clenched her fists and said, "Never!" I responded, "Would you rather keep on hating Fred or go to the Light?" I was surprised when she answered, "Hate Fred! I have even changed the Lord's Prayer. I ask God to give me the vengeance I want." Hilda's dark shadow side was completely out in the open. I had a vision of Hilda dying and her crippled, dark soul leaving her body in a brown, etheric wheelchair and heading straight for Fred and all of the other people that had 'done her in', but especially for Fred. Hilda continued, "I am a stubborn woman and my stubbornness has gotten me everything I have. Without it, I would not be where I am today." I wondered how many of us really listen to what we say. Hilda was not changing her mind for me or for anybody else. One of the hardest lessons that love has to teach us is to give people the space to lead their own lives and learn their own lessons so that their successes will also be theirs. I had to allow Hilda to choose her own path.

At the trial, Hilda's ex-husband, Bob, testified that he never wanted a divorce from Hilda. Attorney Potter testified under oath that he was never hired by Hilda to represent her at the guardianship trial. Things were looking bleak for Hilda and her face and her mannerisms reflected the sad state of affairs. She wasn't even represented by an attorney; they had all told her that she was going to lose because she had signed a promissory note to Attorney Potter before he started working for her. I could feel my heart going out to Hilda and then I could feel it expanding and sending unconditional love to everyone in the courtroom. At that same time, Potter's attorney was giving his summation statement. Suddenly, Potter's attorney said, "It doesn't matter that my client did not show up for the guardianship trial. This case is about the promissory note that Hilda signed." The judge leaned over his desk with his mouth wide open, Potter was turning red behind the ears and his attorney kept on talking. I believe that my mouth was also hanging open. The judge then gave Hilda the opportunity to write a post-hearing statement, which Hilda asked me to help her with. I was shocked later to find that the judge had ruled in favor of Potter. Arizona justice?!? Hilda went into complete denial when she heard the news. Hilda was hardly finished with Potter's suit against her when she learned that Delanti was going to sue her for breach of contract. He wanted Skylark.

In the meantime, Ken and Hilda's old trainer, Butch, kept trying to talk Hilda into taking my horse back from me. Butch was well over eighty, crippled and hauled oxygen around with him in his car. Once, he was drinking at a bar when he found out that his oxygen canister was empty. He called Ken, and Ken got another canister from his trailer and ran it over to the bar at midnight. Butch had visions of showing my horse as a carthorse. How he thought that he was even going to put a halter on my horse, let alone hitch him up to a cart, I do not know. Amazingly enough, Butch's most frequent complaint about Hilda was that she lived in the past.

Between the pressure of the trials and Ken's constant badmouthing, Hilda's physical health and mental state continued to go downhill. One day, Attorney Maroney called me to ask if I would meet him at Hilda's home. She hadn't been paying her electric bill and the electric company was going to turn off the electricity on both of her ranches in five hours. Mr. Maroney and I agreed not to tell Hilda that because of her age and ill health, the electric company was not going to turn off the power to her home. I had come to the conclusion that Mr. Maroney was not just one more wolf at Hilda's door after I found out that Hilda had told me a lie about him. Mr. Maroney was in fact a decent, honest man. I was discovering that Hilda often told lies and then talked herself into believing them.

Mr. Maroney and I spent three hours trying to convince Hilda that she had to pay the bill, which was somewhere in the neighborhood of $15,000. We tried everything - sympathizing with her, going through her bankbook with her so that she could see for herself that she hadn't made out any checks to the electric company in the last couple of months, telling her that if anything happened to her boarders' horses that she could be sued for a lot more than $15,000, that we didn't want to see her sitting at home in the dark at night, etc. Sometimes, she would pout and tell us that we had no sympathy for her; her old car, worth probably $1,500, had been stolen and vandalized and she said that she was mourning its loss. Other times, she would scream at us. She said that the manager at the electric company hated her and was out to get her. She said that she would pay her bill after the electric company put her deposit in an interest-bearing account. I am not sure what finally convinced her to pay her bill, but when she went to fetch the money, Mr. Maroney looked at me and said, "Kathleen, this is abuse that we are taking!" I agreed and silently promised myself that I would never do this again. I think that Mr. Maroney made the same commitment.

I stayed away from Hilda for over a week. When I did see her again, she told me that Mr. Maroney had come to her home and used abusive tactics in order to get her to pay her overdue electric bill. I just listened! Had she forgotten that I had been there too and that I knew what had happened? I always had an impression of being in a no-time zone whenever I visited Hilda; now I was feeling like I was in "The Twilight Zone". Hilda had gone back and forth all summer long on every issue in her life; that included telling one woman in my presence that she was willing the horse to me, and others that she had given him to me. It was now September and I was afraid to ask her if she remembered.

In his efforts to make Frank look bad in Hilda's eyes, Ken never provided Frank with an accurate list of boarders and their horses. Frank told me that Hilda had told him she had given me

Baskabas. So, the next time I was out on the ranch helping Frank count horses, the idea came to me to ask him if I could receive a monthly board bill for my horse. I was pleasantly surprised later when Frank told me that Hilda had OK'd it. Beginning in September, I started receiving board bills with my name and address on it, Baskabas' name (that's what Hilda still called him) and "No charge per Mrs. Hood". I was glad that Hilda had done the right thing. I didn't discuss it the matter with Hilda because I was afraid that she would teeter back to saying that she was willing me the horse. It just felt better to leave well enough alone. Mr. Maroney also knew that Hilda had gifted me with the horse, and when he asked me what kind of documentation I had to prove that Hilda had given me the horse, I told him that I had requested board bills from Frank and he responded, "Perfect Kathleen!"

As Hilda's health declined, she would bring up the fact that she did not have a will. On several occasions, I had seen Hilda's mother's etheric form standing behind her holding a piece of paper that said "Will" across the top of it. I thought that Hilda's mother was trying to tell Hilda to get her affairs in order and provide for her other horses before she passed on. Hilda had a niece that she liked. Hilda once told me that she had tried to "make up for things" by taking her niece places and buying nice things for her. When I asked Hilda what it was that she had to make amends for, Hilda shut down and clenched her fists. The next time she brought up the subject of a will, I asked her if she was going to provide for her niece and her horses. I told Hilda, her attorney and accountant that if Hilda left me anything in a will, I would refuse it. However, Hilda seemed to think that if she made out a will, she would die. She told me that just before she had gone in for cancer surgery four years ago, she had told her attorney to cancel all of her wills. Hilda felt that not having a will was what saved her life. As Hilda told me that story, what I was shown was that death wasn't in the cards for her at that time; it was her ego's total self-absorption and lack of concern for her niece and her horses, and not attending to business that put her back into a wheelchair. Hilda stubbornly refused to make out a will even though she was the one who kept bringing up the subject and asking me what I thought; and every time she brought up the subject, I felt like I was playing the same role in the same movie.

I helped Hilda out every time she asked me. I thought that I had karma with Hilda. When I told this to my friend, Cynthia Kyle, Cynthia said, "No, Hilda has karma with you. It was part of her agreement when she came in to get this horse to you." Well, that explained why Hilda had initially said that she was willing me the horse and then had given him to me. Hilda did not give anything away to anybody. It was like she had a reversal in that she thought that money was love. Cynthia also said, "Hilda's hands are arthritic from clutching and holding onto her money and her possessions." I had told Hilda repeatedly when she brought up the subject of a will that I

23

would not accept any money or property. I thought that everyone should have at least one friend who didn't want their money, didn't want to work for them and loved them unconditionally. I also knew that there was something wrong with Hilda's money. I had seen a visual several times of the people who were out to get Hilda's money and property as cunning, vicious animals. They were all after the same prize, but none of them had the clarity of mind to see that what they were fighting for was a vial of poison. I found it very interesting that Hilda mentioned Scrooge at least once a month. She was highly critical of his greed, but she could not see it in herself. I assumed that it was Hilda's own greed that had made her money and possessions so toxic. As these observations came to me, I had to remain watchful that I did not fall into judgement of her, because I noticed that most of the people whom I had brought with me to meet and visit with Hilda would often get violently ill the next day, if not that evening. Consistently, it was only those who were highly critical of her or judged her who got sick. Those who stayed out of judgement were fine.

Finally in November, the farrier told me that I could start riding my horse and if he did well, that we would be able to shoe him in six weeks. I started working from scratch with Marauder for the third time, only this time very, very slowly. As Marauder was no longer half-starved, I could keep pieces of carrots in my pockets and give him occasional rewards while I was on his back. I was working as hard as I could to put enjoyment into our ride so that he would actually look forward to my getting on his back.

Before I left for New York, Hilda was again going back and forth about willing my horse to me and giving him to me. I watched the gemstone of her soul grow smaller and smaller. Once, a friend called her while I was sitting with Hilda. Her friend was so loud that I could hear both sides of the conversation. The woman told Hilda that she had heard from several sources that Ken was dealing drugs on her property again. Hilda closed up, said that she wasn't going to listen and hung up the phone. I watched her and waited to hear what she was going to say next. "Imagine the nerve of her telling me that Ken is involved with drugs. What do you think about her, Kathleen?" I reminded her that there were children taking riding lessons on her property, as well as adults and horses, and that she might consider checking into it for their safety. Hilda responded, "It is none of my concern. If he is dealing drugs, it doesn't affect me." I saw a vision of Hilda in a black tornado. It was like she was being swallowed down, but there was no bottom in sight. When I told Hilda what I had seen, she looked at me in astonishment and said, "That's exactly how I feel." I also saw glimpses of the people who were after Hilda's money being drawn by their own greed into her abyss. Until she made the attempt to try another way, take another course of action, Hilda would continue to be swallowed by the black hole of her own making.

When I returned from New York, I approached Hilda alone to ask her if she remembered that she had given me the horse. As always, Hilda was glad to see me when I walked in. I told her about my trip and the opera that I had seen. Suddenly, she started to cry. She looked at me and told me that I was the only one she trusted. With her next breath, she asked me to give her back the horse. I could not turn him back over into the hands of abusive trainers. She had to remember giving him to me in order to ask for him back. So, I promised her that I would keep him on her property for as long as she was alive. Then for the first time, with a worried look, she asked me what I thought about Ken. I had been sticking up for Mr. Maroney, Frank and Charles; this time, I could tell her that I thought Ken was the one who was messing up her records. I didn't want to frighten her; so, I did not tell her that several people, as well as myself, suspected that Ken had tricked her into signing a will and that he was actually trying to kill her.

The first two weeks of December I spent in Ireland and then Holland. In Dublin, I stayed at a lovely hotel on the Irish Sea. My dear friend, who is more like a sister, Kathryn O'Connell, came in from Killarney and shared my room for several nights. One evening, she asked me to show her how I dowsed. After she got the pendulum going, I started asking her questions about Marauder. All of a sudden, she looked at me and asked me if I had initiated him into the healing rays. I answered that he was up to the first level of Cahokia. Kathryn said, "I believe it! He is powerful and he has overlaid his astral body over me. He has something to say that you need to hear." What Marauder had to say was that he had loved Lydia until she betrayed him by abusing him. He had a trust issue that needed to be healed and he wanted our help. We sent him healing, which he accepted. Kathryn said, "I have to meet this horse of yours when I come to visit you in March."

When I returned home, I went out to see Marauder and I told him that I understood that he had loved Lydia and that she had hurt him. I also told him that if it hadn't been for Lydia, I never would have seen him, let alone started working with him. I told him that if he breathed away his worries, he would feel better. He breathed a sigh of relief. Some animals understand the spoken word better than others do. Each species has its own communicative gestures, and in addition, communicates telepathically by sending and receiving pictures. Oftentimes, animals understand us better than we understand ourselves.

I had planned a short trip to Europe for both Hilda's sake as well as for my horse. The upcoming trial with Delanti was putting a lot of pressure on Hilda, and more than once she had told me that she didn't think that she was going to make it. When I entered Hilda's home, I found out that she had fired Ken, Frank was on Christmas holiday with his family, and Fernando was with his family in Mexico for the entire month of December. Hilda didn't have much of a family left; she had never seen her ex-husband's illegitimate child. Bob had gotten one of the staff pregnant in the nursing home in which Hilda had placed him before their divorce. After Fred got guardianship of his brother, he kept Bob in the nursing home and actually hadn't seen him for two years. All of Hilda's money that Fred had accumulated by divorcing his brother from Hilda, along with the yearly alimony, was ultimately going to go to Bob's child. I wondered what Fred was doing with the money; guardians are held accountable in other states.

Hilda's brother had been dead for several years and Hilda told me that her sister-in-law started treating her badly after Hilda's mother died. Hilda's nephew, Tommy, had tried unsuccessfully to have her declared incompetent several years ago. When a court representative had come to Hilda's home, he asked her what day it was. Hilda said she did not always know what day it was, but she happened to know on that occasion and she told him. Then he asked her who was president and Hilda answered, "Hillary Clinton!", and slammed the door in his face. So, she wasn't talking to her nephew. Hilda's perception was that before Tommy had started legal action against her, he had been helping her get her affairs in order and they were becoming great friends until one day, he asked her why she inherited all of her mother's money and his father received nothing. Immediately after that incident, Tommy tried unsuccessfully to get guardianship of Hilda.

December 1996 - it was Christmastime and Hilda had been alone and lonely. In her vulnerable condition, Butch had been trying to talk Hilda into firing Charles and Frank and hiring a married couple with whom he was a friend. When I met the couple, Laurel and Ivan Hardy, their energy was dark and heavy. They were too arrogant to see how transparent their motives were. In addition, they were dirty and ill kept. They had recently declared bankruptcy and looked like they had been living out of their old, beat-up car. Hilda's ex-husband, her maid and I all tried to talk Hilda out of hiring them. It was the only time that I offered unsolicited advice to Hilda. The couple had told Hilda that they would work for less money than Charles and Frank, and bring her more money in. That was all Hilda needed to hear. The first week in January, she fired Charles and Frank. The day after she hired the couple, I saw Jacob on the ranch for the first time since May. Not only was this too much of a coincidence, but he pulled his cowboy hat down to hide his face when he saw me. When I called out, "Jacob? ! ?", he answered in his unmistakably deep voice. When I stopped in to see Hilda that day, she was cold and distant.

On January 11 at 11:45 at night, Frank called me. His voice was extremely agitated. He proceeded to tell me that he had been going back and forth in his mind about calling me. He said, "I know that Hilda was my client, but what she is planning on doing is wrong and falls outside of our client-accountant relationship. She told me that after you finish testifying for her against Delanti on February 4, she is going to tell you that the horse is no longer yours. If I were you, I'd call my attorney." I was shocked and asked Frank if he had any idea why Hilda was doing this. Frank answered, "Greed! You don't know her the way I do."

I don't know how many emotions came up for me - fear for the horse, anger at myself for not seeing this coming, the pain of betrayal and rejection, and the realization that I should have taken the time to find out how to register my horse when I got him instead of taking care of Hilda's business. I left a message on Ira's answering machine. When he got back to me on Monday, he informed me that verbal contracts are binding in the state of Arizona unless the value is over $500. In that case, there must be written documentation. He said that the board bills that I had faxed to him were considered written documentation. He told me that the horse was mine and that I should just move him. I began looking for a stable and found a farm close to where I lived. It was clean and the people who worked there were very nice. I also called and wrote to some of the people that I had brought over to meet Hilda. I knew that she had told a few of them about giving me the horse. Cynthia Kyle, Kim Williamson and Maria, Hilda's maid (who was also my maid), had their statements notarized for me and Frank was also willing to testify on my behalf.

Ira had drafted a letter for Hilda to sign that stated that she had given me the horse. I was going to present it to her. If she didn't sign it, I was going to take the legal steps necessary to have the horse registered in my name. Either way, I was still going to testify on her behalf at the upcoming trial. I knew how Hilda could be, but I knew that the truth in this instance was that Delanti was trying to cheat Hilda and I had to testify for her or I wouldn't be able to sleep at night. I also had to let Hilda's new attorney, Daniel Moriarty of the prestigious law firm of Bates, Mallory & Grimes, know about all this so that he would know what questions he shouldn't ask me on the witness stand. Hilda's trust in Mr. Maroney had deteriorated completely, she refused to pay him what she owed him for the work he had done thus far for her, and he quit. The lawyer from his office had been nice enough to continue working for Hilda until she found a new attorney, and when she hired Daniel, Mr. Maroney's law firm gave Daniel all of the work that they had done up to that point. When Daniel heard my plan, he asked me if I would please wait until after the trial to get the horse registered in my name. Daniel said that it would make his job of defending Hilda a lot harder if I proceeded before the trial; I would look like just another example of Hilda entering into a contract and then changing her mind. Instead of being a witness for Hilda, I would become a witness for Delanti. My first instinct was to say, "No!". Instead, I called Ira who thought that I should do this one last thing for Hilda and then simply get out while I still loved her. When I told this to Daniel, he breathed a sigh of relief and then told me that after the trial, he would try to convince Hilda to sign the letter that Ira had drawn up. He said that if Hilda were to take action against me after the trial, that he would not take the case. Daniel then asked me what I was going to do with Marauder and I told him that Ira had suggested that I had enough evidence to prove that Hilda had given him to me and that I should simply move him to another barn. Daniel said, "I am not your attorney, but if I was, I would tell you to do the same thing."

Since I didn't have Marauder's yellow hauling tag, I couldn't trailer him to the new barn. Instead, I was going to have to ride him 2 1/2 miles, and most of the ride was going to be off the shoulder of Santa Fe Boulevard, which had six lanes of traffic. Penny Cantley said that she could help me. So, on Sunday morning, January 19, we went out for breakfast and then we drove over to Hilda's ranch in my car. While I saddled up Marauder, I watched as Hassle Free nervously trotted back and forth. I was afraid that she would work herself into a state and then colic. I had only seen Hilda's new managers on the ranch once since they had been hired and they were more interested in my horse than they were in learning about which ones were Hilda's and what they needed. So, I moved Exquisite, Marauder's mother, into Marauder's run. I used to turn the two mares out together whenever there was a free turnout, and they liked one another. As we rode out, I turned around and saw that Hassle Free had calmed down. I asked the angels to protect the two horses and I saw a soft blue light shower down over them.

Marauder and I made it to Santa Fe Boulevard with only a few short stops. At the intersection, I managed to push the walk button. When the light turned green and the little walking man lit up, we started to cross the street. We made it across the eastbound lane, but Marauder chose to stop in the middle of the westbound lane. He lifted his tail and relieved himself, much to the absolute horror of the woman passenger in the far right-hand lane. I didn't look over to see what was going on with the rest of the people in the cars. In the meantime, our green light had turned red and the little walking man was nowhere to be seen. The traffic waited for us to get across without anyone honking his or her horn or attempting to drive around us. Arizona drivers are seldom this polite! Many of them look like they think they are running the gauntlet. Between the Yahoos, drunks, nearblind and combinations of the aforementioned, Maracopa County must lead the country in traffic fatalities.

Once across Santa Fe Boulevard, we had other less-busy streets to cross, but the worst one was behind us. I chose to ride him on the north side because earlier that week, I had seen that that shoulder was deeper than the one on the south side of the boulevard. I also thought that if we left early enough on a Sunday morning, there wouldn't be much traffic. The traffic was not as bad as on a weekday, but it was still there, including two motorcyclists. It certainly helped when the ambulance driver turned off his siren when he drove by. I knew that Marauder trusted me because he knew that I loved him and respected him, but even so, I was surprised at how well he was doing. Even when the rollerblader went by us twice, he remained steady under my soft but firm hands and voice. When any of us takes right action and allows Mother-Father God to work through us, miracles are probable; however, I knew that if I lost it, he would too, and I would be galloping down a major boulevard on a horse with a fried brain. Once at the new farm, I took off his saddle and bridle and then turned him loose in a large turnout where he spent the day running and bucking. Penny had wanted to wait for me at the new farm to make sure that we made it all right. While she and I watched Marauder carrying on, Barb, the ranch manager, came out and joined us. She was interested in hearing about what was going on with Hilda. Apparently, lots of people knew about the hay running out and the growing manure piles and the theft; it was hard to believe that Hilda had built a multimillion-dollar business. There were also lots of rumors about Delanti taking over Hilda's ranch. I was glad that I had the opportunity to tell her a little bit about what was happening, but I didn't want to pile it all on her at once.

Marauder acted as though he was able to breathe fresh air for the first time in his life. He was more relaxed at the new ranch. James was the only animal abuser on the ranch and he had nothing to do with Marauder. We had just begun to trot before we left Hilda's ranch. When we trotted, I had to be careful not to let him panic and slip into frenzy. If he started to lose it, I would try first to calm him down at the walk and if that didn't work, I would dismount, untack him and let him run and buck it out in a large turnout. Once when I was riding him, another horse was being shown in halter to a prospective buyer. The individual showing the horse had a large bullwhip. The horse suddenly started to act up and while the horse was not being whipped, in Marauder's perception, he must have thought that the horse was being hurt because suddenly Marauder lost it entirely. At that point, I had to calm him down just so that I could get off of him. It took a long time for his brain to cool down. Whipping and bullying has the same effect on horses as it does on people - it just doesn't work!

I still had Maria clean for me. Frank and Mr. Maroney were the only ones who knew that I utilized Maria's cleaning services and that Maria continued to tell me what was going on at Hilda's ranches. One day, Maria arrived at my home with the news that Hilda, at her manager's suggestion, had hired another couple to live with her. The man was a heavy drinker and he kept Hilda's glass full. The woman was supposed to cook, but her idea of a meal was fast-food restaurants. I knew that Hilda had told Frank that she hid close to a half million dollars in cashier's checks and real money in her home. When Hilda had told me this piece of information and wanted to show me the money, I declined. I did not want to know! I never told anyone about the money because I did not want to put Hilda at risk. Maria arrived at my home one day to clean and told me that the couple was gone, as well as Hilda's money. Hilda was currently angry with Maria because this time, she thought that Maria had stolen a bar of soap. So, Maria was not cleaning or cooking for Hilda for several weeks. Either Hilda or her new managers had talked Hilda into believing lies about Maria again. "Thank God I have not been to the house of Hilda. If I had, she would have accused me of stealing her money." I silently thought to myself the same thing. Later, when I talked to Daniel about Hilda's upcoming trial, I told him that at Ira's advice, I had moved Maruader. Daniel again said he would have given me the same advice. When I asked about the theft, he was shocked that nobody had told him.

Hilda's trial was postponed to February 12 because Delanti's lawyer was ill. Frank, a real estate agent any myself waited in the lobby to be called to testify. Frank was going to say that Hilda always had a lawyer present whenever she had sold property in the past; the real estate agent was going to testify that Skylark ranch was worth considerably more that 1.8 million dollars; I was the only one who could prove fraud. The judge had called for a break before Daniel presented Hilda's case. Daniel wheeled Hilda, who looked as though she was having a good day, into the lobby. Laurel and Ivan Hardy followed them. Everyone listened as Hilda asked me why I hadn't been coming around to see her. Ivan immediately interjected, "We were not the ones who had the injunction issued against you prohibiting you from contacting Hilda or coming on the property. It was, ah, one of the boarders who didn't like you." As I had never been served with with any papers, I wondered what Ivan was taking about. Then Hilda asked me if I was still riding Baskabas. In order to test the grounds to determine where I stood with her, I reminded her that she had given him to me. Hilda immediately clinched her fists and shouted, "I said that I was going to will him to you!"

Neither Frank nor myself had been called in to give a deposition; Delanti's lawyer was either overly confident or incompetent or both. On the witness stand, I did the best job that I could of telling the truth. Hilda had her left hand over the left side of her face and would only occasionally peer out at me between two of her fingers. At one point, I could feel my emotions welling up in my throat. Mrs. Delanti's mouth dropped open when I testified that I was with Hilda the day before and also on the morning of the day they had come to her home in the first week in April and that Hilda had clearly told me that they were coming to give her the last payment on the ranch that they had purchased from her, not to give her a $20,000 deposit on Skylark Ranch. Delanti's lawyer was so completely unprepared that at one point, he asked me,

"Isn't it true that you were a witness for Mrs. Hood in her trial with Potter?" I answered, "No, I did not testify; Hilda asked me to be there as a friend to support her in the courtroom." Then he asked me about the statement that I had helped Hilda prepare in her trial with Potter. I also mentioned Potter's testimony and his lawyer's remarks at the August trial. Even though Daniel had successfully removed Potter from testifying, the judge who was hearing the Delanti case was the same judge who had heard several of the hearings between Potter and Hilda. Daniel had told me that Hilda was on record for lying under oath in the judge's courtroom. So, instead of using Potter as an example of Hilda not fulfilling an obligation that she entered into, the incident became a positive one for Hilda's case. Delanti's lawyer then asked me if I was familiar with the fact that Hilda had agreed to sell Skylark Ranch to Delanti for a reduced price in exchange for the development being named Hilda Cauldron, after her maiden name? I looked at the judge and said, "Nobody would know who Hilda Cauldron was! Hilda doesn't even sign her name Hilda C. Hood! As Fred Hood is also a developer in Arizona, it is Mr. Delanti who would not want the name Hood on any of his housing projects." The judge just looked at me and nodded in agreement. Later, Daniel told me, "You were great, Kathleen!" I asked Daniel if he was going to turn Delanti over to the legal authorities on fraud charges if the judge decided in Hilda's favor. Daniel answered, "No, Delanti will probably have to pay Hilda's court costs and that will be punishment enough for him." I wondered how many inmates in Sheriff Joe's internationally infamous desert "Tent City Jail" would gladly pay the state's court costs in exchange for their freedom? Collectively they probably hadn't done as much financial theft or damage as this one developer. Victor's wife had told me that they had been introduced to Delanti the first night that they had moved to Scottsdale. Delanti was drunk out of his mind at a local restaurant and bragging about how he had just swindled somebody out of their property. I had told Daniel about this before the trial, but for whatever his reasons, he chose not to call either Victor or his wife in to testify.

It was Frank who called me weeks later to tell me that Daniel had called him with the news that the judge had decided the previous week in favor of Hilda. We both wondered why Daniel hadn't bothered to call me. When I phoned Ira to find out what Hilda had said when Daniel had taken Ira's letter to her, Ira said that Daniel had not gotten back to him. Weeks later, Daniel told Ira that Hilda refused to sign it. Ira was again trying to legally get Marauder registered in my name.

In the middle of February, I had three women from India come to my home to be initiated into the other rays of healing and learn how to do the Tera-Mai™ Seichem initiations. They left on March 2, the same day my friend, Kathryn O'Connell, arrived from Ireland. Later that week, we were both at my home when I answered a knock at my door. A detective from the Scottsdale police department was investigating a charge that I had stolen a $100,000 stallion on either March 2 or 3. Apparently, Hilda's managers and Butch thought for almost 2 months that Exquisite, a 22-year-old mare with a swayback, was a 7-year-old stallion. The detective also showed me a restraining order prohibiting me from visiting Hilda or stepping foot on her property. It had been issued by Daniel's law firm and certified as having been served. The detective was surprised when I told him that I had never seen it before. The Scottsdale detective believed me! After I had told Daniel that Ira Schwartz had told me to move the horse, Daniel probably drew up the restraining order but did not have it served so as to insure that I would testify for Hilda. However, by having it certified as having been served he could later say that I had been on Hilda's property illegally when I moved the horse.

Kathryn stepped out of the guest bedroom to see who had arrived and then promptly spun around and retreated when she saw his handcuffs and gun. She said later that this would have been unheard-of in Ireland, and that she would certainly have a good story to tell when she got home. I showed the detective my board bills from Hilda's ranch and the board bills that I had from the new ranch for January and February, and the signed affidavits. He said, "You have too much. I am not going to charge you with horse theft. I am going to turn this over as a civil matter." Even though the Scottsdale detective informed the press of his decision, that night the local news reported anyway that a horse thief was on the loose and that a $100,000 stallion had been stolen. Hilda told anyone who would listen that I was the horse thief.

Cynthia Kyle and Kim Williamson both called to tell me about a dream that they had had. In this dream, they saw a man handing me some papers regarding my horse and that I was smiling. They went on to say, each in their own words, that when lawyers are involved, things get sticky, and while events may not look good from the outside, that everything would turn out all right in the end. Ira Schwartz called to tell me that when he had checked the Department of Agriculture's records, he found that Hilda did not have a registration in the name of Baskabas and that she had more than twenty registrations that were listed simply as 'horse'. The descriptions on the 'horse' tags were so general that each one of them could describe a hundred or more horses in Arizona. Ira went on to say that Daniel Moriarty had still not gotten back to him as to whether or not Hilda was going to sign the letter that he had drawn up. Ira also suggested that I use another attorney because he had worked for Hilda for a day, and if she wanted to make a fuss, she could delay things. Ira suggested that I call Edgar Arnold, who had done 'horse stuff' before. When I met with Edgar, he told me that I had a great case. He suggested that because of the overwhelming amount of evidence, we ask for a summary judicial hearing.

Even though there was a dispute over the ownership of my horse, Marauder was not locked up and I was free to ride him at any time. The judge had ordered that Marauder remain where he was until the civil matter was resolved. Ira had suggested that I call the agricultural agent and tell him everything that had happened. When I spoke with him I also told him that the police had turned the case over as a civil matter and that there was a court order preventing him from being ridden or hauled off of the property. When the agricultural agent went out to talk to Barb, she showed him my board bills with "No Charge Per Hilda" on them and openmouthed he said to her, "I didn't know Kathleen had these. This changes everything."

Hilda's managers had come over several times to see my horse, but Barb and the rest of the staff simply told them they could not show them my horse. Maria had told me that Hilda had only received 15 boarders' checks for over 300 horses for the month of February. Hilda's manager's theft was so blatant that Ivan had told one of the trainers on the property to make out his monthly check of $3,000 directly to him and not tell his wife. One of Hilda's boarders called me and I found out that Ivan had been telling boarders to make out their checks to Skylark Ranch. Hilda didn't have an account under Skylark Ranch! In light of this, I couldn't believe that her managers were like 'Laurel and Hardy', calling a great deal of attention to themselves.

Early on the morning of April 1, the agricultural agent told Barb that Hilda had found her registration and hauling tag for Baskabas and that he was going to compare the markings on the state registration with the markings on my horse. He told Barb not to tell me because if I interfered, he would have to arrest me. Early the following morning, Barb called me in tears, saying that the agricultural agent and Hilda's managers had picked up my horse. My heart dropped, and I left an anxious message on my attorney's answering machine. I knew that I had to get into a place of allowing the horse's higher self to do whatever it was that he needed to do; yet, at the same time be able to make choices so that the necessary legal steps could be taken. Hilda's managers had acted as her attorney and interfered with an ongoing civil matter by presenting misleading and incomplete information to a court, which issued an order prohibiting me from harassing Hilda. Spirit sent me a message, "No matter what happens, everything is in Divine Order." When I called the agricultural agent, he suggested that I write to both the International Arabian Horse Association in Colorado and the National Show Horse Registry in Kentucky to check the registration for Baskabas.

I tried to meditate in order to calm myself down; I felt as though a child had been kidnapped. The spirit of Hilda's mother came to me in meditation. I asked her, "What is going on with Hilda? Why does she continually draw to herself problems and punishment?" Even Hilda's own attorneys said that they had never seen anything like it in their lives. Hilda's mother simply showed me a vision of Hilda signing her mother's name on a will and thereby cheating her brother out of his inheritance. Hilda had justified her actions because she felt that she had been cheated and mistreated; Hilda was not conscious enough to forgive and go on. Hilda had been punishing herself ever since, but at the same time, she continued to justify other wrongful actions. Evil begets evil! Hilda hated Fred because he had done the same thing to her as she had done to her brother; Fred hated Hilda because she reflected his own greed and dishonesty back to him.

My attorney, Edgar, decided that the injunction prohibiting me from harassing Hilda was outrageous and he wanted to represent me in court and have the injunction reversed. Less than a week before the court date, I heard from both horse registries. Neither one of them had a registration listed for Baskabas under any possible spelling. Any national horse registration papers that Hilda's managers had come up with either belonged to another horse or were forged. The day before the court date, Edgar called me. Hilda's managers and her law firm lifted the injunction against me. Daniel had been representing Hilda in the matter even though he had told me that he wouldn't. Edgar had him removed from the case, but not the law firm. The law firm wanted me to promise not to try to see or contact Hilda. Edgar also told me that the federal government, specifically the Department of Labor, had indicted Frank. Edgar Arnold was representing Frank. I wondered if it had anything to do with Hilda's illegal Mexican help? Edgar told me that it involved another one of Frank's accounts.

Shortly after the injunction against me was lifted, Edgar had a 180-degree change in attitude concerning my case. Suddenly, according to Edgar, I went from having a great case to a "she said/she said" case and an ordinary hearing. I went in to see Edgar and one of the partners of the law firm, Sam, on the Monday before the horse hearing, which was supposed to be held on May 7, to find out that Edgar had only spoken with the two witnesses who were unable to be at the hearing - Frank and Ira. If I hadn't called Penny, Cynthia, Barbara and Hilda's maid, they would not have made plans to come on May 7. Edgar also informed me that Frank was changing his story concerning Marauder and myself. Frank had faxed two of my board bills to me and at the top of the FAX were not only the date and time, but Frank's initials and FAX number as well. The Phone Company would also have a record of the two calls coming into my FAX machine at the same day and time. The question for Frank would be, "Why were you sending a board bill to an individual who did not own a horse?" Why did you put 'NO CHARGE PER MRS. HOOD' on Kathleen's board bills if you hadn't OK'd it first with Hilda Hood?" If I had been training Baskabas for Hilda, I would have received a paycheck, not a boarding bill. I could hardly believe that Edgar was not advising his client, Frank, that he was playing <u>Monopoly</u> and writing his very own 'GO TO JAIL' card. By Friday, I had come up with a list of twelve reasons why I wanted Sam, one of the partners, to completely take over my case. If Edgar had been bought out, it was not about my horse; it concerned Hilda's $10,000,000+ estate, not just the $30,000 to $40,000 monthly billing that her two ranches pulled in. If 'Laurel and Hardy' were involved, they were hardly capable of pulling this off by themselves. Somebody was behind them. Fred ? ?

The hearing had been moved and I made an appointment to see Sam the following Monday. Sam agreed to take over my case and asked me to contact the horse registries again to find out the names of the horses that Hilda did have registered with them and I agreed to do so. The National Show Horse Registry only showed Hassle Free under Hilda's name; the International Arabian Horse Association had two accounts listed under Hilda's name, and again the only half-Arab horse registered was Hassle Free. There was nothing under Hilda's ranches, Hilda was not incorporated and she was the sole owner of her horses. Where were the other half Arabs listed that Hilda still owned who had been shown in national competitions under their real names? The only reason that Exquisite and Hilda's two half-Arabian stallions would no longer be listed under Hilda's name is if they had been sold. Could Hilda or her managers switched horses, had the valuable horses' papers transferred to the supposed new owners and kept the real horses? As stallions were involved, even Hilda would not have enough money to settle all of the lawsuits. If the swindling scheme extended to Hilda's full-blooded Arabs and Hackney Ponies, Donald Trump would not have enough money to settle all of the claims. When Baskabas was born, Hilda would not have been able to register him under his dame's name if Hilda no longer had Exquisite' papers. When Baskabas exhibited winning qualities, they couldn't show him without national registration papers. It is illegal but not unheard of for a winning stallion to be shown under another stallion's name in order for the owner to collect high breeding fees.

Everyone we meet in life reflects back to us where we are. When I asked what it was that Hilda was reflecting back to me, the answer I received was guilt, and that I was not giving myself permission to experience the extra frills that life offered. At any time along her life's path, Hilda could have taken responsibility for what she had done, or she could have reversed her downward spiral by taking only one positive action that would have been completely out of character for her. By stubbornly holding onto her guilt, even though Hilda was a multimillionaire and had many good qualities, her life was a misery. Her house, beautiful in appearance, was dark inside and filled with cockroaches; the large garage was packed with both junk and nice things that Hilda would never use again. Her house was a Freudian reflection of her life, and Hilda reflects back to all of us our own guilt and denials. I know in my heart that Marauder in another

35

lifetime as a man had done similar things to what Hilda had done. It was my horse's karma to expose the corruption and I was helping him, just as I could have helped Hilda, if she had let me.

In meditation, Spirit showed me that during the last year, I had spent too much time helping Hilda and not enough time writing my second book. So, I had been given this time to be without him as an 'opportunity' to finish my book. I had never meddled in Hilda's affairs, but only stepped in when she asked for help. Somewhere along the way, I became too involved. Hilda didn't know how to return love, and she treated terribly those who had honest motives and were kind to her. Rather than dismiss her dishonest agents, she kept them on so that she could complain and play the role of a victim. Her grasping for every dollar that she could get her hands on was a substitute for love.

Against my attorney's objections, Hilda's relatives' attorney postponed the hearing for a third time. Besides other evidence, they were more than likely using my case as an example of her incompetent behavior. Hilda had no case, no witnesses, and since Marauder would only allow me to ride him and was of no possible use to her, Hilda was spending more money than he was worth trying to get him back. I had four witnesses, board bills, oral contracts are binding in the state of Arizona, and gifts (be that gift livestock or whatever) cannot be taken back by the giver. The judge was told, "Hilda may not be able to testify in her own behalf". When Sam called to give me the bad news, he also told me that he thought Hilda's relatives would sign my horse over to me after they got custody of Hilda. I was also able to have an agent go out to Hilda's property to check on Marauder. Sam decided to look through the Department of Agriculture's records again and found that Hilda did have a yellow hauling tag for Baskabas - it had been issued April 1, 1997. It looked like the agent had come out early on the morning of April 1 to draw my horse's markings on a hauling card, not to compare them with an already-existing hauling tag, which is illegal. Neither Hilda nor her managers knew the exact markings on my horse, which is why Hilda's managers had kept coming out to try to see him. Since they couldn't gain access to my horse, they found another way.

I appointed Barbara as my agent. She brought along a camera when she went out to see Marauder. His supposed trainer did not know where his stall was. When they found him, he looked so drugged that Barbara hardly recognized him. When the trainer took him out to a turnout and asked him to run, he stood for a long time and then trotted with his head down so far that his nose practically touched the ground. Marauder hadn't seen a farrier since he arrived on Hilda's property; his hoofs were long and cracked and his shoes were pinching his feet and hurting him. When Barbara asked Hilda's managers when Marauder had had his last shots or worming, they said that they did not know. I was outraged when I saw the pictures. In addition, Daniel was still involved; his signature was on various legal documents in connection with the case and he had represented Hilda before the judge via telephone. Spirit told me to give them my righteous anger, and as I did I asked that Divine Will and Divine Justice prevail for all parties concerned.

Barbara found a vet who drew blood and sent it to a lab; however, the tests came back negative which would indicate that Marauder was not drugged, but rather in a deep state of depression. However, I discovered later that the vet had ordered a general blood test and not one specifically for depressants. Barbara also took a trainer out with her on one occasion and they found that Hilda's other horses were half starved and in terrible condition; one of the horses was five hundred pounds underweight and looked like a walking skeleton. Hilda was not receiving enough board money to pay her bills, and she was not using her personal money to meet her obligations. When the hay was low on Hilda's ranches, did Hilda's managers tell the workers not to feed Hilda's horses? One of Hilda's prize stallions and five other horses were missing. Did they starve to death or had Hilda's managers sold them to the stockyard? In either of these scenarios, evidence of the illegal horse operation was destroyed.

Maria and Frank went to visit Hilda before the horse hearing. They both tried to convince Hilda to regive Baskabas back to me. Her lawyers and managers had gotten her too worked up over the matter; she refused! Hilda was quite upset with Maria that day because Hilda had found out from Ivan Hardy that Maria was going to testify against. Maria also found out that Buddy had become severely ill shortly after my horse had been stolen and that Hilda had fired 'Laurel and Hardy' but they refused to leave the main house on Skylark ranch and were continuing to collect her boarder's money. After Maria and Frank left, Hilda accused Maria of stealing an unusual antique turquoise ring that she often wore. When Maria told me what had happened, I wondered what else Daniel hadn't told Hilda, and how could Hilda be both calculating and incompetent?

Kim was unable to get off of work again in order to attend the horse hearing now scheduled for June 27. Instead, she was asked to give a telephone deposition. Daniel's law firm had appointed another attorney, Eugene Dufarge, to represent Hilda. Hilda's attorneys had written to Sam saying that, yes, Hilda had told people that she had given Kathleen Baskabas, but what she meant was that it was a gift in a will. Kim kept repeating that the word gift was used, not the word will.

Frank also gave a deposition because he was not available on June 27. Frank changed the facts. He said that was aware of the fact that Hilda had willed me the horse but he was not aware of the fact that she had given him to me. When asked if he could describe the circumstances of how it came about that he began sending me board bills Frank answered, "Kathleen approached me and asked me if I would send her a monthly board bill showing zero balance due and I did so." When asked why he did it Frank answered, "I did that because Kathleen requested that I do it. She was a good friend of Dorothy. I didn't feel there was any harm in it, and also it helped me with my accounting because I could then match an invoice to a stall and to a horse." When asked if he had ever discussed the zero-balance board bills with Hilda, Frank answered that he never had. Later he added, "In hindsight, it probably wasn't the best decision on my part, but I saw no harm in that." Frank also testified that on the way to the Delanti trial in February, Hilda had told him that she would not be giving me the horse after the trial. Eugene confidently asked Frank if Hilda had ever given a horse away before. Frank answered, "Yes! I know that this is true because it was also a tax write off and I had to get documentation as to the value of the horse." Eugene almost fell over in complete shock. As part of her defense, Hilda had told Bates, Mallory & Grimes that she had never given a horse away to anyone and she wasn't about ready to start now. Sam said, "You should have seen him! I thought Eugene Dufarge was going to fall on the floor when he heard Frank's answer." I was shocked when Sam told me about Frank's testimony. I wondered if Edgar Arnold had somehow managed to convince Frank to testify in such a manner? Sam argued in court that because as Hilda's agent, Frank was authorized by Hilda to send out board bills, that his sending board bills to me was strictly a matter between Frank and Hilda and she was stuck with his actions.

Shortly after Kim's telephone deposition, Sam called again to tell me that Bates, Mallory & Grimes had made a settlement offer. They wanted me to purchase the horse for what it would cost me to go through the trial. Sam said that that would amount to two or three thousand dollars and he suggested that I take the offer. I told him to go ahead and tell them that they had a deal. In this way I would spare everyone having to go through the trial. A couple of days later, Sam called to tell me that apparently Bates, Mallory & Grimes had not consulted Hilda before they had called him, and when they presented the idea to Hilda, she refused.

Hilda's first incompetency hearing occurred before the horse hearing. Sam found out that Hilda's managers had testified against her, saying she had short-term memory loss, etc. On June 27, Bates, Mallory & Grimes put Ivan Hardy on the stand to testify as Hilda's attorney knowing that Hilda had fired him two weeks before. When Sam asked Ivan of 'Laurel and Hardy' if Hilda had short-term memory loss, Ivan perjured himself by saying, "No!" even with a copy of his testimony in front of him. Marauder's supposed trainer also lied under oath. Hilda was wearing the turquoise ring that she had accused Maria of stealing. She was completely frazzled during her testimony. Unable to keep her lies straight; she made herself look incompetent.

Sam had asked me before the trial how he should go about questioning Hilda. He said that it was difficult for any attorney to cross-examine an elderly woman without having it look like they were beating up on her. I told Sam that it is hard enough for anyone to keep his or her lies straight. Hilda at 93 and failing memory would not be able to keep her lies logical. My suggestion was to keep his questions simple and be as gentle with her as he could. When Sam asked Hilda if she had ever given a horse away before, she answered, "No! Yes, I think to one of my managers before he left. No! Maybe the horse's name was Trogon. No!" She had pictures of Stormsfury but none of Marauder even though he was in her possession and at one point, she referred to Marauder as a mare. She did admit that she had originally intended to will Marauder to me and later Sam told me, "That counts, if she dies, I am putting in a claim for the horse." Hilda's mind was actually very sharp and calculating the day of the trial. Once, she injected into her answer that she had found out that I did not know anything about horses, but since I was only riding Marauder at the walk that she didn't think I could do much harm. Hilda was already thinking ahead and trying to get out of paying me the $50,000 to $80,000 that she would owe me under the Unjust Enrichment Act if I lost the case. I wondered if Hilda's knowledge about horses was truly so limited that she was unaware of the damage a bad rider can have on a horse even at the walk or if that was the best lie that she could come up with. Looking at her then, I could hardly believe that I considered this woman a friend. I felt like a Piscean fish, who had just been taken in one more time. Why didn't I see people like Hilda coming?

I told my story, and when asked about the board bills I had received from Frank, I stated that in order to put "No charge per Mrs. Hood" on them, Frank would have had to ask Hilda's permission. Maria was also able to testify that she knew from Hilda that I had been given free board. Eugene could neither looked at me when he asked me questions nor when I answered. My witnesses were consistent and the facts that Hilda and her agents had filed a false police report and that the horse's hauling tag had been issued illegally was also brought out. The judge ruled in the middle of the trial that Hilda had given me the horse. According to the gift articles in the state of Arizona: "A gift of any goods or chattels is not valid unless the gift is in writing, duly acknowledged and recorded, or by will, duly proved and recorded or unless actual possession of the gift is passed to and remains with the donee or some one claiming under him." Sam had proved all of the conditions in order for a gift to be considered a gift. Two weeks later, the judge ruled in favor of Hilda because he decided that because she had not given me a bill of sale at the time she gave him to me that that invalidated the gift. Even in Frank's deposition when Eugene asked him, "do you have any understanding regarding whether any type of paperwork is necessary in Arizona to effect the gift or transfer ownership of a horse?" Frank answered, "No, I am not familiar with any procedure." Ira called the ruing nonsense when I told him. He said, "If the judge really felt that you really needed a bill of sale, he should have ordered Hilda to give you one. "

Because of the judge's first ruling, Sam wanted me to appeal the case. He said that he had already proved that a gift had been made and that all he needed to do was prove that the judge's ruling concerning that a lack of a bill invalidated the gift was in error. Sam said that he would keep the costs to a minimum. So, Sam wrote the appeal.

I. STATEMENT OF THE CASE

Plaintiff/Appellant Kathleen Milner brought a declaratory judgment seeking to establish her right of ownership of a horse named Marauder. Marauder is an eight year old gelded horse that Defendant/Appellee Hilda Hood gave to Ms. Milner. A replevin hearing was held in front of a Commissioner of the Arizona Superior Court on June 27, 1997. The Commissioner pursuant to an Order dated July 21, 1997, found that despite evidence of a valid *inter vivos* gift, the transfer of the horse was invalid because a bill of sale did not accompany the gift.

1) STATEMENT OF FACTS

Ms. Milner and the Appellee were formerly very good friends. The Appellee owns two ranches in north Scottsdale. The testimony was that she owns fourteen horses and boards others at her ranches. Ms. Milner provided assistance to the Appellee in managing the two ranches by, among other things, making arrangements for "board bills" to be paid.

According to the Appellee's own testimony, in March 1996, the Appellee agreed to leave Marauder to Ms. Milner in the Appellee's will. Ms. Milner testified that in early May 1996, the Appellee's ranch manager at the time told Ms. Milner "the horse is yours now Kathleen." Ms. Milner confirmed this in a conversation later that day with the Appellee. At the replevin hearing, Ms. Milner introduced the testimony of three witnesses, including the Appellee's former housekeeper, who confirmed the gift had been made. All of these witnesses testified to the Appellee's numerous and unequivocal statements confirming that she had given the horse to Ms. Milner. See also deposition of Kimberly Williamson submitted to the Trial Court by agreement of the parties in lieu of live testimony. The testimony was that horses had been given as gifts on previous occasions by the

Appellee. See deposition of Ms. Hood's accountant submitted to the Trial Court by agreement of the parties in lieu of live testimony.

The testimony also indicated that after May 1996, Mr. Milner renamed the horse and was the only person to care for the horse other than the minimal care provided to all horses boarded at the ranch. Ms. Milner elected to keep Marauder at the Appellee's ranch until January 1997, and then moved the horse to another ranch in Scottsdale. The uncontroverted evidence was that the horse was moved in an "open and notorious" manner, and neither the Appellee nor her agents protested the horse's removal or took any action with respect to this matter until March 1997. The evidence was that action was taken shortly after Ms. Milner acted as a key witness for the Appellee in a lawsuit in which the Appellee successfully rescinded a contract to sell one of her ranches. Ms. Milner brought her replevin action after the Appellee's agents took the horse.

At the hearing, Appellee's counsel asserted that Ms. Milner's claim should fail as a matter of law in light of the Appellee's failure to provide a bill of sale for the horse. The hearing was continued on two occasions, and went forward almost two months after the replevin action was filed. Why the Appellee waited until the date of the hearing to raise this issue with the Trial Court is a mystery to Ms. Milner's counsel. In any event, the Trial Court decided to hear testimony, and permitted counsel to supply post-trial memoranda on the effect of the "bill of sale statute on the law of *inter vivos* gifts. After the hearing, the Trial Court ruled that the Appellee's failure to provide a bill of sale negated the gift and therefore denied the relief requested. Ms. Milner believes this ruling is clearly erroneous for the reasons set forth herein. Ms. Milner sought Special Action Relief with respect to the Commissioner's ruling. This Court declined to accept special action jurisdiction via an Order dated August 12, 1997, and did not reach the merits of the issue presented. This appeal followed.

2) ISSUE PRESENTED

WHETHER THE STATUTE GOVERNING BILLS OF SALE IN THE CONTEXT OF LIVESTOCK INVALIDATES THE COMMON LAW AND STATUTORY LAW RELATING TO *INTER VIVOS GIFTS* AND CONTRACTS.

3) STANDARD OF REVIEW

As set forth above, this case involves strictly a question of law. When reviewing a conclusion of law, the Court of Appeals is not bound by the trial court's conclusions, and will review such question *de novo*. Interpretation of a statute is a question of law that is reviewed *de novo*.

41

4)   ARGUMENT

The Trial Court erroneously held that the agricultural laws requires a bill of sale in the transfer of livestock and that any transfer not accompanied by such is invalid and unenforceable. The contrary, the requirement of a bill of sale for the transfer of livestock does **not** preclude a party from transferring livestock through common law means and does not allow a party to invalidate a valid contract or gift.

In her attempt to renege on a gift that was proven with overwhelming evidence that the Trial Court below, Appellee "grafted" language on the bill of sale statute that is simply not there. A reading of the statute itself demonstrates the fallacy of the Appellee's argument. The statute at issue reads as follows: Upon *the sale or transfer of livestock, delivery of the animals shall be accompanied by a written and acknowledged bill of sale from the vendor to the purchaser.*

The statute is conspicuous in what it does **not** say. Appellee is reading the statute to say that no transfer of any livestock is effective until a bill of sale has been provided. It does not say that. It does not even imply that. If the legislature had chosen to provide that a transfer was not complete until a bill of sale had been provided, it could have very easily done so by language to that effect. There is absolutely no language requiring a bill of sale to effect a transfer. The fact that no such language appears anywhere in the statute is conclusive of the legislature's intent that the statute should not be given the meaning ascribed by Respondent and endorsed by the Trial Court. The law simply imposes upon the seller/ transferor a duty to provide a bill of sale. It seems clear that the purpose of the statute is to avoid conflicts over ownership for livestock roaming on the open range, or as against third parties claiming ownership. The statute serves no other legitimate purpose, and was not intended to provide a mechanism for a seller/giver to avoid his or her promise.

Of great significance, Arizona law provides that in case of alleged theft a bill of sale if "prima facie evidence" of ownership. If a bill of sale is only "prima facie evidence" of ownership, a bill of sale is by definition not conclusive. Logically, other evidence of a transfer is contemplated.

Moreover, it is axiomatic that "Statutes are not to be construed as effecting any change in the common law beyond that which is clearly indicated. ••• If possible, statutory enactments should be construed as consistent with the common law.

Sam backed up his statements with facts and law. His opening brief continued on siting other cases and refuted the case made by Hilda's attorneys. All of Daniel's responses were a continuation of the twisting and misrepresenting of the law that was his trademark. During the ensuing months, Bates, Mallory & Grimes did everything they could to make the case as expensive and as drawn out as they could. Any reasonable request my attorney made was countered with a barrage of legal tactics. Somehow, Daniel successfully argued that the case could not go to appeals. So, my attorney was left pursuing avenues through the lower courts.

That summer I made the choice to go back to Europe to escape the chaos that my life had become. I returned to Arizona the first week in September to the news that Arizona's Governor Symington had been found guilt in federal court of fraud. When he was forced to leave office, among other things, he had left the Arizona school system in a state of disaster. Sam informed me that in July, Hilda's relatives had been successful in having her declared incompetent. However, the judge handed over Hilda's estate to an Arizona bank and the Phoenix Forty Bank was intent on persuing the same insanity over the horse that had resulted in Hilda being declared incompetent in the first place. It looked as though Daniel had created the case for billable time and now Phoenix Forty Bank and Bates, Mallory & Grimes were using the horse as their 'cash cow'. Sam went on to say that because of a letter he received in May from Bates, Mallory & Grimes stating, "Hilda Hood told Ms. Milner's witnesses that Baskabas was a gift in a will to Ms. Milner. • • • " that when Hilda died, I inherited the horse. I wondered if Bates, Mallory & Grimes were even aware of the amusing fact that I was officially the only one on record who was being willed anything? The judge who had presided over the horse hearing was going through a nasty, expensive divorce; if he had received any bribe money, all that he had gotten and more would soon quickly be eaten up by his own lawyers.

It has been my personal experience that our animals pick us. If we should try to own or hold onto an animal that is supposed to belong to another, the results can be disastrous. Before I bought Abez, he had been breaking down fences, butting down gates and raising all kinds of other havoc. After I bought Abez, his outrageous behavior ended. I had boarded him for a short time at a stable where the owner/trainer bought thoroughbreds off of the track, retrained them and then sold them. Once, an Illinois hunter/jumper trainer with a formidable reputation came up to Wisconsin and casually got on Doc. Doc then proceeded to almost kill them both. A week later, a young woman who had just learned how to ride came out with her trainer to look at the horses that were for sale. When she got on Doc he submitted gracefully to her. One would be hard pressed to see how this could possibly be the same horse. I was at the stable when she came back to have a second look at Doc. I could see that he was desperately trying to communicate to her how much he loved her. I called over to her "Doc really loves you." She responded "Do you think so?" I answered "I know so!" Doc looked at me with his eyes filled with gratitude and then resumed pouring his heart out with reintensified determination to the young woman. Three days later, she purchased Doc. Like Doc's episode with the profession from Chicago, Marauder was creating disturbances for anyone who had been involved in his theft or the continuing injustice.

In the beginning of October, I prayed and asked God what it was I should do. Two days later, I received the distinct message to buy another horse. Logically, I thought that I was not ready for another horse, but I also knew that not to respond to an answer to a prayer has the effect of cutting communication to Higher Forces and I had the responsibility to 'check it out'. I was impressed to go back to Barbara and find out what horses Floyd had for sale. Barbara told me that Peter Sikes had died just two weeks before and that the agricultural agent had had a heart attack in September. Later she discovered that he had been asked not to return to work because of my case and others. Karma was coming back to everyone who had been involved in the theft and mistreatment of Marauder. Then Barbara suggested that I try Handsome, a beautiful, black Tennessee Walker. I worked with him and rode him several times. While he liked the extra attention and me I discovered that his musculature made it difficult for him to do dressage.

Floyd had told Barbara that if Handsome did not work out, that I should try Christie, a dapple-gray, full-blooded Spanish Arabian mare. When I heard her name, I felt my heart connecting to her. I checked with Cynthia Kyle to see what she picked up on Christie. Cynthia described Christie and went on to say that Christie would like a woman to own her, namely me. In the middle of October, Christie was trailered down from Floyd's ranch in Verde Valley. I was there when she arrived. She was all heart! The first time I rode her, I felt that she had a great heart and was trying to meet me half way even though she was frightened and didn't have muscles in her back and hindquarters. I didn't ride her again because I felt that I was hurting her. In addition, she had an injury to her right eye which I treated externally with an eyewash made from Eyebright tea and orally with homeopathic Arnica in the form of tiny sugar pills (six pills twice a day). It took a little over a week before her eye was healed. One of my students, Tracy Lawler-Boen, the author of <u>All God's Creatures Reference Guide</u>, had ridden in national competitions. I asked her if she would come out to see Christie. Tracy noticed that Christie had a blown tendon in her left rear leg, that she had a slight clubbed right foot and that there was chronic trauma her spine. We did hands-on healing on her and in less that 12 hours, her tendon was back to normal and the aura around her right foot was electric. As Christie's right leg was not deformed and she was a good mover, her clubfoot could have resulted from flexing the same foot when she was a filly eating grass in the pasture. If their trainers do not repeatedly touch young horses' legs and

44

their hoofs are not kept trimmed properly, one foot can become clubby, or Christie could have had some kind of a problem with her right foot in the past. Christie's muscles may not have developed adequately when she was a filly because the grass in the pasture was her major source of food and did not have the proper nutrients, or because she was kept in a stall. Sometimes people keep good looking horses in their stalls because they do not want a mark on them. The resulting problems from such a practice are far more detrimental to the horse's mental and physical health, attitude and performance.

Christie's price was $8,500, which was half of what Floyd had paid for her. I knew that if Spirit wanted me to do something, the money would be there. I felt that Marauder's spirit had brought Christie to me in part to keep my attention focused away from his pain. Christie was athletic in that when she rolled, she could easily roll from one side to the other; when I walked her around with a lead rope and halter, her back feet would always overstep the imprints left by her front feet. Potentially, Christie was a great dressage horse; on the other hand, her Arab temperament would be a hindrance to controlled dressage movements performed in a show ring. Training and first level dressage train the horse to carry a rider safely and comfortably, and help the rider and horse to become a team. Many horse disciplines are turning to dressage as a foundation for other work because many of the horses that are winning have dressage training. So, if the show ring did not work out for Christie, I would have a sound horse to enjoy. Immediately after I put down a deposit on Christie, Floyd changed his mind about selling her. When Barbara told him that I had already put down a deposit, he was ethical and agreed that I could continue to make payments on her. The window of opportunity for me to buy her had only been open for two weeks!

I started lungeing Christie in long reins and surcingle to build up her muscles so that she could comfortably carry a rider. I purchased the long reins with several yards of thin, cotton rope between the attachment to the bit and the heavier, thicker reins so that if there were an accident, the reins would break and not my horse's neck. Since Christie had had a blown tendon in a rear leg, I wrapped all four of her legs before lungeing her. The purpose of wrapping a horse's legs is to give the legs support without constricting the joints or cutting off the blood supply, and to gently pull the tendon in the back of the leg to the inside, towards the horse. The starting edge of the wrap can be anywhere on the front or the sides of the legs, but not on the tendon and care must be taken to make sure that the wraps are smoothly wrapped around the lower leg and not wrinkled. The wrap is started on the front legs just below what looks like the horse's knee, which is actually the horse's radiocarpal joint or wrist; it is where the radius and ulna end (these two bones are fused together in the horse) and the carpal bones begin (again, these bones are fused together). Hoofs are equivalent to our finger and toenails. On the back legs, the wrap begins just below the ankle joint where the fused fibula and tibia end and the bones of the foot begin.

It was obvious from Christie's behavior that the terrorizing training techniques used to get a horse ready to be shown in halter did not work on her – she was far too sensitive. Typically, horses that are shown in halter are made to run in circles in a round pen while the trainer cracks a whip, or waves plastic bags or tin cans tied onto a stick. The desired result is to have the horse shiny and to float into the show ring with impulsion. Then they are asked to standstill and stretch out while the whip is held in front of them, which is something like spanking a child and then telling them not to cry. Christie was terrified of whips and the round pen! When I rode her, she was continually on the lookout for the 'horse eating monster'. With my pockets full of carrots, I would lead her around the ranch and then down the road. We would investigate signs and mailboxes. I taught her what the word smell meant by saying "smell" and exhaling into her nostrils. I would then put my nose next to the questionable item and repeat "smell". As she put her nose closer to the object, I would give her pieces of carrots until her nose was almost touching the thing she feared. Soon, all I would have to say was "smell" and she would immediately breathe, relax, put her nose down and smell it. If she wanted to eat the grass growing on the side of the road, she had to get used to the noise of the traffic. Slowly her confidence built up and she smiled and looked so proud when I told her that she was getting big and strong like her friend Pooh Bear, a bay Arabian mare. Since Pooh Bear's owners did not come out to see her, with their permission I would sometimes turn Christ and Pooh Bear out together in a large unoccupied arena and let them gallop and play. A hunter/jumper trainer on the ranch had told Barbara that it was dangerous to have horses loose in an arena next to where horses were being worked, so I wasn't able to let them out together often. I noticed that Pooh Bear could also roll from side to side and that she overstepped when I was leading her around. Once when I turned them out in the arena with the jumps in, Pooh Bear canter towards one of the jumps and then effortlessly cleared it. I told Barbara to tell Pooh Bear's owners that I thought that she was a good horse and if they came out and took lessons with a quality trainer, they might just find out for themselves how good she was. Barbara told me later that she had spoken with them, but they still didn't show much interest in their horse.

Finding a good trainer in Arizona was difficult, so I continued to work with Christie on my own. The hunter/jumper trainer at the barn where I boarded Christie was unlike anything that I had ever seen. She rode with the backs of her ungiving hands up, elbows out, knees and feet too far forwards and slouched over in the saddle. When she cantered with chaps on she bounced on the horse's back; when she posted the trot she jabbed her horse in the sides with her spurs at every stride. She jumped without a helmet and many of her students were picking up her bad habits. I once watched her try to lunge Sara with a halter and lunge line only and she couldn't do it; she had to have her assistant come out and help her. Sometimes my students would want to come out and see Christie; those who knew about horses could hardly believe their eyes.

I am reminded over and over again in my life how when I listen with my heart and follow Spirit that that is when things happen. God has an uncanny way of knowing what it is I need and when I need it. On November 11th, the day that an astrologer told me would be the best day for me to assume full ownership of Christie, I gave Barbara the last payment. After lungeing Christie, I walked into the office to find Barbara nearly beside herself. Top Contender, another of Floyd's horses and Christie's half-brother, had come down with what they thought was pneumonia the night before. I had channeled healing for several people and horses on the ranch. I asked her if she wanted me to work on Top Contender. When she said yes, I asked her to tune into the horse and visualize him while I sent absentee healing. Within 20 minutes or so, there was a huge shift that Barbara felt and I saw as a huge flash of light. I found myself saying to her, "This is going to be quick! You will know today one way or the other if he has made a remarkable recovery or if he has made a final transition." I left the office and returned 15 minutes later. The ranch in Montana where Top Contender had been leased out to had called. He had died 15 minutes prior to the call, which was exactly at the time that Barbara, and I felt the shift. The woman in Montana said that she had watched as the beautiful black stallion rolled over, pull out his IVs and die. I received the strong message that his suffering could have gone on for a week. His dying two hours after I officially bought Christie was too much of a coincidence and I had the feeling that Top Contender was Christie's twin flame. When I asked Serge Martel, my Native American, student, teacher, psychic, psychologist, he said that he could see the cord between Christie and Top Contender reaching through the veil and that they would have to be twin flames. Serge saw Top Contender sending Christie confidence. Dapple gray horses are born black, turn gray and then white. Serge saw that Christie would get darker. He went on to say that I had opened a door for Top Contender to go quickly and that he had died with a lot of gratitude.

I had moved Christie to a stall with an attached turnout area which she had access to during the day. I continued to long rein Christie and after a while, I was impressed to ride her bareback at the walk so that I could strengthen her muscles further before I put her saddle on. I checked with Serge first to find out if I had lost my mind or if this is what I was supposed to do. Serge felt that it would not only be good for Christie, but that it would also help strengthen the bond between us. When I rode Christie bareback, I discovered that she loved me so much that if she did startle, she would not run off. I had been giving her homeopathic Hypericum for her spine and the second time that I rode her bareback, I felt and heard her spine readjust under me. I did a lot of groundwork with her, teaching her to move away from the pressure of my hand. In addition, I started leading her around both on and off the property with a pocket full of chopped carrots showing her scary mailboxes, signs and other 'horse eating monsters' while I fed her treats. One of the most important things we can do for horses is to help them move through their fear. Like a vice, fear constricts us; fear's grip also holds onto our gifts so that when we are ready to walk through the fear, we find that our dragons were made of papermachet and that our gifts were there waiting for us all along.

Sam called me one day; he was furious! Daniel Moriarty sent him a letter threatening Sam, Sam's law firm and myself. Sam went on to say that while there was one error that he failed to catch in a document that he had submitted, he said that usually lawyers would simply call one another, point out the mistake and ask that it be corrected.

We received your docketing statement today, which was filed with the Court of Appeals on October 16, 1997. Eugene Dufarge is out of the office and I wanted to respond immediately given the pending Motion to Dismiss the Appeal.

There are several outright misrepresentations in the docketing statement that must be corrected immediately. I understand your position that the trial court's ruling on the provisional remedies request made Ms. Milner's chances of prevailing hopeless. You should say so explicitly in the docketing statement. It is impossible for the Court to do its job if you intentionally mislead it as to the nature of the appeal. We will be forced to inform the Court of the actual facts and your misstatements unless the errors are not corrected immediately. We do not want to do so and do not relish the necessity to seek sanctions against your client and your firm for filing the frivolous appeal. You are only compounding matters by answering the Court's written inquiry in a less than forthright manner.

The specific sections containing misstatements are as follows: . . . *(Daniel listed six errors when in fact there was only one. The other so called errors were Daniel's own misstatements and misinterpretations of the law.)*

These are very serious matters. We still have an obligation to bring these to the attention of the Court unless you take immediate steps to correct them. I believe the misstatements could even trigger reporting obligations to the Bar regarding lack of candor to the tribunal. We have no desire to do either and hope you will fix this immediately and make the issue moot. If we do not receive a faxed copy of a fully amended and accurate statement by tomorrow at 5:00 p.m., we will proceed as discussed above. If you have any questions, please call.

When Sam asked me why Daniel would attack him in such a manner, I answered that I thought Daniel was hoping that I would fire Sam and hire another attorney or give up the case all together. Sam also told me that it was not possible to correct the error by Daniel's deadline and he left a message for Daniel to that effect. I wondered how much Bates, Mallory & Grimes would bill Hilda for the letter?

Some of Arizona's developers coveted the land on which an old movie theatre stood. The screen was the last big screen in Arizona. Ever since I had moved to Arizona, citizens and different groups had tried to save the theatre. It qualified as an historic site, enough signatures had been gathered, but the Phoenix City counsel refused to declare it a historic site. The matter ended up in court but the judge ruled in favor of the developers even though there was nothing in the law to support the developers' case. Fred and many of the other developers were busy plowing under and paving over all the reasons that people had moved to Arizona for in the first place.

Just before Christmas, Joseph Lindquist, the lawyer for Hilda's trust, called Sam with some interesting information. After Phoenix Forty Bank assumed control of Hilda's estate, they tried to sell all of Hilda's property. The Arizona trust not only did not investigate the gross discrepancy between number of horses and amount of deposits, but they kept Laurel and Ivan Hardy on as managers. Hilda fought the guardianship and the bank tooth and nail, and in the middle of December, as a compromise, her estate went into a trust. Her relatives were now involved, but the bank somehow retained some interest in the estate. Joseph told Sam that since the end of July, Bates, Mallory & Grimes had billed Hilda's estate $35,000 for the horse case, and this was in addition to the money for the hearing any other money that Hilda had already paid them. Joseph was shocked to find out that there had been a restraining order on me preventing me from seeing Hilda, and that when it was lifted, I had to promise not to try to see Hilda. Joseph said that the restraining order was not Hilda's idea and that she actually missed me. Joseph suggested that I get together with Hilda to see if we could work things out between us or turn the matter over for arbitration. I told Sam that if I received permission to see Hilda, I intended to sit and listen to her and then introduce the subject of Baskabas, which is what she always called him, and hear what she had to say.

Two weeks later, Joseph Lindquist was fired and neither the new attorney nor Dorothy's relatives nor the bank brought up the possibility of my visiting Hilda again. I told Sam that I could literally see Hilda at one point saying, "Let Kathleen keep the horse." But her managers and Bates, Mallory & Grimes had more than likely fabricated stories and kept the truth from her. Sam went ahead with the appeal and Dorothy's attorneys continued to do everything they could to make the case as long and as drawn out and as expensive as they possibly could. While I prayed for Marauder's highest good when he came to mind, I wouldn't allow myself to ponder the subject. I let my attorney do the work and God just kept getting me the money to pay the legal fees, which were getting close to $30,000. Several people asked me why I just didn't let the horse go and accept the $50,000 to $80,000 under the "Unjust Enrichment Act". If I had felt that that was what the horse and God wanted, I would have withdrawn my character from the bad movie, taken my money and run. I strongly felt as though I were saving the horse's soul, for on some level he was learning that real love not only nurtures and supports and allows, but real love is there when times are hardest. If this were a human soul, nobody would question me. When Kay Scott came to study with me, she told me that she could see that in another lifetime when I was a Native American, Marauder had also been my horse and that he had saved my life; now, I was saving him.

Whenever Christie and I rode by Handsome's barn, he would call out to me. My heart went out to him and I would send a prayer from my heart to God and ask that the right person come and buy Handsome. Just before Christmas, Barbara told me that a man had purchased Handsome for his wife as a Christmas present. Thank you God! I greeted the New Year in New York City. It was difficult to believe that it was 1998.

Christie and I worked for a long time on just the walk. I would collect her and then let her walk on a long rein. We did lots and lots of circles, turns on the forehand and some leg yielding. By the time I started trotting her, she was naturally inclined to go on the bit and engage her hindquarters. Muscles had filled in her back and neck, and there was definite muscle delineation throughout her body. She had become more confident and didn't even look like the same horse I had purchased in October. I bought an expensive dressage saddle, but Christie preferred that I rode her bareback and that fact was clearly evidenced by how much better she moved without the saddle. Liz, who moved back onto the property, told me that while Christie never bucked, she hated the saddle from the beginning. One night, Liz said that she put her saddle in Christie's stall just so that Christie could get used to it. In the morning, there was a big bite mark in the saddle but Christie was at least a little better about accepting the saddle. Christie's training consisted of Liz getting on her to see if she could walk, trot and canter. Afterwards, nobody did anything with her.

Bates, Mallory & Grimes were back representing Hilda in the issue over the horse. Daniel called Sam with another offer. They wanted me to buy Marauder for a ridiculous sum of money and pay Hilda's legal fees, which had gone well beyond the $60,000 mark. Sam said that he was obliged to tell me about the offer but that he also felt that I shouldn't have to pay anything for the horse, let alone $110,000.

In May, Barbara told me that Pooh Bear was for sale for $1,000. If they could not sell her, they were going to take her with them and find a stable to board her. While I was brushing Christie, I explained to her that if I bought Pooh Bear, I was going to have to pay attention to her. If I didn't buy Pooh Bear, the stable her owners moved her to in northern Arizona would probably not give her the free extra attention that Camelot Farm gave Pooh Bear. There was a look of horror on Christie's face and she sent me a picture of a dark, outhouse-like building in the middle of a deep forest with her friend inside. I couldn't laugh because I knew that I would hurt Christie's feelings. I bought Pooh Bear the next day. During the day, they shared Christie's large stall and run. At night, Pooh Bear went back to her own stall and Christie was locked in her own stall and her neighbor got the use of the run at night.

When I saddled Pooh Bear for the first time, I noticed an old scar on her right side where the girth is cinched. While the girth has to be tight so that the saddle and rider stay on the horse, some people tighten the girth too tight as a punishment. What possible good they think they are going to accomplish, I do not know? When I rode her, I knew for certain that she had been abused severely, though not as brutally as Marauder. Pooh Bear was a basket case. I found out later that James, Floyd's former foreman, had ridden her (if you can call that riding) with his large, sharp spurs. Every time my lower leg touched her sides, I thought that she was going to "jump out of her skin". To the many onlookers, it must have looked as though Pooh Bear had never been under saddle before. She was sacred to death that I was going to hurt her or that something awful was going to happen. She didn't have a true walk; rather, she paced, which is a defense against a hard, unrelaxed seat. When I finally got her to walk and breathe, I called it a day and rewarded her.

Vaseline can be put on a horse's scars (not a wound) and within a week, the scar will begin to loosen, shrivel up and fall away. The fresh skin will soon begin to grow hair. Horses are so sensitive that I feel that by gently removing scars in this manner from their physical bodies, it helps to begin healing the more detrimental scars that are left on the emotional body. So, for the next few days I put Vaseline on her scar. Soon all traces of her scar were gone.

To help relax Pooh Bear, since I had a bridle that would not allow the bit to go through the mouth, we practiced sudden stops. With my weight on the inside foot, I would pull back on the inside rein. I would then switch my weight to the outside foot, hold the rein and wait for her to stop. After she stopped, I would hold the reins normally and wait for her to breathe. After she sighed, we would continue. To help her release her fear of the unknown, I slowly got her used to having a towel go down the front of her face. Then I covered one eye and then the other eye. After she adjusted to this, I covered both of her eyes, and she was left totally dependent upon my eyes, voice and touch. We would walk and pause, waiting for her to breathe.

At the end of May, a new judge was going to hold a short hearing and rule on the bill of sale issue. Bates, Mallory & Grimes turned it into a long hearing arguing that the new judge could not make a ruling. So, my attorney and Hilda's attorney had until June 6th to submit in writing to the new judge why he could or could not rule on the bill of sale ruling. While I was going through the transcript from the horse hearing, I saw the copy of the hauling card that the Agricultural Agent had drawn and issued on April 1, 1997. Hilda and her managers had listed Baskabas as a Saddlebred. If that were true, what was the point in telling me that he was a National Show Horse, which he could certainly pass for? Since they had to have the Agricultural Agent draw my horse's markings on the hauling card, they couldn't have found his Saddlebred registration papers or sent for duplicates. And that still didn't explain why Hassle Free was the only half Arab listed in Hilda's account. What in the world had Hilda and her managers been up to over the years?

When the Arizona summer heat arrived, I stopped working both mares and concentrated on keeping them both cool. I had badly sprained my ankle in the spring and even riding made it worse. So, I was glad to have an excuse not to ride. Horses can handle cold better than heat. Their internal cooling system acts like a swamp cooler; so, when it is hot and humid and their lungs are pulling in hot, moist air, they cannot cool down. I would go out to the barn a couple of times a day and hose both horses down with cool water. One day, I noticed black blotches on Christie and was told that it was a fungus and that gray horses were particularly susceptible to it. Apparently, there is so much fungus in the air in Arizona's Valley of the Sun that it is a common problem. Soon Pooh Bear had it too. I used an array of horse products, Tea Tree Oil and other anti-fungal solutions. Desitin was the only thing that worked on Christie. It dried up the fungus within 24 hours and then I curried it off. Then other spots would appear. It took over a month before the fungus was completely gone.

Pooh Bear was well muscled when I purchased her even though she hadn't been worked for a long time; however, she lacked strength in her back and her spine was at least 4 inches lower than it should have been. During the hot months I used my hands and fingers on pressure points on both horses' bodies to lift, strengthen and round their bodies. I also asked them to reach for carrots that I held between their front legs to get them to round their backs; and next to them to get them to stretch. Christie got so flexible that she could almost touch her tail. The hunter/jumper trainer and most of her clients continued to canter and jump their horses. They did not have a clue as to why their horses' legs would swell so that they had to apply ointment and wrap them every night.

Saddlebred trainers will sometimes chain the horse's front legs together and the back legs together in order to get the horse to lift their legs higher in a somewhat forced appearance of collection so that the horse will not stretching out in an extended trot when they are lungeing or being ridden. The classical European method for achieving collection is to build the horse's strength through a graduated series of exercises initially with the trainer on the ground working with the horse and then in the saddle. Slowly, the horse is asked for a few steps of collection by the rider sitting tall in the saddle, playing gently with the reins between the little finger and the ring finger (first one hand and then the other), visualizing the horse in collection and using the lower legs to round the horse. As the horse learns what is expected, the rider's aids become softer with the idea being that "less is more". When I rode Abez, we had gotten to the point where my aids were invisible to the untrained eye. One day the Saddlebred trainer at the ranch had a horse chained and he fell on top of her and she broke one of her legs.

In June, I began using Michael Sarno as a farrier. He pulled off Pooh Bear's shoes, brought them to me and said, "These shoes should never be put on an Arab." After he trimmed her and put different shoes on her, her hind legs, which had been too far under her, straightened out. In ten minutes, he had increased her value by thousands of dollars. Because her old shoes had altered her natural body carriage, she had probably been in pain whenever she had been ridden. Michael also put different shoes on Christie and by the end of the summer, her straight, clubfoot had begun to assume the correct angle.

On September 20th, the new moon, I woke up remembering a bizarre dream. Initially, there was a man, whom I thought was not interested in me, and a loose horse , which was running amuck in the distance. Then the horse came to my front door and asked me telepathically if I would take off his awkward and constricting harness. I did and he stepped into my home. He thanked me and told me that his heart needed healing. I then noticed that the man was eating dinner in my home and smiling at me.

At the end of September, the new judge ruled that there would be a 2-day, jury trial on January 27, 1999. The complete testimony from the hearing would be read to the jury. If he had ruled in my favor, Bates, Mallory & Grimes and the Phoenix Forty Bank would have only appealed it – more billable hours against Hilda's estate. I could hardly believe that these people would want to go to court. Were their egos so large that they could not see how badly they would look to 12 people?

By the end of September, the mornings were cool enough to begin working with Christie and Pooh Bear. I started slowly with the surcingle and long reins since they were out of condition. There was a new riding ring next to their barn and close to the street. Christie had improved a lot since I had purchased her, but she was still leery of noisy vehicles and street activity. I kept a tension on the outside rein when she circled towards the street. At first she was reluctant to go anywhere near the rail next to the street, but as I kept walking her through it and praising her, her fears subsided. Pooh Bear's fear was not of surrounding distractions, it was of me. She would have been willing to run like hell when I lunged her in the surcingle and long reins; however, this would not have developed her muscles for collection and would have been too stressful on her inside legs. The idea is to change gaits often and keep the impulsion forwards without allowing the horse to rush. Apple slices and my voice helped both mares. After the first time I worked Pooh Bear, she figured out that when I came for her she was going to be worked; so, she would duck out the back of the stall and into the run. After a couple of weeks, Pooh Bear's attitude changed. When she saw me coming she would come to the stall door and want to be first. It's strange the way little things can make your heart swell.

Christie was afraid of the noise of the cars, trucks and motorcycles that went by. Since the county closed Pima Road, the traffic driving past the ranch had increased significantly. Christie balked when I worked her too close to the road. There was a very wide strip of grass between the road and the riding ring fence; so, I began taking Christie for walks along the strip. Since her love for grass and weeds was stronger than her fear of the vehicles, she slowly released her fear. One day when we were out, I watched and listened while one of the hunter/jumper trainers tried to teach a small group of students how to half halt. A half halt is a movement whereby the rein is gently drawn back towards the hip as the horse's back moves the rider's hip forward. If it is executed in this manner, it is easy on the horse's mouth and causes the rear leg on the same side to come under the horse and collects the horse. The hunter/jumper trainer did not explain the movement; she simply told her students that it was a transition. She asked her students to canter, and they she yelled out for them to half halt. She called out to her students, "Since you have half halted, you should now have half the canter that you had before."

One day, I was working with Pooh Bear on the ground. She suddenly became nervous and panicked, so, I asked her to halt. I was patting her and waiting for her to breathe when I looked up and saw two of the hunter/jumper trainers riding in the ring that was next to us. One of them was bouncing on the horse's back while leaning forward at the trot and asking for a canter. The horse's head was high in the air and he was shaking it from side to side. When she got, him into a canter his head was still in the air; when she settled back in the saddle, he lowered his head somewhat. She seemed oblivious to what had happened because she went on repeating the same error. The other trainer took a hold of the reins in her left hand, lift them up to her shoulder level and then she extended her whole left arm over to her extreme left. My mouth fell open! I was shocked at what she was doing; I thought her riding was awful. Then I got a second shock – I had fallen in judgement with these trainers. Our judgements act like a trumpet calling our attention to these same attributes that are within us. If we cannot look at ourselves, forgive ourselves and release these attributes from us, we keep calling what we are in judgement of to us. Our teachers become increasingly blatant until we get it! That is, it's not them; it really is us. There are etheric cords between ourselves and those whom we judge. When I got home I used the Hosanna clearing to cut the cords and release not only any ignorance and arrogance within me, but also any injustice that Bates, Mallory & Grimes was reflecting back to me. The trick is to be able to recognize the inappropriate behavior without attaching any adjectives such as "awful" to it. To say that somebody is riding in such a manner as to upset the balance of the horse and hurt his back is a statement of fact. To say that an attorney created a case to produce billable time, or that he was overcharging his client or that he didn't have a case is a statement of fact. To call that same person a "jerk" is a judgement. People who hate homosexuals are often latent homosexuals; look at J. Edgar Hoover. There are Austrians today who remember when Hitler sent SS officers into their country to murder his own Jewish relatives.

On the full moon of October 6th, Sam called me again. Another bank had been appointed trustee of Hilda's estate and they were anxious to settle. They wanted me. Hilda's attorneys had told Sam that people were coming out of the woodwork suing Hilda. Knowing Hilda, there were legitimate claims as well as outrageous claims. For reasons unbeknownst to me, some individuals like Lydia felt that Hilda owed them something. Did they really believe their own fantasyland rationalizations? Well, the feeding frenzy had begun and in my mind's eye I could see the ghastly expressions on the faces of Hilda's relatives as they watched their aunt's fortune dwindle.

When working in hand on the ground with a bridled horse the trainer stands on one side of the horse. S/he holds the bit gently in one hand while the other hand holds the rein and whip. The whip is used to cue or correct the horse, not to punish and the horse is left to deal with it. Christie and Pooh Bear were so 'freaked out' by my dressage whip that they were unable to 'deal with it'. Pooh Bear kept startling; she looked like she was going to jump out of her skin. Groundwork is a wonderful way to teach a horse what is expected of her before actually getting on and asking for the movement. When I did ground work with my mares my only tools were my voice, mental imagery and the reins. A gentle touch is required or I would end up pulling the whole bit through the horse's mouth. I worked patiently and for very short periods of time asking them for a shoulder in, to halt, go backwards, halt and then repeat. I made certain to work both sides equally. Groundwork is a lot harder than it looks. Initially, I gave them a piece of apple or carrot every time they halted rewarding approximate behaviors. Neither of my girls liked my hand on the bit. When they began to understand what I was asking them to do, I dropped the hand that was holding the bit down on the rein and return it to the bit if they resisted my vocal cues or mental imagery. This proved very effective.

After I agreed to sign a statement saying that I wouldn't reveal the terms of the settlement, Hilda's lawyers and trust asked if I would also sign a statement saying that I would take the horse "as is". I knew that Marauder's confinement at Hilda's ranch had been difficult and my heart went out to him. If there were nothing the matter with the horse, then why would they ask me to sign off? A few days later, my attorney told me that Daniel had come up with the idea that the horse was not in Hilda's trust. Thus, the new trustee could not give me the horse. It made absolutely no sense to me. They had taken Hilda's checkbook away from her and she was in her nineties and in a wheelchair. How was she supposed to care for any of her horses? But Daniel could be assured of a prolonged case and more billable time.

It was November. My attorney did get the trust to agree to let Barbara go out Skylark Ranch with a veterinarian to check Marauder. Laurel and Hardy had left the state of Arizona with their new cars and a herd of horses for a ranch that they had purchased in Utah. The new manager at Skylark Ranch was a man named Dave Adams. The first time Barbara called Dave, he told her that she could not come on the property without a court order. I informed my attorney as to what had happened and he called Daniel to find out if we needed to go to the judge to obtain a court order or if indeed Hilda's trust was going to allow Barbara and the vet in to see my horse. Daniel said that somehow Dave had not been informed and that I should try again. The second time that Barbara called Dave, he told her that he wasn't sure which horse was Baskabas and if it was the one she was describing to him, Baskabas was on a list to be destroyed. Dave was off the ranch when Barbara and the vet went out to see Marauder. He was underweight and his hoofs were a mess. Barbara said that it looked as though he had not been trimmed since she had last seen him and that he had just had an emergency trim – but his hoofs were still a mess. When a horse is let go for that long, the farrier cannot take the entire excess hoof back at once; it has to be done gradually over time. His left front hoof was bandaged. When I told my attorney what Barbara had found out, Sam called Daniel and Daniel responded with a letter.

> Dear Sam,
>
> I spoke to Skylark Ranch manager Dave Harrison this afternoon with regard to your telephone call and letter. He indicated that he has never spoken to Ms. Milner. She did not show up at the time arranged and so he was not present when she came to examine Baskabas at Skylark. I have no idea who Ms. Milner talked to. In any event, Harrison confirmed that Baskabas is not on a 'list to be destroyed'. Although the horse is quite old and is somewhat cripple, he will not be destroyed unless there is a sudden emergency health situation, in which case you will be contacted beforehand.
>
> Mr. Hayes was aware of the situation with the horse's foot and has been attending to the horse. The farrier the ranch uses will be seeing the horse this week and will take care of the problem. There is no need for Ms. Milner to send her farrier to deal with it. If you have any further questions, please give me a call.

I had told Barbara before she went out to tell Marauder that I was still hanging in there for him and that he would be coming home soon. She did. I could feel that it gave him hope and a reason to hang on.

When the blood report came back, the vet called Barbara to tell her that Marauder had a major parasite infection. They obviously had never wormed him. A parasite infection of this magnitude can eat away at the insides of a horse and kill him. Barbara called Dave Harrison to tell him about the report and that the vet was going to come back and tube worm Marauder. John told Barbara that he couldn't understand the report because Baskabas had just been paste wormed. Barbara told John that when a parasite infestation becomes as bad as Marauder's, only tube worming would clean out the horse. The vet went back out to tube worm my horse.

Over the next several weeks, the weight of Hilda's deception and the greed of her trustees and lawyers continued to cave in upon them. I was impressed with the thought that I should begin to look around for a stable to board Marauder when he returned. I felt that Marauder would be uneasy at the stable that he had been stolen out of. I had met a man on a plane the weekend of Halloween who gave me the name of two stables. When I went out to check the first stable on my list, I had to explain to Andrew that I wasn't sure when I would be getting my horse back from Hilda. As soon as I mentioned Hilda's name, rage flashed across Andrew's face. He told me that he had had a fire at his ranch during the summer, which destroyed one of his barns. The ranch Hilda lived on had been sold to a developer and among other things, the barns were being sold. Andrew had gone out to look at the barns but what he saw made him leave in disgust. Hilda's horses had been kept in their stalls 24 hours a day without bedding and the ground they were standing on wasn't even. Every time the stall cleaners took out the manure, they took a little dirt with the manure and they had gradually created a valley in each of the stalls. Their hoofs were all a mess – it looked at though they hadn't been trimmed for two years or so and none of them looked healthy. When Barbara had spoken with John Harrison, he also had told her that half of Hilda's horses had been put down the week before. Andrew must have seen them just before they were destroyed. The laws in Arizona against animal abuse are so weak and antiquated that my attorney told me in order to have Marauder moved to a neutral location where he would receive proper care, we would have to prove that he was in imminent danger of dying within the next few weeks. According to the law, in order to bring charges of animal abuse and cruelty, we would have to prove recklessness.

My second stop was Santa Rita Stables where the man I had met on the plane was training his horses with Alice Sarno whom he had raved about. Four horses had just moved out of a barn that had only four stalls. In the back of this small barn was a small turnout area that the four horses took turns using. Santa Rita had two regulation dressage arenas, a jumping arena, three other riding arenas and a 10-acre event course. There were mountains between Santa Rita and the brown-colored smog air of Phoenix. Even so, between construction dust and car exhaust, the air was not the best anywhere in the county. Two days later I moved Christie and Pooh Bear into the barn with four stalls. I told Christie that we could try to get ready for dressage competition, but if she chose not to perform in the show ring, the training would enable us both to enjoy our riding time together.

One day, while grooming my horses, a woman approached me. She owned a buckskin mare and had moved out of the same stable I had just moved my horses out of. She told me that she had boarded her horse at Skylark Ranch during the summer for a short period of time. The first time she tried to move her horse to Skylark Ranch, she paid somebody to trailer her horse there. Since she couldn't be there herself, she had made arrangements with John Harrison to meet her horse and the woman she had paid to trailer her mare. When the woman arrived at Skylark Ranch she waited for over two hours for John Harrison to show up. He never did, so she had to trailer the buckskin mare back to her old stable. After she finally got her horse stabled at Skylark the hay was changed. Now horses have a very delicate digestive system and hay that cannot be fed to horses is often fed to cattle. The new hay they were feeding at Skylark Ranch was so hard and moldy that it would have been thrown out before it would ever have been fed to cattle. The thought crossed my mind that Hilda's old trustee was trying to force the boarders so that they would have an excuse to sell Skylark Ranch and earn their percentage from the sale. Righteous anger had been welling up inside of me. I sent a prayer, a cry, a scream up to God demanding that something be done and the justice prevail.

Sometimes people or animals go through amazing spurts of growth and are able to make quantum leaps. As an affirmation that this is where she belonged, Christie suddenly stopped falling on her forehand at the trot and moved forwards and balanced at the trot working off of her hindquarters. After adjusting to the new stable, I took a lesson with Alice on each horse. She was very helpful because she knew what she was doing. Before I left for England on November 30th, I watched Alice ride each of my horses and made the choice to pay Alice to ride them while I was gone. While Alice was riding Christie she asked me if I thought Christie was ready to canter and I said "yes". I watched while Christie demonstrated a voluptuous, round, balanced canter. While I was in England, Christie strongly impressed two messages into my thoughts. The first was that I had to stop blocking and allow events to occur naturally. The second was that she was ready to be shown in the International Arab Show in February. When I returned from England, I had the show's coordinator fax me the entry forms and I filled them out, paid the fees and mailed it off on the last day that entries were being accepted.

During the ensuing week, Christie showed both Alice and myself that I had made the correct choice in entering her in a big show. Christie released more of her fear, and since she was not as distracted by her surroundings she was paying more attention to what it was she was supposed to be doing. She became more responsive to my leg. She was beginning to stay on the rail (next to the fence line) when she cantered forwards in a straight line. And at the trot she could go from a collected gait to stretching down her head and neck, which stretched out and freed up her back and shoulders.

My sprained foot had completely healed by September and since I had returned from England my sinuses were clear enough to start working out. In 1989, I had been involved in two car accidents that had left my life at a standstill. My doctor had told me that most people in my condition would have crawled into bed and stayed there for the rest of their lives. During the slow healing process, I found myself returning to the spiritual awareness and mysticism of my childhood. After my back had completely healed, I became aware of the pain in the tendons that went across the top of my upper legs. Whenever I finished riding my horse, Abez, it felt as though somebody had tried to amputate one of my legs. I felt fortunate that the intense pain was usually one leg or the other and rarely in both. By 1996, my healing had progressed to the point that I could dismount from Marauder pain free. By January 1998, I felt that my body had healed to the point that it would benefit from exercise beyond the stretching exercises that I had been doing.

The exercise room in the apartment complex I lived in did not have equipment to exercise the legs; so, I joined a gym that was close to where I lived. Every other day, I would take 2 to 3 capsules of a combination of L-Arginine & L-Ornithine with a glass of water the first thing in the morning on an empty stomach and then workout. I could feel my body becoming stronger and fit. The thought behind riding is to encourage the horse to willingly submit to the rider's aids, not to bully the horse. The strength in my legs helped me to effectively use my body to communicate to Christie what it was that I wanted her to do. When my adductor muscles were able to press 60 pounds comfortably, my lower legs were able to stay on Christie's sides. Working out enabled me to have a better sense of holding my horse between my leg and the rein.

Bach Flower Remedies help to release negative emotions and transform them into positive qualities. Horses, especially Arabian horses, seem to have some kind of group karma whereby they have elected to work through fear. Because in addition Pooh Bear had been abused and Christie had been terrorized when they tried to train her for halter class, I had been giving both of them Mimulus (overcome fears and anxiety) and Walnut (to release the patterns and bonds of past patterns). As Bach Flower Remedies are preserved in brandy, I used distilled water to dilute them and stored them in clean glass bottles with a glass eyedropper so that the brandy would not eat away at the plastic.

On January 7, 1999 when I came out to the stable, my intention was to start with Pooh Bear. However, my eyes focused on Christie's halter and leadrope. I grabbed it and got Christie. As I squirted the liquid into her mouth, the glass eyedropper came out of the plastic top and onto her tongue. I grabbed hold of her lower jaw but I could not get it in time. I watched horrified as she swallowed it whole. I took Christie over to Sue, who was leasing Santa Rita, told her what happened. Sue told me that there was a vet on the property and where he was. The first thing he asked me was whether or not she had chewed it. Because she had swallowed it whole, he told me to pray and that she would probably just pass it. Since the eyedropper was glass, he didn't want to oil her because he said that the digestion would go around it and it would not move through her. The only thing he could suggest was roughage. So, I grabbed some hay and led Christie back to her stall. For two hours I worked on Christie while both horses ate in their hay in their paddock. The good news was that I could feel her aura; if she were going to die, her aura would already be leaving her. The bad news was that the energy at her solar plexus was wild. I didn't know if the unstable energy was from the glass eyedropper in her stomach or if Christie's emotional issues were coming up. The solar plexus is a touchpoint for emotional release and it really doesn't matter how many legs we have, we all hold a lot of emotional garbage in both our solar plexus and neck. I could visualize blue coating and protecting her entire digestive track and at the end of two hours, I could no longer sense the presence of the eyedropper. I left Santa Rita so that I could keep my colon therapy appointment with Rosemarie.

Rosemarie is also quite psychic. When I told her what had just happened, she also felt that Christie was going to be all right. Oftentimes, when I am going through therapy, somebody that I know will come into my aura and ask if they can also go through the release. After I agree to their request, they typically come in and out of my awareness. When I am aware of their presence, I can see their 'stuff' in my mind's eye. I ask the angels what the individual needs and watch them as they work. Sometime, I use my physical hands to grab the 'stuff' that is being freed up or to simply hold the area while the angels bring in healing energies.

I fully expected Christie to come in during my colonic; instead, Pooh Bear showed up. When I looked at her, I could see a large black mass that Rosemarie, my colon therapist, could also see. Before the end of my appointment, the negative energy had been released from Pooh Bear. As I was getting off of the table, I was given a strong psychic awareness – Christie had taken Pooh Bear's hit! Because Christie was clear enough emotionally and mentally, the glass eyedropper could pass through her. If the glass eyedropper had come loose in Pooh Bear's mouth, it would have cut up her tongue, esophagus and stomach – out of kindness, she could have had to have been put down. Rosemarie got chills up and down her spine when I told her.

Christie had always loved doing flying lead changes while she was running free – whenever she turned she would always switch to the correct canter lead. When she began having a problem picking up a right lead canter, I had asked Tracy Lawler-Boen to come out and look at her to see if she could find any muscular or structural difficulties that Christie was having. Pooh Bear's ears laid flat against the back of her head whenever I started to trot her, so, I also asked Tracy to look at Pooh Bear. One week later, Tracy came out to Santa Rite to do massage therapy and Dr. Regan Golob's Bio-Energy Analysis Therapy. Dr. Golob's nutritional, muscle and nerve reflex points can reveal energy blocks that create musculo-skelatal and nervous system problems. Energy blocks along either side of the spine can often be visually observed as mangled hair growth that no amount of brushing can comb out. When the block is released, the hair lays down smoothly. What many people have found is that healing energy can be channeled while using low-force techniques to facilitate the elimination of energy blocks and synchronizing energy flow, thereby relieving pain and allowing the brain to send out instruction and to receive important feedback information from the body. *(Regan Golob, B. A. D. C., P. O. Box 1278, Issaquah, Washington 98019)*

Christie had more places to be worked on; Pooh Bear had fewer active points, but she experienced more pain during the release. While Tracy was working on loosening the block in Pooh Bear's neck, tears into Tracy's eyes and she said, "This mare is so willing, she is trying to do this by herself." It felt like Pooh Bear had had enough and Tracy agreed to come out the following week. For the following seven days, I continued using low-force techniques on my mares. When Tracy came back, Christie's right ribs had gone back out, but it wasn't as severe. Pooh Bear's right ribs and left hip were badly out of place, and I thought that it was a good thing that I hadn't been doing very much with her. Her muscles at the base of her neck were still very tight and sore from having been ridden with her head high in the air and her back hollowed out. Just from doing belly lifts, lungeing her on the long reins and surcingle and riding her at the walk, Pooh Bear's spine had come up at least three inches since I had purchased her. Her crest (the topline of her neck) was slowly coming along.

In between Tracy's visits, Dr. Carbo came out to freeze-dry several small growths on Pooh Bear and float both of my mare's teeth. Horses can grow points on their teeth, which interfere with eating and having a bridle in their mouth. Dr. Crabo has electrical dental equipment, which I believe is more efficient and kinder to the horses mouth. Dr. Crabo and his assistant had set up their equipment in Pooh Bear's stall. Pooh Bear was anesthetized even though the process was painless; Christie watched from her stall in horror, especially when the headset was placed in Pooh Bear's mouth to keep it open. So, I kept petting and reassuring Christie. Pooh Bear was then led out into their run and Christie kind-of willingly was moved into Pooh Bear's stall. Dr. Crabo found that her wolf teeth were present. Wolf teeth are something like our wisdom teeth; however, they grow where the bit is placed. While Christie's wolf teeth were all very small, one was loose and had obviously been bothering her when she was bridled. While Dr. Crabo was pulling her wolf teeth, I held my left hand in the aura under her jaw and held my right hand and arm at my side with my fingers pointing towards the earth in order to drain the pain. Even though Christie was under anesthetic and her brain was unaware of the pain, it was still there!

In this manner, I was helping to release the trauma, which in turn would help the wounds heal faster. It is my personal opinion that it would benefit every doctor and veterinarian and their patients if medical practitioners were initiated into at least Reiki I. Because the issues behind Pooh Bear's growths were not yet completely resolved, shortly after the growths had been freeze dried, two bumps appeared on her spine. I started giving Pooh Bear homeopathic Hypericum and worked on the touch points for emotional and mental release. I also applied Tea Tree Oil directly on the inflamed areas. As the bumps went down, I started lungeing her. When I was able to ride her again, she was more comfortable physically as well as mentally and emotionally.

Just on a chance, I had written to the American Saddlebred Association to see if they had a listing for Baskabas under Hilda Hood's name. Bingo! I was shocked to find out that Hilda had lied to me. Did she tell me that he was a National Show Horse so that I would look in the wrong places for Marauder's papers? Was this her 'ace up her sleeve'? Was she hoping that if I did find out that he was a Saddlebred that it would be after I testified for her? The illegal horse operation may not be what I had imagined it to be. However, the American Saddlebred Association had no records of Baskabas being shown! Lydia had told me when I initially began working with the horse that Baskabas had been shown as a National Show Horse and she even knew the people who had shown him. Baskabas (also known as Marauder) did not have a typical Saddlebred head and could easily pass for a National Show Horse. Lydia and I were not the only ones who thought that he was a National Show Horse – every 'horse person' I showed him to also took him for a National Show Horse. And then there was the horse with all of his bones showing – he was definitely not an Arab! I wondered if anyone would ever discover what had been going on and everything that had gone on at Hilda's ranches?

On January 20th, a week before the scheduled horse trial, the new judge ruled on the first judge's "bill of sale ruling". After six months, the new judge decided that he could not make a ruling on another judge's ruling and the upcoming trial was cancelled. My attorney wondered why he couldn't have made this ruling in June? Why did he have to wait until a week before the scheduled jury trial? Sam went on to say that the appeal that should have been filed a year and a half ago could be rushed because of the abuse issue, but even at that it would take three months before a higher court would hear the case. The thought that went through my mind was that it was Hilda's original intention to will me the horse and perhaps that was the best way for Marauder to come back to me. A spirit guide sent me a message, "Since Hilda refused to make out a will, everything that has transpired established her intention to will the horse to you so that when Hilda dies the horse will be yours."

Periodically throughout my whole life, I have been able to see an individual's higher self come down into the body. When this occurs the physical body assumes a larger stature and the individual's eyes and voice communicate with authority. When the higher goes up, sometimes the individual remembers and accepts what they said, sometimes they shake their heads and mutter "Why did I say that?" This phenomenon happened on one occasion while I was speaking with Hilda. Hilda was complaining that both her lawyer and accountant were encouraging her to make out a will and she was dead set against doing it. Unexpectedly, her higher self came in! Hilda sat up tall and straight in her wheelchair; she looked directly at me and said "If nothing else Kathleen, you are going to end up with that horse!" After Hilda's higher self left she looked surprised.

Daniel Moriarty told Sam's assistant that he was going to have the plaintiff changed to the trust rather than Hilda Hood. Such a move would allow Daniel to bill the case in house; that is, every time he or anyone at Bates, Mallory & Grimes mentioned the case, they could bill Hilda's trust. It was blatantly obvious that Hilda had retained a lawyer and a law firm that was just like her. My attorney's assistant's response to Daniel's intention was "How can you do that if the horse is not a part of the trust?" Sam told me that he was going to write a letter to Hilda's trust through Daniel saying that if the horse is a part of the trust, the trust has already said that it is willing to give the horse to Kathleen. I also suggested that it was time to tell Hilda's trust that Daniel's letter and Hilda's testimony counts. When Hilda dies, I am willed the horse and that under no circumstances should he be placed on a list to be destroyed. Now that I knew where Maruader's papers were, all that I would have to do when Hilda died was get a copy of her death certificate and mail it to the American Saddlebred Association along with Daniel Moriarty's letter and they would send me Baskabas' papers.

Dear Daniel,

This is simply to confirm the proposals conveyed in our earlier telephone conversation to resolve this matter. As I indicated, Ms. Milner plans to appeal the summary judgment and have the appeal accelerated. Since this matter has already been fully briefed, it should not be as expensive as most appeals. On the other hand, it will involve the additional expense that either Ms. Hood or the Trustee will need to bear. As I read the Trust documents you previously provided, the Trustee has the legal authority to resolve this lawsuit by simply conveying the horse to Ms. Milner, and the exclusion of the horse from the trust assets was a mere oversight and does not affect the Trust's ability to settle this case. As we discussed some time ago, the Trust is not enthusiastic about having to litigate this case. By contrast, Ms. Milner feels quite strongly that she has been wronged and that the gift of Marauder has been and can be proved to clear and unequivocal evidence. In short, we feel quite confident about our position regarding the necessity of a bill of sale and anticipate that we will eventually be trying the case. In light of this and Ms. Milner's undying desire to right the wrong that has occurred, Ms. Hood and/or the Trust will continue to spend money litigating this case. Moreover, Ms. Hood testified to the fact that she intended to will the horse to Kathleen. In light of Ms. Hood's advanced age and the high cost to the Trust, it would seem reasonable that the Trust would now give Ms. Milner back her horse rather than litigating the claim in probate court, assuming the Trust has or can obtain authority to do so.

Additionally, this will confirm that I have been authorized to offer to pay for the cost of Marauder's continued care and upkeep, provided this occurs in a "neutral" location acceptable to Ms. Milner. As I indicated, Ms. Milner has great concerns about the continued well being of the horse, which she can support with appropriate testimony from the veterinarian and other witnesses. I believe that the appellate rules provide that the Court can entertain motions in the nature of a temporary restraining order to maintain the status quo between the parties. Of course, if Marauder dies, the status quo is not being maintained. Ms. Milner would like to simply resolve this issue amicably without the necessity of filing papers to have Marauder moved to a neutral location. It is difficult to see how this could be detrimental to Ms. Hood or the Trust's interests. In essence, Ms. Milner would be saving either Ms. Hood or the Trust money by paying for the entire upkeep of the horse that I understand no one is riding anyway.

As indicated, I would appreciate hearing from you regarding the foregoing. Absent resolution of these matters, Ms. Milner has instructed us to proceed with all due haste.

Our first time in the show ring was at Santa Rita on January 31st. It was a disaster! I braided Christie's mane three times only to watch it come undone shortly thereafter. By the time I found out that I did not have to braid her mane for a schooling show, I only had ten minutes to acquaint her with the new things on the ranch and warm her up for the first test in Training Level. As soon as she got into her fear, I lost my connection with her and we lost our chance. Fear, worry and hatred pull anyone, no matter how many legs they have, out of their center and away from God - the result being missed opportunities. I had not been feeling well and while Christie was warmed up for the second test, by that time, I had a fever. Besides coming above the bit, pulling on the bit, swishing her tail, twisting her neck and head and zigzagging, I messed up by giving her the wrong cue or cued her too late. What was disappointing was that neither one of us did out best.

The following weekend, we were entered in a large dressage show at Santa Rita. I purchased deep setting gel number 8 only because 9 was not available. Christie's mane stayed braided! We were better! Christie ended up with a third and fourth place in her classes and her scores were not bad. I showed her the yellow and white ribbons that she had won and praised her. Christie was proud and it felt as though her confidence had grown.

Before the big Arab show, Frank, who was still Hilda's personal accountant, called me and asked me for my maid's phone number. Then he asked me how the 'horse thing' had turned out. It felt like he was on a fishing expedition. So, rather than confront Frank with his lies, I played along and told him exactly what had transpired and that I fully intended to go ahead with the appeal. Frank was shocked to hear about the false police report and was stunned when I told him that my attorney had already proven that Hilda had given me the horse and that all he had to do was prove that a gift did not require a bill of sale. I knew for certain that Bates, Mallory & Grimes had not been entirely truthful or upfront with their client. I asked Frank, "How many married women would you find in Arizona if they had to ask their fiancés for a bill of sale for their engagement ring?" Frank confirmed that both the first trust company and the law firm had gotten a lot of money out of her and that the second trust company had sold one of her ranches without consulting Hilda or her relatives and Hilda was now on her third trust company. Frank then told me that the trust had no intention of paying for an appeal. A pretty interesting statement from somebody who didn't know how the 'horse thing' had turned out. I told Frank that if the trust was smart that they would stop fighting me and use my testimony to sue Bates, Mallory & Grimes and get Hilda's money back. When my attorney called, I told him what had happened and he said, "Good!" He also told me that Daniel Moriarty had said that he wanted to be the first to file for the appeal. That was weeks ago! Sam said he was not willing to wait any longer and that he was going to take the first step.

Arizona has always been a transient state – the 120 degree-plus summers are difficult and the energy of the land brings people's issues to the forefront. Arizona in general and Scottsdale in particular have paved over the very reasons why people moved to the state in the first place. Scottsdale officials would like to tear down all or part of historic Old Town and put up a shopping mall. Beautiful ranches have been replaced with gingerbread, cookie cutter housing developments; so, the movie star/horse owners no longer come to visit their rancher friends. The Scottsdale Arabian Horse Show used to be huge and was international because of the people who came. People could show their horses and then ride them in the surrounding desert. Now, if people can get to the show through the never-ending, massive road construction-destruction-reconstruction that will supposedly end in the year 2007, they are left contemplating the surrounding overdevelopment while breathing hazardous air. The same officials who authorize and profit from overdevelopment were left wondering why tourism was down – they will probably form a million-dollar committee in hopes of discovering the answer. Even though the Scottsdale Arabian Horse Show is not what it used to be, it is still a big show!

A good dressage horse's performance is like a controlled explosion. So, while we made mistakes, Christie's periods of brilliance in particular moves kept her scores up. In her class for Training Level I and II for Arabians and half-Arabs, Christie won a fifth and a second place. Alice came with us to the Arabian Horse Show; she felt that Christie was improving daily. And in dressage, the real horse and rider that anyone is competing against is you and your own horse. Most of the horses had been body clipped, supposedly to give them a sleeker look. In the morning, they just looked naked and cold to me! You could spot the horses that hadn't been clipped even from a distance by the rich color of their outer coats. Many of these owners had done what I had done – simply clipped the ends off of the longest hair.

Pooh Bear hadn't taken any notice to our leaving; she was in heat and was madly flirting with the gelding next door. When we returned to Santa Rita, Pooh Bear was still in her own world. Psychics have always seen Christie with a baby and Pooh Bear would probably enjoy the experience if she were out in a green pasture with Christie. That is the only way that I would breed my mares and I certainly would not breed them every year. Young horses need to be with their mothers. If a mare is rebreed immediately after giving birth, then the young horse has to be taken away from its mother so that the mare's body will stop producing milk and nourish the growing fetus. Overbreeding dogs produces diminished quality of puppies and ruins the breed; breeding mares every year also substitutes quantity for quality. Many horse breeders are afraid that if they miss a year, they will miss that 'once-in-a-lifetime great foal'. Actually, when any of us honors our horse as a being with a soul, the Absolute rewards us. When we are open to possibilities and not attached to outcomes, our lives take off. Before I breed Christie and Pooh Bear, I will see how far Christie and I can go in dressage and allow Pooh Bear to have the experience of how pleasurable riding can be.

Daniel had told Sam that Bates, Mallory & Grimes would like to be the first one to file papers to start the appeal process. Sam agreed to this!? Two weeks later, Daniel still hadn't started the appeal process and Sam called to tell me that he was going to begin the process. On March 16th, I received a letter from Sam stating, "The appeal process has been delayed somewhat, since in addition to submitting their own proposal on the judgment, Bates, Mallory & Grimes has also requested an award of their attorneys' fees of $30,551, which is only for the hearing in May 1997." Sam submitted his opposition:

DEFENDANT MAY NOT NOW SEEK AN AWARD OF FEES, AS THE JUDGE DID NOT AWARD ATTORNEY'S FEES. Following a hearing the judge issued his Order for the provisional remedy on July 7, 1997, a copy of which is attached hereto as Exhibit "A". The judge specifically ordered "each party shall bear their own costs and attorney's fees." As the Court will recall, the Court ruled that "the judge's ruling should be considered as the law of the case." Accordingly, this Court determined that it could not revisit the judge's ruling regarding the effect of the "bill of sale statute", and should also accordingly not revisit the issue of attorneys' fees which were declined to be awarded by the judge. Defendant, however, hopes that this Court will rule exactly the opposite when such a ruling would be to Defendant's benefit. The duplicity of Defendant's position is obvious. Defendant cannot have it both ways, and consistent with this Court's prior ruling, this Court should not revisit the ruling declining to award fees.

UNDER THE CIRCUMSTANCES OF THIS CASE, A FEE AWARD IS NOT MANDATORY. . . . Moreover, Defendant conveniently overlooks the fact that the judge held specifically that a fee award under the circumstances of this case is not mandatory. This Court should exercise its discretion and not award fees in this matter.

THE AMOUNT OF ATTORNEYS' FEES REQUESTED IS NOT REASONABLE. **The Requested Fees are Not Properly Calculated:** Calculating the hours for each attorney at their respective rates, the fees total $24,746.50 and not the $30,551.00 claimed by Defendant's Affidavit in Support of Attorneys' Fees. Mr. Moriarty computed for 48.6 hours at $1,85 per hour ($8,991)' Eugene Dufarge computed for 114.1 hours at $130 per hour ($14,833); CTM computed for 2.7 hours at $125 per hour ($337.50); and KJR computed for 6.5 hours at $90 per hour ($585). This error raises a serious question of the reliability of opposing counsel's method of keeping, recording and calculating fees.

Defendant's counsel has incorporated the time entries with their Affidavit of Attorney's Fees and is not submitting these records as they are kept in the normal course of business. As a result of the significant error in calculation and the manner in which they have been presented to the Court, the fees submitted should be carefully scrutinized.

Attorney's Rates: Ms. Ronstreet, a summer clerk for Bates, Mallory & Grimes during the summer of 1998, has been charged at a rate of $90 per hour. Mr. Ronstreet's rate is excessive for her level of experience. In addition, the Affidavit in Support of Fees identifies an individual with the initials of HJH as having a "conference regarding hearing on order" on April 23, 1997 for 1 hour. HJH is not identified in the Affidavit, so it is not possible for Plaintiff to comment on the reasonableness of the time spent or rate charged for this entry.

Specific Objections to Itemizations: Attorney time spent on a matter in Scottsdale Justice Court is not properly charged to this case or Plaintiff, even though the parties within the Justice case were the same. Mr. Moriarty's Affidavit itemizes entries for the dates of April 22, 23, 24 and 25, 1997, for numerous attorneys in excess of $2,000 working on an unrelated case in Scottsdale Justice Court, which did not involve the merits of the case before this Court. It is, therefore, inappropriate to assess these fees against the Plaintiff in this case. If appropriate, Mr. Moriarty should have requested those fees from Scottsdale Justice Court.

On June 3 and 4, 1997, Mr. Jones itemizes time spent for consideration of whether his firm has the authority to continue representation of the Defendant due to pending conservatorship proceedings. As the issue of the Defendant's conservatorship proceedings was wholly unrelated to the merits of the replevin hearing, it is not appropriate to charge time to this case for time spent on conservatorship issues. The time spent, in excess of 5 hours ($650) should not be assessed against the Plaintiff.

The itemizations of May 26, 28, 29 and June 1, 1998, delineate work on research and preparation of a Supplemental Memorandum regarding whether the judge's ruling is the "law of the case". The Supplemental Memorandum consists of five pages and six Arizona case citations. This motion apparently demanded the time of both an attorney and a summer clerk for a whopping total of 13.3 hours and in excess of $1,800. This is an unreasonable charge for the amount of time necessary to prepare such a memorandum.

The Total Fees Claimed is Wholly Unreasonable Given the Nature of This Case. Even taking into consideration the adjustment for calculating errors, the fees remain unreasonable in light of the uncomplicated nature of this case. This case consisted of two telephonic depositions; one-half day provisional remedy hearing; and a motion for summary judgment before this Court. $24,000 is simply unreasonable for the scope of work necessary to defend the foregoing matters.

CONCLUSION! In sum, the judge did not award attorneys' fees and this ruling should not now be revisited. As such, Plaintiff hereby requests this Court to deny Defendant's Motion for Attorneys' Fees. If the Court finds it appropriate to award fees in this case, Plaintiff requests that they be drastically reduced in that Defendant's attorneys' fees were improperly calculated and are wholly unreasonable given the simplistic nature of this case.

After the horse hearing Bates, Mallory & Grimes argued that the case couldn't go to appeals court even though the judge had signed an order sending it to appeals court. Then after numerous delays, the new judge finally set a date for a jury trial and then decided in favor of Bates, Mallory & Grimes a week before the jury trial by saying that he could not hear a lateral court's decision. Now this! The whole thing was becoming overwhelming. I cleared my mind and focused within. I asked Holy Spirit, "What needs to transpire so that this situation can be resolved for the highest good of all concerned?" I listened with my heart. After I had been meditating for about fifteen minutes or so, I felt hidden guilt rise up inside of me. A part of myself was guilty because Hilda's manager may have persuaded Hilda to give me the horse. Then an inner knowing reassured me that my actions and intentions had been honorable. Nobody tells Hilda what to do! Hilda had her own motives for giving me the horse. I exhaled! The guilt released! I felt a shift! On April 20th, the new judge denied Hilda's request for attorney's fees. Sam is now free to move the case to appeal. It will be interesting to see what Hilda and her trust will do.

However Marauder comes home, I will have to start from the very beginning to calm him down and reestablish his trust in people and myself in particular. But he will know the staying power of real love, and that a real friend is a friend regardless of how many legs that friend has. I have been the defendant in court and won against injustice; as the plaintiff in the horse case, I stood up for both Marauder's rights and my own. They never thought that I would take legal action. They thought they could steal my horse and that I would do nothing but cry. My efforts to protect and reclaim Marauder were a labor of love. Love does not hurt; love brings up issues for healing. In releasing the past, I forgave Hilda and everyone else involved for the pain that they have caused through their deception. Why Hilda's trust would continue legal action against me just so they could destroy the horse while ignoring those who had swindled Hilda is a question beyond my comprehension. By remaining in the present I can stay focused on the task at hand so that like the reed, I am able to bend with each changing direction as the case twists through legal trappings. In releasing the future, I am allowing Great Spirit to surprise me with the best results.

Holland and Rembrandt's Daughter

Reincarnation & the Spiraling Dance of Life

The Rijks Museum in Amsterdam literally comes to life whenever I enter through its doors. As though there were a cord attached to me, I am drawn to the Old Dutch masters. The first time I stood in front of Rembrandt's The Night Watch was the summer of 1995. Suddenly, energy poured out of the picture. I felt its comforting, loving essence surround and go through me. Jane Rijgersberg turned and looked at me with her mouth open. She felt it and we both noticed that other people were also feeling it and looking strangely around them. Then I found myself talking to one of the curators and he brought up the subject of authenticity and artists' signatures. For whatever reason, I pointed out Rembrandt's signature and he said, "I've been looking for that." He then asked me a question about The Night Watch. I answered his question and then continued talking about other aspects of the painting. Suddenly, I was aware that twenty or more other people were standing around me, listening to my dissertation. I came back to another more logical place in my brain and asked myself, "Unbelievable, what are you doing, Kathleen?" I excused myself and quickly looked around for Jane. She asked me, "What were you doing, Kathleen?" I answered, "I do not know. I think that I was one of Rembrandt's students."

The next day, I asked one of my psychic Dutch students to see what she could pick up. She told me that she saw me as Rembrandt's illegitimate daughter. "You can't be more than three or four years old and already you are mixing and using the paints in his studio." Then I heard a man's voice speak these words, "Why her, why not my son?" I knew that it was Rembrandt's thought three hundred years ago, when he wished that his son had been born with artistic abilities. I was very much an unwanted child and I could feel his cold resentment going through me like a sword piercing my heart.

When I returned to Arizona, I went up to Sedona to see my friend, Pamela Hoffman, and to heal the pain that had been brought up to the surface in Holland. Solar, a healer and psychic, went out into the red rocks with me one day. I told him about my experience in the Rijks Museum and that my student had seen me as Rembrandt's last student. He tuned in and said, "When you say that you were Rembrandt's student, I receive an affirmative, and when you say that you were Rembrandt's daughter, I also receive an affirmative. Kathleen, what I am getting is that you were both. Rembrandt's illegitimate daughter was his last student." He saw the emotional pain that I had experienced during that lifetime and he added, "Towards the end of his life, Rembrandt accepted you." Was he now reaching out from the grave to heal both of us?

I sat down and meditated among the red rocks, listening to the deep wind-like sound from the belly of the mountain as it pushed me further and further back into my mind. I saw a vision of an experience I had had when I took the Sylva meditation class. At one point during the class, we were all instructed to go down to our laboratory and find our male and female guides. Typically these are aspects of ourselves; sometimes, they can be people with whom we still have issues, such as ex-partners, or it can be a guide who has come to work with us. I don't even remember who my male guide was because when the elevator doors opened to show me who my female guide was, I saw a beautiful woman, with her blond hair pulled back into a single French braid, huddled in the corner of the elevator. She was dressed in rags, but I knew at the time that those garments did not reflect her station in life, but rather how she felt about herself. Now, lying against the side of the mountain, I knew that I was looking at myself in that lifetime as Rembrandt's daughter and feeling the deepest pain of rejection. The energy that I had experienced in the Rijks Museum was fatherly love from Rembrandt asking me to forgive him.

I went back to Europe in November of 1995. I had told Jane about my experience with Solar and she had made arrangements for us to go back to the Rijks Museum. This time as I stood in front of The Night Watch, the whole picture came alive. I felt as though I could step into the action if I wanted to do so. Then my conscious brain took over, I thought about the man who had taken a knife and slashed the painting several years ago, and as my fear took over, the scene changed back into a painting.

Then I began to look at the paintings that had been done by students of Rembrandt. I found a painting of a nobleman that had been painted by a man named Arent van Gelder, whom they attributed to be Rembrandt's last student. I knew that women frequently painted under their father's or husband's name or an assumed man's name. (This practice continued well into this century. For example, everyone assumes that the author, Taylor Caldwell, is a man. Her real name is Janet Taylor Caldwell.) Still, I asked Mother-Father God for proof that Rembrandt's daughter had painted this picture. I kept on gazing into the painting, and suddenly the man started to grow a beard and age before my eyes, while his eyes held their loving attention on me. By the time the picture returned to its original state, Jane found me looking at it. I asked her, "Who painted that picture?" And she started to read the plaque. Suddenly, she jolted back, looked at me and said, "You did, Kathleen! You did!"

A year later, I went back to the Rijks Museum, but this time with Erik Homan. We watched together as several of Rembrandt's paintings changed before our eyes. He was glad that he had come with me; I was providing great entertainment for him. When I showed him the painting of the nobleman, I asked Erik to see if he could pick up any impressions. My logical brain was thinking that the man in the picture might be Erik because I was with Erik. No, Erik did not think so. What he did pick up was a great deal of 'animal magnetism' and he said, "The two of you had a very enjoyable life together." Erik was right! The man in the painting was not he.

Oftentimes, we come back to complete unfinished affairs. One Australian astrologer, whose name unfortunately I do not know, did a reading on Princess Diana's chart and believes her to be a reincarnation of Mary Queen of Scots, whom the people loved. The people still loved her! She had a major role in exposing the Crown, which she and Fergie refer to as The Firm, and to help the English people recognize themselves as citizens, not as subjects. The most common reason for re-experiencing past lives, either in déjà vu or past life regression is that something needs to be healed and released. Sometimes, what heals us is the awareness alone that we actually did the unconscious acts for which we now hate others. Oftentimes, individuals work out past life issues through a professional talk therapist or a true healer. Even after déjà vu experiences people seek out counselors or healers. Many people know that they have lived before. Reincarnation: The Phoenix Fire Mystery, compiled and edited by Joseph Head & S. L. Cranston, is filled with examples of some of the most famous people in history who came to this realization. When we heal the past, we can release the guilt of not living up to other people's expectations, and we are able to consciously live the lives we desire. Rembrandt's daughter needed to release the guilt of not being the son that her father wanted and the resulting festering, low self-esteem.

One of my students, Shantarisumari, had gone to Holland in 1994 and taught Reiki. She went back again to give them initiations into fire, which she had thought up. One initiate smelled sulfur for six months afterwards. During the initiation, another woman heard a voice from the pits of hell shouting, "Who dares to wake me up?" The would-be initiate called out one of the names for God three times - the entity left and so did the initiation she had paid for. Robin Hormann said that the initiation into fire he received simply did not last. When Shantarisumari's Dutch students asked how they could get in touch with me, she answered that I was always traveling and completely unavailable. When Jane Rijgersberg called me the first time to tell me about all of this, she asked me if I would come to Holland and reinitiate and teach Reiki because they were not certain about what they had received from her. I allow my students and students of my students to repeat Reiki Mastership with me on a donations-are-accepted basis. I agreed to go to Holland.

It is an interesting fact of reincarnation that we are not only drawn to those and that which we love, but also to those and that which we hate. In Ireland, I have found many reincarnations of former popes. Most of them, like Kathleen Dillan, are so guilty that they cannot let go of their need for self-punishment. In the Shamanic Workshop, Kathleen Dillan had found a comrade in crocodile. She always had felt that she needed to be in control of the healings she was facilitating. At one point in the class, when we were using journeywork to do a healing, crocodile held Kathleen so that she could not look to see what was happening and thus control the outcome.

Sometimes, people need to feel the pain before it can be released. When it was Kathleen Dillan's turn to receive hands-on healing from the class, she realized that she had been a pope and that she was responsible for the torture and burning of thousands upon thousands of people. Then she flipped into a past life where she was being burned as a witch. Her agony went on and on. She repeatedly refused to forgive herself. Then, I finally said to her in a very calm, gentle voice, "OK, if that's what you want, then keep on burning." She answered, "Wait a minute. What was it that you said I needed to do?" I answered that she needed to forgive herself and would she like the angels to come in and help her. She said, "No angels." Then I asked her, "Whom would you accept to come in and help you?" Her response was "Crocodile!" He came in, laid over her and began talking to her. "I have eaten many people. Let go of your anguish and guilt. Just don't do it again." She started laughing and broke her reincarnation cycle of self-inflicted torture.

Some psychics and healers have found reincarnations of former SS officers in Israel. I found reincarnations of former Nazi officers in my class in Holland. One of my students became so ill during the class that she was unable to leave Jane's home at the end of the class. I worked on her until almost ten o'clock with no relief in sight because she could not see her issue. Finally, I asked her if she would like me to tell her what I saw, and she answered affirmatively. As gently as I could, I told her that she had been a German officer in World War II. She freaked out and shouted emphatically, "No!" Very calmly, I said, "OK then, why don't you ask your own guides if what I am telling you is the truth or a lie." She smiled and confidently closed her eyes. I knew that she was expecting her guides to tell her that she was right and that I was wrong (oftentimes with auditory and visual messages, we hear and see only what we want to hear and see). Suddenly, her eyes popped open, she started crying and stated in a most amazed voice, "You are right." Then she told me of how as a child she had gone to the Black Forest with her parents on vacation. She was severely ill the entire time. She said that she had unnaturally vomited and had diarrhea long after there had been any food or liquid inside of her. While the healing energy was running through me, she released guilt and pulled in unconditional love. She also found out while she was lying on the massage table, that the shadow being who had been haunting her during my class was not the devil; rather, it was the Nazi officer that she had been whom she could not forgive. When she could forgive herself in that lifetime as a German officer and integrate her shadow side, she was able to leave Jane's home. Power without love is what we call 'evil run rampant'; love without power is what we call 'Mr. Milktoast." We need both and we need them to be in balance in order to create beauty and harmony within and without. Until we are able to integrate our power and our love, we live in duality, going back and forth from one extreme to the other. Working out past life issues is one way in which to combine our love with our power. When we see ourselves living lives that embarrass us, we have a difficult time judging other people for living unconsciously at the far extremes of duality. There is similarity in these outer limits and it is where we find ourselves inflicting harm upon others as well as ourselves. For example, politically, the far left (Communism) and far right (Nazism) both take away personal freedom and property, freely torture and execute citizens, and impose rigid regulations for the benefit of a few.

There was a man in the same class of whom I had visually gotten a clear picture as a German officer just before I reinitiated him into Reiki. The view I had of him was looking down at him from behind and slightly to his right side. It was like I had wings and was flying or hovering over him, catching a glance of the side of his head. Immediately, the word Hitler came into my mind and just as quickly, my logical right brain dismissed the idea. When I did the Sakara initiations on him, I did not feel the energy of the initiation go into him. When I initiated him into Angeliclight, I did not see the angels do their usual thing. Rather, I saw his handsome face turn into a sinewy corpse and he turned and looked at me. I was impressed to continue, even though the initiation was not taking place. The last thing the angels need people to do in the Angeliclight initiations is to speak while they work on the initiate's throat and third eye. What I ask people to say is a variation of Dael Walker's Light Invocation which also has elements from The Course in Miracles and The Teachings of the Inner Christ. It goes like this: *From the Lord God of my being to the Lord God of the Universe. I call forth the love, light and power of the Christ within. I am a clear and conscious channel, healing with every thought, word and deed. Transforming any and all darkness into love and light from within and without in Divine Order and for the highest good of all concerned. So be it and so it is.*

I didn't think that this prayer would offend anyone, especially when I explain that Christ is not just Jesus; it is the All-Prevailing, all-knowing, All-Loving Light of Creation. My student repeated it three times, drank his glass of water and left. I knew that I had to speak to him alone before he left and also give him back his money. I continued initiating people and when I was finished, I found Jane. She said, "He is very upset with you, Kathleen. He keeps saying that you made him repeat a vow that he could not and did not want to say. You know that there are words that black magicians can never say, and your prayer is filled with them?" No, I was not aware of that fact!

I met him upstairs. He was so angry that he could hardly speak. I started by telling him what I had seen just before I reinitiated him into Reiki. He responded, "I felt someone had seen me, I just didn't know who, but I thought that it was you. I know that I was a German officer and responsible for the torture and deaths of thousands and thousands of children, but I cannot be responsible now for what I did then." For some reason, he went on to tell me that because of a decision he had made many lifetimes ago, he was unable to have normal sex. He was consciously aware of the fact that he had been born to his mother as her first son who died as a baby. I knew for sure that he really was a reincarnation of Hitler. I know that there are stories of how the body in the bunker was too short to be that of Adolf Hitler, and of the rumors that he and other officers had fled to South America (the Catholic Church never spoke out against the Nazis during W.W. II and could have protected them afterwards). Albert Einstein proved years ago that time and space do not exist the way our limited brains conceive them. It is possible for a soul to live simultaneous or overlapping lives. The man who stood in front of me was not aware that he was a reincarnation of Hitler; his conscious mind would not have been able to handle the realization. Then he went on and on about how I had made him repeat a vow. When I asked him why he repeated the 'vow', as he called it, if he didn't want to, he answered, "Because you have a lot of power over people." He was absurd in blaming me for what he said. I knew then that it was his own higher self that came in, demanding that he do something to begin the reversal of the downward spiral. He told me that he had not gotten what he had expected to get out of the class and added that he hated the Hosanna symbol. I felt that that was good news for the rest of us. He left with the Reiki, but not the other rays. Spirit let him keep the Reiki because he had repeated the 'vow'. There was now a glimmer of light where there had been only darkness. Mr. Hitler may very well get to heaven in some future lifetime, but first he told me that he was going to visit his grave (the grave of his older brother).

When we heal our own past lives, we may also be releasing a part of our own soul that has remained earthbound. When we help earthbound spirits go to the Light, we may possibly be healing someone else's past life or a soul fragment that is in torment. I was in Juliet, Georgia in the summer of 1996 with Kathryn Odom. Just across the street from the restaurant where the movie, Fried Green Tomatoes, was filmed are several antique shops. We went into one of them while we were waiting for a table at the now very popular restaurant. When we walked in the door, I was halted in my tracks. I looked over at the woman whom I had presumed to be the proprietor and asked her as carefully as I could if she thought that there might be any chance that she had a ghost in her cellar. "Yes, I do! Her name is Juliet. She died under unusual circumstances. Most folks think that she was murdered." When we die, we bring our state of consciousness with us - be it fear, guilt, rage, etc. For example, the 39 Heaven's Gate members who committed suicide in California were disillusioned and controlled when they held professional, corporate jobs. When they bounced to the other extreme as 'social dropouts', a phenomenon Flo Conway and Siegelnassiegelna refer to as Snapping in their book with the same title, they were still disillusioned and controlled by their cult leader. In their deaths, they did not go to a spaceship orbiting the comet; they remained bound in their disillusioned thought forms, which is what has been controlling them from the start. Juliet was still chained by her emotional state at the time of her death.

The proprietor of the antique shop in Juliet, Georgia continued and asked me why I was asking. I looked down the cellar stairs and saw pitch-blackness. "Well, I think that Juliet has got hold of my ankles and is asking me to help release her from the thought forms that are binding her so that she can go to the Light." The owner of the store smiled at me and then added with a frown, "Many people come here hoping to have the opportunity to see Juliet, and I sell books on the ghosts of Georgia." Juliet clutched onto me as if I was a lifeline. For her sake, I did not dare to move, although I didn't really know if I could move. Then the proprietor said disappointedly, "Well, if she really wants to go, please help her." I asked for the angels, felt their presence, and then a column of Light descended. I talked to Juliet and asked her to take the hands of two of the angels and simply rise up with them. When the angels were finished helping Juliet, the energy vortex stayed, and I was told to tell the shopkeeper that she would still have this story to tell and that people who came to her store could take advantage of the healing energy in the spinning vortex.

The only difference between Ted Bundy and Jeffrey Dahmer is that Ted Bundy blamed everyone else for his crimes but himself, and he remained unrepentant to his death. I had gotten up early the morning Jeffrey Dahmer was murdered and heard about his death on the morning news. I had completely forgotten about it by the time I went back to my bedroom to get dressed. Suddenly, Jeffrey Dahmer appeared in front of me. I quickly said, "If you have come in the name of my Lord Jesus Christ, please stay. Otherwise, go away and stay away." I repeated this three times, fully expecting Jeffrey to go. He didn't! He then pointed out to me that he was wearing a white shirt, which actually looked as though it was from another century. I asked what was going on. He said that he needed help going to the Light, and he needed to do it quickly before too many people judged him. So I asked the angels to come. I felt them bring the Light. I instructed Jeffrey to take the hands of two of the angels, step into the Light and rise up with them. He did this very quickly. I knew that he must have had a change when he was in prison, so I decided to watch the television special on him that evening to find out what exactly Jeffrey had done.

When Jeffrey Dahmer's trial was going on, I lived in Milwaukee. I honestly do not enjoy watching things like that, but it seemed to be on every channel because whenever I turned my television on (which isn't much), there he was! On one of these occasions, I heard that Jeffrey had been involved in black magic at a young age. I knew then that he had contacted an evil force in his youth that had stayed with him and 'messed up' the rest of his life. Evil hides and festers under a cloak of black. It is not that black is evil, it is that black, like nighttime, has the ability to conceal. When evil is exposed to the 'light of day', we can see what has been going on. The more we can stay out of judgement, the clearer we see.

When I watched the evening special, I listened to an old interview he had given. Jeffrey did not blame his parents, teachers, society or evil spirits. Jeffrey had taken full responsibility for what he had done. Jeffrey went on to say that he had begun searching for God, he was remorseful and that he had worked on forgiving himself. His physical body is gone, but Jeffrey saved his soul.

When we ask God for Divine Justice, place all parties involved in love, and refuse to participate in games, the best prevails. When we take joy in another's death because we judge them to be evil, we can be assured that there is a similar lifetime within us that needs to be healed. Everyone I introduced to Hilda who fell into judgement of her, her managers, her trainers or Fred became ill because they were pulled back into the game of duality rather than stepping back and looking at what within themselves was being mirrored by Hilda. We can only see who we are.

Past lives come up not only to be healed, but also to help us connect to Spiritual gifts and talents that we had in other lifetimes. Energy patterns on the planet shift; for example, the quality of the energy in Israel today is not the same as it was 2,000 years ago. So, when we go to places where we have lived before, it is not to connect to the power, but rather to bring up the memory. When we listen with our hearts, we know where it is we must go. When I visited Dorothy and Gordon in England, they said that they would take me anywhere in the British Isles for a long weekend. I chose the Isle of Iona, which is off the Isle of Mull in Scotland. The Isle of Iona is tiny. In Celtic times, like Inishfallin in Ireland, it was a place of learning the Old Ways. Today, there are a few inhabitants, the ruins of an old monastery, a retreat house for burned-out American attorneys, and a golf course complete with grazing livestock. My experience on the island was not overwhelming, but I suspected that something had happened. When we got back on board the ship, I felt a small tug in the top pocket of the jacket that Dorothy had given me to wear. The pocket itself was thin and long. At the bottom of the pocket was a teaspoon of sand. There was no other sand on the jacket or in any of the other pockets, and I had checked all of them when Dorothy had given me the jacket to make certain that none of her belongings were in any of the pockets. I had not lain down in the sand on the beach while I was on the island. It was like the spirits of nature and the angels were leaving me with a small reminder. I still have the teaspoon of sand.

I returned to Holland again in the spring of 1998. Once again, Jane accompanied me to the Rijks Museum. Several paintings in the Golden Age of Dutch art caught my attention. The executioner in Carel Fabristins' "The Beheading of John the Baptist" had an uncanny resemblance to Rembrandt. The facial colors that Ferdinand Bol used in his "Self-Portrait" were completely different than the oil colors he used for the hands. The left hand lacks the internal structure of bones, tendons and muscles that the right hand has. In addition, the left hand is noticeably smaller than the right hand and appears feminine in nature. It is our right brain and the leftside of our body that are our feminine, creative nature; our left brain and the rightside of our body are our masculine, intellectual nature. Even so, it is blatantly clear that two different people had worked on the piece. Bol's "Self Portrait" was supposedly painted as a gift to his fiancée. Oftentimes during the Middle or Dark Age, women worked in their father's or husband's art studios and painted under their father's or husband's name. Bol's "Self Portrait" was not a contract of his faithfulness to his fiancée, but rather her contract to Bol, allowing him to take credit for her work.

Our last stop was Rembrandt's "Still Life With Peacocks". While it is clearly Rembrandt's signature, there is no "t". A small blond-haired girl in the background is looking at the scene in front of her. Proportionally the birds are too big, but they would have appeared that way to a little girl. Up close, the painting is loose and impressionistic; stepping back, it appears realistic – not Rembrandt's style. There is a composition problem in that an apple and a peacock are fighting it out to see which one will be in the foreground – a dilemma that Rembrandt would have easily resolved. Rembrandt didn't paint "Still Life With Peacocks", the little girl did.

Women artists were forced to paint under a man's name in their husband's or brother's or father's studio during the Dark Ages of the Holy Catholic and Apostolic Inquisition. The inquisitors were always on the look out for those with any wealth as well as heretics. The witch's family was forced to pay for all those involved from the time of the arrest to the execution. The cost of torture was based upon how many tortures the witch or heretic had to go through before the individual confessed. Many confessed to unspeakable crimes that they never committed simply to save their families from poverty. The Witches' Hammer is evidence of the clergy's loathing of sexuality, it is a perverted handbook on witchcraft and a series of "yes" or "no" questions complete with standard answers that was used to interrogate witches. This is the reason why in the documentation that survives trials and interrogation, all of the women gave identical answers. After paying off the jailer, torturers, judges and executioner, the inquisitors kept a portion of the money and the rest went to Rome. Later popes even tried the dead. Thus, a man could wake up one morning and find that all of his earthly possessions had been confiscated because a dead relative had been found guilty of heresy or witchcraft.

"When Napoleon conquered Spain in 1808, a Polish officer in his army, Colonel Lemanouski, reported that the Dominicans blockaded themselves in their monastery in Madrid. When Lemanouski's troops forced an entry, the inquisitors denied the existence of any torture-chambers. The soldiers searched the monastery and discovered them under the floors. The chambers were full of prisoners, all naked, many insane. The French troops used to cruelty and blood could not stomach the sight. They emptied the torture-chambers, laid gunpowder to the monastery and blew the place up." Vicars of Christ: The Dark Side of the Papacy by Peter De Rosa
(While this book went through 7 printings and was on the New York Times list of best selling books, it is difficult if not impossible to obtain a copy. The manager of the largest bookstore in Denver, Colorado said, "If the book is as hot as Kathleen says it is, it is not unheard of for a large institution to buy up every single copy and stop the publication.")

In the Dark Ages there was legitimate reason to fear the Inquisition and for a woman to hide any talent that another might envy enough to accuse her of being a witch over. The papacy's attack on women and the rewriting of the Gospels extended to the women in Jesus' life. Jesus may very well have saved a prostitute from stoning by saying, *"Let ye without sin cast the first stone."* However, according to the Dead Sea Scrolls, Mary Magdalene was his wife. What I felt from "Still Life With Peacocks" was the remorse and resentment born from the Age of Darkness, which forced me to paint in the manner of my father. The heaviness was in my chest and over the next year, I worked with healers, in meditation and with the Bach flower remedies to release these dark emotions and open my heart to forgive everyone involved and myself. The more that my heart opened, the more that I could connect to Holy Spirit, the Absolute and my own higher self! To get to the place within of inner knowing, which is actually the highest and most accurate psychic ability, our emotions have to be open and clear and negative thoughts have to be released and healed. Suppressing negative emotions or thoughts is something entirely different – these are the underlying causes behind dis-ease, pain and suffering! In releasing our self-created torture chambers we are free to choose to release our destiny to the Absolute. It is then that we discover our life's plan and life flows like the application of oil paints to canvas.

England and Anne Boleyn

The Dance Continues

When I wrote about my past life experiences as Anne Boleyn in <u>Reiki & Other Rays of Touch Healing</u>, Anne Boleyn was not popular! I chose to write about my efforts to heal that lifetime so that other people might be helped to look at lifetimes and issues they were having difficulties with. When I was asked to come to England in the summer of 1995 to teach a Reiki Mastership class, I was not thrilled! Most of the people who wanted to take my class had done a Reiki Mastership class with another teacher the previous year. This Reiki Master had given them a symbol, which he said came from Tibet, as a symbol of initiation. Several of the students later ran into a Tibetan Buddhist monk in London. In their excitement, they showed the monk the symbol they had been given and told him what they were using it for. According to the account that was given to my by several people, the Tibetan Buddhist monk 'freaked out' and told them that it was a symbol used for exorcisms and said something like 'crazy Westerners'. As an enticement for me to come to England, Dorothy and Gordon said they would take me for a long weekend anywhere in the British Isles that I wanted to go; I picked the Isle of Iona in Scotland.

I almost missed my plane from Phoenix and somehow got turned around in New York's JFK Airport. When we deplaned in London, it was so hot that walking through the aluminum octopus arms of Heathrow Airport was like meandering through furnace vents. I wondered what the English did with foreigners who fainted in their airports. I was feeling quite nauseous by the time I got onto the plane to New Castle. After I found my seat, I placed my hands over my stomach and tried to breathe the sick feeling into my hands. I was actually doing better; however, it was a breakfast flight and they were serving an English breakfast of sausages, bacon, ham and blood pudding. The stewardesses parked the serving next to my aisle seat. I was going to ask them to please move it, but I thought they would be through soon. Instead, the busy stewardesses seemed to serve the whole small plane from the centrally parked cart. By the time we landed, I could feel that my body was flushed and I was sweating. Even though there wasn't anything in my stomach, something told me to grab the emergency airsickness bag that was in the flap of the back of the seat in front of me. Dorothy recognized me immediately and was excited to see me. She was sweating profusely because she was not used to the extreme heat that was plaguing Europe that summer. Having just come from Phoenix, temperatures in the middle to upper 80's was a relief. I thought that I had made it 'home free'; however, when Dorothy's car started moving, the carsickness I suffered throughout my childhood returned and I began heaving uncontrollably as though I was being purged. When I could grasp my breath I apologized but she simply waved it off and kept talking to me. I was very grateful. By the time we arrived at her beautiful English home, I was feeling better. I cleaned up, went to my room and passed out on the bed.

I was grateful to wake up rested and feeling better. I went for a walk in Dorothy's wonderful English garden and then began meeting the people who had come to take the class. Jane Rijgersberg had come from Holland to take my classes in New Castle so that when I left England to teach in The Hague, she could pay attention to the needs of the people who came to the class – European hospitality is gracious! When I began talking to her in Dutch, she almost fell over. Jane had never heard Dutch spoken with an English accent before. Whenever there was a free minute, she helped me learn Dutch.

Usually, I offer Reiki I & II classes for review on a donations-are-accepted basis prior to teaching the Reiki Mastership class. However, Dorothy and Gordon had not set it up that way and since everyone was already a Reiki Master, I thought that they would have enough experience in facilitating healings and working with the energy sending distant healings that this would not be a problem. I was wrong! When they asked me to do healing demonstrations prior to the class they seemed astonished that healings were happening. Nobody had any idea what to do when one woman went through an exorcism – at one point, her body was wildly contorted and appeared almost suspended over the table as the demon was leaving her body through her mouth. It was too late to change the class agenda and all I could do was suggest that they read Reiki & Other Rays of Touch Healing.

After the Reiki Mastership class began, many of the students in the class started to ask questions about healing. Every time they asked, I would politely say that we had to stay on track so that they could learn how to do initiations and suggested that they read my book. That was not the only problem! Sometimes when I would answer a question, if the student didn't like the answer, they would keep asking the same question. Several people asked me about the YOD initiation before I gave it. I answered simply that it is the first initiation in the Egyptian symbols, they were given to me by the same Higher Beings who gave me the missing elements of the Reiki initiations and that initiates have found that YOD opens their intuition. Opening up to psychic impressions helps indirectly with healing in that it helps the healer communicate with the celestial angels who are the ones doing the healing and also to tune in on the healee. My explanation didn't satisfy one German woman in particular, and she and a few others repeatedly questioned me about YOD for 30 more minutes or more. I kept repeating that I had told them everything that I knew about YOD and I had no intention of simply making something up so that their curiosity would be satisfied. After even more questions about YOD, I suggested that I postpone doing the YOD initiation until after lunch, we would go on and work with the symbol Halu. During lunch, the German woman and everyone else who had doubts could meditate and ask their guides whether or not they should do the YOD initiation. YOD was not a part of Reiki Mastership; it was something extra that I did in the class. So, if there were people who did not want to have this initiation, there was no problem. After lunch, I invited everyone who didn't want to do the YOD initiation to step out of the room. Nobody left! Even the German woman stayed! I was tempted to escort her to the door myself.

There was also one student who kept trying to take over the class. At one point, Robert said that he belonged to a Reiki society in Japan that traced back to Dr. Usui and he even took out some symbols that he claimed were the original symbols that Dr. Usui used. As half the class started to get out of their chairs, I politely suggested that Robert show them the symbols during lunch or after the class. All of the students who had been moving towards Robert sat back down again. Later, I took the man aside and asked him, "If your organization goes back to Dr. Usui, why are you taking my Reiki Mastership class?" He responded that he planned on taking the energy back to Japan and putting it into initiations that he considered proper Oriental initiations. That is, the initiator takes the initiate to a door and then leaves. If the initiate takes the initiative to open the door and walk through, he is initiated. I asked him, "If these initiations don't work now, what makes you think that they will continue to work if you take the energy from the initiation you received from me and put them into a new pattern?" Robert did not answer. He stiffened his body, leaned his body into mine and with his eyes 2 inches from mine, glared at me. I found out that most of the people in the class were planning on taking the energy of the initiations they received through me and put them into other Reiki initiations they had learned. I asked them, "If the other initiations you learned did not work after you received them, why would you put the energy you received into them now?" I did not receive an answer but they were intent on going ahead anyway. I asked them, "Have you considered that if you change the pattern of the initiation, you alter the energy?" Nobody answered!

After the class received their Reiki Mastership certificate which had "Tera-Mai™ Reiki" instead of "Usui Shiki Ryoho" at the top, while I slept, most of my students stayed awake all night complaining and plotting how they could get me to give them different certificates. The next morning, they invited me into the parlor where they were seated in a circle. A spokesman for the group expressed that they would like certificates that said "Usui Shiki Ryoho" at the top. I answered simply that that was not a problem but since I didn't have any certificates that said

"Usui Shiki Ryoho" at the top with me that I would have to mail them back from the States. It was like I was standing in a circle of hot air balloons and suddenly they all deflated at once. When some of the students said that they only wanted their Reiki Mastership certificate so that they could be official and to be able to go off and 'do their own thing' I said, "That's it! Enough is enough! You ask me the same questions expecting me to give you a different answer. It is this simple, you have a choice, if you change the initiations, you are obligated to tell your students. If you use the name Tera-Mai™, you must keep the initiations standardized. As for not teaching you healing techniques, you all knew before you came here that there would be no Reiki I or II review. The energy will teach you if you will just read the book." Jane said later that she had been waiting for me to speak up and stand my ground for two days.

Sophia told me years later that once, when I left the room most people were talking about how they wanted their old, comfortable Reiki back. They didn't like dealing with other people's issues; they were uncomfortable facing their own torture chambers. Of all the people who attended the class only Sophia, Jane from Holland and Andre´ from Belgium stayed with the Tera-Mai™ initiations.

Some of the students in the class had heard that I could do table tipping and they either wanted to experience it or learn it. Table tipping is a lot like using a Ouija board in that a spirit from the other side of the veil comes in and moves a marker across a board which has the alphabet and "YES" and "NO". However, in table tipping the spirit tips the table – two taps for "yes" and one tap for "no". It is important to establish and be very clear about what "yes" and '"no" are before beginning. Precautions such as lighting a white candle, mentally and psychically surrounding the group with cobalt blue, releasing negative energy and calling in the Higher Forces are exercised before inviting a spirit to come in and communicate with the group. After the spirit is called in, the group questions three times by asking if the spirit has come in the name of Jesus, or in Divine Truth, or the light and love of Christ. If conflicting answers are given at anytime, a negative spirit has peaked its head in. Sometimes the heaviness can be felt immediately. If the spirit is negative, it must be exorcised. Sometimes it takes an hour or more of clearing before the negative spirit is impeached and a spirit with a high vibration can come in. I feel that oftentimes, earthbound spirits will use the opportunity to come in so that they can be released to the Light or Heaven. The problem in New Castle was that Gordon had come up with a table that had metal wheels on it. When the spirit came in, it was unable to tip the table; the spirit was only able to shake the table back and forth from above the metal castings. The woman from Switzerland had suggested that 'yes' be any movement and 'no' be no movement whatsoever. Most of us were laughing so hard that we were crying; the woman from Israel and a few others tried not to laugh and kept looking under the table to determine if anyone was using their feet to create the bizarre, erratic table movement and the rapid halts. After we cleared for almost two hours and sent dishonored knights, witch hunters and others off with the celestial angels, we were able to attract a higher force. We were still laughing and the laughter was breaking up the negativity.

Just before we left for Scotland, Gordon checked the weather forecast. Scotland was the only place in the whole of the British Isles that weekend that was not scheduled for rain. My memory of Scotland is unlike that of most other people; I remember a sunny land with yellow-green grass everywhere. The Scottish cattle have long, hairy coats and many of the Scots themselves are tall with large bones. The Scottish warriors must have struck a cord of terror in the English knights five hundred years ago.

We stayed at a beautiful bed & breakfast on the Isle of Mull. The major town on the island could serve as a movie setting. Saturday afternoon, Dorothy and I had been exploring the town on our own. When Gordon found us he told us that that night, one of the local pubs was having an Irish band play. We all thought that it might be fun to go to the pub after dinner. The band was great; when they played the drums in an ancient call to battle, it was as if Gabriel and his legions were rising out of the music and traveling across the water calling civilization to awaken to the Golden Age of the Return of the Angels. When they were through playing the piece, they looked at each other wondering what it was that just happened.

We had gotten to the pub early and had front row seats on a long bench. There were five or six small square tables in front of the bench. Dorothy and Gordon sat immediately to my right and we pushed the two tables that were in front of us together. A lattice panel was next to Gordon and we could see the bar on the other side. Immediately to my left was a group of people who were busy drinking and talking amongst themselves. The band was in front of me and slightly to my left; I could see the front door to my right, which was on the other side of the bandstand. I am not a great drinker, so I was drinking mineral water, talking with Dorothy and Gordon and listening to the band. Then a tall, dark haired, handsome man walked in and he simply stopped in his tracks and stared at me; the Italians have an expression for it, they call it 'thunder struck'. His friends were sitting next to me and he sat down at the table to my left facing me. Now, in order to see the band, I had to look over his head. I noticed that he was staring at me; so, I simply smiled. I think he was terrorized but he managed to kind of smile back. I continued talking to Dorothy and Gordon. The next time I looked at the band and saw the man staring at me, I smiled and he looked down to check something out on the floor. Then a young teenager who was sitting a few people down from my left somehow managed to spill drinks on the couple who was sitting between us. They left in a huff and the boy and everyone else slid down towards me so that they could have more room between them. The boy was now sitting immediately to my left. So now, I would talk with Dorothy and Gordon, listen to the band, have brief conversations with the boy and every time I looked up at the band, I would see the questioning face of the tall, dark haired man. Somehow, the tall, dark haired man and myself started talking, he introduced himself as Chris and the terrified expression left the Englishman's face. After a while, he motioned for the young teenager to come with him, he excused himself and they went to the other side of the lattice panel. Gordon could see and hear everything; he told me later that Chris had given his son 100 English Pounds Sterling to go back to the yacht where he and his friends were staying. Before he left, the boy and Chris came back to the table and sat down. When I looked at the boy I noticed that he was counting a wad of bills that he had pulled out. I suggested that he put the money away while he was in the pub. Dorothy and Gordon told me later that when his son had taken out the money, Chris had a look of horror on his face and he was desperately trying to signal his son to put the money away. Shortly afterwards, his son left and Chris got up and sat down next to me.

I had sworn off men a year before I left for Arizona and I had told Dorothy and Jane this during one of our conversations in England. Now I found myself sitting next to a man who was obviously interested in me. While I truly believe that every woman should have the kind of experience I was going through at least once in her lifetime, I didn't want to encourage Chris either. He had told me that he was an engineer on an oilrig in the North Sea off the coast of Scotland and that he had come to the Isle of Mull with some men that he worked with and his son. I knew that the Scots were not being paid for the oil that England was drilling; so, when the conversation turned to how much England had done for Scotland, I said, "I think England ought to give Ireland back to the Irish and Scotland back to the Scots." Chris roared, "Are you crazy saying that in here? They don't even want to have their country back." I paused, considered his statement and then leaned over and asked the man sitting next to Chris, "Excuse me! Would you like to have your country back?" The man was stunned at first and then answered, "Yes!" We could all tell it was very clear that Chris was shocked and his feelings were hurt. I felt terrible and I couldn't leave him like that. So, I said, "It's not that we don't like you, because we both like you. It's just that they would like to have their country back." Chris reconsidered his position and began talking to me again and occasionally to Dorothy and Gordon. Chris was calm, confidant and enjoying himself. When he held my hand in his I noticed how huge his hand was. Then he asked me what I did for a living. I answered that I held seminars and had written a book teaching people how to tune into and explore their psychic and healing ability. Chris dropped my hand and raised both of his arms above his head, slammed his huge hands down on the small table. For a moment, I thought it was going to break. All he said was "That does it! That's it!" I smiled at Dorothy and Gordon and excused myself so that I could find the lady's room. Chris was facing his friends and grumbling when I left. When I returned to the table, Chris started up another conversation.

At that point, I simply relaxed and began enjoying myself. Chris then asked me what I was drinking and then excused himself to go to the bar. The man from Scotland who wanted his country backslid next to me and we began talking. Chris returned with a bar tray full of after dinner drinks for his friends and himself. Chris smiled and motioned with his head for his friend to move, but the man from Scotland wasn't budging. Chris gave his other friends their drinks and then waved a drink under the Scotsman's nose. The Scotsman still wasn't budging. Chris then put his drink and his friend's drink down on the table, reached over and picked up his friend, moved him over and sat down next to me. I think that I was not the only one who sat openmouthed while Chris did this. In a very calm, friendly manner, Chris started asking me about my book and he gave me his address in England so that I could mail him a copy. He asked for my address several times and finally Dorothy gave it to him. Chris asked me if I would go golfing with them Sunday morning, but I explained that I was with friends and that we had made plans. When his friends got up to go back to the yacht he kissed me goodbye.

When Dorothy asked me, I told her that I wasn't planning on writing Chris. I really couldn't see myself with somebody who drank a lot. Dorothy told me that she felt that Chris and I had known each other in another lifetime where he had fallen in love with me but it hadn't work out. She felt that God didn't want me to shut off the possibility of the right man coming into my life. While Dorothy was talking I had a vision of myself walking hand in hand into the sea with other women who were considered witches while Chris and other soldiers looked on. We had taken some kind of mushroom or plant to ease the fear and chosen our watery death to avoid humiliation and the fire, and also to save our family's possessions from the Inquisition. Later, when I went to Ireland and told Kathryn O'Connell about what I had seen, she told me that to this day there are stories told in Europe about thousands upon thousands of women who committed suicide in the identical manner that I had observed in my mind's eye.

The Isle of Iona was extremely small and very interesting. There weren't many buildings - one of the homes had been converted into a retreat for stressed out American lawyers. Sheep roamed the golf course. Saint Colombo had driven the Druids out of Scotland. A church and monastery had been built over the Celtic site of learning on the Isle of Iona. While psychic forces had once been abundantly present, they spirit of the land had moved on long before. What remained was the remembrance and there was still some magic in the air. The vision I had seen of myself walking into the sea with Chris sadly looking on had been so vivid that I sat down to meditate and ask if I dare begin to open myself to the possibility of another man in my life. I knew that I had to release my fears of being in a relationship because it was my own fears that were creating my worst nightmares. It came to me to simply write to him and be watchful. When we returned to Mull I found a postcard with a photo of the local cattle. I wrote to Chris, "Did your tongue perhaps feel like this fellow's coat in the morning?" I also gave him Jane's telephone number in Holland.

Jane and Ger picked met me at Shripol Airport in Amsterdam. It was wonderful to see her again and she was excited to see me. I told her about Chris and that he might be calling. She told me that she thought that Dorothy was right and that it was time for me to bring joy into my personal life. Chris called within minutes of our arrival and we talked for a long time. He said that he had been looking for me all day Sunday and asked where I had been and where I had stayed on the island. He also told me that on Monday, he couldn't find my address, and he thought his son, not wishing to see his father get into a relationship with anyone but Chris' ex-wife, had taken it. If I hadn't written to Chris, I never would have known that his interest in me went beyond a superficial pub encounter. He found me attractive and interesting; he was beginning to make me feel good about myself. He asked me again for a copy of Reiki & Other Rays of Touch Healing. Jane had extra copies of my book. I hesitated and then mailed him a copy.

Chris later sent me a postcard that had a picture of the oilrig he worked on. He said that if there had been a cure for hangovers in the book that I might have converted him and that he would write again. I answered his letter, but I never heard from him again. Dr. John Gray refers to the process of introspection that men go through as "going into their caves" and when they are ready to come out, they snap back like a rubber band. If I had been a bank president or a cleaning lady, Chris could have accepted me; when he read my book Chris went into his cave and I broke his rubber band. We were in each other's lives briefly to open the door to a new reality. Whether or not he closed or walked through the opening to the possibility of metaphysics was entirely up to him; whether or not I chose to leave myself open to the possibility of another man coming into my life was up to me. Spending the summer of 1995 in Europe changed my thinking and the whole rest of my life. A healing process had been initiated within me and there was no turning back. However, I wasn't sure that I wanted to go back to England. A thought deep inside of me surfaced – they still don't like me. Consciously I reasoned that my life didn't work in England.

What we resist persists. In the spring of 1998, I returned to England and this time I stayed in Brighton by the sea. Sophia and I had the opportunity to spend a day in London - we began at the Tower of London. The Yeoman who guided our tour injected a good deal of humor into the telling of the path that led prisoners to their execution. Sophia kept looking at me with a worried look on her face; she was wondering how I was taking his jokes. I found myself laughing along with everyone else and it was just what I needed. When a prisoner was brought to London Tower, the horror began with seeing the severed heads that lined the wall, which had been stuck on spears. The blackbirds would have been picking away at them with the first thing to go were the eyes. After being tortured and tried, the condemned was taken to a public place of execution. To insure that his death was quick and merciful, he was expected to tip the executioner. When the head was chopped off, the crowd would cheer – it was public entertainment. The Yoeman told us the story of John Sullivan who refused to tip the executioner – after several unsuccessful whacks his head was still half on. It was then that the executioner took out his knife and slowly carved what remained off of the body. Heads were added to those on the Tower wall. When we were in St. Peter ad Vicula, the Tower church, the Yeoman told us that the headless bodies were all brought to the church and thrown into the basement of the church unburied. Anne Boleyn and Catherine Howard had private executions on the Tower Green, their heads were put back on their lifeless bodies and they were buried under the altar, a place of honor. I wondered who else could see that what the Yeoman was describing was a black magic ritual that could only have been ordered by the highest church officials and the king himself. Black magicians instill terror into their victims (usually helpless animals) before killing them and their black magic spells are sent out on the vibration of horror that was created. I could see clearly that the midnight ceremonies at the Chapel Royal of Saint Peter ad Vincula were considerably different than Sunday service. I could feel the souls who were still trapped by their fear as well as the trapped souls who had used other's fear for their own evil purposes. I prayed for them all and watched as a column of Light filled the chapel giving the long departed an opportunity to be released and experience love and joy.

While our tour group was standing next to Traitor's Gate and the Yeoman was explaining that Anne Boleyn was brought to the prison through this entrance, I heard Sophia whisper in my ear, "You are giving off so much heat, you could probably heat the whole complex!" I was not aware of any temperature change. So, I asked her what it was she was feeling. Sophia answered, "You are releasing rage." I heard the words, "How dare they do this."

Later, when we were on our own exploring the Tower I looked down from a window onto the Tower Green. In my mind's eye I could see the tortured, mangled bodies of the men who had been accused of having sexual relations with Anne Boleyn being carried into the church one by one. I realized that Anne had carried the guilt of their deaths with her when she died. On a subconscious level I was afraid of getting into a relationship in this lifetime because of the fear that something awful might happen to the man. I was trying desperately to breathe away the toxic emotions of guilt and terror and clear my mind. I again gazed down at the Tower Green and the headless bodies were gone. I was relieved. With my mind once again at peace, I found myself going within into a place of no mind. Suddenly, I was struck with the inner knowing that after Henry's death, his son, Edward VI, did not die a natural death; he had been murdered. That reality was so clear, it was as if an etheric note had been sounded and the vibration of that truth was momentarily suspended in the air.

When we stood at the scaffold site on the Tower Green, Sophia suddenly turned to me and said, "You didn't go to the Light after they executed you. You stayed to protect your daughter, Elizabeth." On the way to Westminster Abbey we walked by the Raven held in a small cage. Legend has it that should the Ravens leave the Tower, the monarchy will fall.

Entering the Abbey through the Great North Door we then proceeded to tour the tombs of kings, queens and others, who now unknown, had been wealthy or famous in their day. One important aspect of architecture is that a statue or monument fit the space. Westminster Abbey was jammed packed with large, obtrusive crypts and sculptures. One small, uncluttered room at the end of the abbey was enclosed by glass and was set aside for prayer. I had been praying for quite a while when I heard a voice from deep within me say, "I forgive them all. Please help them, Father."

Neville Kim Sing had made plans to take Sophia Lucia and myself to Hever Castle, the childhood home of Anne Boleyn. Diane Shillingford had told me a few days earlier that I would enjoy the outing as Anne would have been very happy there. I wondered if that was true. The night before we left, I couldn't eat dinner; when I woke up the next morning, I felt sick to my stomach. Even though I was supposed to give a lecture and demonstration that evening, Sophia felt that it was important for me to go. Sophia is so efficient! Before I got out to the car, she had put blankets and pillows in the backseat along with a bucket so that I wouldn't spoil Neville's BMW, household cleaner and a rag to clean the bucket with, and a jug of water and some cups. Sophia's neighbors probably thought that they were taking me to the hospital.

I know why they call it Hever Castle! When I wasn't passed out on the backseat, I was retching in Sophia's bucket even though there wasn't any food in my stomach. A few times I tried to drink water, but it just came up and I would pass out again. Then Sophia handed me homeopathic Arsenicum and said that it would make me feel better. Within less than a minute, I was heaving uncontrollably. When I finally stopped, I took a sip of water and Sophia handed me homeopathic Belladonna and said that this one would surely make me feel better. Again, I heaved uncontrollably. I managed to gasp, "I thought you said this would make me feel better." She answered, "It is! You need to get the toxicity out of you." When I finally stopped heaving, I took another small sip of water and passed out again. When I woke up, I needed to use the toilet quickly. I told Neville and he pulled into the parking lot of a hospital. Sophia came with me and told the nurse at the door that she had an American lady who needed to use the toilet. They didn't have too much to say; they pointed and said it was at the end of the hallway. I managed to say thank you before we left and Sophia and I walked out and got into Neville's car. Before I laid down on the backseat, I turned back and saw the speechless faces of four of the hospital staff who were standing openmouthed in the front entrance looking at us. I took another sip of water, was grateful that I would never see these people again, lay down and passed out.

The next time I woke up, we were at Hever Castle. It had been raining and the air was clean. Dark gray and black clouds filled most of the sky. Yet, some of the sun's rays managed to pierce through the clouds to light the landscape. The whole scene looked like it could be a cover to a Steven King novel. I threw up again in the parking lot and then somehow managed to walk to the castle. Going over the drawbridge, my eyes drank in all that was around me and I found myself wondering where the horses were. Inside there were several portraits of Anne Boleyn including the one that is usually used; the one where Anne looks like one of Cinderella's wicked stepsisters. When we walked by the children's rooms, I was struck with the knowing that as a girl my brother had repeatedly raped me. I knew that I did not want to marry Henry whom I perceived of as a man who forced his will upon others. I was going in and out of the consciousness of Anne Boleyn. When I was in my own consciousness in my own body, I was aware that I was not feeling well. I told Sophia and Neville that I had to see the life-size wax figures of Henry, Anne and his other wives. I had to look at Anne. When I saw her, I was surprised to see that she was very pretty. Abuse victims tend to have both low self-esteem and guilt. Perpetrators tell children that they are being abused because it is their fault. Somehow the child is made to believe that they are the ones causing the predator do horrible, unspeakable acts. What I had been throwing up all morning was toxic shame.

In the consciousness of Anne Boleyn, suddenly, I heard Henry asking me to marry him. I knew I shouldn't tell Henry but I did it anyway; I told him that I couldn't marry him because I wasn't a virgin; that my brother had raped me. Henry was angry! He roared out of the castle. I heard hoof beats galloping down the road and a part of me was relieved because I thought that it was over. But he returned and asked again. As his subject, I couldn't say "No!" to the king. Later, after the birth of their stillborn boy, Henry thought that he had jinxed himself by not marrying a virgin. Henry knew that he couldn't simply use Anne's brother, George, to have her declared a traitor; so, he and his ministers falsely accused and tortured five other men along with George. Five of the men refused to falsely accuse an innocent woman. After being tortured, they were hung, released just before drawing their dying breath and then drawn and quartered. Henry had George buried next to Anne under the church altar as an insult to her. Only the minstrel, Sincaton, broke under torture. Throughout Henry's life, the testimony of the five men nagged at him in a tiny corner of his brain and manifested as his gout.

Feeling Anne's remorse, I asked Spirit, "What should have done?" The answer was that if I had asked God what to do, I would have received my answer. Henry had had Cardinal Wolsey break Anne's engagement to Lord Henry Percy, the youngest son of the 5th Earl of Northumberland so that he could marry Anne. If I had said "yes" to Henry the first time he asked, his love for me was great that his love would have healed my wounds. Henry would have had two sons with Anne. However, Anne would not have grown old with Henry; Anne would have died in childbirth with their second son. There are framed letters from Henry to Anne hanging in the castle; she was the love of his life. The rumor that Anne Boleyn played with men's emotions and withheld sex from King Henry so that he would marry her was propagated by Henry's ego, nursed to maturity in his brain, birthed by his emotions and rationally excused by his desire for a son.

Consciousness-raising experiences whereby an individual is fully participating in another reality are what Native Americans refer to as a vision quest. When I am having an experience as the one I just described, people who are with me also have unusual experiences. I turned and looked again at the wax figures. Some of them were moving. Sophia was standing next to me and I asked her if she noticed anything about the wax figures. She said, "Yes, some of them are moving."

We must have set the record for the fastest tour of Hever Castle ever. Once outside, Neville handed me a plastic bag and I heaved in that. I looked up and saw the horrified expressions on the faces of some more people. Neville got permission to drive his car into the grounds so that I wouldn't have to walk. I took another drink of water and slept all of the way back to Sophia's home where I cleaned up and went to sleep until it was time for me to get ready to go to the lecture/demonstration I was supposed to give. When I woke up I was feeling and looking a lot better, but I knew that I would not have the energy to both talk and do healings. So, I asked seven of my students to come on stage with me and then invited seven members of the audience to come up who wanted to experience healings. I talked, answered questions and then went down the row talking to healers and healees and asking them what they were experiencing. It worked out very well.

When I saw the movie, Hope Floats I felt that Gena Rowlands could have been talking to me when she said to Sandra Bullock, "You know your love life has always been a disaster area. They ought to have those big orange cones all around you." While my current relationship was indeed a huge improvement, I had to ask myself why I couldn't experience a healthy relationship and what the man I was dating was reflecting back to me. The answer was my own fear of being in a relationship. Even though Anne Boleyn died bravely, fear and mistrust of relationships followed her to the grave. The man I had been dating was showing me my fear in order for me to release it, just as he had shown me my light so that I could shine. I prayed that someday he would be able to release his fear so that the special qualities I had seen and loved in him could come forth. To be totally released from the cycle I had to forgive and love myself unconditionally. I took the flower essences Mimulus to release fear and Walnut to break the cycle and prepare for new beginnings. My two mares, Christie and Pooh Bear, were also reflecting my fear back to me; so, I also gave them Mimulus and Walnut. (For animals put a few drops in their water dish or water bucket.) I purchased two crystal necklaces at A Peace of the Universe bookstore/crystal shop. The first was a Native American-looking silver necklace that had been made in Turkey. It had a single orange carnelian stone (protection and banishes sorrow). It had an extremely strong but positive masculine energy; it gave me the feeling that God the Father was holding and protecting me. The other necklace was pink quartz (love) and apatite (apatite can be used as the stillpoint between consciousness and matter). Judy felt that it would help me with self-love. I was still healing. When a personality dies before their time, I believe God provides that soul another chance to reincarnate when they are ready so as to resolve and heal issues as well as to experience the missed opportunities that were cut short.

Somebody once sent me a card with a picture of an angel in complete surrender basking in God's love. Sometimes Pisceans can get too emotionally invested in the outcome. I tried to envision myself like this angel simply letting go and letting God do the work.

I returned to England for the third time in December 1998 and stayed with Diane Shillingford. She told me later that she knew that I was coming to finish the healing of Anne Boleyn and also to help to heal Great Britain. I never made it out to Hampton Court. I was given a book, which is now out of print, to read, A Tudor Story: The Return of Anne Boleyn by Canon W. S. Pakenham-

Waish. The book went through five hands in order to reach me. It seemed so important that I stayed up and read it in one night.

In the 1920's and 1930's this clergyman was strongly impressed that Anne Boleyn was innocent and he wanted to write a play on the subject. While most historical accounts hold the opinion that Anne withheld sex from King Henry so that he would fall in love with her and marry him, Sir Francis Bacon had written a play defending Queen Anne. There are many metaphysicians who believe that Sir Francis Bacon was Saint Germain and that it was Sir Francis Bacon who wrote the plays that are attributed to Shakespeare. The legend of John the Beloved is that he chose not to die but to remain on Earth to help usher in the Aquarian Age, the Golden Age of the return of the angels. The television series, The Pretender, touches upon the possibility of changing identity. Sir Francis Bacon and Chief Joseph may possibly be two of Saint John's identities.

In his quest for material for his play, the clergyman, W. S., visited many spiritual mediums. It was through these mediums that he obtained information for his play and later the book I was reading. Anne initially appeared as an attractive, well-dressed woman of the 15th century. While she did not give the medium her name, the clergyman could tell by what she was saying that they were speaking to Anne Boleyn. The medium was unfamiliar with British history but she was picking up things particular to Anne Boleyn. She felt terror and the sense that a great tragedy had occurred. C. W. asked Anne for little-known facts about herself that he could research so that he would know for sure whom he was speaking to. Anne gave him five things and over the course of several years, he verified everything including the facts that her favorite white horse led her coronation as queen, she owned a small dog and that she wore a small, oval amethyst ring.

When Anne was asked if she had gone to Heaven (the Light) after her death she responded that she had had some things to take care of first. When Anne was asked about her marriage to Henry, she refused to speak about it and said that it was a closed book. Over the years, Spirit worked through the mediums and the clergyman to help heal her wounds. As Anne healed, other personalities from her life began to appear along with her. Kathryn of Aragon appeared as a Light being very much concerned about her "beloved Henry". Jane Seymore, the pure and demure 3rd wife of Henry VIII, showed up as a dark heavy soul who had never gone to the Light. I wondered why, but neither the mediums nor W. C. asked her the question. Henry appeared initially as a soul who was just awakening after four hundred years from the crushing weight of his earthly choices. He insisted upon being called King Henry, even though nobody on the other side recognized him as a king. When Henry was asked that if at the time he had known that Anne

Boleyn was innocent, he responded, "Yes, but by divine right of kings I held the right to hold her guilty anyway." Slowly, with Spirit's help and through his own prayers, Henry began to heal and feel remorse over the way he had treated those around him, in particular Lord Henry Percy. On one occasion, Henry showed up furious at Jane Seymore. He was holding some documents while he roared, "Where is she? Where is Jane Seymore? Jane never told me about these contracts."

As I continued to read, I could hardly believe that nobody asked Henry what the contracts were or why he was so angry. It bothered me so much that later I meditated to see if Spirit would tell me the answer. The answer almost knocked me over. Henry was right, he'd been bewitched! But Henry had the wrong woman. Jane Seymore had put a spell on Henry because she wanted Anne's life. Well, Jane got Anne's life in spades – Jane Seymore died in childbirth. Something was lifted off of me; it was the last of the spell that Jane had cast upon me. Evil has to have a vehicle with which to enter and Jane's black magic had a choice of models from which to choose in order to have its effect on Anne. There was the shame and guilt from being raped by George, or her unforgiveness of Cardinal Wolsey for carrying out Henry's instructions and having her engagement to Henry Percy broken, or her unexpressed anger towards her father for helping to arrange her engagement to Henry. King Henry VIII also afforded Jane Seymore's spells the possibility of any number of different avenues of entry. While Henry began as an intelligent, well-intentioned and honorable man, he is a primary example of how "All power tends to corrupt; absolute power corrupts absolutely". *Bishop Mandell Creighton, 1887*

Later, when I told Diane what had happened, she said, "Do you know the reincarnation of Jane Seymore in your current life?" The first name I heard was "Shantarisumari". Diane got the same thing. What I wasn't clear about was whether Jane cast the spell on Henry and Anne herself or whether she paid to have somebody else do it. I found it mildly amusing that after five hundred years, she was still trying to live my life. The Tudor Story: The Return of Anne Boleyn talks about how Jane Seymore was healed by Spirit through the mediums and the clergyman. However, when Shantarisumari was confronted with the same dilemma that Jane Seymore faced and had to choose which path to walk, Shantarisumari's choice again was the illusion of glamour. Rather than exploring the depth of possibilities within herself, she wanted somebody else's reality. Shantarisumari then compromised her ethics and justified wrongful acts. Real evil does exist and evil has about it an illusion of glamour. Those who think they are taking a shortcut to fame and riches through black magic fail to achieve elegance or find joy or true love. The black magician stands in the middle of a pentagram (a symbol of protection not of evil) to protect him/herself from the demons s/he summons to carry out unspeakable deeds. S/he lacks the foresight to see that when s/he dies, there is no pentagram. The demons s/he thinks that s/he is controlling will control him/her. The possession can last for lifetimes until finally the personality admits that there are problems and seeks out help. Oftentimes when I am facilitating an exorcism, I can see the past life where the possessed individual I am working on used the same demons inside of them to cause horrific acts. How can we tell the difference between the illusion of glamour of evil and God's Truth? "Seek (out the Truth) and ye shall find." "Ye shall know them by their works." *Jesus Christ*

Shantarisumari in this lifetime publicly talks about the fact that she and her boyfriend do not have sex; she attributes it to her piety. From working with many people, what I know to be true is that individuals who use black magic to entice another to fall in love with them in one lifetime cannot have normal sex in subsequent lifetimes. The reincarnation of Hitler shared with me that he was unable to have normal sex and he said that it was because of a decision he had made many lifetimes ago. While he did not elaborate, I could see clearly that it was the one where he thought he could use black magic to secure the love of another.

There were other things that the clergyman either did not pursue or made left-brained assumptions about. W. C. asked the first medium if the spirit she was talking to could describe her home and Anne gave a perfect description of Hever Castle. The medium went on to say that the spirit of the dead woman was showing her a castle that was half in the light and half in the dark. Rather than asking why, the clergyman assumed that it was a shadow. W. C. also assumed that George was Anne's beloved brother – abuse victims are often extra nice to the one who is abusing them in an attempt to avoid abuse by pacifying the abuser.

And likewise, just because a spirit is speaking from the other side of the veil does not mean that they know everything. When Anne was asked if Henry's daughter, Mary, was currently reincarnated, Anne responded that since Mary was with her that she couldn't be reincarnated. While Anne had some idea of the illusion of time on the earth plane, she didn't comprehend that it was not only possible to live simultaneous lifetimes, but it is possible for one personal aspect of a soul to show up in spirit form while simultaneously being reincarnated.

In January 1536, Anne caught Henry in the closet having sex with Jane Seymore. Shortly thereafter, Anne gave birth to a stillborn boy. The soul may have taken one look at his soon to be parents and opted not to breathe the first breath whereby the soul enters the physical body or perhaps the stillborn birth could have been a part of Jane's curse. W. C. was curious about where Anne was from January 1536 until May 1536, when she was tried and beheaded. In last chapter of <u>A Tutor Story: The Return of Anne Boleyn</u>, Anne relates how she walked terrified through

Hampton Court gardens knowing that the stillbirth of their son sealed her doom. She fled to the home of a friend and Henry followed her there. When he arrived, he grabbed her by the arm and dragged her across the floor, up the stairs and down the hall to a bedroom where she remained locked up until her trial. Anne said that Henry had broken her arm. As I read, I was exhaling horror. I knew that Henry had beaten Anne before locking the door. It would have been impossible for him to drag Anne with her arm broken without pulling it off. One of Henry's complaints to W. C. about Anne was that she was always crying. More than likely this was not the first beating Henry had inflicted upon her and may have been the real reason for the stillbirth. It was nearing dawn but before I put my head on the pillow, I prayed for myself and tried to send forgiveness to everyone known and unknown who had harmed me and asked to be forgiven by any and all whom I had harmed. Several hours later, I woke up, pushed my body off of my stomach and screamed out in pain. If felt as through the humerus of my right arm had been broken. For over a month, the pain continued intermittently as the cellular memory was released and my arm healed.

Henry once complained to the clergyman about his former wives. He felt that the problem was theirs. I would bet a lot of money that all of the later incarnations of any of Henry's wives had serious relationship issues.

Anne was not the only lifetime I healed while I was in England. In one past life regression many years ago, I had the experience of being a priestess in Greece when the Roman soldiers came through and decimated the temples. I hated the Roman soldiers! In my next lifetime, I came back as a pillaging, marauding, raping Roman soldier. As the Roman soldier, I was murdered at night in my bed, and with my dying breath I was remorseful and filled with guilt. When I reincarnated as Anne Boleyn I suffered a hundred times over the deeds of the Roman soldier that I had been. The Roman soldier was charged with destroying the Druids; Anne Boleyn's family could trace their lineage back to both the Romans and the Celtics. Anne's intuition and healing abilities and knowledge came from her Celtic ancestors. We are always drawn to what we hate as well as what we love. When Diane Shillingford and I went to the ruins of the old Roman Palace at Fishbourne (born of the fish), I knew that Jesus was with me and that something was going on. It was like blessed Divine grace was assisting my soul to release guilt and breathe in forgiveness. Perhaps that is the function of grace and that it is a gift that we can all experience when we are ready.

I came home to Phoenix on Monday, December 14th looking five years younger and weighing five pounds less. Amazing what manifests when we are willing to work through and release our issues. While I had been in England, I had been fighting off one of the various infections that were going around. The long trip home without a good sleep only made it worse. By Wednesday, I had again started to feel better, so I kept the massage appointment that I had made with Shari Sage before I had left. She did a lymphatic massage to help my immune system but she couldn't find the infection until she got to my right foot. She told me, "When I touch your left foot, it radiates a golden light. When I touch your right foot, it is like there is a hidden agenda that is apart from and contradictory to your life's agenda." While I did the Hosanna clearing, Shari used Tai Chi to remove the blockage from my foot and escort it out the backdoor and into the Light. After my massage, I had scheduled a foot massage and reflexology appointment. I had never done this before and even when I had made the appointment, I wasn't sure why I was doing it. As I sat with my feet in the bubbling, hot water, I marveled at how God provides for each one of us when we can love and forgive ourselves and surrender to our own unique divine plan.

The following day, I went in for my colon therapy appointment with Rosemarie Siciliano. When I told her what had happened at Fishbourne and then at the Lee Robert's Spa in the Scottsdale Borgotta, she laughed. "So, you went to the Roman palace to heal the Roman soldier." The architecture of the Scottdale Borgotta is like an old Roman castle.

My chiropractor, Hermine Muellerleile, treats the whole person and is always interested about what is going on with each of her patients. I told her about my experiences in England and also that Christie was making quantum leaps forward and I had entered her in the Scottsdale International Arabian Horse Show in February. Hermine responded, "Perhaps, it is Christie who is mirroring back to you what is happening in your own life?!!! "

In February 1999, I returned to England. There are many portraits of Queen Elizabeth I in the National Portrait Gallery. It is clear that her sunken eyes developed later in her life. Her father, Henry VIII, died from the long-term effects of syphilis. If Elizabeth had contracted syphilis early in the womb from her mother, she would have been sickly and weak like her brother, Edward VI. Elizabeth was infected either later in the pregnancy or by coming in contact with her father as a baby or toddler. Yes, syphilis is that contagious! Henry VIII in all likelihood contracted the disease from Jane Seymore. Elizabeth's sunken eyes were an outward sign of the interior breaking down of her fine muscles, which was caused by syphilis. I believe that Elizabeth knew she could not have children and that is the reason why she never married. When she was 29, Elizabeth I almost died from small pox. She probably began wearing heavy white makeup and wigs to cover up the scars left from small pox, and in light of Elizabeth's sunken eyes, the makeup also covered a copper-colored tint to her skin resulting from syphilis. However, as the movie, Elizabeth, suggests, the cult of the queen was deliberate and was advanced through both subtle and obvious means.

The earliest reference in the portraits to the cult of Gloriana with moon symbology occurs in a miniature by Nicholas Hillard (1506-07). The origins of the moon cult of the queen began with Giordano Bruno when he made references to Elizabeth in "larger than life" verbiage whose influence was capable of creating a "new-world order". Sir Francis Drake spread the moon cult of the queen as a replacement for the Virgin Mary, and he gave Elizabeth a half moon in 1587. November 17th, Accession Day, and September 7th, Elizabeth's birthday, took the place of holy days honoring the Virgin Mary. In 1588, there were many church eulogies personifying the queen as the goddess Diana with cosmic powers. In Raleigh's portrait of 1588, in the top left-hand corner there is a small crescent moon. With the defeat of the Spanish Armada that year, the cult became public. In a 1588 work by Sir Christopher Halton, he alludes to the queen as the goddess Astraea who is ushering in a new Golden Age. In the 'Armada' portrait Elizabeth's sleeves have jeweled Enochian magic symbols, her collar has equal armed crosses and her fan is made of lacy crescent moons. In John Case's woodcut, he depicts Elizabeth embracing the solar system with Earth at the center. In the 1592 'Ditchley" portrait by Marcus Gheeraerts the Younger, Elizabeth is standing on a map of the world with her feet planted on England. Her dress is covered with various symbols containing equal armed crosses, all of which are connected in diamond patterns which connect and form six-sided figures with a central focus which in turn alludes to the seven directions – north, south, east, west, above, below and within. The portrait of Elizabeth completed in 1600, shows Elizabeth with a radiating crescent moon on her bodice. One of the side effects from syphilis is delusions of grandeur.

When Henry VIII and his men drove the Catholic priests, bishops and archbishops from the churches and abbeys, they would have found some of the secret mantras, rites and Enochian Magic practiced by Jesus and his original followers. Elizabeth I practiced a system channeled by Dr. John Dee and Edward Kelley, which they also called Enochian Magic. John Dee was an astrologer and he picked the day for Elizabeth's coronation and instructed her in arcane matters. He was also suspected of being an espionage agent for the queen and signed his correspondence to her "007", just like Ian Fleming's character, James Bond. John Dee was not psychic! It was Edward Kelley who perceived information from the Otherworlds during their scrying sessions while John Dee took notes. The angels they were involved with are highly suspect as they gave the men both white and black magic - although the angels did tell the men never to use the system of black magic, why did they even introduce the men to black magic? Both Dee and Kelley had warnings that the whole system was suspect when the angels threatened to put a curse on John Dee and his progeny for five generations because he was not doing their bidding fast enough. The "angels" also told Kelley that he had to get married even though he didn't want to get married. Then the "angels" told Dee and Kelley to swap wives. Interestingly, while Dee thought the "angels" were genuine, Kelley, the psychic, felt that the "angels" were deceiving them. Dee and Kelley worked together for five years and the Otherworld communication stopped when the two men parted.

The unnatural storm that rose up from nowhere and defeated the Spanish Armada was the result of using Enochian Magic, secret rites of the Church and Elizabeth's inherited psychic abilities. It was the destiny of the Tudors and England to halt the rampages of the Roman Catholic Church's Holy Inquisition. In truth, England would have defeated Phillip II and Spain without the use of black magic. The Spanish ships, manned by soldiers, were cumbersome and their firepower was less effective than that of the English. English ships, manned by sailors, were smaller, closer to the water and more maneuverable. Through the right use of magic, 1588 could have been the beginning of an age of Piscean enlightenment for not only England, but also the whole world. Instead, it was the zenith of Elizabeth's reign. By the time Elizabeth died, James VI inherited a depleted treasury, discontent and the rise of Puritanism, which while oppressive, never matched the Gestapo techniques of the Inquisition (in 1967 it became the Congregation for the Doctrine of the Faith). When Natural Law is forgotten, wrongs by the aristocracy or government are masked with moral indignation and propriety. Those with the most sins cast the most stones!

I never know where I will receive insights and knowledge. York turned out to be more than memorable. York is one of the most haunted cities in all of Europe! York's violet past has produced an abundant population of trapped souls who were unable to go to the Light after they died. Some 150 ghosts have been repeatedly seen and identified; notables include the Black Abbot of St. Mary's Abbey, Thomas Percy, 7th Earl of Northumberland, and a troop of Roman soldiers who walk a buried road and have been seen marching through the basement of The Treasurer's House. What is interesting about the troop of Roman soldiers is that they were seen before anyone knew of the buried Roman road. When the road was discovered it proved to be the exact depth of the soldiers' feet in The Treasurer's House basement. Vikings, Scots and Romans all invaded York. Witches were tried and burned in York. In 1190 AD hundreds of Jews were burned in the castle where they had sought refuge from a riot started by Englishmen wishing to avoid repaying their debt to the Jewish money lenders. Both the debtor's prison and the women's prison were in York. As we visited York on a Monday, we missed Mad Alice's nightly ghost walk. We did visit the castle, the museum that was built over the women's prison, the beautiful Minster and we walked along the old streets. After we returned to Sheffield, I was aware that one of

York's spirits was behind me. I knew that he had been a man and had been looking for a way out of York for a very long time. I invited the celestial angels in and then created an opening of white light by energizing the symbol, Johre, with Cho Ku Rays. He stepped into the circle quickly and went with the angels to a place of healing and rest. I then used the Hosanna clearing for myself, the house and every being in and around the house.

Several days later, because of avalanches followed by freezing rain in the alps, rather than going to Austria to go skiing, I went back to Holland with the nursery rhyme, "The Jolly Old Duke of York", playing off and on in my head. Jane Rijgersberg has always been a good psychic. She got the same thing that I had; the ghost from York was already trying to communicate with me. The nursery rhyme stopped playing as a confirmation that we were right. I did a Tarot spread on the ghost from York to see if the cards would speak to me. The man had been a nobleman. He was also a highly evolved being who had gotten caught up in the mindset of the Dark Ages. The card in his immediate past was a queen. The energy lifted off of the card and I was shown that in York he recognized Anne Boleyn because he had known her when she was queen. Initially, he was surprised to see her walking around York with her head on; then he saw her as a forgiving soul who could help him. The devil was how people in York perceived him. The final outcome was Thoth - he wanted to help me personally, and he was interested in healing through other Tera-Mai™ practitioners and myself. The man from York told me that the shame and guilt, which he had suppressed in life, kept him earthbound after his death for he was one of the nobility who had judged Anne guilty of the charges brought against her by Henry. He went on to say that it wasn't only Henry VIII who had known that Anne was innocent. The only nobleman to verbally object to Anne's trial and walk out of the trial was Lord Henry Percy, who died the following year. The man from York also told me that it was easy for Henry Percy to speak out because Henry VIII would not have wanted to make an enemy of the Earl of Northumberland, who was already offended because Henry VIII had had his son's engagement to Anne Boleyn annulled.

Robin Hormann came to me for a healing on Saturday, March 6th. Robin had a lifetime that he refused to forgive himself for; he couldn't even look at it to identify it and it was holding him back. During the session, Robin was still unable to look at his past life, so, I asked him if he would like me to tell him what I saw and he answered "Yes!" I told Robin that I saw him as a priest in the Aman Brotherhood in Egypt. Immediately, Robin saw a man in black robes. After a while, I asked Robin what was happening. Robin said that he was trying to turn the robes gold but they kept turning back to black. I asked Robin to find out what the Aman priest wanted. Immediately, his robes turned to gray and through Robin he said, "We have a question to ask you. We have been told that the balance between white and black is gray. Is this true?" I tuned into my guides and said, "I feel that the gray you are speaking of represents the mundane. In truth, like a well-tuned instrument, it is the middle road that offers the most choices, opportunities and freedom of movement. In terms of colors, the rainbow itself expresses the balance between white and black."

As the Aman priest and the man from York were both working through the same issues, I asked the Aman priest if the man from York could come in to assist in the healing. At first the Aman priest could not look at the man from York. The Aman priest did not like what he saw because he was seeing himself. When the Aman priest became aware of this and could look at both the man from York and himself, they both left the dark room that they were in and went up a flight of stairs to a large open room. They each went to what Robin described as an open coffin and lay down. There were other souls in similar 'coffins'. I knew immediately that the 'coffins' were like meditation chambers and that the souls who were there had come to be released and healed. Many of these souls had also been members of the Aman Brotherhood or the English nobility during the 16th century. The members of the group then merged with the peace of the Almighty and I asked them to be aware that they were breathing in love and forgiveness and exhaling guilt, fear and other emotional garbage. I looked over at Gaza, Jane's dog, and felt that he, too, was healing a former reincarnation when he lived as a man in Europe during World War II.

When Robin opened his eyes and was ready to get off the table, I thought that we had worked for twenty to thirty minutes. No! Almost four hours had gone by. Where had I been? Had the angels unconsciously taken me out of my body to work with all of the souls who had gathered? Then Robin told me that during the healing he was aware that he and Gaza were breathing together. When Jane came into the room, she said that she had laid down on her bed for a short rest and found herself being healed with Robin. Jane also felt that aspects of people I know in this lifetime had also come in to be healed.

What I noticed in the ensuing days, was that Gaza was being presented with the option of bringing these new options into physical form or continuing with the old patterns. In Gaza's case he opted for new behavior. I knew that every soul who had participated in the group healing would also be given the free will choice of instituting new ways of thinking and behaving in their current life or, if they were not currently in body, to bring about change in their next reincarnation. Just like Shantarisumari, they would be given the opportunity to choose the old path or walk a new one. Until thought is acted upon and becomes experience it is only an idea. There are many psychics who believe that the individuals that I am standing up to in order to save and reclaim Marauder are the same individuals who were responsible for Anne Boleyn's trial and sentencing.

Holy Kabbalah

A Look at Ourselves & Our Relationship to God
As Seen through Oil Paintings

After viewing a series of abstract tapestries on the Holy Kabbalah, I imagined the possibility of depicting the Kabbalah in concrete forms. In 1987, I worked on a series of oil-on-canvas paintings on the Kabbalah, commonly called the Tree of Life. Each painting, every character took on a unique look and life of its own. After the last painting had dried, one of my neighbors, who was a rabbi, sent me to another rabbi in Milwaukee who had done extensive studies on the Kabbalah. Through our conversations and the books he gave me to read, I began to piece together the meanings of the images that were created on my canvas. Not everyone considers these paintings to be art. Their technical merit leaves much to be desired. They are included in this chapter because of their energy and the story behind them. Some people are disturbed by their appearance, others say the pictures are too dark, and then there are those who have been healed.

As a healer, I am a channel for healing. All healing comes from Mother-Father God. As a painter, I am a channel for creativity. All creative inspiration comes from Mother-Father God. Hands-on healing and painting are art forms. When I am clear and allowing, the breath of Mother-Father God can play through me and take physical form. If I am going to worry or exert my will or use only my left brain, the eternal symphony becomes a policeman's whistle.

It is not that I do not use my left, logical brain in the creative process - of course I do! God gave it to me for a reason, but I use it in harmony with my right brain. If I should attempt to shut off my feminine side, my creativity, and compensate by exerting left-brained knowledge only, I leave my audience cold. Examples of left-brained dominance can be found in healing and art: 'Modern' allopathic medicine treats symptoms, not the cause of the pain or disease. We can find paintings that are perfectly drafted but have no life, no feeling, and no right-brained inspiration.

On the other hand, if I am lazy and do not take the time to learn my craft, inspiration has no outlet in which to take physical form. In hands-on healing, I have to be open to healing energy, but I also need an understanding of how healing energy works. The basic foundation of healing is that the healing energy is allowed to flow from God through the healer and into the healee. The healing energy allows 'negative' thought forms and emotions to dissolve or be pulled off and the void is then filled with healing energy. When the source of the disease or pain has been released, the physical body can be healed. Each healee goes through his/her unique process and searches

103

out different modalities to support the healing process. For example, some people seek out a Chinese herbologist, others go to chiropractors, some find comfort in counseling, etc. In this manner, the healee takes responsibility for his/her own healing.

Correspondingly, in art we can find paintings that have feelings but no understanding of draftsmanship, color or perspective. The disharmony affects our perception regardless of whether or not we are aware of it. Corot's mitten-like hands are a distraction; and in his paintings where the hands are drafted correctly, it is obvious that someone else painted them and this, too, is a distraction. In art, the painter learns the rules of draftsmanship, anatomy, perspective, and color. In the application, the artist becomes a channel for creativity, yet at the same time the left-brained knowledge that has become so familiar flows with the right-brained creativity. In this creative process, because the painter has taken the time to learn the rules, s/he can then break them and bring about new and exciting images.

In both healing and art, observation is mandatory. In healing, the healer works with the client's symptoms. The healer becomes aware of these symptoms by listening to the client and observing the behavior. The healer also uses his/her third eye to look beyond the surface and through the masks. Many psychic readers are simply reading the individual's aura or projected thought forms. The mystics and prophets are able to look beyond and see the Truth of what is, not what it is that the client wants to hear. Leonardo da Vinci was able to create remarkable images in large part because of his power of observation to see what is. Leonardo's studies on water movement, a major subject of his manuscript called the Codex Leicester, are still used today. A secondary subject of the Codex Leicester is light and the way water reflects light. With knowledge that comes from observation and study combined with artistic ability, water and nature can be expressed on paper or canvas with authenticity and sensitivity. The character perceptions that lie behind the portrait that we feel from great works of art have also been observed and felt by the painter or sculptor, and during the creative process, it, too, has been laid out before us in paint or marble or clay.

The quality of healing or creative energy is dependent upon the healer or the artist. Healing energy is supposed to run smoothly through the healer and into the subject. Healing energy can be distorted when the healer refuses to look at and work through his or her issues. Man-made initiations into healing can create distorted energy patterns or create no energy at all, which means that the healer is giving of her/himself. Multiple, dissimilar initiations into a single ray of healing create chaos. Artwork may contain energy, but the energy may not be the kind that you want to hang in your home. I once went to an art show at the Museum of Modern Art in New

York with my friend, Charlotte Liss. She was really excited about the energy that was coming off of the paintings. Yes, granted there was energy all right; however, the artist was an unrepentant, convicted murderer on death row. Need I go further? Is this the kind of energy you want hanging in your home or office?

With this brief background on the correspondence between healing and art, what follows is an expanded dissertation that I wrote in 1988 for the gallery who represented me. Unfortunately, neither these thoughts nor the paintings ever reached Chicago because shortly after writing it, I was involved in two car accidents, which occurred three months apart. I owe much of what I wrote about the Kabbalah to the rabbis to whom I showed my paintings and the books that they gave me to read on the subject. The books I read all began by stating clearly that the Holy Kabbalah is not to be taken literally. The first few pages talked about the esoteric qualities of the Holy Kabbalah and then the rest of the book fell into a left-brained, literal discussion. The authors do exactly what they warn their readers not to do. My neighbor, the rabbi, told me that he had once attended a weeklong conference on the Holy Kabbalah given by a world-famous expert on the subject. My neighbor, a very intelligent man, informed me that he was able to follow the speaker for perhaps the first twenty to thirty minutes and after that, he said that he was lost. He also shared with me that he strongly suspected that he was not alone. When we put aside our fears of looking foolish we find out that our questions are valid and frequently shared by others.

The qualities of Mother-Father God are multidimensional and greatly beyond our understanding. In Hinduism, white creates, blue sustains and red destroys. All three are necessary and ongoing in every moment. It is easier for us to think in terms of physical forms rather than just colors. Thus, white becomes Brahman, creator of the universe; blue is Vishnu and Red is Shiva or Mahesh, annihilation and destruction. These same colors - white, blue and red - are used in Buddhist practices. (They are also the same colors used in the flag of the United States of America. That, along with the five-pointed star of the ancients, denotes the spiritual role that the United States is supposed to be playing.) In much the same manner as Hinduism, the Holy Kabbalah expresses energy patterns and traits in different physical forms.

1. The Intellect - Keter, Bina and Hochma

Divine Intelligence sees the hidden patterns that form the ideal plan. We as humans not only fail to see order amidst chaos, but we cannot even find the thinker behind our thoughts. Keter represents that elusive thinker who in reality is both our own higher self and our connection to Mother-Father God. Bina (who in this picture reminds me of Quan Yin, the Chinese goddess of mercy) is wisdom and Hochma is intelligence. Yellow is the color for mental activity, and the symbols themselves represent abstract thought. There is an eleventh sephira, Dwatt, who represents both the connections between the thinker and the thought as well as bridging the gap between intellect and emotions. Here, Dwatt's form is that of a symbol.

1.   Keter Sending Out Netza

Keter is the initial spark of creation and also the spark of inspiration that comes to us from seemingly nowhere. When our brains are clear, when we are free from worries and release our 'negative' programs, we become receptive to thought forms from our own higher self, God, and the angels and spirit guides who travel with us on our life's path. Our brains are like radio receivers, and in this respect, one could say that we are all channels. When we release our own negative programming and the insistent chatter, our brains become clear receivers of insights and inspiration. Through meditation, we open the door for psychic impressions to come in. Some call this the work of the devil. However, Jesus spoke prophesy and so did the fathers of the Old Testament. The Bible was not written by God but by men who were called prophets or psychics. Jesus was a prophet, a psychic, a healer and he encouraged meditation to discover and know the answers that lie within. The major difference between possession and using psychic abilities is that with possession the messages from the other side of the veil are constant; the entities literally run the thought processes and the life of the individual.   These lives are out of control!

I had a friend who learned to channel and was 98% accurate; however, she refused to check out who she was channeling and if indeed the messages she received were in Truth, and soon she was 98% inaccurate. Her dependence upon the guides she was channeling was obsessive-compulsive to the point that she let them tell her every move to make. I once asked her why she was doing this and her response was that her parents and teachers had left her with such feelings of inadequacy that she did not trust her own decisions. Her guides also told her that she was going to save the world single-handedly. Thus, my friend suffered from both low self-esteem and egomania simultaneously. Through 'the guidance' of her guides, she lost over $6,000,000, and yet she continued to misplace her trust in them. One definition of mental illness is that the same behavior is repeated over and over again with the same results but with the expectation that something different is going to happen.

So how do we protect ourselves and check out messages? The Mayans, Aztecs and Egyptians all painted the ceilings of their temples cobalt blue to draw in higher forces and repel lower forces. We can ask for cobalt blue before we meditate and before we go to sleep at night. When we hear or see spirit, we can ask three times if it has come in the name of Christ or in any of the 1,001 names for God.

While I was painting Keter's face, it insisted on being long. When spirit comes in this strongly, at some point, there should be a confirmation that yes, this was indeed the correct course of action to take. I received my corroboration through the rabbi who told me that Keter was often referred to as "the long-suffering face of God". He also told me that thousands of years ago, humans had large, thick ears and noses. The almost Egyptian-like headdress is a reminder that the Kabbalah comes from Egyptian archetypal symbols. Moses was next in line to be Pharaoh; he would have studied metaphysics and gone through the initiations in the temples. After he led the Jews out of Egypt, he taught them the magic of Egypt. After Moses returned from India (not just the top of the mountain) and found the Jews worshiping a golden calf and preparing to offer a sacrifice, that is when the knowledge was taken away from the populace and taught through the Essenes. Mary, Joseph and Jesus were Essenes. The Essenes were Jews; a fact that radical Christians forget.

Keter's spark of inspiration can trigger a series of events if we are open to following through by taking action. Keter is cloaked in mystery, but it is the mystery of life that we all discover when we allow our lives to play out, when we remember that the journey is the goal. In the Kabbalah, it is also Keter who sends out the other sephirot, or archetypal constructs, which is why Keter is referred to as the crown. It is these emotions and our mind that the sephirot represent and that we are supposed to be the masters of, rather than allowing negative thought forms and negative emotions to run our lives. Being true to ourselves; not worrying about what others think of us.

Keter on one hand looks biblical, but on the other hand, he is dark blue in color because Keter is not just one man. Perhaps this greater concept is the reason why the Jews discouraged the painting or carving the sephirot because in so doing, there was the risk that these Divine aspects would become narrowly defined. An example of limiting God to a single man occurred at Niccaea after Christianity became the official religion of the Roman Empire. Here Constantine declared Jesus, God's only Son, to be 'one substance' with the Father. Thus began the falsification of the Gospel and forged documents supporting heresy, which created the papal system. From the 10th through the 15th centuries, the papacy stood for everything Jesus opposed. Among other things, they sold offices and indulgences – Sextus IV came up with the idea of selling indulgences for the dead to their living relatives. In 1789, Pius VI admitted that the Pseudo-Isidorian Decretals were a forgery. These forgeries were so good that they had fooled both Gratian and Thomas Aquinas. Correspondingly, in matriarchies that are out of control, we find that rather than honoring all of nature, one artifact from nature becomes Goddess and along with that, the rules that define how humans interrelate with one another and the environment become stringent and oppressive. It is in the extremes that we find similarities.

Here, Keter sends forth Netza, whose element is water. She represents the timelessness of the ocean as well as higher love. Visually, Netza is symbolized with the scales of the sea creatures and a headdress of ocean waves. Just as I could not make Keter's face shorter, Netza's face would not lengthen. The rabbi told me that Netza is called "the short-faced one". Netza breathes back life to Keter, for it is in the physical expression that Keter exists in the world around us. In Taoism, God is an active verb Who is found in nature and in each and every one of us. When we honor nature, others, and ourselves we honor God and become expressions of God.

We are never alone. The illusion of separateness begins when we fail to surrender to God and to our Divine Plan that we co-created before our very conception. The positioning of the planets at the time of our birth is called our natal astrology chart, which is the map of what we came into this lifetime to learn and experience. As our astrology chart progresses throughout our life, we are given clues of 'what's coming up next'. When we are 'clued in' and clear, we are open to the messages Keter sends.

3. Hochma and Bina Giving Birth to the Other Sephirot

In the old texts, Hochma was depicted literally as impregnating Bina. From this union of intellect (Hochma) and knowledge (Bina), the spark (Keter) sends out the other sephirot. In this painting, the sephirot of emotional qualities are conceptualized first in thought and then sent out through the Earth Mother (Bina) as colored rays of light, each color representational of each sephira's unique attributes. Hesed, loving kindness and mercy, is pink, the color of compassion. Gevurah, power and law, is the energy of red. Tiferet, beauty and harmony, begins to take form in the calming blue ray. Netza's form becomes more pronounced in the yellow ray of eternal thought. Hod, in purples and dark blues, represents the majesty and glory of God as well as man's true purpose as co-creator. Hod appears somewhat oriental, showing the viewer that he is wise like the ancient sages of the East. His eyes reveal sensitivity and strength, making known that he is the emperor who rules with fairness and justice for all of his subjects. White is the full spectrum of all colors; Yesod is the foundation and the concentration or manifestation of the other sephirot. Malkhut, the kingdom, is represented by silver, the color symbolic of the moon and feminine energy. The ancient Jews saw Malkhut as being in exile. As a patriarchal tribe who felt that women did not have souls and who denied the Goddess (the feminine aspect of the Creator), they were in part responsible for this excommunication. Whenever a society or an

108

individual denies one aspect of its nature, be it feminine or masculine, paradise on earth is an illusion at best.

4. Hesed and Gevurah Forming Beauty and Harmony

Power without love is what we call "evil run rampant"; love without strength is what we call Mr. Milktoast. Both Mr. Hitler and Mr. Milktoast are out-of-balance, extreme conditions and potentially harmful.

Gevurah and Hesed are multidimensional aspects of Tiferet. A few of the facets of power (Gevurah) are mastery, influence, passion and authority. Aspects of love (Hesed) include affection, nurturing, devotion and admiration. When Gevurah and Hesed come together, they form Tiferet, or beauty and harmony. The relationship between Gevurah, Hesed and Tiferet is dynamic, just like the qualities represented by these sephirot surface and play out in our lives in varying degrees and in different sequences and combinations. That is, we project or reveal different faces and facets of ourselves in different circumstances. Other people perceive us through their own masks.

The dragon of the West guards the two things he cannot possibly use; that is, the virgin and the gold. Here, the dragon of the East who brings good fortune and treasure to mankind represents Tiferet. Tiferet is the stabilization of opposing forces and is expressed in artistry, ethics, nature and healing.

5. Yesod Balancing Netza and Hod

These three sephirot are similar to Tiferet, Hesed and Gevurah in that Yesod, Netza and Hod take the same emotions and archetypal constructs to a level of understanding that is beyond our lives on a 3-dimensional planet. Netza is eternity. The woman holding two balls has a snakelike body, which meets to form an endless circle - a timeless symbol for eternity. Hod is majesty. The lily is symbolic of the kings of France.

In one sense, Netza is like the Oneness that we are all a part of and Hod represents our individuality. When we forget that we are unique expressions of the Creator, eternity becomes monotony. When we forget that we are a part of the Whole and our egos get out of control, absolute power corrupts itself absolutely.

Yesod is the stability that comes when all aspects and talents of an individual soul are allowed to play out and shine with consideration for the rest of creation. When humanity's strengths and purpose are in alignment with the Divine Eternal Plan, there is a foundation for the manifestation of heaven on earth represented by the Star of David.

The two triangles of the Star of David also depict the sephirot of the intellect merging with the sephirot of emotions. On another level, the Star also represents the lower sephirot of emotions (Gevurah, Hesed and Tiferet) whose actions are manifested in this world, coming together with the upper sephira (Hod, Netza and Yesod) whose attention lies on the other side of the veil. When we live consciously in this world and we are aware that our actions have consequences in the next world, we are both grounded and open to the possibility of the gifts of the Spirit. It is this consciousness that opens us to Malkhut, the kingdom.

6. Malkhut and Christ

Both bridge the gap between heaven and earth. Jesus was born a Jew and taught that we are all sons and daughters of Mother-Father God. Through responsible living and meditation, we can live in this world yet be of the next. Jesus said that the kingdom of God is found within. How else do we go within besides meditating?

The legend of Malkhut is that when people misused the gifts of the spirit (psychic gifts), the bridge between heaven and earth was broken. Humans fell away from the One to create a play of their own making. The bridge that was broken is the link between our conscious reality and the reality of our own higher self and our relationship to God. In so doing, we lost our humanity.

Hon Sha Za Sho Nen is a symbol for healing karma that within the painting bridges the gap between Judaism and Christianity and between this world and the next. Hon Sha Za Sho Nen is one of the symbols that was traditionally taught in all Reiki II classes. Somehow when I took Reiki II, I totally missed the part about the symbols being secret. It seemed perfectly logical at the time I painted these pictures to incorporate their potential energy of healing into art.

7. Veils

When I painted this, my idea behind it was that the sephirot could be looked upon as garments or attributes that we all take on. We show the world different aspects of ourselves just as our appearance alters when we change clothes. From the initial thought (Keter), we expand outwards.

Gloria, a woman who had done extensive study on the Holy Kabbalah, called and asked me if she could come over to my home and see the paintings that she had heard about. When she saw **Veils** and heard my explanation, she told me that I was completely wrong. She said that it was actually Tiferet who was in the middle of the painting, and as the fulcrum in the Holy Kabbalah, Tiferet balanced the other sephirot.

My neighbor, the rabbi, also told me that my explanation was wrong. He said, "Those are not garments, they are wings." He even ran home to get his bible so that he could show me that he was right. When he returned, he opened his bible and read to me a prayer in which the faithful calls upon God to send angels' wings for protection and guidance.

I told another Jewish man who came over to see the paintings my explanation, Gloria's explanation and the rabbi's explanation. He responded by saying, "You and Gloria and the rabbi are all wrong. These are not garments, they are not the sephirot and they are not wings. They are the veils of the Holy of Holies. I know this to be true because I can feel myself walking through them as I look upon this painting." In actuality, we were all right and so is a myriad of other explanations.

8. Yesod as Joseph in His Coat of Many Colors

Joseph has his hands extended in a typical rabbi's blessing. The old Hebrews saw the sephirot as clearly depicting characteristics of Fathers of the Old Testament. Joseph, the Pharaoh's storekeeper, through wise management was able to feed many people from many nations during the time of a great drought. Joseph's own brothers came to him for Egyptian wheat, the foundation of many diets. The other sephirot are represented symbolically: Hesed as Abraham's knife, Gevurah as the sword of Isaac, Tiferet as Jacob's ladder, Malkhut as King David's harp, Netza as Moses' horn (in this case the horn of plenty) and Hod as Aaron's censer.

In essence, this viewpoint of the Holy Kabbalah gives us a working psychological profile of ourselves and our relationship to God. Often the Holy Kabbalah is depicted as a tree, and this also teaches us in a very visual way that we are a microcosm of the greater macrocosm. However, the Old Testament tells us that Moses and the priests and priestesses of Ancient Egypt were able to perform miracles or high magic. The concept of our inner reality as a tree is shamanic in origin. The veil of Isis was the shaman's blindfold, which was used to aid the shaman in his/her journeywork by keeping his/her inner movie screen as dark as possible for better viewing and more active participation. The priests and priestesses of Ancient Egypt were shaman. As Moses was next in line for the throne of Egypt, he would have had to have studied and gone through the rites of initiation in the Egyptian mystery schools for the purpose of learning esoteric knowledge and empowerment. Indeed, Moses was truly a great shaman.

All of the books on the Holy Kabbalah that I read ten years ago allude to the mysticism and magic that can be found in the Holy Kabbalah, but none of them state where it is or how it works. In my last book, Reiki & Other Rays of Touch Healing, I mention that the Kabbalah and the Tarot can both be traced back to Egyptian symbology. It is in ancient Egyptian symbols where metaphors go beyond psychological principles and into esoteric language (meditation, healing, divination and magic). The essence of the energies depicted in Egyptian symbology is the forces of the Creator and the gifts of the Holy Spirit that are bestowed upon humanity when humanity is clear and conscious. Whenever the gifts of the Holy Spirit were misused by society, they were taken away from mankind. In these dark ages, occasionally a psychic or mystic is born with the gifts of the Spirit or they are granted through prayer. (Edgar Cayce read the Bible three times.) They came to remind us what we had lost, not to be put on pedestals out of our reach after their deaths.

There is a definite relationship between the ten sephirot and the ten principal archetypal Egyptian symbols, which are represented by gods and goddesses. The Hebrews, a patriarchal tribe, removed the goddess aspect and feminine principle out of Egyptian mysticism and this is clearly shown in the painting, "Yesod as Joseph in His Coat of Many Colors". Through this and the other pictures, I have presented a psychological study that, on one level, works. When I compare the Kabbalah to Egyptian knowledge, you are going to have to put aside what you just read. While there is a correlation between the sephirot and Egyptian gods and goddesses, this is an entirely different approach. Just as the Hebrews saw leaders of the Old Testament as having predominant character traits that were found within each sephira, the Egyptians must have seen that their ancient heroes, who later became memorialized as gods and goddesses, epitomized the essence of specific forces that govern the universe. Neither the Kabbalah nor Egyptian symbology is to be taken literally; their esoteric messages come from the subconscious and superconscious and beyond.

Within Egyptian symbology can be found the original intent and multidimensionality of each archetype. An archetype represents principles, which can be personified. They are like heroes whom we can emulate. **Keter is Osiris**. Osiris is like the wise, kindly father who is loved and respected by his children. The positive energies of Osiris are those of a wise leader such as King Solomon - wisdom, justice, integrity, stability, respect and responsibility. The reversed energies of Osiris can be found in religious mania of grandeur and is exemplified by the greedy, self-serving King Midas. Osiris is like the elusive spirit and the strength that can be found in the Christ Light.

Bina is Isis. Isis is like the nurturing, compassionate woman who listens with her heart to the requests of her children. Isis and Thoth are the two magicians in Egyptian symbology. The opposite energies of Isis occur when magic turns to superstition or when the ego gets lost in separatism and possession.

Negativity happens when the personality is out of balance; the further away from center that the soul sways, the denser the energy becomes. **Hochma is Set**, the Prince of Darkness and Enemy of Osiris. Like the Old Testament, Set murders his brother, Osiris, out of jealousy. However, since Egyptian symbology came before the Old Testament, it is more accurate to say that the story of Cain and Abel is like the story of Set and Osiris. If Set is active intelligence, it is those thought forms that rationalize evil or the guilt that keeps us prisoners in the torture chambers of our own minds. The only positive aspect of Set is the strength we gain from overcoming everything from obstacles to pure evil.

Hesed is Bast, Goddess of Joy and Patroness of Cats - symbolic of psychic abilities and intuition. It is the pleasure of love that comes from a clear mind and generous heart, which opens the heart to devotion. It is the joy that manifests itself in music and dance. The energy opposing Bast is mental illness, depression, withdrawal and uncoordination.

Gevurah is Anubis, the Protector and Guardian. Anubis is like the knight who uses his strength to protect the kingdom and the subjects. It is the strength we exert to overcome adversity, as well as the power that comes from within to move through our own fears. The only difference between a hero and a coward is that the hero walks through fear to see what is on the other side. The reversed meaning of Anubis is both vulnerability and the bully.

Tiferet is Horus, whose attributes include beauty, harmony, artistry and creativity. Horus is also the Patron of Homes and Families, where beauty and harmony should begin. There is also an interweaving or overlaying of the energies. While the energies of Bast can promote mental healing, Horus' healing energies are for the physical body, particularly the eyes. The opposite meaning of Horus is both low self-esteem and egomania.

Netza is Thoth, Lord of Time, Lord of Karma and Patron of Healers. The caduceus, Thoth's symbol, is used by the American Medical Association. The strong energies of Thoth are not only for healing the physical body, but the emotional, mental and spiritual as well. The opposite meaning of Thoth is quackery, pseudo-intellectualism and disease.

It is Thoth and Set who are the two spiritual energies that guard the Spear of Destiny, the spear that pierced Christ's side. It is the reason why evil has been able to use the energy of this talisman, but only for a short time because the Lord of Karma steps in and plays his hand. When it is time for the spear to change hands, nothing can stop this event from occurring. Hitler and the Nazis lived high on the hog for a period of time, but when the end came, it was painful and humiliating. (The Spear of Destiny by Trevors Ravenscroft)

Hod is Ptah, Architect of the Universe. On a personal level, it is the mastery that is acquired by the soul through the lessons of many lifetimes. "Each constructive lesson that is learned represents a brick in its spiritual foundation, and as the edifice gradually takes shape the true character and identity of the psyche is established." (The Way of Cartouche by Murry Hope). Ptah is the inventiveness and tenacity of the human spirit. The opposite meaning occurs when an individual is not self-realized. When we cannot look within and find our own gifts and talents and we are living out somebody else's reality, our lives become banal and destructive.

Yesod is Hathor, the energies of nourishment, fortitude, organization and confidence, which are all qualities exemplified by Joseph. If organization is Heaven's first law, then to be organized, we need to be able to utilize the energies of the other universal constructs. The reversed meaning of Hathor is deprivation and intimidation.

Malkhut is Nephthys. Nephthys is the mysticism and psychic gifts that we have denied ourselves and in so doing, we have destroyed the bridge that connects us on earth to heaven. The opposite energy of Nephthys is disillusion - the disillusion that happens when we get caught up in the material world and forget that we are part of the Whole. To reconnect to the Whole and reclaim our psychic abilities begins with meditation.

While Egypt lay in ruins, the knowledge and magic of Egyptian symbology was carried by nomadic people who later became known as Gypsies (they were called Tinkers in Ireland). Hitler wanted the Gypsies exterminated because he saw them as a threat to his black magic. Hitler even had his metaphysical teachers murdered after he studied with them so that he could perceive himself as superior and without competition (The Spear of Destiny by Trevors Ravenscroft). The wanderers carried the Laws and Great Teachings on 78 cards whose images were called the tarot (Torah is Hebrew for The Law). The energy of the ten sephirot was qualified and represented on the 22 cards of the major arcana (from the Latin meaning secret). While the Hebrews, a patriarchal tribe, took out the feminine aspect from the Egyptian symbols, the tarot retains both masculine and feminine aspects of Divinity.

114

The Roman Catholic Church is responsible for rewriting and altering the meaning of the true teachings of Jesus and his apostles (Vicars of Christ, The Dark Side of the Papacy by Peter De Rosa). For example, some people believe that the world is coming to an end because of the Apocalypse of Saint John. First of all, the writing style and content of the text itself is completely different from anything else that John the Beloved wrote. Secondly, there is repeated reference to Satan in the Apocalypse. Satan would not have been in Saint John's vocabulary as being the devil. The Roman Catholic Church during the Inquisition invented Satan! Kramer and Sprenger wrote Malleus Maleficarum (The Witches' Hammer) in 1486; Innocent VIII wrote the preface. Likewise, the Church's depiction of Mary stepping on a serpent (symbol of the Celtic Druids) is representative of the Church's efforts to crush the Goddess, suppress women and keep mysticism away from the populace. God is both feminine and masculine, and so are we.

Keter's energies are found in The Emperor, The Hierophant and Justice. The Emperor commands others for the purpose of achieving his goals; Keter sends out the other sephirot so that the Divine Plan might be realized. The Hierophant is the merciful, spiritual guidance that interfaces heaven with earth. Keter is the wisdom that sees all sides of an issue and cuts through obstructions to reveal the truth so that Justice might prevail.

Bina is The High Priestess and The Empress. The High Priestess is magic, the psychic energy of the moon and of the Goddess. She is typified by the wise women (witches) like Joan of Arc. The Empress is the bounty of the Earth Mother.

Hochma is The Devil and Death. Real evil does exist and The Devil epitomizes the bondage that greed, ignorance, limitation and lack of compassion create. "'Devil' is 'lived' spelled backward. It is living and looking only to what has been." (Carol Bridges, The Medicine Woman Inner Guidebook). When we live in the present moment, we are able to move ahead. When we stop recreating the past with our actions and thoughts, we set ourselves free of what many indigenous people refer to as the Trickster. The Trickster is not The Devil! The Trickster is the master trickster who tricks himself by falling into his own trap. The Trickster mirrors back to us our own unconsciousness until we at last become conscious of our own foolishness. When we become conscious, we die to our old nature and are reborn with profound change. The Death card is not always in reference to the physical body. The transformation that the Trickster makes possible is Death to the old thought forms.

Hesed is The Lovers and The Moon. The Lovers personify the joy of true love that can be found when two people who are complete and at peace within themselves find one another. Each mirrors back his/her own inner beauty, balance and confidence. The Moon represents intuitive knowledge and the feminine principle.

Gevurah is The Chariot and Strength. The Chariot is the hero warrior; the personality who has taken charge, who holds the reins of power. Strength is not the forcing of will, but rather the courage that comes from listening to one's own heart.

Tiferet is The Tower and The Star. In all mysticisms, the creator God or Goddess is also the Destroyer. Kali, Shiva's consort and goddess of creativity, is like the warrior maiden, Brunhilde. The lightning, which strikes The Tower, breaks up the old patterns, which no longer serve our highest and best good. "The explosion has a liberating potential; it has cleared a site for new growth." (Amy Zerner & Monte Farber, The Enchanted Tarot). We cannot build new structures on top of garbage; the old must be burned away before the new ideas can take form. The Star then brings us illumination and inspiration that when acted upon brings our dreams and wishes to fruition.

Netza is The Magician, Temperance and Judgement. Magic requires occult adeptship, which is the ability to bring about transformation, requires the power and knowledge of the elemental forces and psychic intuition. Magic also requires discipline, patience and timing. We are all potential alchemists; when we change the way we think, we change our whole lives as well. Everything is within us; however, that does not mean that we cannot learn from another individual. Both extremes of consciousness, "I don't know anything" and "I know it all", close us off to the Mind of God. Our thoughts are things that create the world we live in as well as our bodies. One reason why our bodies age is because we have bought into the idea that they are doomed to deteriorate. They are not supposed to! Our bodies are our vehicles for exploring this reality and they are supposed to be healthy, youthful and whole throughout our lives.

Thoth is the original symbol for what was later called Netza. Thoth and Isis are the two magicians of Egyptian symbology. They are both healers - healing is magic. Besides being Lord of Time, Thoth is also Lord of Karma. Karma is the judgement that we inflict upon ourselves. Thoth, Netza, The Magician, as well as the energy of the other sephirot are potentially found within all of us. Karma and the divine Trickster can push us to our limits and force us to deal with our issues or collapse under the weight of our own making. Beneficial energies are available to us when we make the effort to look within to discover the source of our anger and pain. Then we are free to grow, study, learn from one another, travel, etc.

Hod is The Sun and Wheel of Fortune. The sun represents spontaneous, passionate, masculine energy. The Wheel of Fortune is destiny that is played out in what appears to us as endings and new beginnings. Reality is that as one door closes, another one opens. The goal is this journey! Like the spin of the wheel, we ride out the rhythms and cycles of life. Within the Wheel of Fortune, like The Chariot, is the reminder that nothing and no one stays on top forever. Every thought gets to be played out in the physical reality in one way or another; every soul has its day in the sun.

Yesod is The Hermit and The Fool. The Hermit's knowledge is of both this world and the next. He is the enlightened teacher who patiently waits for those students who are ready to seek him out. He is the sage to whom others look for advice. The Fool is the unconscious, a seed that has not yet germinated. He is innocent and knows only to tell the truth. He is beginning his path towards enlightenment. The Hermit has the insight to realize that he is as much the fool as he is the sage; that is, he can never possibly know all there is to know. With all his wisdom, what he knows is but a drop of water in the vast sea of universal knowledge. He is neither the know-it-all nor the know-nothing. Every morning he awakens with an open mind and heart to begin anew his sojourn home to Greater Reality.

Malkhut is The World and The Hanged Man. Earth is our mother; our physical bodies come from the Earth and to Earth they will return. Our body is the temple that holds our soul. If we don't take care of our bodies, then where are we going to live? Everything we need to heal our bodies is found in nature. We are a part of and connected to nature; without nature, our world ceases to exist. When we honor the natural world, we are connected to the Goddess and the feminine principle. The Hopi's understanding of nature went far beyond the physical world, and this connection brought them psychic abilities that rivaled the priests and priestesses of ancient Egypt.

In indigenous cultures around the world, in order to possess psychic abilities of prophecy, healing and magic, the shaman had a near-death experience, fell to the pits of hell and was raised to the heights of heaven. In order to do this, the shaman would go on what Native Americans call a vision quest where he would deny himself food and water and push his body to physical extremes until he collapsed from sheer exhaustion. In this altered state, he had the potential of tapping into esoteric knowledge and psychic powers. The Hanged Man is like Odin, who hung for nine nights by one leg from the world tree without food or drink until at last he spied the Runes. The symbology of the Runes is Universal in nature and has a direct correlation to Egyptian symbols; they were used as oracles and for magic. (Ralph Blum, The Book of Runes)

Robin Hormann of The Netherlands, who has been initiated into the elemental rays of healing as well as Egyptian Symbology, wrote to me of his experiences using the Egyptian symbols as well as the Runes: *"A year ago I injured both my knees badly. Resting and cooling down my knees with a coldpack was not enough to get them back into shape. As soon as I was initiated into the Cartouche (Egyptian symbols), I started to use Thoth, a symbol for the healer and healing. I also used Ankh, which is the amplifier in much the same way as the Cho Ku Rays energize Reiki symbols. To activate the energy of Thoth, I went into deep meditation and asked for healing. I visualized Thoth in my inner eye and then projected the symbol through my solar plexus so that it was in front of me. Using my breath, I blew the symbol into my cupped hands. I did the same with Ankh and asked Spirit to amplify the power of Thoth. As I repeated this three times, I felt the energy building up between my hands. In my inner eye I could see that a golden ball was being created in my hands. I brought the energy to the injury and let it sink into the injury. I experienced different sensations each time that I did this. Then I gave thanks to the angels and spirit helpers as well as to the symbols (everything comes from God, everything has a consciousness).*

When I initially started to treat my knees, I was going to treat only my right knee. As I took the golden ball to my right knee, it suddenly split into another golden ball of exactly the same size. The energy level of the second ball was also exactly the same as the first. Then I brought the golden balls to both my knees and felt all kinds of sensations - cold, heat, electricity, vibrations, etc. It took awhile for the energy to be completely absorbed. Pain and tensions in my knees were gone after this first treatment. I repeated this procedure several more times and my knees are almost completely healed. It appeared to me that the treatments mobilized my body's own healing capacity and took away the blockages.

The Cartouche also helped me with my studies. For wisdom, Osiris showed me the big picture. For education, Thoth brought me insight into mathematics. For intellect, Air proved to be good for memorizing data, such as historical dates. It is possible to combine these symbols, but it is difficult. Egyptian symbols are less suitable to combining than for example those of the Runes. The difficulty is due not only to the fact that the Runes are more suited to combining, because of their less complex design than the Cartouche Symbols, but also because of the more independent nature of the Cartouche Symbols. There are Bind Runes, but no Bind Cartouche Symbols. My experience is that the use of only one Cartouche Symbol energized with Ankh results in a more focused handling of energy."

It was in connecting and remaining connected to nature and the elemental forces that the shaman or wise woman (witch) or Egyptian priest or priestess was able to draw in the elemental forces in order to perform alchemy or magic. Buddha, like other shaman worldwide, retreated into nature before he performed miracles and taught. Likewise, Jesus' 40-day retreat into the desert was shamanic in nature. The elemental forces are an integral part of magic and are found in Egyptian Symbology. In the minor arcana of the Tarot, the four elements are represented in the four suits. The suit of Wands corresponds to the element of fire and the energies are passion, creativity, illumination and transformation. The season is spring and the direction is east. The suit of Hearts corresponds to the element of water and the energies are love, devotion, healing and the development of our psychic abilities. The season is summer and the direction is south. The suit of Pentacles corresponds to the element earth and the energies are grounding, foundation, introspection, prayer and abundance. The season is fall and the direction is west. The suit of Swords corresponds to the element of air and the energies are wisdom, knowledge, communication and gratitude.

Books on high magic discuss the enormous force of will that is required to bring in the elemental forces. This force of will is required if the individual is not attuned to the elemental forces or if the magician's intent is to manipulate and control (what we call black magic). There are stories based in reality of individuals making a pact with the devil or other evil forces, and this is the source of the energy that the black magician draws upon to exert his/her will. To be attuned to the elemental forces is a psychic gift that an individual can be born with; however, if this gift is utilized for evil, it is those same forces that the magician draws upon. What the black magician fails to realize is that the forces that s/he perceives that s/he is in control of are the very forces that control him/her after death. Real evil does exist! While the Creator always gives us free will choice, the reason that evil will always fail is because manipulation of another's free will choice and the decimation of nature operates outside of the natural laws of creation. The Absolute, which permeates all, always levels extremes.

Buddha was born into luxury and was completely unaware of the very existence of impoverishment. After meeting a beggar, he abandoned his secular world altogether and became a poor monk. One day, while he was meditating by the river, he overheard a conversation. A man was playing a stringed instrument and a passenger in the boat asked him how it was that the strings were able to produce lovely sounds. The minstrel answered thusly, "If the string is too loose, the sound will be muddled; if the string is too tight, it will break." That is when Buddha realized that the middle road is the path that offers the richest possibilities and is the way to enlightenment.

Individuals wishing to work with the elemental forces can be attuned to them in an initiation. Individuals can also acquire access to the power of the elementals through a series of consciousness-raising experiences. People who have near-death experiences often bring back healing or psychic abilities from the other world. Deep meditation can open the meditator's intuition (perception beyond the physical reality), which is another aspect of magic, healing and simply living one's life to the fullest.

What has been lost to humanity is the means of using the knowledge of the Holy Kabbalah, the Tarot and the Runes in magic and healing. The Hindu Atharva Veda, which is related to all magic rituals, is missing. A few rituals have been passed on by word of mouth through families, but the energy of the elemental forces is not there unless the individual family member was also gifted with elemental healing energy.

Religions keep the truth from the masses in order to control them with the result being that true spirituality is lost and is replaced by religious fanaticism. For example, the Shroud of Turin depicts the front and back images of a man who was 5' 9" and weighing about 178 pounds with the identical wounds Jesus Christ received just prior to and during his crucifixion. Most people are familiar with the 1988 scientific study the Vatican funded to determine once and for all if the Shroud was the burial wrap of Jesus Christ. It was a one-man venture! This man said that the Shroud carbon dated to the 16th century and that the red was paint pigment. Greg Braden was given the scientific data and 30,000 slides documenting the 1978 multi-scientific-disciplinary, 5-year study of the Shroud of Turin involving some 40 scientists. These scientists found that threads of the Shroud dated back 2,000 years – in the 16th century, there was a fire (which would have created carbon) in the church where the Shroud was kept, which would explain why the shroud could be carbon dated to the 16th century. In addition, they found blood and blood serum on the cloth – there was NO paint pigments whatsoever on the shroud! The study concluded by stating that the image was the result of a rapid, intense, biological, internal heat source and that either the Shroud passed through the body or the body passed through the Shroud. This study has never been carried by any news media. Why is the church trying to distance itself from the Shroud? According to the Mormon Bible, which is based on the golden tablets written in ancient Hebrew that were found in colonial Pennsylvania, Jesus performed his greatest miracle – he raised his own body from the dead and continued his teaching. Hands-on healing is often accompanied by intense heat and often during sessions, time is illusionary. Jesus' body probably was displacing back and forth in space during the healing, which would account for the image on the burial shroud. Jesus NEVER claimed to be the only son of God; the Council of Chalcedon in 451 decided that Jesus was divine as well as human. By placing Jesus on a pedestal the Catholic Church put him out of reach for any human to try to emulate? Yet, Jesus said, "Ye shall do greater things than I have done!" There was a time when magic was in the earth and messages were carried on the wind. With the Church's decisions to alter Jesus' teachings, magic was left primarily in the hands of those that would manipulate and conjure for their own greed.

So-called black magicians use a force of will to call in the elementals and then use their own anger pushed to the point of rage to send it off for the purposes of what amounts to manipulation and control. There are black magicians who have access to secret doctrines, but for them the growing problem is their inability to summon in the elementals as this world moves into the Golden Age of the Return of the Angels.

Part of the trick of magic is to find the right key with which to open the door. The following invocation is a variation on the ritual used in the movie The Craft and comes from Invocation of the Spirit. I have placed the elements in a different way than the movie. What I have found in my studies is that Native American tribes differed from one another (and also the movie) as to the placement of the elements. This is what works for me: The east traditionally represents the creative spark – that is fire! Porcupine, who represents innocence, the child's heart which trusts the love it feels, often sits in the south of the medicine wheel – that is water! Bear medicine is the power of introspection as he hibernates within the earth – introspection is a quality of earth and bear is most often in the west! Buffalo resides in the north and he represents wisdom – that is air! So, in this light, in order to connect to the elemental forces, before beginning, I place a candle in the east to represent fire, a vessel of water in the south, a rock or crystal in the west and a feather or a knife with a white handle in the north to represent air. Incantations are more powerful if they are spoken without inflection but with emotion. The Guardians are the Ancient Ones.

> Hail to thee guardians of the watchtowers of the east. Powers of fire and transformation. Hear me. Open the gates. Come to me now.
>
> Hail to thee guardians of the watchtowers of the south. Powers of water and intuition. Hear me. Open the gates. Come to me now.
>
> Hail to thee guardians of the watchtowers of the west. Powers of Mother Earth. Hear me. Open the gates. Come to me now.
>
> Hail to thee guardians of the watchtowers of the north. Powers of air and invention. Hear me. Open the gates. Come to me now.
>
> Bring your power and your might, your insight in this night to empower my incantations, to bring form to my magical workings. I am imploring Thee Manau, Brahman, Allah, Creator and by all of Your great and Holy names. Ancient Goddess by all Your great and Holy names I am

calling Thee • • • *Isis, Asatare, Diana, Ostara, Hava, Inanan. By the power of the moon in* (name the astrological sign that the moon is in) *I call Thee. By the power of three times three I invoke Thee. Hoc est corpus meum* (Repeat three times three. It comes from Jewish magical rites and was changed later to 'hocus-pocus'). *I am calling upon the angels of* (prosperity, healing, joy, justice • • • or whatever the rite is that needs to come into physical manifestation. It is far better to concentrate and focus on one thing at a time; it makes the magic more powerful.). *Hear my voice ancient wise ones. I summon and stir thee from primal abodes. Lend me your powers. Show me your glory. Teach me your way. **If this is Thine Will, Mother-Father God, so must it be**.* (This last sentence is how all magical workings or prayers are best ended. That is, leaving everything in Mother-Father God's hands rather than us trying to force our will.)

Once the magic, prayers or ceremony has been completed, the magician closes the gates, thanks and dismisses the forces, guides, angels, etc. and asks them to complete the task assigned to them. Again, I cannot stress this enough, instead of saying "This is my will, so must it be!", it is far better karma and much more effective to say, "If this is Thine Will, so must it be!" Once the forces have been dismissed, it is best to let go and not think or talk about the petition, the magic or the possible consequences. If energy is put into talking, it pulls energy away from the magic. When the forces and spirit helpers have been dismissed, oftentimes the participants will feel the energy leaving. Just before the magic begins to come back (which could be days or weeks later), there will be a calm (something like being in the eye of a hurricane). Just before the consequences of the magic are realized on the physical plane, the magician will experience the sensation of the power of the force of the magic, images or impressions, and a feeling or an inner knowing of how things are going to work out. This is definitely the time to give thanks and gratitude, and again silence must be maintained. Black magicians do not experience these same sensations in the same way because they send their magic out through proxies; black magicians do not want to experience in any way the magic that they have sent out. They may postpone their karma, but in so doing, the consequences for them may be dire. An example of this type of diversionary tactic, which allows the originating party's reputation to be unscathed, is the fact that the United States government leases the CIA ultimately from the Royal Crown of England. MI6 and CIA are one and the same. So, while the CIA is on the wrong side of every issue on this planet, it is the United States that takes the blame for the actions of the CIA. Because black magicians use proxies, they also give away a good portion of their control over the situation; therefore, it is easy for a white magician, who can work without judgement, to alter or 'dis-spell' black magic. The last step is the physical manifestation of the magic, and again it is proper and right to give thanks and praise. It is also the responsibility of the magician or shaman to give back to Earth and to the community a generous portion of what has been gained through magical means.

In order for the magic to have power behind it, the individual needs to be able to draw upon the rays of power from earth, air, fire and water. Healing is magic, and connection to the Universal elemental healing rays enables magic to occur. A Reiki initiation that opens the crown chakra fully connects the initiate to the elemental earth-healing ray. This brings about a consciousness- raising experience and is an initial step in becoming an alchemist. It is basic because the other elemental rays will not be grounded without elemental earth. Universal initiations into elemental healing rays were never meant to be altered or personalized by mankind. In particular, to play with fire is as dangerous in other dimensions as it is in our three-dimensional world. There are hundreds of documented, witnessed accounts in both Europe and the United States of individuals who for no apparent reason burst into flames. I personally believe that spontaneous combustion occurred because either they somehow incorrectly connected to the elemental fire ray or they misused this element in another lifetime, if not this one. One woman burst into flames while she was sitting in a chair. She burned from the knees up and the chair was not even singed. The trigger or match that caused her to incinerate came from another dimension. The fire that burned her was five times hotter than the fire used to cremate a body. One salesman in Georgia survived spontaneous combustion because only his lower right arm burned. The doctors who examined him said the fire was internal in origin.

Prayers can also produce miracles or magic, especially when they come from the heart. The following is a Hindu prayer. In it, we can find elements of later religions, such as Buddhism and Christianity. We can also find similarities with the invocation on the preceding page as well as references to the holographic nature of the universe. We are not as different as we would like to think we are. It is when we recognize the similarities between races, cultures and religions, that we can see for ourselves that we are not humans separated from one another and God - that would make us godless. We are immortal beings connected to one another, nature, all of creation and God. Yet, we are all unique expressions of an Infinite God; not even two snowflakes are identical.

OM ASATHOMA SATH GAMAYA TAMASOMA JYOTIRGAMAYA MRITYURMA AMIRUTHAM GAMAYA ON SHANTHI SHANTHI SHANTHI

May the Sun be good to us. May Varuna be good to us. May Indra and Brihaspathi be good to us. Prostration to thee O Vayu. Thou art indeed the visible Brahman. I call thee just. I call thee true. May that protect me. May that protect the teacher Om Shanthi Shanthi Shanthi.

Lokah Samastha Sukhino Bhavanthu Lokah Samastha Swastino Bhavanthu Lokah Samstha Shantiho Bhavantu Om Shanthi Shanthi Shanthi.

May that protect us and cause us both to enjoy the bliss of Mukti. May both exert to find the true meaning of scriptures. May our studies be fruitful. May we never quarrel with each other. Om Shanthi Shanthi Shanthi.

May who is Supreme among the vedas, who is of cosmic form, who was born of the immortal vedas, who is the Lord of all, strengthen me with wisdom. May I become the possessor of all wisdom that leads to immortality. May my body be fit for meditation. May the tongue be extremely sweet. May I hear much with my ears. Thou are the sheath of Brahman enveloped by intelligence. May thou protect what I have heard. Om Shanthi Shanthi Shanthi.

I am the mover, cutter of the tree of existence. My fame is like the mountain's peak. Supremely pure am I. I am the immortal one as He is the Sun. I am Lustrous wealth. I am great wisdom, Immortal, Undecaying. So runs Trishanku's teachings of wisdom. Om Shanthi Shanthi Shanthi.

The whole is that, the whole is this. Taking the whole from the whole, what remains is the whole again. Om Shanthi Shanthi Shanthi.

May my limbs, speech, prana, eyes, ears strengthen and all my limbs grow vigorous. All is the Brahman of the Upanishads. May I never deny the Brahman. May the Brahman never spurn me. May there be no denial of the Brahman. May there be no spurning of the Brahman. May all the virtues recited by the Upanishads repose in me delighting in the atman. May they repose in me. Om Shanthi Shanthi Shanthi.

My speech is rooted in my mind. My mind is rooted in my speech. Brahman reveal, reveal thyself to me. Ye mind and speech enable me to grasp the truth that scriptures teach. May what I have heard not slip from me. I join day with night in study. I speak the truth. I speak the just. May that protect me. May that protect the teacher. Om Shanthi Shanthi Shanthi.

1. The Intellect - Keter, Bina and Hochma

2. Keter Sending Out Netza

3. Hochma and Bina Giving Birth to the Other Sephirot

4. Hesed and Gevurah Forming Beauty and Harmony

5. Yesod Balancing Netza and Hod

6. Malkhut and Christ

7. Veils

8. Yesod as Joseph in His Coat of Many Colors

Hawaiian Shamanism and the Goddess

The Other Side of the Veil

Mayan religion and language are rooted in Tibetan Buddhism; Hawaiian shamanism has its origins in India's Hinduism. Both Hindus and Hawaiians had a caste system ranging from the untouchables to the superelite. Buddha did not come to destroy Hinduism, but rather to break the caste system. Hawaiian gods and goddesses are the same as Hindu gods and goddesses, but with different names. The Goddess aspect of The All, which manifests through us in intuition, other metaphysical skills and the creative expression of living one's life to the fullest, is apparent in both Hinduism and Hawaiian shamanism. Just as we as individuals play out different roles in our lives and explore various talents and aspects of ourselves in different lifetimes, so too, God explores feminine and masculine aspects of The One. It is when these aspects are pushed to extremes that we forget who we are and how powerful God is. "*Nothing in excess* was the second phrase written over the gateway to the temple at Delphi. The first counsel was *Know thyself.*" (Ralph H. Blum, The Book of Runes)

Matriarchies and patriarchies pushed to extremes by individuals tampering with spirituality in order to control through domination by spreading fear and ignorance bring about their own downfall. In both matriarchies and patriarchies, similar patterns arise; such as, too many rules, many of which are contradictory. These rules are designed to keep a small percentage of the population in control of the masses. Patriarchies and matriarchies both give birth to fanaticism and dogmas, which replace an individual's right to seek the Truth. Citizens and religious followers are taught to 'buy into' whatever the politicians and religious leaders say is fact. In both extremes, women are encouraged to have as many children as possible without regard for their own needs, their partners' needs or the best interest of the firstborn. This leads to overpopulation and economically based wars. Wars are started by the few and fought by the many. The masses are told and sold the emotional ideals of honor in battle, while at the same time are taught to hate the opposition so that they will be emotionally detached from or overjoyed at the death of the enemy. Public citizens are never told the true status of the war (Presidents Nixon and Johnson) and are never told the real number of casualties (Americans were told that only a handful of soldiers died in the Gulf War). Saving Private Ryan is the first movie that depicts war as it truly is. George Washington warned Americans to stay out of international confrontations. Switzerland is a very wealthy country in large part because it has managed to remain neutral during international conflicts. Tyrants remain as heads of states because citizens are indoctrinated and terrorized into to believing that they have to accept the status quo or another country is supporting the despot in return for natural resources. In all of the above scenarios, the welfare of the individual and thinking for oneself is discouraged.

In patriarchies that are closed to Mother-God, technology plays havoc with the environment, resources are kept limited and controlled by those controlling politicians, and wars are tools to gain economic advantage. Women are encouraged to have as many children as possible to insure a cheap labor force and provide cannon fodder for wars. The warrior aspect of Father-God, who is supposed to protect the citizens and the kingdom like the knights of the Round Table, becomes the bullying agent of tyrannical politicians and heartless industrialists. The planet becomes an uninhabitable, barren wasteland devoid of wilderness, or the search for the ultimate weapon ultimately destroys everyone. There is an asteroid belt between Earth and Mars that holds enough material to form a planet that many people feel really existed until the residents there blew themselves up.

Matriarchies that are closed to Father-God have their own unique set of problems. Women are encouraged to be fruitful, like the Earth Goddess, and have as many children as possible. Honoring of nature turns to superstition. Rather than being on equal terms with nature, which is also a reflection of God, humanity becomes less than nature. Nature becomes the enemy because too many illogical and conflicting taboos are zealously enforced with extreme punishment or death. Human sacrifice is practiced to appease the spirits of the land represented by various gods and goddesses, who become more and more angry with each generation until they reach a state of rage. Technology and science are stifled. In extremes, men are stripped of their masculinity and serve as a slave work force. Matriarchies come to their ultimate demise because the warrior who is supposed to protect the kingdom has been suppressed along with the other masculine aspects of teacher and consoler.

Outward reflections of our society represent our inward denial of our own nurturing, creative, intuitive feminine nature, and this is true in both men and women. Women are born with 2/3 feminine energy and 1/3 masculine energy; men are born with 2/3 masculine and 1/3 feminine energy. Helen Keller very much represented the forsaken Goddess left deaf and blind because femininity was denied expression. Helen's battle for self-understanding and self-expression paved the way for other women to explore and give form to their feminine nature. She also opened the door for men to be open to their own 1/3 feminine nature and thus more fully express their masculinity in harmony with the Creator. When we integrate our own feminine and masculine nature and create beauty within, we create a wonderful world in which to live. This is the Spirit of the Times that we are all helping to create, which some call the Golden Age of the Return of the Angels. This change in the Universal Calendar has been predicted by all great cultures that have come before us - Mayan, Incan, Aztec, Egyptian and even the Australian Aborigines.

Duality within us also takes expression in our relationships. When some men fall in love with a woman who has balanced love and power, they become afraid because they haven't integrated these two aspects within themselves. Their rough, macho exteriors hide their low self-esteem. The frightened little boy inside, who is expected to live up to his father's and mother's and society's expectations, is filled with guilt and does not know what to do with a woman who can love him and allow him to be who he is. So he puts her in a corner and pulls her out only occasionally. When the woman gets tired of being ignored and leaves him, he cannot understand what happened and his heart is broken. So he goes to the extreme of bringing in women whom he does not love, thinking that they cannot hurt him. Since he doesn't know how to be a good partner in a good relationship, he pulls in women who also don't know how to be both supportive and allowing. These women are demanding and use sex to control him. Sometimes when men cannot commit to a loving relationship, their fear goes back to another lifetime; more often the issue began in childhood when their mother broke their trust in women. He fails to see that Miss Poison Ivy bears remarkable similarities to his own mother and that his own fear will prevent him from experiencing the joys of true love. Unfulfillment will be a pain that is carried to the grave. Mother will always be a wedge between him and his heart's desire until he can see his mother clearly, cut the umbilical cord and establish an adult relationship with his parents. To release his fear, anger and misconceptions of women and love may very well require a healer who can bring up emotional issues, psychological counseling and possibly hypnotic regression with a healer or psychologist.

Women who are in duality see a man's excessive striving for financial success or his obsession with sports as greed or self-absorption, when the real issue for the man maybe that he needs to release his fear and guilt, love himself and integrate both sides of his nature. He can then step out of duality and live his own life in his own wonderful, unique way. In this state of consciousness, he can find the right woman - a woman whom he loves and will love him in return. All of the above with a slightly different twist can be applied to women because we all pull in relationships that are a reflection of who we are. Oftentimes, when a woman meets a man and falls in love she assumes that this is "the man of her dreams" and projects ahead rather than taking the relationship one step at a time. She becomes disappointed when he doesn't live up to her expectations. Truthfully, the only thing we can expect from anyone is to be him/herself and to act accordingly. When we can truly love ourselves, focus on what we do want in our lives and do the things we love to do for their own sake, that is when love finds us. In a "healthy" relationship, the woman's nurturing womb of creativity provides a fertile ground for his ideas and dreams; the man gives her driving force and protection. Their relationship is supportive, loving and allowing.

In The Accidental Tourist, William Hurt speaks to Kathleen Turner about Gena Davis. "I'm beginning to think that maybe it's not just how much you love someone. Maybe what matters is who you are when you are with them." • • • "She's given me another chance to decide who I am. To step out of the weary groove and stay out." To do this, each partner slowly opens him/herself emotionally to the other person so as to feel as well as to see what is being reflected back.

Rewriting of history has prevented us from learning the lessons of our ancestors. The history of the world as taught to young schoolchildren up through university classrooms is a pale reflection of both the achievements of humanity in golden ages, as well as of the great destruction caused by societies where greed, control, corruption and ego brought about the demise of government and culture alike. Deleting of the Goddess began as early as changing Brigit, the Celtic Goddess of poetry, healing and smithery, into a worshiper of Jesus and a Catholic saint. Spanish soldiers burned the Mayan library. British history books, probably more so than those of any other country, belong in the fiction section of the library. I have students and friends in England who have told me that until the movie Gandhi came out, they had no idea of the oppression inflicted on India by the Royal Crown and English government. Many were ashamed to call themselves English. Max Muller, a religious fanatic, intentionally set out to destroy Hinduism by alienating Hindus from their culture and religion. Among other things, Max Muller referred to the singa lingum, an amorphous stone representing formlessness of God or the Stillpoint, as a phallic symbol.

Christian missionaries in Hawaii literally enslaved the natives, took their land and quashed the Hawaiian religion to the point that very little knowledge remains about either shamanism or the Menehunes, the 'little people' who were Kauai's first residents. These elementals have different names in different indigenous cultures around the world. They sometimes appear in miniature human form. These elementals live in another dimension or what some refer to as a parallel universe. When the veil between our reality and theirs becomes thin, then we can see them. When I was in Kauai, I saw these elementals twice as earthy-colored balls of energy. When

I asked if the natives of Kauai had had similar experiences, I was told that if they had, they were not talking because of the fear that had been instilled in them by Christian indoctrination.

The Garden Isle of Kauai is the only Hawaiian isle with navigable rivers and is separated from the other islands by treacherous waters. Jurassic Park was filmed on Kauai and the hurricane in the movie was the real hurricane that hit Hawaii. Mark Twain referred to Waimea Canyon as 'the Grand Canyon of the Pacific'. It is to the shores off of Kauai that the Humpback Whales come each year to give birth. Kalalea *(the sun that shines on the edge of time)* Mountain is said to be the first place where Mother-God entered Earth. This mountain looks over Anahola *(time measured)* and is a place set outside of time. Angeline Locey (one of only 6,000 people put back on the land in 1995 after Congress voted in the 1920's to give 200,000 acres back to the Hawaiians), has her home set up to practice the ancient art of healing in the form of colonics and Lomi massage. Here in Anahola, with a perfect view of the sleeping-goddess-like form of Kalalea Mountain, people can break the bondage of time so that healing can transpire.

Kauai is also the site of a new Hindu temple. 108 is an important number in Hinduism; but there were only 107 known Hindu temples. One thousand years ago, it was written that another temple site existed in Kauai, which was nine hundred years before the existence of Kauai was known. Satguru Sivaya Subramuniyaswami, whom his followers lovingly refer to as Gurudeva, saw this temple in a vision and is currently rebuilding that temple on the heart chakra of the Wailua *(Great Spirit)* River, a place called Where Heaven Touches the Earth. The Hawaiians utilized this natural place of high energy to teach spirituality and for the attainment of spiritual gifts. Each temple along the Wailua River corresponded to one of the river's seven major chakras. These spinning energy circles have direct correlation with the consciousness of the aura, the energy field (which has been photographed and measured) surrounding people and animals alike. In similar manner, Egyptians had constructed temples of learning and worship along the bank of the sacred Nile River. In Hawaiian and Egyptian temples, seekers were taught divination, shamanic journeywork, healing and other metaphysical skills. It is when society or individuals forget that these spiritual gifts come from God and lose consciousness of the fact that these are tools to assist in remembering the journey home that society decays or individuals fall deeper into duality.

The root chakra, which is located at the base of the spine, grounds us, as well as our thoughts, into physical form. The root chakra is directly related to the astral body, which looks very much like our physical body because it holds the perfect blueprint of the physical. As we move into The Golden Age, our astral bodies are manifesting more and more through the physical, and this phenomenon has been referred to as 'acquiring a light body'. Like the human body, the astral body can become diseased and distorted with heavy emotions and dark thoughts. When I teach people how to read past lives, it doesn't matter how physically beautiful or handsome the individual was in that past life; if the personality was engaged in greed, jealousy, fear, etc., then the astral projection from that life will reveal those same distorted, unconscious qualities as plainly as <u>The Portrait of Dorian Gray</u> depicted the evil in his soul. The astral body is attached to the physical body by a silver cord, and it is the astral body that travels during our dreamtime, out-of-body experiences and during shamanic journeywork. The astral body typically leaves through the open crown chakra, although Edgar Cayce's astral body was observed leaving through his solar plexus when he did his psychic or medical readings.

The second chakra is located below the navel in the front of the body and at the lumbar spine in the back. An energy line runs from the crown through the root chakra; the other chakras (front and back) are attached to it. The second chakra corresponds to the first emotional body and is a center for creativity as well as the 'inner child'. When we are driving our car and we somehow get from 42nd Street to 95th Street, it was the child who drove the car. Trauma from childhood is held in this chakra. In spiritual work, the shaman holds ceremony through the use of the second chakra. In order to do this, the shaman has to be channeling creative, healing energy from Mother-Father God. A so-called black magician uses demons as his/her source of energy, which some can feel as heavy and dense. We can tell the difference between the two because as Master Jesus said, "Ye shall know them by their works." A so-called white magician holds ceremony in a circle and s/he begins by opening his/her heart and calling in Holy Spirit helpers - guides, angels and other souls of higher consciousness - who step into the expanding aura of the shaman. All healers who are channeling Universal energy can hold ceremony. The circle of energy expands so that all of the participants are held within the field. It is this cosmic force and Holy Spirit working through the shaman which affords the opportunity for healing and conscious awareness. The participants can contribute to the ceremony and what they bring to the circle is directly correspondent to the energy level that they are able to channel.

The solar plexus or third chakra is located below the sternum in the front of the body and just opposite that point on the back of the body. The color is yellow and the solar plexus corresponds directly to the first mental body. It is also a touch point for the release of emotional (thoughts with feeling attached) issues. There is a will center located behind the solar plexus. People who are possessed have given away their will and frequently the healer or shaman will find that the entity hides in this chakra. The healer is there to provide enough energy so that the demon can be released to the Light for transformation and to assist the healee in taking back their own authority. When the psychic channels of this chakra are opened in either Enochian Magic initiation or because the individual has brought that ability with him/her when s/he was born, it can be used for healing.

The heart is the gateway to the higher chakras. Without heart-love energy, access is denied. Calling in demons is not a metaphysical skill of the throat chakra; anyone who does not have the foresight to see *'that what goes around comes around'* can make a pact with the devil. Ancient wisdom cannot be spoken and given earth form unless the heart is open to listening to the Voice of Creation. Using inner sight to bring about one's own will is not the receiving of psychic impressions of the Truth of What Is, which is a metaphysical skill of the third eye. When the spirit, mind and personality become corrupted, the crown chakra, which is located at the top of the head, closes and the individual cuts him/herself off from Source and becomes entrapped in a world of his/her own disillusionment.

While the heart chakra, or fourth chakra, of the Wailua River is the site of the future Hindu temple, the fifth or throat chakra lies at the base of the crater. The seventh or crown chakra is at the top of Mt. Waialeale, Earth's wettest weather spot. Energy pours into the crown and then flows into the third eye, or sixth chakra, which is located between the top and base of the mountain. The root chakra is located at the mouth of the river. The second or creative chakra is found at the birthstones located off of Kuamoa Road and close to the ocean. The third chakra had been turned into a cattle pen and is now being renovated. Each year, the Hawaiian priests and priestesses would travel up the Wailua River and up Mt. Waialeale as a spiritual quest and to regenerate their bodies. It is believed that there were healing stones placed at the top of the mountain. Using natural places of high energy to teach spirituality and for attainment of spiritual gifts has been used by other cultures honoring the Goddess.

Hindus believe that creation is broken down into three different worlds; the physical, the astral (which is the realm of spirit and also where our souls travel in our sleeptime), and a world where souls who, after countless reincarnations of learning, achieve a state of bliss. Hindus believe in one God who manifests in many forms throughout creation. Hindu gods and goddesses personify various attributes of the One God, Brahman.

Pele, the Hawaiian goddess of fire and volcano, is Kahli, the Hindu goddess who possesses the same attributes of creativity and destruction. Pele and Kahli are most powerful forces that demand human respect. These goddesses are both a little bit strange or eccentric; they are tantric and capable of changing form. They are fluid in manifestation.

131

Lono, whose form is that of a pig, is Gnosha, the Hindu elephant god. Both are nonhuman deities. Both are endearing and accessible, easily invoked and approachable. They are bringers of fertility to the earth, deities of agriculture, abundance, and worldliness in a positive way. Lono and Gnosha are close to families and family needs.

Kane, the ultimate Hawaiian god and man, is the Hindu god Vishnu or Krishna. They are creators, preservers and destroyers. Aloof, they are too pure to approach.

Ku, the Hawaiian sun god of war and sorcery, is the beautiful Murga, who is closest to healing. The magic and healing aspects of Ku have been lost; however, there are Hawaiians who are born as healers, some of whom bring this spiritual gift in through ancestral lineages. Siddha medicine focuses on power and perfection. Poisons are treated homeopathically, hands-on healing is performed in ritual, and tribal medicine is found in ceremonies. To this end, herbs, essential oils, mantras, yantras (mystic diagram or pattern composed of geometric and alphabetic figures used for concentrating spiritual and mental energies) and yogas are used. Healing practitioners have to meditate with 'medicine' before it is used. This statement describes shamanic, indigenous cultures around the world. It doesn't matter what our background is - European, African, Indian - we all trace our roots back to a time when Mother Earth was honored and the other side of the veil was a reality that could be utilized to make this reality a better one.

Hula and Lomi are two surviving ancient Hawaiian healing art forms. Hula is like India's classical dancing called mudra, which uses subtle hand gestures. The hula visually depicts the source of creation; Lomi creates from Source and is a way of living. Lomi is loving hands and loving the body. Lomi is an ancient Hawaiian massage using herbs, sea salt, and clay to remove misqualified energy so that the body, mind and spirit can be in flow. Angeline Locey says, 'Lomi does you'.

What has been lost to both Hindus and Hawaiians is shamanic journeywork and the shaman's drum. It is the rapid, non-varying beat of 205 to 220 beats per minute which quiets the active left brain and sends the shaman into altered states of consciousness. The overtone of this drumming harmonizes and balances the two hemispheres of the brain, and may be the reason why we feel dissociated from our bodies and participate fully in our imagery. It is more powerful than virtual reality. When we visualize ourselves, we activate the holographic mind; therefore, a shaman who is channeling sufficient Elemental Universal Energy can effectively bring about changes in the hologram simply by altering his/her piece of the hologram.

132

When the drum begins beating, the shaman sees him/herself, in the eye of the inner mind, standing in a beautiful place in nature and looks for an entrance into the Underworld. S/he typically travels down a slanted tunnel and comes out into a beautiful place in nature. Sometimes shaman travel into the Underworld through tree roots or simply takes a leap of faith by jumping into a hole. The Native American shaman of the southwest traveled into the earth through a hole in the kiva. The wise women of Europe lay on the hearth next to the fire so as to keep their bodies warm while their astral bodies journeyed. The Underworld has gotten a 'bad rap' from the Catholic Church. It is a place of creativity - Walt Disney found Mickey and other famous cartoon figures here. The Underworld is a wondrous realm inhabited by nature spirits, devas, power animals and elementals whom the shaman uses for divination, healing and other spiritual work. Henry Ford and George Washington Carver worked with these intuitive forces to bring about new innovations and inventions.

There are numerous entrances to the Upperworld of the angels. Some shaman travel first to the Lowerworld and ask one of their power animals to take them to the Upperworld. The shaman can see him/herself traveling to the Upperworld on a rainbow or through a star gate. In the Celtic tradition, shaman travel up the world tree to and through the North Star. It is here that the souls of the departed are often seen and the Truth of What Is can be accessed. Angels, spirit helpers and the spirits of the ancestors can all be used for healing, magic and divination.

The Middleworld is most like that of our physical, three-dimensional reality. It is here that the shaman can travel with his/her spirit helpers to visit a friend or attend to an individual in need of healing. In the Middleworld, the shaman can see the cause behind the disease, which manifests as bad smells, reptiles or insects, or dark or murky objects. The shaman uses his spirit guides or angels to remove the spiritual infection and heal the area. If the shaman is working in accordance with Natural Laws and channeling enough elemental energy, the Holy Spirits will come to his aid and the work that is done in these other realities will be experienced in the physical reality. Danuska came to me and asked if I would shamanically journey to her mare who was pregnant with twins. In order for a baby horse to survive, it must be born full-term. If the mare is carrying twins, there is a danger that the foals will be born prematurely. If the mare does carry them both to term, she may reject one because she does not have enough milk for two babies. When I journeyed to Danuska's mare, I watched the spirit helpers attending to the mare while I saw myself initiating her into Reiki. Several months later, I spoke with Danuska. Her veterinarian had examined the mare and heard the two foals' heartbeats the week before she delivered. He knew for a fact that there were two foals; however, the mare delivered only one healthy colt. The other foal completely disappeared. Danuska said, "You should have seen him looking through the afterbirth and examining my mare. He didn't have a clue as to what happened to the other foal."

In Celtic tradition, the Otherworld consists of three realms of Land, Sea and Sky. In the center, the Sacred Fire burns in the Sacred Grove, where the Worlds flow together. These realms directly correlate to the four elements, the power that the shaman connects to and utilizes in journey and magic work. The World Tree connects the Land and the Sky and is the vehicle by which the Celtic shaman travel into the Otherworld. "Among these worlds, all common life is sustained between the Chaos of Potential and the World Order." (Druidheachd, Symbols and Rites of Druidry by Ian Corrigan). As the shaman's journey is within and our bodies are a microcosm of the Universe, the shaman's spine is representative of the World Tree. Yoga is a shamanic practice that was used to prepare the shaman before performing rituals, magic or journeywork. The Mayan high priests (shaman) used to sit on top of the pyramids in full lotus position after performing other Yoga postures for the purpose of bringing Light into the land and the people.

The imagery and events that occur in the Upperworld, Middleworld and Underworld go beyond what the human brain can imagine. Three women from India came to be initiated and to learn how to do the Tera-Mai™ Seichem initiations. They also wanted to do the Shamanic Workshop that I teach; however, by the time I found out about their request, it was too late to advertise and find other students. I initiate my shamanic students into healing so that when they do soul retrieval, they are able to heal the soul before they bring it back. When I taught the three Indian women how to do soul retrieval, I had two of them working simultaneously on the third member of their group. I had never done this before. When they shared their experiences, they found out that both individuals who were involved in the soul retrieval had the same bizarre experiences. When Joyothi Bathija and K. N. tried to retrieve Prabha's soul fragment, they both ended up going into a cave of brimstone and fire inhabited by Satan and other demons - a scene that Joyothi previously thought existed only in horror movies. When Joyothi asked what kind of healing Prabha required, her guides told her that Prabha needed a new, loving, kinder heart. While Joyothi watched, at the same time Holy Spirit burned out Prabha's black heart and replaced it with a compassionate one, K. N. smelled sulfur burning. shamanic journeywork is not an end in itself. What must accompany the work is a change of both heart and attitude on the part of the healee. In Prabha's case, she refused to give up her old ways.

In India, the only surviving link to the shaman's drumbeat can be found in the Hindu funeral march. As the body of the departed is carried through the streets of India, the rapid, repetitive drumbeat is played. Today, people come out to pay their respects. Originally, beating the shaman's drumbeat after physical death was the vehicle by which the soul set off on its last journey. The worlds that the shaman psychically journeys into are the same worlds that the souls of the departed inhabit. Our life's experiences determine how limited or how expansive our soul's experiences will be; thus, we really do create our own hell or heaven. Soul fragments that are lost in places like dark caves are visages of ourselves that are experiencing a hell of our own creation. Sometimes during the Shamanic Journey class, when I teach my students how to travel into the Upperworld, people will come back and tell stories of how on the way up, they saw groups of souls in various box-like rooms. The rooms or buildings are open but the inhabitants cannot seem to find the way out of the particular space where they are confined. These souls are also completely unaware of the journeyer. These are souls who during their lifetime felt that their religion or their way was the only way, and they are living their reality with those of the same limiting consciousness. The only way out is a change of mind. When we change the way we think, we change our whole lives.

France is an example of how our thoughts create our environment. In Paris, there are plaques, statues, engravings and pictures memorializing and depicting events such as witch burnings, Nazi atrocities, bombings, shootings, etc., which has the effect of keeping people chained to the past. The city is dirty because the thoughts are heavy. It would be difficult to imagine a statue of Lincoln after just being shot lying in the Capitol rotunda in Washington D.C. - most people would agree that the majority of politicians are heavy enough with corruption without weighing them down with even more negativity. In cities where the individual(s) is/are honored and remembered, the energy is lighter. In the French countryside and in the French towns, it is clean and the attitude of the French people is completely different.

In order for the shaman's journeying or medicine to work, s/he needed the help of the spirit helpers and power animals. Just as we function on other planes of reality (our subconscious and superconscious are but two examples) as well as on this physical one, the 4-legged, winged, finned, etc. are also multidimensional. Each species in the animal kingdom brings a spiritual gift with them for the benefit of humanity. Medicine Cards by Jamie Sams and David Carson beautifully describes these attributes - a few brief examples are Crow (law), Lynx (secrets), and Eagle (spirit). So, if a shaman were carrying Crow medicine, s/he would be able to journey into the Underworld, find crow and ascertain whether or not the healee had broken Natural Laws, or discover the karmic lesson behind the healee's disease or pain. Powerful shaman carrying this medicine are able to shape shift or change their form in physical reality. It is called shape shifting because the illusion comes from within; that is, as the shaman's physical form changes, s/he experiences an inward shift of energy to one side. Even though there is a physical manifestation, the ability to shape shift does not come from the physical; it comes from beyond the physical. This phenomenon can be experienced in journeywork, whereby the shaman can travel with the power animal or ride upon the power animal or, other times, become the power animal.

Lynx is the keeper of secrets. "Some medicine people believe that the Sphinx of ancient Egypt was not a Lion but a Lynx." (Medicine Cards) The secret that both the Sphinx and Lynx guard is the secret of animal medicine. Contrary to some belief, animal medicine is not gained by killing the animal, but rather by contacting the spirit of the animal and respecting its physical form. A shaman who has Lynx medicine has the ability to work with all forms of animal medicine.

Animals are here to serve as caretakers for Mother Earth and they do this through what we call 'the delicate balance of nature'. Eagle bridges the gap between heaven and earth. The Native Americans have a saying, *"When the Eagles are gone, so then will Earth be gone."* Money-oriented industrialists, financiers, and power-hungry politicians are too shortsighted to see beyond today. Desert-like planets in science fiction movies are not habitable for advanced life forms. Eagle can only survive in the wilderness. When the wilderness has been cut down and stripped away, eagle will disappear as well as the living habitat which sustains us. shaman who have Eagle medicine are easily able to petition Higher Forces and make the invisible visible. People who attend ceremonies that are held by a shaman holding Eagle medicine often see spirits or feel spirits moving past them. *"Ye shall know them by their works."*

A shaman has the ability to journey for another for the purpose of retrieving lost power animals. We lose our power animals through disuse or disrespect. My lost power animal, Owl, was my lost childhood abilities of intuition and healing. I am grateful that I live in a time, unlike my mother's, where retrieval is a possibility.

The books and teachers of shamanism will indicate that the shaman goes within him/herself to his/her own piece of the hologram. My experience has been that the powerful shaman has the ability to go within the healee's inner landscape for the purpose of retrieving power animals or soul fragments and this is evidenced by dramatic physical, mental or emotional changes. While this can be a powerful force for good, it is also the reason why the shaman needs to protect his/her body during sleep or meditation. There is the Taoist morning practice of releasing one's own higher self (guru) from the heart and up through the crown to remain watchful during the day in a position just above the head. Before going to sleep, one's higher self is pulled back into the heart to guard the body at night. The Mayans, Aztecs and Egyptians used the color cobalt blue to draw in higher forces and repel lower ones. The simple act of asking celestial angels to bring cobalt blue light before we go to sleep protects us. I have even had clients who have had abduction experiences in the past, asked for cobalt blue at night, and the abductions stopped.

To be able to work with Holy Spirit at high levels of consciousness, the shaman must keep his/her body, mind and emotions clear. In 'New Age' dialog, this translates as 'working out our issues'. There is a ceremony, which is referred to as Death of a Shaman, whereby the shaman journeys to the Underworld alone to face that which s/he fears the most. S/he may or may not be consciously aware of his/her greatest fear. When the shaman finds the thing s/he fears, the shaman then asks what s/he fears to eat him/her. The shaman is not killing his/her soul or committing suicide; what is being eaten is his/her fear. It is a process of death and rebirth; death to fear and rebirth in joy. It is not a painful experience once the shaman has walked through his/her fear and consented to be eaten. The shaman's head is usually the last thing to go. After being eaten, the shaman is given a new body and returns to consciousness cleared of the fear-based emotion.

I have been studying shamanism longer than I have studied Reiki. I went through this ceremony almost 20 years ago and was surprised when darkness ate me. Since then, I have been releasing my fear of small, enclosed, dark places as well as my fear of working with the Great Void that is found within. From my Shamanic Workshop students, I have discovered that this fear often comes from past lives where we were burned alive or otherwise tortured for being a witch. In my classes, I explain Death of a Shaman and then give them a break, allowing them the freedom of choice as to whether or not they are ready to journey Death of a Shaman. If they run into other people on their break who ask what it is that they are doing, I typically hear, "We are going to be eaten!" I could write a whole chapter or perhaps even a book on my students' experiences, but I will give a few examples.

A clergyman in New York returned from Death of a Shaman with this tale. He had gone into the Underworld searching for something to eat him. He ran into a handsome young man who asked him what he was doing. The clergyman responded, "I am looking for something to eat me." With that, the handsome young man turned into the devil himself, frightened the clergyman and then proceeded to eat him. When the devil was through, he turned back into a handsome young man again and the clergyman got a new body.

Edde Sailer went into the Underworld to find something to eat her and found a snake who ate her whole. As she was passing through the body of the snake, she became frightened, but she remembered that I had instructed them that they could call upon their power animals, angels or other Holy Spirits to help them or to answer questions. In the belly of the snake, Edde called out to her guide to ask why it was taking so long. Her guide responded, "It's all right! Relax! I am right here!" Edde did as her guide instructed, came out, got a new body and came back to consciousness.

Ian went into the Underworld, but rather than looking for something to eat him, he decided that he would take on anything that tried to eat him. Ian was successful because nothing in the Underworld can make the shaman do anything that he does not want to do. The only exception is that for those individuals who work with demons in black magic rituals - in the Underworld, these entities control the shaman. I have had one such student who came to the conscious realization after journeying that these demons also controlled him in his consciousness. After a while, Ian got tired of chasing off his fears, and he asked his guide, "What is it that I am learning from this?" He was told, "Nothing!" So, Ian consented to be eaten. With that a large bird snatched him up, flew very high in the sky and then dropped him. Ian landed on his head, which split open. All kinds of ugly, rotten things came out. Then an array of insects and reptiles consumed him. He got a new body and returned to consciousness visibly shaken, but with conscious clarity of mind.

Evelyn Kerns' journeys belong in a class all by themselves. Evelyn went into the Underworld, but no one or nothing would eat her. She was about to give up hope when she ran into a cartoon-type creature, but he told her he was afraid she wouldn't taste very good. Evelyn offered to pour honey over herself, but he still didn't think he would eat her. When she asked him what would make her palatable, the dragon pondered and said that maybe if she doused herself in mustard, he could swallow her whole. Evelyn obliged, she was eaten and then she proceeded to poke him from inside. He jumped up and down. Then he expelled her and she floated out whole inside of an iridescent bubble.

Autobiography of a Yogi by Paramahansa Yogananda gives numerous accounts of various metaphysical abilities that East Indian gurus are able to do. Gurus accomplish physical manifestation when they are able to change the vibratory rate of electrons and protons. In order for an object to remain in physical form, the guru needs to be able to reach beyond the astral plane to higher vibrations. It is considered very bad karma for a guru to manifest something of great value, like a ruby necklace, and sell if for a 'reasonable sum of money', knowing full well that the necklace will soon disappear. Among other things, levitation, the ability to bring in aromas from other levels and stepping into 'time slowed down' is discussed.

Cultures honoring the Goddess performed rituals for the purpose of staying close to the earth, to contact spirit guides, for healing and cleansing purposes, for divination, for empowerment, etc. Without the honoring of nature as an aspect of Divinity, the attainment of these true psychic abilities is impossible. Modern farmers believe that they are entitled to 100% of their crops or herds; they have forgotten that their livelihood comes from the Earth and that they are expected by the Natural Laws of the Absolute to release a small portion back to Mother Earth's creatures. Whenever any of us forget to give thanks, the cycle of giving and receiving is broken and we receive less and less because we give less and less. Mother Earth Spirituality by Ed McGaa, Eagle Man, explains the purpose behind many sacred ceremonies as well as how to do them for the benefit of ourselves and our world. The power of ceremony to facilitate beneficial change is impossible without the elemental forces of nature, which are also the forces within us. Earth, air, fire and water are the building blocks of this Universe. As we move into the age of enlightenment, the first step in connecting or reconnecting to the elemental forces is respect for Mother Earth.

Even the art of divination is possible through the elemental forces - crystal balls, water divination (scrying), reading tea leaves, listening to the wind, etc. Within both the Tarot cards and astrology charts can be found the elemental forces. Most people who do psychic readings are reading the individual's aura, which like our bodies, is also composed of the four elements. To give the Truth of What Is and not what it is the reader wants to hear, the reader needs to be connected to the Goddess, which is the intuitive aspect of Divinity. In order to connect to the Goddess, we have to be connected to the Earth Mother in a healthy, respectful manner. An age of enlightenment is such that the presence of both Father-God (Enlightenment) and Mother-God (Potential) are in balance. This means that we do not see or hear spirits all of the time; rather, we use our psychic abilities and intuition as a tool and in combination with our logic and intellect to create a better world for ourselves. It really is that simple.

Book of the Hopi by Frank Waters, which is based on Chief White Bear's knowledge, discusses the journey patterns of the Hopi which enabled them to remain close to Mother Earth and keep in harmony with the universe and within themselves. This book tells a few stories that give a small insight into the metaphysical mastery that was acquired by different Hopi tribes. Each tribe within the Hopi Nation by focusing on a particular animal or aspect in nature was able to develop extraordinary psychic abilities. Some shaman were so attuned that they could shape-shift and become their tribal totem. Other tribes were able to psychically manipulate the elemental forces that comprised their tribal totem. All shamans develop their psychic abilities through careful observation and harmonic interaction with nature. Shamanic gifts that are birthed and nurtured in one lifetime can take form in a new way in another lifetime.

When I went up to Sedona, Arizona with Kim Williamson and Crystal Wilk in November, 1996, we stayed at the home of Naomi White Bear (White Bear's widow), which was in itself a miracle. Naomi was tight-lipped, yet, at the same time, she was drawn to me, and she asked me to sit down next to her. As she gazed into my eyes with her soft eyes, I could feel that she was psychically reading me. Then she asked me if I would do a healing on her. As soon as I put my hands on Naomi, she could feel the energy moving in her body. At one point, Naomi blurted out, "You are doing what the Hopi medicine men do when they heal, but they do their medicine four times for the four directions, not three times like you are doing." What I personally believe is that the healing techniques I used on Naomi, which are found herein, are the same healing modalities that have been used by Hawaiian shaman, East Indian gurus, African shaman, the wise women of Europe, Jesus and his followers, the priests and priestesses of ancient Egypt and other shaman throughout time.

Ama Deus

Shamanic Healing From the Jungles of Central Brazil

Ama Deus (I Love God) was brought to the United States by Alberto Aguas. It is sacred healing and has been used for thousands and thousands of years by the Guarani *(Gau ra nee)* Tribe or los Guaranis located deep in the central jungle of Brazil. These people lived close to nature and the Goddess. From their passionate love for the earth was born a shamanic language that has been untouched and unpolluted by the white man; thus, it remains easy and effective. Simplicity is not synonymous with complacency. Working with the mind and the heart of God is never contrived or complicated; the Truth is always simple. It is when man steps in and out of ego, fear or greed and decides that he has the right to alter sacred knowledge that things get 'messed up', and this is evidenced by a steady, inexorable decline in the healing energy.

When Alberto taught Ama Deus in the United States, he never taught all of the symbols in any one place. Alberto also combined Ama Deus with the crystal work that he did and subsequent followers have utilized it within other healing modalities. One of the keys to using Ama Deus is that it is not to be combined with other symbols. To do so is considered impure or sacrilegious.

I neither studied with, nor did I ever meet Alberto Aguas, and I have been told that he has passed on beyond the veil into the spirit world. I learned Ama Deus from a man *(whom I will refer to as Charles)* who called me and wanted to do an exchange with me. In return for my initiating him into Sakara, Sophi-El and Angeliclight, he had a l o n g list of different Reiki and other healing modalities that he was willing to share with me. I do not see Spirit often with my physical eyes in my ordinary life, and not all of the time when I am facilitating healing work. However, I spoke with Charles, the spirit of a shaman appeared to me and asked me to go to Charles and learn Ama Deus. I have since come to believe that it was the spirit of Alberto Aguas who came to me. So, I told Charles that I would simply like to learn Ama Deus.

Several weeks later, I was flying on a plane, eager to learn Ama Deus. I even had a present for Charles, as he had told me that his birthday was that weekend. After I reinitiated Charles into Tera-Mai™ Reiki and initiated him into Sakara, Sophi-El and Angeliclight, Charles decided that because I would not show him how to do the initiations into the other rays of healing, he would not teach me Ama Deus. Charles knew beforehand that Spirit had asked me to set up a school to insure that the initiations into the elemental Universal healing rays would be handed

141

down and taught in their pure form, and that I couldn't show anyone until the school had been set up. That fact is even in my first book, <u>Reiki & Other Rays of Touch Healing</u>, which he told me that he had read. I felt totally naive and betrayed. Disheartened, I thought that I had let down the shaman who had encouraged me to come. It was as though I had been raped, and I wanted to go home, but the shaman appeared again and asked me to stay.

Against my better judgement, Charles reinitiated me as a Seichem Master and gave me some other material. I wondered why the shaman had asked me to stay. At lunch, Charles asked more questions, and I ended up talking about a Chi Kung Master from Hong Kong that I had studied with in New York. This piqued Charles' interest and he wanted to learn what I had learned. This time, I had Charles show me Ama Deus first before I taught him. Of course, Charles had to tell me that he already knew what I had taught him. But I had Ama Deus. I excitedly returned home to Arizona.

My enthusiasm was short-lived. The pneumonia I came down with when I had moved to Arizona returned with a vengeance. In looking through the instructions for the Seichem initiations Charles had initiated me into, I saw that they had been drastically altered and that the master symbol or Dai Koo Mio was actually a symbol which pulled energy out of the individual. It is a common law of physics that if the signal is changed, then the wave produced by the signal is inexorably altered. What is true on one level has a corresponding truth on other levels. When a teacher changes an initiation, then the energy is altered. If the initiation is manmade and no longer "it" then either the energy transfer will not hold, not take place at all or it will set up a negative vibration. I had to see a doctor and be put on antibiotics, went to healers who could help take out the symbols and energy pattern Charles had initiated me into and did clearings on myself. Charles proved to be one of my best teachers, he taught me a lot!

When I tried to use Ama Deus, I discovered that something was missing. I had an inner gut feeling that Charles had left out the closing symbols intentionally, but I called Charles in order to give him the benefit of the doubt. When I reached Charles, he told me that if I showed him how to do the Sakara initiations, then he would give me the rest of Ama Deus. I responded by telling him that that wasn't the deal that we had made. When I had initiated Charles into Sakara and the other elemental rays of touch healing, he had been amazed at the energy. On the phone, Charles arrogantly told me that he had felt nothing from the initiations I had given him. The shaman showed up by my side and he spoke these words which I repeated to Charles, "By your very words, it is so." Even over the telephone, I could feel the initiations leaving Charles.

The shaman then told me that I would find the missing piece of the puzzle. He guided me to work with two women - a psychic from Phoenix who calls herself simply, Kathleen, and Susan Friedman Kramer. The following month I was teaching a class at The Source of Life in New York. A woman in the next seminar room was teaching a class on crystals, and I found out that she had studied with Alberto Aguas. I showed her the closure symbols that we had been given psychically, and she confirmed that both the symbols and the procedure were those that Alberto had taught her. In return, I gave her a copy of the class agenda for Ama Deus I had typed up which had all of the symbols in it that Alberto used.

If after reading through this chapter, you decide that your intent is to work in purity with this healing system, repeat this vow:

"I now vow to be a part of sacred traditions and lineage of the Guarani shaman healing practice which I will always carry out in a sacred and honorable way."

Shamanic Breathing: Breath is the link between our physical body and our soul. To breathe deeply, inhale through the nostrils, expand the diaphragm and stomach, and hold. Exhale through the mouth. The consciousness behind the breathing before practicing Ama Deus is to become the breath of God. Purposefully think and take in the Light of God. Become filled with the Light of God. Feel yourself as a never-ending channel of love; breathing love in and exhaling love out. This emotional feeling of love is vital in sending out symbols. Open the heart and use feeling. At the moment of sending symbols, the shaman is All Love and is in the moment, in the Circle of Life with Mother-Father God and All Creatures. The emotion of love swells within while the symbols are visualized and held. The symbols are released to do their work on an out breath or exhale.

Symbols are not for decoration. When the shaman sees them in the mind's eye, they do not necessarily have colors. If colors are needed, the spirits of the shaman and spirit helpers brings them in. Again, symbols are always sent with love.

Spiritual Routine for sending symbols:

1. Say "Ama Deus" *(I Love God)* 3 times.

2. Breath of God as described above 3 times.

3. Cone the fingers of the right hand and touch coned fingers to heart chakra. Feel heart opening. Feel love.

4. Remove the right hand and cone the fingers of the left hand and touch coned fingers to heart chakra. Send love to 3rd eye.

143

5. Love from the heart is imprinted on the 3rd eye and activates that part of our 3rd eye, which is used for healing.

6. **Imprint on palms symbols one at a time with the 3rd eye:** It is called imprinting because you will feel your palm chakra and even the hands themselves expanding. The energy of the symbol in your hand will feel like tiny pulses of electricity. To do this, visualize the symbols one at a time beginning with Symbol One. While visualizing Symbol One, focus attention on the left hand. When the energy is experienced in the left hand, begin concentrating on Symbol Two and focus attention on the right hand. The other symbols come in on the vibration of the symbol in the left hand and are grounded with the symbol in the right hand. *If you have trouble visualizing, stare at the symbol and then close your eyes and visualize it. Repeat until image is in mind's eye.*

This particular healing system works because everything, including our body, is in our mind. By following this spiritual ritual and honoring the symbols and Holy Spirit, we connect to a tradition that is thousands and thousands of years old. Anything that has been around for this long has stood the test of time because it works.

Tips from Alberto Aguas:
1.   Everything I do, I try to bring healing to it.
2.   After the healing, let go and don't talk about it. Don't ask the person later what happened during the healing. If you need to find out what's going on during the healing, the time to ask is during the healing.
3.   Don't interfere with God. Let go! If you talk too much, you're interfering with energy. If the symbols are used in shamanic journeywork, it is appropriate to see yourself in your mind's eye asking questions of the spirit helpers and the spirits of the shaman.
4.   Music, crystals, totems or herbs can be used during Ama Deus healing.
5.   The shamanic breathing or Breath of God can be done the entire time during the healing by the shaman, or by the healee who is receiving Ama Deus healing.
6.   Have holy attitude when healing.
7.   Do healing work before eating, not after.
8.   Be clear about the purpose and release the outcome to God.
9.   I am here as a vehicle.
10.   Healee can do spiritual routine before receiving healing symbols.
11.   To alter symbols or use with other symbols is considered impure. Not only is the vibration altered, but the spirit guides and souls of the Guarani shaman will "back off" as well.

<u>Irapuru`</u> is the sacred bird of the Amazon Jungle. Can intone "Irapuru`" 5 times to raise the energy vibration and to connect with ancient shamanic spirits and spirit helpers.

<u>Symbols</u>

All symbols have depth, memory and dimensionality. They are not flat. Like everything else, they come from God. The system is simple and it works. If it's not broken, don't fix it!

1.   Imprint **Symbol One** on left palm to claim or draw in the energy of God. Symbol One acts like an energy wave on which other symbols ride in. *Hold symbol in mind's eye for <u>one minute</u>. It may change shape in the beginning when you are new at holding an image for that long. Do not consciously try to change shape. If it does alter, <u>gently</u> bring image back. If you need to look at symbol on handout again while visualizing, do so. Do the best you can. It does get easier.* Left hand brings in symbols and healing energy.

2. Imprint **Symbol Two** on right palm. This symbol anchors and holds the energy for the symbols that are to be used in healing. *So much is done with the palms of the hands in this healing system that often when you see Guarani shaman who are in spirit coming to assist you, their hands are huge & filled with Light and energy.* Right hand sends healing from the heart that is filled with love on the out breath. *Hold symbol in mind's eye for <u>one-minute</u>* • • •

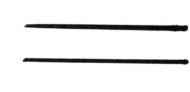

3. **Absentee healing:** Do spiritual routine. Imprint Symbols One and Two in the palms of the left and right hands. To use this symbol for absentee healing, see golden light like brilliant ball. You may see it come in on the wave in your left hand and anchored within the lines on your right. Hold the image. You can also put other symbols from this system into the golden ball when it is appropriate to do so.   See the

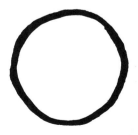

145

symbols you are using above eye level or above the imaginary horizon line in your mind's eye.

4. Symbol Four is used to lock in the healing, send the symbols back to God and end Ama Deus healing. During the healing process, the symbols are visualized. The shaman is the silent observer, watching the events that transpire. When it is time to end the session or move onto another type of healing modality, Ama Deus needs to be closed by sending the symbols that have been used back to Source. First, visualize the wave looping up. Then visualize Symbol Two within the wave. Then close the wave by visualizing a single horizontal line over the wave. *(It is like the energy of Symbols One and Two are being stabilized.)* Next, visualize the symbol(s) you have been working with within the two lines. Do this after working with <u>most but not all</u> of the symbols. To complete the closure, on an out breath of air, send symbols back where they came from. <u>Give thanks and gratitude to symbols, guides, spirit helpers and Mother-Father God.</u>

5. Is used for **Purification**. Like any language, Ama Deus has its exceptions to the rule. <u>Do not use Symbol Five with spiritual routine.</u> Never use combined with any other symbol - always use alone. Can be used over food, medicine, water, other drink, etc. In other words, it can be used for everything that is put in or on the body. It can be used to remove implants, needles, transplants, and germs - anything that has entered the body. It can take out emotions; for example, when eating in a restaurant, if the cook is upset, that emotion can go into the food that is being prepared. Simply visualize this symbol over what needs to be cleared. Placing the fingertips together and forming a "V" with the hands, and then moving the hands down and through what needs to be cleared can also be very effective.

6. It is neither a heart, nor is it necessarily pink or any other color. **To Rescue a Dying Person** - to help them in their choice to die or to live: Do spiritual routine and imprint symbols in palms. Always have candle lit, or see a candle in mind before beginning healing. Using a feather-like touch, the shaman holds onto the second toes of the dying individual. Shaman's third finger is on the top and at the base of the second toe; shaman's thumb is underneath and at the base of the second toe. Symbol Six is sent on the breath and up through the meridian lines to individual's heart as many times as is needed. This entire procedure is done for 3 consecutive days, and then it is stopped for 3 consecutive days. Shaman has to be faithful. This 6-day process can be repeated as many times as necessary until there is a decision on the part of the individual. Release the individual to God and then lock in healing with Symbol Four.

Absentee: Send symbol within golden ball (Symbol Three) to their heart. When finished, lock in healing with Symbol Four.

It is my personal belief that if a shaman were holding enough energy and if the spirit of the deceased were willing, this symbol could bring back the dead. (It is not unheard of for a shaman in journeywork to retrieve the soul of the departed, bring it back and bring the dead back to life.)

7. **To Help the Dead Travel Speedily to the Light** - It is used for those persons who have been dead for less than 21 days. If it has been longer, use Symbol Eight. Symbol Seven is used exactly like Symbol Six. Do spiritual routine, imprint symbols in palms. If the body is present, use thumb and third finger. Then blow Symbol Seven up through feet, up through the tunnel and into all of the subtle bodies. It is important to have candle lit while working. Continue absentee healings up to 21 days from date of death and then do not use again on this soul. Lock in healing with Symbol Four.

<u>Absentee</u>: Do spiritual routine, imprint symbols on palms. Exhale golden circle with Symbol Seven. Visualize it going into the soles of the feet, through the tunnel and up through subtle bodies to the total being, not a specific part of being. Lock in healing with Symbol Four after each session.

8. For **earthbound spirits**. Do spiritual routine and imprint Symbols One and Two on palms of hands. If the earthbound soul cannot be seen, imprint Symbol Three (absentee symbol - golden circle) before imprinting Symbol Eight on the third eye. If the spirit can be seen (earthbound soul has materialized), do <u>not</u> use Symbol Three. Burn a white candle while working. If it is not possible, see one or build one in the eye of the inner mind. Symbol Eight is used for those who have been dead longer than 21 days. Lock in healing with Symbol Four after each session.

9. **To bring in a spiritual guide for self.** Do spiritual ritual and imprint Symbols One and Two on palms of hands. Can either use absentee symbol, or simply imprint Symbol Nine in inner eye. Hold the image in mind's eye and observe what transpires.

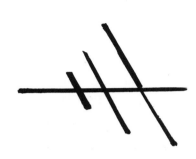

<u>Symbol Nine is for personal use only</u>. Use in a meditative state to bring spiritual guide, power animal or master. Can light a candle and put it in a safe place before beginning. *(The color of the candle is up to the meditating shaman. South Americans light black candles and pray to St. Martin to help them with their psychic abilities. Cobalt blue draws in positive forces and keeps unwanted influences away.)* After spiritual routine, Symbol Nine is projected into air in front of the shaman. The image is held in the mind's eye. This symbol is never sent to another. At the end of the meditation or journey, when communication is over, use Symbol Four and on an out breath, send symbols and energy back to where they came from (the ethers, God, Universal Mind). This same process can be used with present spiritual guides to divine answers to questions. The intention is set before beginning Ama Deus.

10. **Healing to self** - Works with our own heart, and also to mend our broken heart. In silence and privacy, do spiritual routine and imprint symbols. Symbol Ten is visualized in front of the shaman. It is then scooped up with the hands and brought to the heart. *Hands can also be held in the aura over the heart without touching the body. The heart is experienced or visualized as moving into the hands that are holding Symbol Ten. Love, clear, cleanse and caress heart. Then put heart back into the body with symbol in it.* Symbol Ten is the seal, not Symbol Four. In other words, Symbol Ten is left in the heart. Symbol Ten can also be visualized for 20 or so minutes after doing spiritual routine. The shaman simply watches the symbol to see what transpires. S/he may see him/herself and sometimes the symbol becomes a physical object, which the spirit helpers use to heal the shaman.

Can <u>very rarely</u> be used with someone else and only if the shaman is <u>very, very</u> close to the individual. If Symbol Ten is used on someone else, Symbol Three is always used with it, even if the person is in the same room. <u>If this is used on someone else, the shaman must be there for him/her afterwards.</u> The shaman has taken responsibility. What I have found is that when people do not take responsibility for their own healing or participate in the healing process, the healing either does not hold or does not happen at all. Personally, I feel that using Symbol Ten on somebody else is interfering in their lives every bit as much as if I were to tell them what to do. Also, unsolicited advice is unwelcome advice and is very rarely acted upon.

11. **Emergency** for self or other people! Does not have to be used with healing routine - can use Symbol Eleven by itself. Very powerful! Spiral is drawn quickly - from center outwards in both clockwise and counterclockwise directions. Can use both hands and arms. In an emergency, healer does very fast spirals over the head, in front and in back, and then zeroes into the injured area doing the same. Person should be lying down, but in emergencies, <u>it is best to let qualified medical staff move the injured.</u>

Absentee: Do spiritual routine, imprint Symbols One and Two in palms. Think of person and then imprint Symbol Three. Then work symbol; that is, physically move hands in spiraling motion. Requires great concentration.

Concentrated, focused attention is the key to this healing system!

Symbol Eleven does not have to be drawn with the arms. It can also be sent with concentration and the results can be a very powerful energy. Can be used on self or others. Can be used with injuries or any pain.

Symbol Eleven can be used in an emergency when many people who know the symbols are together. Sit in a circle, do spiritual ritual, imprint symbols into the palms of the hands. One person passes the symbol on the breath to the person on their right. Continue around the circle, faster and faster until the circle becomes the symbol. Can do it for political situations, political leaders, etc. Don't use with someone who has a bad heart. Works with very ill and very depressed. If you do spiritual routine, lock in with Symbol Four.

12. This symbol can also be used in an **emergency** when many people who know the symbols are together. Use with ritual. Pass the symbol around the circle in the same way Symbol Eleven is passed. Seal with Symbol Four.

13. For **animals**, birds, etc. Do spiritual ritual and imprint symbols in palms. If absentee, use Symbol Three before imprinting Symbol Thirteen. Can be used for emotional or physical issues, individual animals or species. Lock in with Symbol Four.

14.   To treat or **heal planet Earth.** Do spiritual routine and imprint symbols in palms. Imprint Symbol Fourteen in mind's eye. No absentee symbol is needed because we are on planet Earth. Lock in with Symbol Four.

15.   Use with spiritual routine and imprint symbols in palms. Use this symbol to send a blessing to ourselves or to somebody else on their **birthday**. Our birthday is the beginning of our New Year; in astrology, it is called the solar return, and each solar return has its own sphere of influence until the next birthday. Use Symbol Fifteen for clarity, perception, courage and balance. Lock in with Symbol Four; however, the two horizontal lines of Symbol Fifteen overlay on top of the two horizontal lines in Symbol Four.

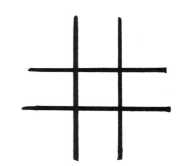

16.   Use with spiritual routine and imprint symbols in palms. Transfer this symbol to a stone. Visualize symbol in your mind's eye, hold the image, and on an out breath of air, send it to the stone. Then go to sleep; it will **invite dreams**. Have paper nearby to write down dreams (all aspects of the dream). Brings about a dream for breakthroughs. Only to be used for the self to help make choices or to determine answers. Don't use every night; use for a turning point. Do not seal with Symbol Four.

17. **To bring into consciousness**, lie down alone in a quiet place. Do spiritual routine and imprint symbols in palms of hands. Hold image and then on an out breath, send Symbol Seventeen away to the ether or Akashic Records. Ask to receive what's useful at this time or ask, "What is it that I need to know at this time?" Symbol Seventeen can bring recollections and visions of past lives. Used only on self. Called mastermind symbol because it connects to superconscious. Close with Symbol Four.

18.   Use on **world leader** or **world situation** or **important causes**. Do spiritual routine and <u>do not</u> ask for a specific outcome. Allow it to work. Can be used with Symbol Fourteen. Afterwards, lock in energy with Symbol Four. This is an adaptation from a time when Symbol Eighteen was sent to chiefs of neighboring tribes.

19. When other symbols don't fit, use Symbol Nineteen to deal with **unknown situation**. Can be used in absentee healing or if person is present. Can be used on self. Do spiritual routine. Imprint symbols in hands. Seal with Symbol Four when finished.

20. For use on **other people's hearts** - physical or emotional. Do spiritual routine. Imprint symbols in palms. Visualize Symbol Twenty and send it to person's heart. Can send it absentee or use it if person is present. Seal with Symbol Four when finished. Personally, I prefer to use Symbol Twenty rather than Symbol Ten for other people. I feel that I have enough of my own 'stuff' to work through without taking on that of somebody else.

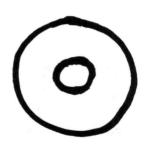

21. **Asking at the time of the full moon** for a particular wish, or to receive an answer to a question. Be clear about request or question before beginning. Do spiritual routine. Imprint symbols in palms. Visualize mastermind symbol (Symbol Seventeen) in third eye. Visualize Symbol Twenty-One in third eye. Images of symbols are held in front of the shaman. Let go and let God. When finished, symbols are sent back to Source where they came from. Do not use absentee symbol. Do this on the evening of the full moon. If full moon is in early morning, can do this the evening before (or evening after). The energy builds up just before an astrological event. This is why the energy is more powerful just before or during an astrological occurrence than the energy just afterwards.

22. Symbol Twenty-Two is used to bring about an **Exorcism**. Symbol Twenty-Three is used to protect the shaman and all who are present. First of all, the individual needs to be aware that an exorcism is going to be performed. Next, do spiritual routine and imprint symbols on palms.

152

23. Begin with Symbol Twenty-Three. It is visualized over the heads of the shaman, all animals who are present and everyone who is in the house except the individual who is being healed. Symbol Twenty-Two is visualized and sent to the individual. When the entity has been freed from the individual, use Symbol Eight and give that spirit the option of going to the Light. Seal with Symbol Four, but keep Symbol Twenty-Three. Symbol Twenty-Three is the last thing that is seen before opening the eyes. At this point, Symbol Twenty-Three can be visualized over the head of the healee. Person has to be willing to let go of the entity.

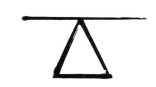

At the end of this chapter, I have included "Procedure for an Exorcism" that was written by Peggy Settle, one of my Tera-Mai™ Seichem Masters. Peggy wrote this during the Shamanic Workshop after watching me use Ama Deus to perform an exorcism on one of her fellow classmates. I believe that her account will also give you an idea of how Ama Deus can be practically used for healing purposes.

24. **To visit a friend.** Do spiritual routine. Imprint symbols in palms. Do not use absentee symbol. Release Symbol Twenty-Four to a friend. Used for friendship and out of love. For use with people who are in body on planet Earth. To find a missing friend or someone else's loved one. Must release outcome to God. No conditions! No exceptions! Seal with Symbol Four.

25. **Eyes** - to help people with their mental, physical and metaphysical vision. Use with spiritual routine and imprint symbols in palms. Visualize Symbol Twenty-Five and send to person's eyes. Symbol Twenty-Five can also be used on self. When finished, picture Symbol Twenty-Five as a seal on eyes.

26. For **infants** - it is gentle enough to be sent absentee or used when baby is present. (Other symbols are too powerful for a newborn. Babies are delicate and healing modalities that are fine for an adult or a child may be too much for a baby; for example, the color purple is too strong for a baby.) Symbol Twenty-Six is used on newborn babies until they are 3 months old for the purpose of sending Light and helping the baby make a smooth transition and ground into the physical body. Do spiritual routine and imprint symbols in palms. Visualize Symbol Twenty-Six. When through, seal with Symbol Four.

When the fetus is in the womb the mother protects it and the soul can attach to the fetus at any time. What I have found is that when pregnant mothers become fully initiated Reiki Masters, their babies are safely born as Reiki Masters. The soul enters the body of the infant with the first breath and it leaves the body with the last breath. In the case of a stillborn, the soul has not been able to enter the physical body. It is far more difficult to come into this world than it is to leave it. When hands-on healing is used on infants, the healing energy will stop flowing when the baby has had enough. When the shaman adds the focus of his/her attention, the energy can quickly become too much. The lines at the top of Symbol Twenty-Six act like a safety valve, releasing excess energy when the baby has had enough.

Personal Observations

1. Before meditation, try repeating "Ama Deus" 3 times and then breathe the breath of God in meditation for 20 minutes. The focus of this exercise is to be in a state of unconditional love.

2. All healing energy that the shaman is attuned to will work with the Ama Deus symbols. The shaman does not have to make a conscious effort to bring in healing energy.

3. In self-healing, individual may see the symbol or self, or both symbol and self in mind's eye.

4. In absentee healing, see symbol and the individual may come into the inner eye as well. The shaman may also see him/herself working with the symbol and spirit helpers. Whatever happens, happens. To try to control the symbol or the outcome interferes with the process.

5. The same holds true when the healee is present. It takes practice and patience. I have my students work on themselves with Symbols Ten, Nineteen, Twenty-Five, Nine and Seventeen before I have them practice on one another.

6. Can use Ama Deus healing system before or after other healing work that is done. If the shaman is impressed to use symbols other than those of Ama Deus, then the system is closed with Symbol Four before any other symbols are used. The more Ama Deus is used, the stronger it gets.

7. Cutting the heads off of black roosters and similar practices work on an extremely low vibration of magic and shamanism. We are moving into a more conscious state of awareness, and with knowledge comes responsibility. I do not recommend practices that involve the sacrifice of another living creature.

8. In journeywork, the shaman always sees him/herself in the mind's eye at the beginning of the journey; in Ama Deus, the shaman begins by seeing the symbols.

9. Journeywork can be accomplished without the steady, repetitive beat of the drum while the shaman is working on his/her clients, or when talking a client through a past life regression. The shaman simply sees him/herself in the mind's inner eye with his/her client. *(The drum integrates and produces higher wave patterns in the brain, which makes journeywork easier.)*

10. Shaman typically work with a small altar nearby whenever doing any kind of shamanic or journeywork. This altar honors the 4 elements and 4 directions. While different indigenous cultures place the elements in different directions, I have found that the following works for me: Fire (candle) in East, vessel of water in South, stone or crystal in West, knife with white handle or feather in North.

11. Healee can visualize him/herself in mind's eye and observe healing process, can center in his/her heart chakra, or breathe the breath of God to help initiate healing.

Procedure for an Exorcism

1. Have a white candle burning.

2. Ask for angels of protection and angels of love to stand on either side of everyone present.

3. Ama Deus spiritual routine.

4. Visualize Symbol Twenty-Three and energize with 3rd eye. Visually place this symbol over self and over anyone else in the room. Sometimes this symbol is seen over the head; other times, it encompasses the entire body.

5. Hold client's second toes with your thumbs on the bottom of the toes and middle fingers on the top. Visualize and energize symbol Twenty-Two in mind's eye. Energize the symbol with heart love energy and breathe it out your mouth and up through the meridian lines and/or through the central channel. Focus on the crown chakra when breathing in; never breathe in through your mouth the negative energy from the client. Repeat the process of sending Symbol Twenty-Two to the client several times while holding onto the toes. Check in with client by asking him/her what s/he is experiencing. Oftentimes, they will have an uncomfortable sensation in their abdomens. Our will centers are found behind the solar plexus and 3rd eye and are the locations for most entities. So, also blow Symbol Twenty-Two into these locations for exorcisms. Again, never breathe in client's negativity. After breathing symbols out of the mouth, lift your head, focus on your crown and breathe in through your crown. Once Ama Deus is opened, any of the Ama Deus symbols can be used, such as Nineteen (unknown situation), Twenty (other people's hearts) or Twenty-Five (eyes) at the 3rd eye.

6. Send the entity to the Light (or its rightful place in the universe) with Symbol Eight. Tell them that they are loved, blessed, healed and forgiven, and ask them to take the hand of an angel and go to the Light. Also, have the client repeat three times: FROM THE LORD GOD OF MY BEING TO THE LORD GOD OF THE UNIVERSE. I FORGIVE MYSELF. I LOVE MYSELF UNCONDITIONALLY. I AM THE ONLY AUTHORITY IN MY LIFE. SO BE IT AND SO IT IS.

7. This procedure can be used to integrate the shadow self. This is an eye-opener for many people when they discover that the entity who has been haunting them is actually a past life. Symbol Eight can help that part of the soul reach a state of forgiveness and bliss.

8. Ask the client to bring in the pink light of compassion and exhale it to the entity(ies).

9. Visualize Symbol Twenty-Three again and see it on the client (if cleared), yourself and anybody else who is in the room.

10. Close with Symbol Four and place all symbols except Twenty-Three in Symbol Four.

I have found during the Shamanic Workshops that I teach that 98% of the people who take the class are able to see and experience themselves journeying in the three spiritual worlds that I describe in the chapter, "Hawaiian Shamanism and the Goddess". Those who cannot journey are those who have problems visualizing, and I highly recommend that people practice visualization exercises that are found in either Reiki & Other Rays of Touch Healing or other books before

156

taking the Shamanic Workshop. Visualizing with the mind's inner eye is a skill that can be learned.

I have also found that of those who are able to journey, only those who are channeling healing and psychic energy are able to do effective healings and divinations in the Otherworlds. So, I added a series of initiations to the Shamanic Workshop so that the participants would be able to participate. These initiations include the Order of Melchizedek and the first Enochian Magic Initiation (both of which are described in the chapter, "Initiation"), Violet Flame Attunement (transformation), YOD (intuition), and the Seven Rays (balance).

The initiation into the Seven Rays is at the heart and opens the jewel-like chakras in the palms and fingers. When I was in Holland in November 1996, Mary revealed to me that within her heart are not seven sorrows or seven swords! What is in her heart is that which is in the heart of all true wise women, shaman and magicians; that is, she is connected to and receives Universal Energy from what the Native Americans refer to as the seven directions. These directions are east (fire), south (water), west (earth), north (air), above (Father-God), below (Mother-God) and within (where our own individuality takes form within the greater Universal Mind). This connection expands our awareness, helps us to see all of the aspects of an issue and enables us to help keep our perspective of who we are in relationship to the Greater Whole.

When we are connected to the Universal Patterns of Creation, we are in tune with the Mind of God. That in turn brings about synchronicity, which creates a joyful flow to life. In healing and divination, this means that the channels connecting us to the Seven Rays are open, which allows information and energy to come to us from these sources which are supportive to all metaphysical work that is done. Once these channels are open, it is up to the shaman to keep them open by honoring nature, Father-God (teacher, consoler, protector, left-brained technology), Mother-God (nurturer, creator, destroyer, right-brained creativity), and him/herself.

When we can honor ourselves, we can honor others and nature. We can also clearly see our own truth and how closely our personal truth comes to Universal Truth. We can see where it is that we are only kidding ourselves. While we may be able to deceive ourselves for a short time, we can never fool God. When we can feel and release our buried terror, rage and grief and forgive ourselves and others, then we can let go of our ego-centered agendas and connect with our own higher selves. One way to release unresolved, negative emotions is to work with a healer. As negative emotions come up the healer encourages the healee to feel the emotion and go with it to see where it leads. Fear might lead to a childhood incident where anger was suppress; childhood anger might lead to suppressed rage from a past life. It is like these negative emotions are connected to a dark, unseen timeline. There are blockages along the timeline when in a particular time and place emotions were trapped. As we feel and release these negative emotions, we can begin to let go and let God. Then with a consciousness that is at peace and with an open heart, Truth can bring us back to wholeness, joyful anticipation and participation.

Healings become multifaceted when the healer is connected to and is utilizing the healing rays from all four elements (earth, air, fire and water). The healing energy becomes intense and viewers can become participants as they are drawn into the drama. I was a workshop facilitator at a conference on angels when CBS was in New Mexico filming the material that they were going to use for a segment on angels on Connie Chung's Eye to Eye. Some of the organizers of the conference were going through their own issues, which proved to be so draining that I asked two women to work on me as we were driving out to an old mission. When we arrived at the site the film crew set up their equipment outside and I did a small ceremony honoring the four directions and at the same time, called in archangels to assist in healing. I do not see spirit often! When I do see them I know that something is up. As I called in the spiritual forces, I heard the elementals in the trees and then I happened to look over at the cameraman – there were elementals all over him. (Later, Jay told me that if he had spent $60,000 he would not have been able to get the beautiful color effects that he had gotten during that filming.) Then I concentrated my attention on Deborah Forill, who had asked for a healing. During the healing session she had a dramatic emotional release! When we were through the producer could barley walk over to where we were standing. He leaned against the stone altar and said, "I felt everything that she went through." He had gone through his own healing release while Deborah went through hers.

Ama Deus and other forms of legitimate healing are more than a warm, comforting touch. In addition, it is possible to heal someone who is not in the same room or even the same state. Einstein proved that our concept of time and space is an illusion. Time and space are interconnected. So, if our reality is relative and I am speaking to somebody on the telephone, if I can honestly listen to that person then s/he is drawn into my space. If that individual feels that I am listening compassionately then I am drawn into his/her space. *"Dear Kathleen, I heard you speaking and healing on the radio 99.5 WBAT in New York late one night. I was amazed at how you could hear a voice and make a spiritual connection and begin to heal and clear blockages on people and how they would respond and say yes that they felt something moving inside of them or other sensations. It was truely amazing."* Miguel A. Torres, Elmhurst, New York

Tera-Mai™ Seichem I

Using Healing Energy Without Outside Aids

Traditional Seichem passes down fire energy with the grounding qualities of earth (Reiki). Tera-Mai™ Seichem is an initiation into all 4 elements:

Earth (Reiki) healing energy is experienced as hot and cold (just like the surface of the planet). Grounds all other healing energy. Hand positions parallel to Earth's surface are most effective.

Fire (Sakara) is **clearly** and **immediately** distinguished as pulses of low-voltage electricity which feels like the prickling of pins and needles. Works in the aura as well as the physical body.

Water (Sophi-El) waves of cool energy. Brings up deep emotional issues for healing.

Air (Angeliclight) 2-fold energy of air & spirit. Brings about mental healing and enhancement of the power of the third eye and spoken word. Healer and healee often experience the presence of angels.

Initiation: The group sits in a circle with their backs to the center of the circle. The chakras are more exposed on the back, so in this way, initiates may feel somebody else being initiated. The intention of the circle is to help the initiate integrate the initiation so that s/he can more fully participate in practicing the ancient art of hands-on healing. Prior to the initiation, I call in the angels and guides and then lead the group on a meditation to help them to prepare for their initiation. I will then come to each person in the group. I will place my hands on their shoulders. Then I will draw and then breathe symbols into the palms of their hands. When I tap the initiates on the shoulders the first time, they put their hands in prayer position above their heads. I will blow the symbols into the palms of their hands and then gently clap the outside of their hands so as to seal the energy in. I will then gently lift their heads by placing my thumbs on the mastoid process (the bump in the skull that separates head and neck) - this runs the energy through all of the chakras. After the crown has been opened, the same process will be repeated at the third eye, throat and heart chakras. Afterwards, everyone will have an opportunity to share.

All healing comes from Mother-Father God; we are facilitators of healing energy. The initiation opens the initiate to healing qualities of the 4 elements as described briefly above. The initiation also starts a 21-day cleansing cycle of the 7 major chakras - 3 cycles beginning at the root chakra. During this time, the initiate is wide open; that is, it is an excellent opportunity to release old 'stuff. However, if the initiate chooses to hold onto heavy thoughts and dismal emotions, then more of the same will come the initiate's way. This is one reason why I offer reinitiations on a donations-are-accepted basis; if the initiate gets into trouble, s/he still is afforded another opportunity to connect to healing rays.

Laying on of hands: We will not be working with crystals, herbs or essential oils. We will learn to trust the Universal healing energy that flows into our crowns and out our hands. Each class member will be worked on and have the opportunity to practice on fellow students. One person will lie on the table and everyone else will simply pick a spot. We will allow the energy to run for awhile and then I will ask the individual who is lying down what they are seeing or feeling from, let's say, the hands that are on his/her head. After the healee responds, I will ask the individual who belongs to those hands what s/he is seeing or feeling. In this way, initiates will gain a healthy confidence, and at the same time, observe how healing energy can be experienced in many different ways. Initiates will begin to understand how to ask questions of their clients and get them actively involved in the healing process. Initiates will begin learning how to communicate with the angels and spirit guides who are the ones doing the actual healing.

Some of the things initiates learn firsthand:
• It helps to talk to the client before the session to find out what their symptoms are.
• Sometimes, the healer experiences heat while the healee feels cold energy coming from the healer's hands, and vice versa. Other times, the sensations are similar. This is one reason why hands-on healing is called an art form - there are no hard-and-fast rules as to how the healings will transpire.
• If there is throbbing under the healer's hands, negativity is being broken up as though a spirit jackhammer is being used. Keep hand(s) there until the throbbing stops. Sometimes, the healee will experience throbbing and the healer doesn't. In this case, the healee needs to tell the healer when the throbbing is finished. Other times, both the healer and healee will experience throbbing.
• If healer's hands become heavy, they are filling with negativity and this heavy sensation needs to be pulled off of the client. This is done slowly! So as not to trash the room with psychic debris, by the healer's intention, psychic debris is taken up through the 7 levels to the Light for transformation or sent down to the central fire, into the Violet Flame or into a physical dish of salt water (that is next to the client and healer) for transformation. Some healers like to feed the trees; that is, just as trees transmute carbon dioxide into oxygen, so too, they transform our negativity into positive energy. (Tree huggers are not as foolish as they appear on the outside, and both of these qualities inherent in trees are very good reasons to stop cutting them down and

160

use hemp (marijuana) for paper and alternative building materials.) Whenever negativity is pulled out of the healee, the healer needs to fill the void with healing. The healer simply placing his/her hands on the healee accomplishes this.

• Sometimes, heavy negativity will come up past the healer's hands and be released through the healer's wrists or elbows. If the negativity goes past the elbows, the healer simply excuses him/herself, goes to a sink and washes his/her arms with cold water. This cleanses and releases misqualified energy in the hands and arms. Some healers do this after each session in order to keep clear.

• After grabbing the "negativity", the healer makes counterclockwise circles to help loosen the "stuff". One clockwise circle helps to "stir up" the energy, then the healer can continue with counterclockwise circles. Again, the heaviness is released to the Light, fire or water, as described on the previous page.

• "Negativity" can also be released by the healer laying his/her hands over the area, closing his/her eyes, and visualizing his/her physical arms turning into the arms of a large electromagnet. Negativity is drawn up to the healer's arms just as iron pellets are drawn to the arms of the magnet. Lifting his/her arms slowly, the healer lifts the "stuff" up through the 7 layers (which are associated with the 7 chakras). The healer will feel as though s/he is lifting a noticeable weight; the healee may either feel the pull as the debris is going out of him/her, or the healee will feel noticeably lighter afterwards. At the 7th layer, the healer flips his/her hands over (which changes the polarity of the magnet) and sends the "negativity" into the Light. The healer's hands give an additional push to send the misqualified energy into the Light for transformation. This is the first step in learning psychic surgery.

• To drain any residue: Left hand in the <u>aura</u> above the issue; fingers of the right hand are pointed straight down to the earth. The 'stuff' comes into left hand, moves to right hand and then shoots down to the central fire for transformation.

• After pulling off and draining, clean hands by shaking them and clicking fingers. By the healer's intention, the psychic debris is sent down to the fire or up to the Light for transformation. Then the healer places his/her hands back on the client and fills the void with healing. Healer and/or healee can visualize and observe. Oftentimes, they both see the same colors or events transpiring; other times, they see the same results but different metaphors.

Sometimes people ask me to assist them in understanding their visualizations. Virginia was having trouble letting go of her issue of control. I suggested that she ask her angels to show her what her foundation of control looked like. They showed her a filthy, black square. Rising up out of the square was a white podium for her to stand upon. When I asked her what shape the podium was, she answered, "It is a square." I responded, "This is what I am getting. First of all, if goodness and evil were shapes, goodness would be a circle, which is open, free and allowing; a square is tight, closed and rigid. What they are showing you is that you are trying to build a new foundation on top of the old one which has outlived any possible kind of purpose it might have originally served. You cannot shake off your panic and fear. Work in meditation with your angels to blow up the black square and bring in a solid new foundation. When I did this exercise with my angels, they had me carry bags of smelly, old garbage out of my house. I continued to do this for months, and then one time I thought to ask them to show me what I had cleared out. They showed me a mountain.

• When in doubt, the healer asks his/her angels and guides what to do. The healer does this simply by closing his/her eyes, asking what needs to be done and then waiting to see what messages spirit brings. But even more importantly, it is up to the healer to keep checking in with the healee to find out what is going on with him/her.

• When we visualize ourselves, we are activating the holographic mind. By the nature of the hologram, when we make changes in a part of the hologram, we make changes in the whole of the hologram. When we are using Universal healing energy in nonordinary reality, we bring about changes in this reality.

• Healees can also activate the holographic mind and utilize healing energy channeled by the healer to make changes. Further participation from the client can be solicited by asking questions: "What does the negativity look like?" Or "Ask your own angels to show you what the negativity looks like." Then, "How do you want to release this?" They can visualize fire, Light, water, angelic dynamite, or ask for angels, nature spirits or power animals to assist. The possibilities are endless.

• Before working on the symptoms, the healer cleans up mental and emotional issues behind the dis-ease. (Emotions are thought forms with a learned sensation.)

• Mental healing - (Is described later in this chapter under "Touch points to hold for specific issues".) Healer can also make suggestions such as: Breathe away judgements and breathe in allowing. Breathe away destructive programs about yourself and breathe in positive affirmations that your family and friends love and like about you. Breathe away thought forms that are outside of Universal Truth. See them leaving like old, dusty library books, and breathe in sunshine yellow light and Divine Truth.

• Emotional healing - (is described under "Touch points to hold for specific issues") There is a will center behind the solar plexus. People who have negative thought forms that have taken them over have given their will away. These entities often harbor in the solar plexus. Be watchful and listen to what the client is saying. Should they say that a voice speaks to them from the solar plexus, know that it is not their own voice that they are hearing. My sister-in-law, Jill Milner, who is also a nurse, said that what I wrote about the grays in <u>Reiki & Other Rays of Touch Healing</u> made a lot of sense to her. That is, rather than having mental patients deny their experiences or drug them out so that they will not remember, have them work through their experiences and then give them tools to use, like cobalt blue. She suggested that this same process could also be used with people who have other kinds of mental torture chambers. "Mental patients" who see and/or hear spirits all of the time are psychics that are out of control. They are lacking what, for practical purposes, might be called an etheric filter. They are letting everything from other dimensions in. <u>Variation of Rosalyn Bruyere's Chelation:</u> This is magnetic healing, so once the healer's hands touch the healee's body, the healer keeps at least one hand on the healee at all times. To prepare, rub hands together. Then rub the right hand down (down only) the left arm, and then the left hand down the right arm. Healer centers him/herself at Hara (about 3 inches below belly button) and feels the vertical line running through his/her center. Following that energy channel down to the heart of Mother Earth, the healer grounds and feels healing energies from Mother Earth coming back up through the channels to the solar plexus. Here, the healer feels the will center in the solar plexus and follows the vertical line up past the crown and up to Universal Source. The healer brings back Universal Energy into the crown and down through the vertical channel. Then the healer visualizes colors running into and through the chakras. *(This is also a good way for a healer to end a session; that is, by talking his/her client through the visualization.)*

• Begin session by holding onto the bottoms of both feet. Specifically, touch the solar plexus point in the center of the foot and any other point on the foot that calls out for attention.
• The healer keeps his/her hand on the sole of the foot furthest from him/her and moves the other hand to the ankle of the same foot. Healer runs energy between his/her hands. The energy sensation starts out like a ping-pong ball and increases to a buzz. Then the healer allows his/her etheric hand to slip into the ankle (guides and angels assist the healer). Negativity may look like a dark spot or it may present itself as a visual metaphor, and this is grabbed hold of with the healer's etheric hand. It may explode in his/her etheric hand. Or s/he can grab it with his/her etheric hand and then will his/her etheric hand back into his/her physical hand. When the negativity is in the healer's physical hand, s/he pulls it out slowly and throws it down to the central fire, violet flame or dish of salt water, or takes it up to the Light for transformation. Sometimes, the healer will find a plug that has a mucus-like substance behind it. If so, the plug is removed, the mucus is scooped out and the area is drained. If the plug has an etheric cord attached to it, this cord represents a timeline that travels back through to past lives where this issue has also been a problem. The healer pulls out the plugs and cords until s/he reaches the root cause of the pain or disease. Sometimes, the healer needs to yank quickly to pull this final plug out. Again, the area is scooped and drained. When it has been cleaned out, with clean hands, the healer places his/her hands back on the body, fills the void with cobalt blue and then seals

163

with the color(s) the angels bring in. Often, the sealing color is gold. *(Sometimes, if the client is strong enough, the angels will fill the area with gold rather than blue and then seal in another color.)*

• To clean his/her hands, the healer can shake the debris off or click his/her fingers with the intention that the debris go to the fire or Light for transformation. It is important to do this every time misqualified energy is pulled off of the healee.

• Next step: Slowly, the healer moves his/her hands (one at a time) to the sole and ankle of the foot that is closest to him/her and follows the same procedure as described above.

• Next step: The healer continues up the healee's body, joint by joint, alternating from one side of the body to the other. So, the next step would be the ankle and knee of the leg that is furthest away from the healer. In the following order, the next steps are:

• Ankle and knee of the leg that is closest to the healer.

• Knee and hip joint of the leg that is furthest away from the healer.

• Knee and hip joint of the leg that is closest to the healer.

• Then move one hand to the second chakra and place the other hand between the legs of the client **at his/her knees.** The healer should never become a part of the healee's problem. Clean out the root chakra **in the aura above the root chakra** (the healer does not touch the healee's root chakra with his/her hands - the healer should not become a part of the healee's problem), using the same technique that is used on the joints.

• The healer continues to work up the chakras, remembering to keep one hand on the body at all times.

• Hands and arms can be worked on in the same way in which feet and legs were.

• This same technique can be used up the spine.

• When the healer is through, it is helpful to clear the aura and place the client in a ball of golden light by asking the angels to do this. The healer can ask the angels to fill the golden ball with high vibrational healing energy and then ground the golden ball in ruby red. It is the angels' idea of a bandage.

To begin seeing into the human body (Angeliclight aspect of Tera-Mai™ Seichem helps to do this): This is what I do, and I know that other psychics work differently. Lots of techniques work! The third eye has two centers - one at the forehead and the other between the eyebrows. Focusing on the center between my eyebrows, keeping my physical eyes soft, I ask to see inside of the body. Sometimes the organ or bone will appear in a vision above the physical body; other times, I will see into the body. Sometimes, I will see the organ as it is in physical reality or only parts of it at a time. Sometimes, I will see organs as a cartoon-like representation, or I will see the physical problem as it exists, or I may see the thought form behind the dis-ease. *For example,*

*I once saw a large, coiled snake in Randi Wann's belly, and it looked more real than any snake I have ever seen. **But** it was like the vision of this snake was cut into squares. It was as though I was viewing the snake through nine different television sets, but not all of them were turned on at the same time. Thus, I never saw the snake in its entirety; I only could see one or more parts at a time. When I caught a glimpse of the snake's jaws, I could see that they were holding onto a section of her small intestine. When I touched Randi's body at that point and asked her what was going on, she told me that that was where her most severe pain was. I asked the angels what to do. They told me to close my eyes and visualize myself opening the snake's jaws and then lifting it out of Randi's belly. As I did this visually, I moved my physical hands and arms, using the same movements as I saw myself doing in the vision. Randi's pain subsided after the snake was removed. I then scooped out the mucus-like residue left behind, drained, cleaned my hands and then filled the space with healing.*

<u>Touch points to hold for specific issues.</u> Many of these are derived from Hanna Kroeger's video tape, <u>Hands-On Healing</u> and her book, <u>New Dimensions in Healing</u>: If the client is in so much pain that s/he cannot identify what is going on, I do the pain drain first and fill the space with healing so s/he can concentrate on what the angels bring up for him/her to look at. In almost all other cases, I do the emotional and mental releases first:

Emotional release: Healer places his/her left hand on the solar plexus and keeps it there no matter what! Healer moves his/her right hand to the following points on the healee's body: Palm of right hand, left shoulder, palm of left hand, right shoulder. Fear can be found anywhere in the body, but it is commonly held in the throat. When we clutch, often we cannot utter a sound. So when the healer's hand is at the healee's shoulders, fear from the healee's throat can come into the healer's hands to be removed. Sophi-El will form the 'negativity' in the solar plexus into a ball. The ball will either be burned up under the healer's hand by the Sakara energy, or the ball can be pulled out after the healer touches the healee's left shoulder. The whole process takes about 20 minutes. When the ball is pulled out, it can look like barbed wire. The neck and solar plexus are drained and filled with healing.

Mental clearing: Place the palms of hands on the head of the humerus as it drops from the shoulder. Healer's fingertips should be pointing towards the healee's hands. Healee should have hands off of his/her body because the mental negativity often flows down and out through the healee's arms, hands and fingertips.

Brain integration: Left hand on the forehead, right hand at the back of the head.

Bones: Right hand at the back of the neck (the touch point is between the 7th cervical and 1st thoracic vertebrae, left hand on the inside of upper left arm.

Dropped organs: (a cup is formed at the throat by the collarbones and sternum). Healee lies on his/her back; healer is at the healee's right side. 1) <u>Healer puts middle finger of his/her left hand in the cup and pulls **slightly** towards him/herself</u>. The healer's right hand sweeps **slowly** up the right side of the body about three inches above the body. The healer repeats this sweeping movement three times (or in multiples of three). When the healer brings his/her right hand back to begin the sweep, s/he raises his/her right hand way above the aura so that s/he does not pull the organs back down again. 2) <u>Healer moves middle finger of left hand to the top of the sternum</u> and gently pushes down, sweeping with his/her right hand in the same manner, but this time up the center of the body. 3) As this is magnetic healing, the healer touches the healee's body as s/he moves to healee's left side. <u>Middle finger of healer's right hand is placed in the cup and s/he pulls slightly towards him/herself</u>. Healer sweeps up the left side of the body in the same manner as described above. 4) To ground the healing, the healer holds the healee's ankles on the inside of the legs until throbbing stops.

Glands: On the front of the body - hands over floating ribs. On the back of the body - hands over the adrenals.

Heart: For physical healing, right hand holds heel of left hand. Left hand to left shoulder and then left hand to right shoulder. For heart issues, left hand holds heel of right hand.

Kidney: On the back, place right hand on left kidney and left hand on right kidney.

Ligaments: On the upper right arm - left hand on the point where the biceps becomes tendinous and right hand on the point where the triceps becomes tendinous.

Lungs: Right hand on the forehead and left hand at the back of the head. Also, on the chest between the 2nd and 3rd ribs.

Lymph system: Right hand under the left armpit, left hand on back of neck.

Muscles: Point just below the flexed calf muscles of both legs.

Nerves: Just below top of the knees at the kneecaps.

Reproductive organs: Inside lower leg just below the knees (not if woman is pregnant - can cause miscarriage.)

Spine: Right hand at the back of the neck and left hand on the tailbone.

Spleen: Right hand in the right armpit and left hand just to the left of solar plexus (over spleen).

Tailbone adjustment: Healee is lying on his/her stomach; healer is standing at healee's right side. 1) Hold touch point for the spine. 2) Move right hand to tailbone and take hold of the ankle of the right foot. **Gently** (knees are very sensitive) move foot towards buttock and find the resistance point. Gently move lower leg slightly past resistance point three times or repeat movement in multiples of three. 3) Hold lower leg perpendicular to table and move lower right leg gently towards the left leg and find resistance point. Gently move lower leg slightly past resistance point three times or in multiples of three. 4) Hold lower leg perpendicular to table and move lower right leg gently away from the left leg and find resistance point. Gently move lower leg slightly past resistance point in the same manner. 5) Healee's right leg is lying on the table. Take hold of the whole leg from underneath and circle inward three times or in multiples of three. 6) Move to healee's left side, healer places left hand over tailbone and repeats entire process for left leg. A cracking sound can be heard as the tailbone slips back into place. The client's leg should be completely relaxed during the process. People who have trouble sitting for any length of time typically have their tailbones out. Hanna Kroeger uses this on leukemia patients. She has found that because the tailbone is out, the lymph is not being pumped, and this is what causes leukemia. (Liposuction to remove fat also removes lymph, which is why people who have had liposuction can later look like cottage cheese.) When the lymph begins to be pumped through the body, the leukemia is reversed. This whole procedure is demonstrated in <u>Hands-On Healing</u> and can be easily and painlessly performed by a qualified therapist.

Toxins & parasites: Make claws out of the hands and sweep through the aura, starting at the back of the head, and **slowly** move down the front of the center of the body (2 times). Throw "stuff" down to central fire and wash etheric hands. Clear the chakras by clawing slowly through the aura above each chakra. Do this in both directions - left to right and right to left. Praying or visualizing always helps. Other techniques for clearing, such as sacred geometry from the Circles of Life, works. 8-7-3-1-2 is God's telephone number. For clearing or releasing, circle counterclockwise with left hand while repeating 8-7-3-1-2. For integrating healing, circle clockwise with right hand while repeating 8-7-3-1-2. I have personally found that people who cannot hold a spinal adjustment from a chiropractor, or who have many allergies, have extremely toxic physical bodies.

To close any session: Client is lying on back. 1) Healer's right hand on the solar plexus and left hand at the very top of left leg. 2) Switch - left hand on the solar plexus and right hand at the top of the right leg.

Variation of SHEN, as developed by a Texas physicist which works with the meridian lines and chakras of the human body. It also works on the reverse flow of the natural energy movement in the human body; that is, we usually bring in prana through our left hand, left foot and the left side of our body. Because we are not stagnant, energy leaves through our right hand, right foot and the right side of our body. SHEN is like reversing the flow of a river so that the debris that has wedged its way snugly into the river bottom can be exposed, brought to the surface and released.

If I want to dowse the chakras before beginning to see where the healee is at, I ask to see the health of the chakras. The pendulum should move in a clockwise circle, and all of the circles (chakras) should be roughly the same size. The entire process is demonstrated on the <u>Healing Animals</u> video. Using the Angeliclight, my voice activates the energy as I talk my client through the process:

"See the color red at the sole of your right foot. Beautiful, bright, clear shades of red. Scarlet, crimson, rose red. Bring this red color into your right foot and fill your right foot with red healing color. Move the red color up to your right ankle. Into your lower right leg. Into your right knee. Right thigh. Up to the right hip." As Sakara works in the aura field or astral body, I use my hands and move the energy up through the aura above my client (I do not touch the physical body) while I am talking my client through the process. Speaking helps move the energy and initiate healing. *"Now move the color red across and through your root chakra to the left side of your body. Feel the red color cleanse and heal the root chakra. Release any misuse or abuse of power. Feel any psychic debris being released and transmuted. Feel the root chakra opening and receiving earth energy. Feel the cleansing within your body. See the color red moving into your left hip and down your left leg. Through the thigh to the left knee. Feel the release. Down through the lower left leg to the left ankle. Into the left foot and out through the bottom of the left foot. Down to the central sun for transformation."* Repeat 2 more times for a total of 3 times.

Continue same process for the other chakras, using colors and descriptions that are appropriate - Orange for the 2nd or creative chakra (inner child). Yellow for the 3rd chakra (will center). Green for the heart chakra - (love and compassion). Blue for the throat (creative expression and release of fear). Indigo for the third eye (love and will center). Purple for the crown chakra (surrender to God and identification of true self). I can work with the symptoms exhibited by my client; for example, if my client has thyroid problems, I may want to add, *"Move the color blue from the left side of your neck and into the throat chakra. Feel, see the blue color in the thyroid gland.* • • • I can finish with the color gold and move it up the right side of the body, through each chakra and up to the solar star chakra that is about 3 inches above the crown. *"Feel the Light pouring from the Soul Star into your crown chakra and down through the left side of your body. Feel the healing energy moving freely between the soul and your physical body. Feel the healing energy touching the chakra that is 12 inches below your feet. Ground."*

Psychic Surgery, utilizing the other rays of touch healing. Prior to psychic surgery, I find that it is helpful to discover where and what symptoms the healee is manifesting. I can call in guides and angels to assist. I can visualize cobalt blue:

1) **To open the aura**: Malachite and azurite stones are placed on the solar plexus. If I do not have those stones, I ask the angels to give them to me. Reaching up with my left hand (receiving hand), and feeling the weight of each stone in my hand, I then move my hand slowly to the solar plexus, and place the stones one at a time on the solar plexus. Clients often feel the weight of the stones on their body. Some people see the etheric stones. I can also put azurite on the throat. Coning the fingers of my left hand so that the Sakara energy comes out in a single beam, in the aura over the part of the body I am going to work on, I make four right-angle cuts with the beam of electricity that is coming out of my fingers. There is a <u>noticeable</u> difference in the field above the body. Clients may feel colder in that part of their body. (In the class, students also feel a noticeable difference before and after the aura is cut open. Or if just part of the aura is cut open, there is a noticeable difference in the energy field where the aura has been cut open and where it has not been cut open.) If clients need a blanket or want their coat thrown over them, the healing energy will work through cloth.

2) **To cut out psychic debris**: Oftentimes, I see a field of cobalt blue within which are black forms. In a counterclockwise motion, I trace around the outside of the black objects over and over again with the coned fingers of my right hand in the aura. As I do this, a line of white begins separating the black from the blue. Sometimes, these forms have roots that go to other parts of the body. If so, I can open the aura further as I am working with the beam that is coming out of my coned fingers, and then trace around the roots with my coned fingers. If there is a bad smell or if I see rust, these are indications that the issue is very old and I am going to have to spend more time on that particular issue and blockage. I keep talking to the angels and asking what it is they want to do. Angels have a sense of humor and will bring in such tools as "angelic rust dissolvent". I can ask my client what s/he is feeling or seeing. While I am working with my right hand, I can hold my left hand parallel to the body. My left hand works like a suction tube, drawing psychic debris into my left hand, which is then burned and transmuted by the Sakara energy. When the white line becomes thicker, I can drop my etheric hand into the body and take out the foreign objects as the angels cut them free. (In class, for those students who cannot see as yet, I ask them to go through the motions or rely on what their feelings are telling them to do and ask for feedback from the individual they are working on. <u>It is not as important for the healer to see as it is for the client to experience an actual healing.</u>)

I do not see Holy Spirit often with my physical eyes. When I do, I see beings that are more colorful and real than exist in form in our 3-dimensional reality. We all exist on other realities; for example, our astral body is seen in the same dimension that angels and spirit guides are seen. Sometimes, I can see the whole astral body of the healee when I am working or I will see the organ that the angels are working on. Sometimes, I will see the organ hovering over the physical body as it is supposed to look. I watch as the angels take away the diseased or deformed image of the organ within the body and replace it with the healthy image that was above the body. My students and clients refer to this as an organ transfer (only they do not need $30,000 worth of drugs each year to keep the body from rejecting the angelic replacement). In England, Sophia Lucia felt a hole in her body where her liver used to be. Naturally, she was a bit disturbed but was able to relax when she experienced a new liver coming in. Then, Sophia realized that the reason she was not taking oxygen into her lungs was because they were no longer there. Because the angels had worked on her liver first, Sophia had confidence in them to 'fix her up' with new lungs. When the angels do this, I believe that what I am observing is what 'modern medicine' refers to as spontaneous healing and I never know when these kinds of healings are going to occur. In addition, my students have gotten back to me with similar healing incidents that came out of nowhere, which left the doctors perplexed.

The key to psychic surgery, or actually any kind of healing, is to work with the angels and spirit guides. If I have a question, I ask them what to do. As the angels are the ones in charge and know what it is they are doing, everything that comes up for release and healing are issues that they can take care of. Once when I opened the entire aura of one of my clients, one of my students asked why the crown chakra was not cut. I answer by saying, *"I am not the one who is doing the cutting; the angels are."* The spiritual healers and angels are the ones who are doing this psychic surgery. The visuals I am given, what I hear and feel, are messages sent to me by the angels as I work. When in doubt, I ask 3 times if they or the message is in the Light of Christ or in Divine Truth. Clients can also provide important information in the form of feedback, or help by visualizing their own body to see what is going on. This is only one way in which the angels work. When my daughter dislocated her left knee while skiing, stretching tendons and muscles, after cutting the aura and removing negative blocks, I was impressed to make counterclockwise circles with my coned fingers. As I did this, she could feel the tendons and muscles becoming tighter. When the angels are through, the energy flowing from my hands lessens considerably, so there was never a danger of too much tightening of her tendons. The next day, Jennifer had light, thin, feather-like marks that resembled stitches after surgery on the back of her left knee. I think that the angels were trying to tell her, *"We are here."* Jennifer's knee stopped popping out.

During what I call psychic surgery, I can place my hands on the injured, diseased or troubled area, or on the corresponding touch point on the body for the tissue, organ or gland, and the angels will slip their hands through mine. In this case, I do not move my hands - although I can watch with my eyes open or closed to see what they are doing, tune into movement under my hands and ask my client questions, if that is appropriate. In cases where the individual does not want to be touched or cannot be touched physically, it is possible to do the entire healing process in the aura.

3) **To drain:** When the last of the negativity or the last plug has been pulled off, I scoop and drain the pus-like substance. I may want to begin filling the void with cobalt blue before I begin draining, which helps to sanitize the space. If there is a lot of mucus, I may want to start by asking the angels to fill large buckets with the mucus. When I see that the buckets are full, I grab hold of them, first with my etheric hand and then with my physical hand, and take the buckets up to the Light for transformation. If the draining needs to go on for several days (the angels will let me know), I ask the angels to put in etheric drain tubes - some of which go up to the Light and others go down to the central fire. So that the draining does not create a void, I ask that an etheric I.V. be placed in the crown. Oftentimes, these tubes can physically be felt. They will be there for 3 days unless the healee continues to visualize them; that is, the healee asks the angels if the tubes still need to be in place, and if so, the healee asks that this particular healing modality continue. Asking the angels to bring in cobalt blue cauterizes, sanitizes and heals. The area is then sealed with gold. If the angels bring in other colors, then that is what is needed.

4) **To give healee back his/her aura:** I take off the etheric azurite and malachite with my right hand (giving hand). Moving my hand up slowly, I give the stones back to the angels and thank them. I ask the angels for pink quartz for the heart. I reach up and take the etheric stone in my left hand and slowly bring it down and place it on the healee's heart. Then I ask for amethyst for the third eye, and I repeat the same procedure. I move my hands in the field above the body. That's it! The angels give the healee back his/her aura. **It is important to give the healee back his/her aura!** The healee would get his/her aura back in a matter of time, but I would not want to send anyone away without one.

Where did the aura go when it was cut away? I believe that the angels take it to another dimension and work on it. I never have a sense of it being anywhere around the healee or myself, and it comes back in better shape than before it left. If any additional aura work is required, this is the time to do it - when the aura has been returned. The healer cannot work on the aura if it's not there. Individuals who say that they can see etheric holes in the wall or holes in the sky are in reality seeing holes in their own aura. To permanently heal the aura, the thought forms behind the holes need to be changed, or the healee needs to address alcohol or drug issues.

5) **Angelic bandage:** I ask the angels to surround the healee in a golden bubble and to fill the

bubble with high vibrational medicine - symbols, musical tones, flower remedies, herbs, colors. Then I ask the angels to ground the golden bubble with ruby red. To help bring this into physical form, I feel the golden bubble with my physical hands as it is being created. This, too, will last for 3 days unless the client reactivates the energy. These healings often continue for a month or more.

I have seen instant physical healings, while other people need time. There are no guarantees; however, changes in the spiritual subtle bodies will bring about changes in the physical. It is the nature of the hologram. Also, "as above so below." Thus, it is important for the client not to keep talking about how s/he used to feel, or s/he will re-create the disease and/or pain. This is especially true in the 3 days following a healing when the new energy patterns are becoming established. If the client can stop talking about old ways of feeling and verbalizing destructive thoughts, this shows willingness on his/her part to let them go and change.

Moving energy using only physical eyes: When doing psychic surgery, other techniques, like visualizing my arms as electromagnets and moving the misqualified energy to the Light, are certainly possible. Likewise, I can move energy with my eyes during psychic surgery or during other healing work. Angeliclight provides the healer with this ability. To do this, I keep my eyes open and soften them by not staring and by using my peripheral vision. I ask the angels to show me the misqualified energy. As I move my eyes slowly down, the angels move the negativity out of the body, typically through the bottoms of the healee's feet. The energy follows my eyes. In like manner, I can bring in healing energy. To do this, I look above the crown and move healing energy that the angels are bringing in down into the body and ground it into the chakra that is about 12 inches below the feet. If I see other visuals, I ask the angels what to do.

Violet Flame Attunement

I have been including this attunement in my Tera-Mai™ Reiki I and Tera-Mai™ Seichem I classes because I have found that many individuals take the first-level class to have the energy for their own healing, which is the best place to start. If we cannot heal ourselves, how are we going to help anybody else?

I teach those individuals who take Tera-Mai™ Seichem Mastership how to do this initiation. I found that when I taught Reiki (earth) Masters how to do this initiation, they were unable to pass the Violet Flame on to others. Why? Because the initiator needs to be channeling enough clear fire energy to be able to pass this initiation on. The Violet Flame, whose nature is purely transformational, is an aspect of fire.

To use this energy of transformation on oneself, call upon the Angels of the Violet Fire and Saint Germain before going to sleep at night. Ask the angels to work on whatever issue has come up for healing. Typically, in the morning, the issue has been released. If the problem is deep, it is recommended that the recipient repeat the procedure for 21 to 30 nights in a row.

To use this energy on others, call upon the Angels of the Violet Fire and Saint Germain. Then, the healer visualizes him/herself amongst the angels or in a field of violet. Healer (absentee or hands-on) sees him/herself, the angels and the color violet transforming healee's issues.

The visualization of oneself in journeywork or in working with the Angels of the Violet Fire helps keep the healer/meditator/shaman out of the way and it allows the Truth of What Is to come through. To use the third eye for the purpose of getting somebody to do something or to exert self-will is considered manipulative. For example, Virginia's issues of control were 'in her face' long before she met me. Virginia told me the story of how she met her last boyfriend at a dance. After he asked her to dance, he told her that he had been visualizing his idea of the perfect woman to come into his life. When he saw her, he realized that she was the one. While he may have brought her into his life and their relationship was good for a short while, it quickly got ugly and fell apart. I told Virginia that he was reflecting back to her what she was doing. If he had asked the angels to show him the perfect woman for him, that would have been a different story with the right woman and a different outcome.

When several people who have been attuned are gathered in a circle to do a group healing, the Angels of the Violet Fire and Saint Germain are called in. The color violet comes into the crown and out the root chakra; thus, grounding the energy. This is repeated for a total of three times. The circle is seen as filling with violet as the healers in the group continue to bring in the energy of transformation. When the energy has been built up, one healer at a time names a person, place or event. The whole group works together with the Violet Flame, leaving each healing in Divine Order and for the highest good of all concerned. Participants may want to share their experiences before going on to the next person, place or event, or remain in meditation and share after everyone has had an opportunity to present a person, place or event.

Using the Violet Flame as described above is a healing variation of creating a circle of Light. To create a circle of Light, each healer in the circle draws Light into his/her crown and out his/her left hand and foot to the person on his/her left. Energy can be felt moving around the circle and coming back magnified and intensified to each healer. The process is repeated for a total of three times. The circle becomes filled with Light. For planetary healing, see Mother Earth in the center of the circle. See her in the Light, with the angels, masters, power animals, and other Christed beings working on her. Then pull off and drain negativity (in your vision and with your physical hands), and then fill her back up with healing. The attention of the healers is brought back to the circle of Light. Before continuing, the healers can be reminded that there are angels of healing and protection surrounding them and that they can ask for a confirmation that they are indeed present. Earthbound spirits are then invited to take the hand of an angel, step into the circle and go up to the Light. The angels are then asked to bring into the circle any black magic that is ready to be released to the Light and transformed. Finally, the angels are asked to fill any voids with high-vibrational healing energy. Oftentimes, healers in the circle experience personal healings - what goes around comes around!

Mankind is once again returning to the Golden Age of the Return of the Angels. We have a brief glimpse of what this Golden Age entails in the legends of King Arthur and Camelot. When the Romans invaded England, they murdered the Druid priests and priestesses and brought in technology. They were master builders of roads and aqueducts and among other things, used cement. The Roman soldiers also intermarried with the Celtics. When the Roman army was called back to defend Rome, for a brief time, there existed on earth a balanced harmony between Mother-Father God and between technology and nature.

Granted, throughout time there have been shifts in thinking. For example, I personally believe that the reason that there are no great modern operas is because the individuals who are capable of creating operas, like Andrew Lloyd Weber, are focusing their attention on musicals. Broadway musicals are our modern operas. The great operas are still performed because they are so wonderful that they survive the passage of time. Educated and talented singers like Andrea Bochelli and Sarah Brightman are easily capable of singing both opera and classical music. The shift we are headed for involves more than how we earn a living. The paradigm shift we are entering is much more profound than going from mechanical watches to quartz crystal watches. The paradigm shift of the Golden Age has already started and will be happening on many levels.

It is medically proven that we were once more highly evolved. For example, we are actually missing DNA strands (we are supposed to have 13), and we are currently using less that 10% of our brains. As we open up to the totality of which we really are we are becoming cosmic humans. If Albert Einstein used only 15% of his brain, can we even begin to comprehend what it would be like to use 100% of our brain? In the movie, Phenomenon, John Travolta has more active areas of brain function than anyone in recorded history had. Because of his expanded brain use, his IQ is "off the charts" and he is able to demonstrate telekinesis (the ability to move objects without applied physical force) and other psychic abilities. His character states, "I am the possibility." This possibility is available to everyone who enters the Golden Age. The Golden Age is going to be a quantum leap. To describe the Golden Age would be like trying to tell the residents of Pleasantville what color is and what it is like to live in world where the roads do not circle back into one another but go on. In both movies, some characters either refuse to accept or are afraid when the unfamiliar is introduced into their universe. The mayor of Pleasantville states, "It's a question of values. It's a question of whether we want to hold onto those values that made this place great?" First, there is a violent reaction to "the coloreds" and then a Pleasantville Code of Conduct & Laws of Common Decency is drawn up denying civil rights. If anyone thinks that a government can run a police state effectively and humanely, look at our federal prisons, which are euphemistically called correctional institutions. Nowhere else is there a greater possibility of being robbed, beaten, rapped, contracting a life-threatening disease or a premature death.

In both Phenomenon and Pleasantville, the message is that the possibility is in each one of us. It's inside if we have the courage to look. The Gospel message that *we must lose our lives in order to find it means* simply to surrender our lives to God, which is actually the plan that we ourselves created before we were born. In order to reach the place within us where our potential resides we meditate, pray, release toxic thoughts and open up to our emotions and then release the negative ones. The popes and church councils rewrote Jesus' spiritual message, which means that modern Catholicism and even other Christian religions are based upon forged documents and heretical, intentional mistranslations of the spiritual message of Jesus. For example, nowhere in the New Testament is there any reference to Purgatory. Purgatory was created by the papacy so that the masses would be forced to turn to the church for salvation and so that indulgences could be sold. The truth is, that as in What Dreams May Come, we create our own after-death reality right here on earth. In the spring of 1299, Boniface VIII had ancient Palestrina with the exception of the cathedral leveled and 6,000 people were murdered for disloyalty to the pope. For this act, Dante buried Boniface VIII in the Eighth Circle of Hell, head down in the fissures of a rock.

Christianity is not alone; followers of other great teachers also changed their master's message. Each one of us is faced with the task of sorting out the Truth and unweaving the fallacies so that we might find out whom we are why we came here and what our potential is. The real miracle is that we are all sons and daughters of a God Who is both Feminine and Masculine and our potential has no limits. For whatever reason, the centuries have been what they have been. Salvation and forgiveness is available for everyone, including Boniface VIII and the other popes. It is time to forgive everyone including ourselves so that we can move on to fulfill the prophecies.

As we become cosmic humans, we open the possibility of connecting to other Christed beings on other worlds. In healing circles, we can extend healing from individuals who are physically present to those who are not (with or without symbols). Then we send healing to Mother Earth. Healing can also be sent to other planets, solar systems and worlds that are within our galaxy. The next progression is to send healing to other galaxies that are within our universe, and then other universes. It is an act of healing as well as an exercise to expand or stretch consciousness.

Those present can use the energy for their own healing by seeing themselves in their mind's eye walking into the Light and asking the celestial angels to work on them. Or giving permission for any past lives that require healing to go into the Light and be healed by the angels. Visualizing or feeling release; breathing in compassion and love. Seeing anyone whom they have ever injured mentally, physically or emotionally going into the circle of Light, feeling self-forgiveness and then breathing compassion and love to those souls. Another method is for each person in the circle to name a particular body part that they would like to have worked on. Everyone then either touches themselves on the affected area or the corresponding touch point on the body.

Both the white Light and Violet Flame can be used in combination, or in combination with healing symbols. Hosanna would be particularly appropriate to use with the Violet Flame. Healing circles can be combined with candle magic. We can only do good magic so long as everything is left in Divine Order, for the highest good of all concerned, and that the angels and other spirit helpers are asked to do what needs to be done.

I have people work with the Angels of the Violet Fire before and after attuning them so they can see, feel and experience the difference for themselves. In meditation, I guide the prospective initiates to a lake in Northern Ireland, Washington D.C., Sedona and Kauai, Hawaii, and I suggest that they ask the Angels of the Violet Fire, "How can I help?" Typically, the angels have the meditator watch them while they work. (This is an exercise anyone can do, and you may ask your angels to take you there in meditation so that you can witness all of the work that has been accomplished.) After I initiate the class participants, I repeat the same exercise. The second time, the initiates discover that they actively work with the Angels of the Violet Fire as though they too were Angels of the Violet Fire.

176

Healing Process

Ancient Art of Hands-On Healing as It Is Practiced Today

Simple formulas for successful living and being are in front of our eyes, but we shake our heads in disbelief. We say to ourselves, "It cannot be this simple." But it is! All we need to do is stop making excuses and pay attention to two things. First, in order to find the qualities we desire in ourselves, we must see them in other people. Then, we need to acknowledge that individual or make him/her feel special for having these qualities. It is at this point that the seed of possibility is acknowledged and allowed to come to fruition within us. We can only see who we are. Secondly, when we see qualities in others that we find distasteful, we need to acknowledge that these qualities are within us. We can only see who we are. At this point, we seek out help. Then, we go through a process of peeling away the layers of misconceptions, inversions, distortions, reversals, omissions, misfilings or denials that reveal their presence to us as pain, disease, jealousy, greed, guilt, rage, etc.

Healing is a process that is different for each one of us, but before we can heal, we must acknowledge that there is a problem. Alcoholics or drug addicts have to admit to themselves that they are addicts before they can be successful candidates for therapy. In order to admit that they have a problem, they have to 'hit bottom' or come to such a low point that they are literally forced to seek out an alternative solution beyond alcohol or drugs. 'Bottoming out' occurs at different levels for different people. One man's hell may look like heaven to another man who is lower still on the ladder of despair.

Addiction to drugs or alcohol is not the only behavior we engage in that take us off of our path towards enlightenment. Drug addiction, etc. is a destructive behavior stemming from a distortion in the conscious or subconscious mind. Distortions produce what we refer to as negative thoughts or emotions. Drugs, alcohol, sex, food, etc. serve as substitutes for genuine feelings of joy. However, since the core issue is not resolved, any happiness from the 'quick fix' is temporary and there is no peace of mind. An example of this is King Midas, who substituted his greed for opening up to and experiencing his emotions. When King Midas was given the 'golden touch', he busily pursued turning anything and everything into gold with total disregard for nature and disrespect for his subjects. It was only after discovering that his 'golden touch' destroyed his food, and then turning his own daughter to gold, that he had a change of heart. When he repented and asked from his heart that his gift be taken back and his daughter brought back to life, he broke the downward spiral. This one act of mercy and compassion opened the way for new behavioral patterns.

Oftentimes, we do not allow the ones we love to hit bottom. We want to save people from themselves, when we should be stepping in only when that person is harming another individual. A woman (let's call her Carla) approached me last year, asking me to interpret her dream. "I was in a room with my mother. I managed to get her from that room into the next. It was a struggle, but I did it. As we were walking, a baby elephant appeared and started walking with us. When we got into the second room, I could see the door that opened to a beautiful New World. My mother refused to go any further. I knew that I could step through the door, but I didn't want to leave my mother behind. The baby elephant, my mother and myself were stuck." I told Carla that while one dream has many levels of interpretation, my understanding was that she had to let go of wanting her mother to live up to her expectations. I also felt that her mother was very jealous and often 'cut off her own nose to spite her face,' and that Carla was often kept busy trying to save her mother from herself. I saw the baby elephant as representing a past life when Carla was a sage in India. If she could allow her mother to walk her own path, Carla and the baby elephant would walk through the doorway. Once on the other side of the door, Carla could begin to nurture herself and her latent gifts, as represented by the animal. Carla responded, "You do not know this, but even though I am of Spanish descent, when I was young, I was often mistaken for a little girl from India. I have always been drawn to India, its culture and mysticism. And yes, you are right about my mother."

Children who grow up watching other sibling(s) being physically or sexually abused have tremendous guilt because they are not also being abused. As children, and later as adults, they are always trying to fix things and people and to make everything right. They do not see their behavior as interfering. When guilt is enormous, and looking at the reality is too great a burden to deal with, as a protection, the mind denies that the abusive parental behavior ever occurred. I had one client (let's call her Betty) who as a child had been repeatedly and severely beaten by her mother. One time, mom beat Betty to the point that she thought that she had killed her daughter. Mom then dragged her daughter's body outside, dug the compost hole a little deeper, threw the body into the hole, and was in the process of burying her daughter alive when a neighbor stopped her. Betty's most painful memory of that incident is that her mother's reaction was to bury her where they put the garbage, and not in a beautiful, peaceful spot near the woods. Betty's two sisters and brother to this day are in complete denial that mom ever did anything to hurt Betty. When the time is right, they too will take the lid off their denial and release their pain.

178

Children who are abused often 'check out' when the abuse is occurring; that is, the personality leaves and another aspect or past life comes in who can deal with the pain. In extreme cases, the personality is shattered, and distinctly different reincarnations come into consciousness at various times. The former incarnation who takes the abuse can be a lifetime where s/he was abusive, or it can be a personality who is strong enough to handle the torture. I was once regressed to a time when I was a little boy in southeastern Wisconsin. I loved to paint, but my father did not consider it manly. The last time he abused me, he took a board and beat me to death. My body was a bloody mess; even the femur of my left leg was broken. The last thing I asked for before I died was for parents who would leave me alone. We always get what we ask for, and in the next lifetime, I had parents who didn't love me and completely ignored me. However, when I was regressed to the lifetime that was directly related to the young artist, I found myself as a young Native American boy who had already earned his first eagle feather. This was the personality who had the strength to come in when my father beat me.

In this lifetime, as a child, my physical body still held the trauma from these beatings and subconsciously I reversed the definitions of love and hate. If love wasn't painful, then it wasn't love. So I pushed away healthy relationships and drew in toxic people. During my healing process, I began to recognize and see what it was that I was doing. At one point, I even met the man who had been my abusive father. It was so easy for me to read him; that is, psychically perceive him. He was impotent! In part, this was due to his karmic debt; in part, this was due to his constrictive nature. He had difficulty giving his money, love or his own sperm. He had gone from the extreme of being a tyrant to a weakling. When I forgave him in my heart and released him to his highest good, I broke the pattern. If he wanted to play out his aggressions in this lifetime, then he was going to have to find a different dance partner. Although he, too, had the option of looking at his distorted view of masculinity, healing and moving into the middle ground of teacher, consoler, and warrior who protects the kingdom.

It is far easier for us to deny that we have a problem and blame everyone else. Our denials can become so extreme that, like the abused child, we check out. The personality of mothers of sexually abused children can leave while the abuse is occurring. They cannot face or begin to deal with what their husbands are doing to their daughters. Survivors of incest come to me to heal the inner rage they believe that they still hold for their fathers, only to discover during the healing session that it is their mothers with whom they are most angry for not stopping the abuse. One woman, let's call her Rhonda, related an incident in which while her father was sexually abusing her at the kitchen table, mom stood at the kitchen sink with her back to them. Mom wasn't there!

Rhonda's mother is in total denial of the incest, and was calling her daughter every Saturday morning to verbally abuse her. When Rhonda's husband answered the phone, he would fetch his wife by saying, "It's time for your punishment." Rhonda did come to the realization that she did not have to endure the weekly Saturday morning torture chamber. Rhonda is still trying to work things out with her controlling, mentally and emotionally abusive husband. She was encouraged after his prostate surgery because he became impotent and he could no longer sexually abuse her. Rhonda is now seeing a professional psychologist and exploring other alternative healing modalities. It was not my place to recommend that she leave her husband.

Sometimes, the issue is not a reversal, misconception, inversion, distortion, omission, misfiling or denial. Sometimes, the healee is simply working through karma and goes to a healer to bring resolution to the karma; othertimes, if the karma has been worked through, the healee simply release the physical manifestation of disease or pain. As an example of the latter case, this is Doug Dickson's personal account of healing:

Glands: "I would like to relate a true story about healing. To me it is a miracle, because I found relief from constant pain. It seems unusual because of my complete lack of understanding and the little faith that I had in religion or alternative-type therapies. I have eliminated specific names in this account, as my father is a prominent physician and I appreciate his efforts and those of his close friends who have done their best in order for me to become whole.

When I was young, I played sports from the time I could walk. Whether it was skiing, football, or rugby, I played it from little league through the collegiate level. Sports have always been something in which I excelled and truly enjoyed. During my years of sports, coaches made steroids and other substances available to us in order to enhance players' ability to play. I believe that these poisons were the very root of a problem that was to plague me for almost a decade.

When I was 25 years old, I developed extremely sharp pains in my chest. The pain developed over time and was centered in my right and left breast. After about 6 months of waiting, I finally mentioned the problem to my father. He examined me and decided that I should seek the advice of a close friend, who was also a general surgeon.

I made an appointment and upon examination, he correctly diagnosed my condition as gynecomastia, a condition where hormonal imbalances create swelling and sharp pain in the chest of males. The solution, he said, was simple. If I elected to have surgery, the swollen glands in my chest would be removed and the problem would be corrected. I was very concerned since this seemed to attack and remove my symptoms without solving the problem. The other option was to continue dealing with the pain and maybe someday the situation could resolve itself. I decided to wait it out instead of having surgery and gave my body time to heal.

Several years went by and I dealt with the pain by avoiding any contact to my chest, but the problem persisted. I then sought the help of a specialist in endocrinology. I was examined carefully and given many blood tests. All the tests confirmed the first diagnosis of gynecomastia. The physician was concerned because of the huge imbalance in my body's hormones and thought that I may have a small cancer creating the problem. He referred me to another well-known physician that specialized in gynecomastia and was a world-renowned expert on sex hormone pathophysiology.

Exhaustive testing was then completed including blood samples, ACTH stimulation tests, ultrasound and a MRI. I suffered through it all including the injection of radioactive isotopes into my bloodstream. The results were analyzed by leading medical centers and universities from all parts of the United States. It was expensive, costing well over $10,000. The results of all tests concluded that I had Bilateral Tanner Stage II Gynecomastia, but showed no cancer or other specific problems with any organ of my body. My condition was well diagnosed, but no solutions were available.

The last step was to submit all this data as a case study for a weeklong world conference of endocrinologists. They carefully examined the testing, discussed the situation at length and concluded in a letter to my doctor that the problem was caused 'presumably due to one or more environmental estrogens, not presently identifiable.' A fancy way of saying that there was no specific cause identified and no solution. I gave up hope and decided that I would live with the pain. It had been almost 6 years and no one had any answers.

I met Kathleen Milner about 3 years later through work. I am in the graphic design and printing business and another client referred her to me. After producing advertising and printing for her books, we talked at length about healing. She suggested that I see her and that she might be able to help my condition. I dismissed the suggestion at first, but it seemed to gnaw at me over several months. Although I was quite skeptical because of my ignorance, I agreed to have her perform a healing.

We met at her home and she had me lay down on a table. It reminded me of the massage tables used while I was playing sports in college. She spent a great deal of time getting me to relax and then started the healing session. As she went over my body and asked me to visualize, I felt my body changing temperature. Some areas were getting cold and some were very hot. It was a strange feeling, but I really tried to believe and followed her instructions. My body didn't feel as if anything changed in the process, but I had strong contractions in several muscles that I couldn't control. After we were finished, I still had the pain, but something felt different.

Several days went by and it seemed that my chest was starting to feel better. My condition seemed to slowly improve over the next couple of weeks and there was some relief of the pain for the first time in almost ten years. The pain kept dropping until it was completely gone over about a two-month period. It has now been almost 9 months and I have not felt any pain or symptoms of any kind since meeting with Kathleen.

Although it has been a fairly short time in the history of my problem (almost ten years), I truly feel that I am whole again. I have none of the symptoms that have hurt for so long. I look back on this journey and feel that the traditional medicine I was raised with gave me great diagnosis, but only Kathleen gave me healing. I am at a loss to explain how she could have performed this miracle, but I am forever thankful that she did." **Doug Dickson, Tempe, Arizona**

When I worked on Doug that evening, I began as I usually do; that is, I listened to him so that I would know what his symptoms were. I had him lie down on the massage table and laid my hands on the touch points for mental clearing, then the touch points for emotional clearing and then the touch point for the glands. I then sat behind his head and laid my hands on his chest. He said that I was 'right on target'. When his body convulsed, I reassured him that this sometimes occurred when the angels or spirit helpers were removing toxins. I asked him if he felt 'stuff' running down through his legs and out his feet. He confirmed that this was true, and then he relaxed. After that, the convulsions were not quite as shocking to him as the first had been. Doug was doing a great job of visualizing, so when his curious left brain asked me where the healing was coming from, I asked him to ask his angels to show him. They showed him a tall column of light that flowed into my hands and then into him. The angels told him that the healing rays came from God.

There was a time when I felt that the angels completely took his consciousness out of his body so that they could work on him without his brain getting in the way. When his body had had enough, the healing energy that I was channeling stopped flowing. When we were through, I told him the same thing that I tell everyone else, "The healings usually go on for a month or even longer. If you feel that you need to see me again, just give me a call." Almost a year later, Doug was taking a combination of herbs on a regular basis. For no apparent reason, one day the pain in Doug's chest returned, but it lasted for only several hours and then it went away. Oftentimes, herbs will bring up any remaining residue or consciousness of former diseases in the body for one final cleanses and release. Some people find that when they are detoxing, bentonite clay and water help to pull the toxins out of the body.

Growths: "On the evening of August 6, 1996, my friend told me that she had been experiencing soreness in her mouth for a few days. It was in an area, where eight months prior, she had had two teeth extracted. She had thought that it was just a large blister, and disregarded it. That morning she was in such pain that she had to leave her office and go to her dentist. Her job as an office manager requires extensive verbal communication and she was barely able to move her mouth. Upon examination, the dentist discovered she had a growth, which covered the entire area of the extracted teeth. He stated that he had never seen anything like that before, and didn't know exactly what it was. He referred her to an oral surgeon and asked that he perform a biopsy on it. The earliest appointment was the next morning.

That evening, she asked me to give her a Reiki treatment. I had just received my Tera-Mai™ Reiki attunements 1 1/2 months before. She was familiar with the energy that I channeled before I received Tera-Mai™, but had not experienced a treatment from me since my Tera-Mai™ attunement. As I approached her, and was about eight inches away from her, she literally jumped back and said that she felt very cold waves coming from my hands. She stated that she was startled because I had not touched her when she felt the cold coming from my hands. She asked me to put my hand on her arm, and when I did, it felt warm to her. I then put my hand on my own cheek, and it felt like a normal hand to me. When I put my hand on her cheek, she said it felt very, very cold. She said it felt wonderful and that the pain was completely gone. Before leaving, she again commented on the powerful energy she had experienced through me and thanked me for the treatment.

The next morning the growth had completely disappeared, and instead of keeping her appointment with the oral surgeon, she returned to her dentist. He asked her why she wasn't at her consultation. She asked him to look at the growth. He was astonished that it was no longer there. He couldn't understand how it had disappeared overnight." **Marian Wilson, Cartersville, Georgia**

Eyes: "One day Joan and I went to a shop to look for some crystals. While talking to the owner, we found out that her daughter had done Reiki I and II. Just as we were talking, the daughter came home after running a few errands. She told us that she had two surgeries on her left eye because she has a slight deviation; that is, her eyes were unable to focus synchronically. As a result of the operation, she has some optical cicatrices. After she had eye surgery, she had a dream in which a man whom she never met appeared to her and told her that she never should have had the operations. A few days later at a little house party, the same man who was in her dream was there. He came up to her at the party and said, "Why did you have surgery on your left eye? It was needless, a waste of time and money. If you undergo another operation, you will die." I have been doing absentee healing for her on her request for three weeks now. According to her, she is getting a tremendous relief, and is now able to work for an extended period without her eyes getting tired." **Henk J. Schoonhaven, Suriname, South America**

Shoulder joint: "I have been practicing Reiki for about two months. In that period of time, I've noticed miraculous changes in my life and my outlook is much more positive. I am able to release painful and negative situations quickly. I am constantly amazed at how my life is coming together so clear and precise like the perfect puzzle. But what amazes me the most is on a physical level, my left shoulder had been dislocated numerous times in the last four years, to the point that I was in need of surgery. Any wrong movement caused it to pop out. From my first Reiki attunement with Sue Szymanski, I felt healing changes taking place. I no longer have problems with range of motion, dislocation or chronic pain. My shoulder has completely self - healed in the last ten months." **Dawn Graham, California**

"Dawn, a young personal trainer, came to me in early 1995 for her first Reiki class. When giving the Reiki attunement, I felt her left shoulder move and adjust itself under my hands. I had no prior knowledge of her injury until after the class. Dawn went on to study massage, Reiki Mastership, crystal healing and psychic awareness in the following year and is now a very talented healer and psychic. She was recently featured on the television show Strange Universe.

As for myself, I know Reiki has really opened up the creativity in my life and of my students. Last year, I was guided to create several flower essences for use in the healing process. One specifically works to help people release old issues and helps students during the 21-day cleansing period following Reiki and Seichem attunements.

Reiki was a major factor in my recovery from Chronic Fatigue Syndrome six years ago, and now is the spiritual foundation which guides my work of teaching and facilitating others to learn self-healing and empowerment modalities." **Sue Szymanski, R.N., The Healing Heart, Los Angeles, California**

High blood pressure: "I am here in East Tennessee to help take care of my 89-year-young Grams, Ann Flannigan who had lost the will to live and did not want to be a burden on anyone. She weighed all of 80 pounds and had survived eight different surgeries, the last one in July 1996. Grams has bolts, plates and pins in both hips from different falls. She has been a spiritual pioneer in my family in her quiet way. I am happy to be here for her.

Grams has been doing so well and appreciates my presence. Last month after her initiation into Tera-Mai™ Reiki II, her doctor took her off the blood pressure medication she had been on for years. With regular Reiki treatments, massage, aloe vera juice, ginkgo biloba, vitamins, healthy, fresh food and love, we have increased her joy or quality of life and decreased her painful discomfort. We've even eliminated what she called "zingers" in her brain from a stroke. Grams is happy, has gained 12 pounds, looks forward to each new day and can still beat me in a game of Scrabble.

I continue daily my growth and expansion through a variety of avenues - prayer, meditation, Reiki, nature. I learn as I teach and I teach what I learn through experience. I am committed to doing my part in building an army of healers on this planet." **Lynn Rose Downey, Cosby, Tennessee** (Besides her grandmother, Lynn has also initiated her mother, Rita Majer, into the healing rays.) So, there are now three generations of Reiki women in her family.

Neck: "Gregory Lemenov, one of my Tera-Mai™ Seichem I students, works in a clinic as a massage therapist. He was helping a lady who was in much pain. Her neck would only stay up with a cumbersome harness, which interfered with her career. She was told that the only way out of her harness was via a very dangerous operation. She had seen many doctors and she was frightened.

Gregory is a truly dedicated healer whose goal in life is to learn to help others by relieving their pain. Each day he went to the hospital chapel to meditate and hold Tera-Mai™ Reiki symbols to his heart, hoping to increase his healing ability. Afterwards, Gregory went to the woman and placed his hands on her. She started getting pain relief right away. After 31 days of treatments, she removed the harness and is totally free of pain for the first time in years. She does not need an operation and has called Gregory frequently to thank him." **Gabriel River, San Anselo, California**

Moving Chi (energy or Qi) through the body: I had mentioned in my first book that I had initiated animals into healing. They have souls and chakras and are every bit as much God's creatures as we are. I have found that after they are initiated, they became more intelligent and are able to heal. Both of my cats, Ziggy and Janis, frequently help me in facilitating healing. Oftentimes, they will do it on their own. For example, one of my Tera-Mai™ Seichem Masters was a bit overwhelmed and anxious trying to integrate his initiation. After watching Gabriel intently, Janis leaped up and touched the points where the energy was blocked and released it. Gabriel was shocked to see 'this most remarkable demonstration of moving Chi,' and the fact that it was coming from a cat made it unbelievable. He later wrote her the following thank you letter.

"Dear Janis, Being new and inexperienced at both Reiki and the other healing rays, as well as fan mail, I shall keep this brief. Thank you for helping me integrate the initiations I received from our esteemed Reiki Master. I admire your sensitivity and your simple direct skill in action as well as your knowledge of acupressure and the touch points. I shall endeavor to model myself after you so I can better utilize this gift of healing. Sincerely, **Gabriel River**"

Pulled muscles: "I frequently take my dogs out walking in the desert park, and at the top of the hill, I send out healing. I had pulled a muscle in my back and was in severe pain. So, on that day I decided that I was going to really concentrate and work on myself. About a week before, you had attuned me to Tera-Mai™ Seichem, and I was totally blown away with the increase of the healing level from Reiki to Seichem. On the hilltop I visualized white strings of healing rays zapping me. I put one hand in the front of my body and the other hand on my back where the pain was. It was a matter of seconds; I received an instantaneous healing. It was unbelievable to go from being in so much pain one minute to having it gone the next! I was dancing on the hilltop." **Teri Francis, Scottsdale, Arizona**

Accident: "On the evening of August 17, 1996, Rich and Karen Kopf of Seymour, Connecticut were involved in a serious boating accident on the Housatonic River in Shelton, Connecticut. Four underage boys had taken their parent's boat out and crashed into the Kopf's boat doing about 25 - 30 miles an hour. There was another couple on the boat with the Kopfs; they were killed on impact and it took divers 18 hours to recover their bodies. Karen and Rich were taken to Yale New Haven Hospital where they were listed as critical. Both had head injuries. Even though I had been initiated as a priest into the Order of Melchizedek, I was not permitted to see them until 11:00 A.M. Rich's condition had been lifted from critical to guarded overnight. He had sustained a skull fracture, abrasions about the face and a broken elbow. He was resting peacefully while I treated his head area for about an hour and his elbow for another hour. Later I learned that the doctors were amazed that his elbow healed so quickly that they never put a cast on his arm.

Karen had received a severe blow to the head, her neck was broken and she was in a coma. The doctors were convinced that if she were to make it, there would be brain damage. She was strapped into the bed, her head was shaved, there were tubes in her mouth and nose, a brace on her neck and numerous wires attached her to various medical machines. Then I got a vision of how Karen used to be - beautiful, radiant, whole, chattering, and full of life and laughter. I told Rich's brother, Bill, that Karen had come to me for Reiki treatments before her accident and that I wanted to start sending her healing. He said that if it could help, I should go ahead. Just as I was about to start, a nurse came by to check on Karen and asked me what I was doing. She indicated that Karen was hooked up to what is called a C.S.F. monitor. Apparently, Karen's brain was swelling and the doctors wanted to monitor the pressure exerted on the cerebrospinal fluid compartment of her brain. The nurse said that I could send healing to Karen while she watched. Within seconds, I heard Bill exclaim that the C.S.F. monitor that had read 38 the whole time had moved down to 32. I looked up and watched the monitor move down to 25. The nurse said, "If this Reiki relaxes her that much, then keep on doing it." I noticed that when I removed my hand from her, the monitor would begin to travel up again and when I resumed treatment, it moved back down. After doing Reiki for a couple of hours, the monitor stabilized at the lower level. Within two days, Karen was removed from the C.S.F. monitor and made a complete recovery in the next 4 - 5 months." **Charles Ferraro, West Haven, Connecticut**

Spiritual healing: "Having called upon the Reiki powers and entered a state of stillness, I cut the aura around the whole of the body with my hands and sat at the head of the healee with my hands positioned on her shoulders. The cool pulsing flow of Sophi-El and the gentle almost breeze-like quality of Angeliclight were immediately apparent. I had the sensation of heightened physical awareness whilst being in a deep meditative state.

I moved to the left side of the healee and asked for azurite and malachite as you described. Then with my left hand on her solar plexus and her left hand in my right hand, the still blackness in front of my closed eyes opened to reveal an impenetrable wall of stone. An intense energy began to flow through me to the healee. This stone was the very stuff of existence - the gross material from which we have evolved. I found myself back at the very beginning of time with the healee. I shattered the rock with the sudden knowledge that I could take the healee on a journey of release. All I needed to do was hold the stillness and use the green healing ray that suddenly appeared and shone wherever I put my attention.

The wall of rock had given way to reveal a chamber hewn out of the rock from which radiated raw menacing energy. I then saw a stone sarcophagus, and at this point, I found myself describing the scene to the healee and explaining to her that something extraordinary was occurring and that this was not the usual way in which I would conduct a healing. I surrounded the sarcophagus with a green aura. The sarcophagus melted away revealing a still form, which I knew, was the healee's psychic double.

I then journeyed away from this scene, traveling through clouds until a beautiful landscape of green undulating hills was below me. I scanned the land and found the place I had to take the still form from the chamber. I returned to the rock chamber and the form moved with me back to the hillside where the air was quiet and fragrant with flowers.

Throughout the session, I changed my hand positions on the healee's body moving my right hand to her right shoulder, her right hand and then her left shoulder, all the while keeping my left hand on her solar plexus (touchpoints for emotional clearing). Each time, just before I moved my right hand, I was prompted from within; each move resulted in a shift in scenery. Occasionally, I was moved to drain negative energy through my right hand. In those instances, I moved my right hand behind me and pointed my fingertips down to the central fire of Earth.

Then I witnessed a book's pages turning over slowly and on each leaf, I laid the golden green ray. The pages were transformed as the pain of time itself was erased. In this process the healee's emotions were freed and her astral form gained consciousness. Everything had been done or undone. I told the healee that she was safe, that any healing now had to occur in the very slow time of existence and that only she could instigate that and move forward.

I removed the azurite and malachite and asked for pink quartz and amethyst, which I placed on her body. Closing the aura, I acknowledged the magnificent energy and thanked the powers for this wonderful healing." **David Driver, Shropshire, England**

Healing during a psychic reading: "On February 14, 1997, I was doing a reading for Tom and Peggy Yost. They sat on the sofa and I sat in a comfortable chair facing them at a distance of about ten feet. Normally, I would have been closer, but I felt as though I needed the space. I thought perhaps it might be because I was doing a reading for a couple and the energy would be a lot more intense. I called for my guide, Ezekial, who is himself both very direct and forceful. I could feel his presence as he came in, and then I saw him to my left dressed in Old Testament Robes, striped cloth and a turban. His dark hair was partially visible. Ezekial has a very

188

Arabian body and coloring, and a dark beard. The angels also came in, and together they started feeding me information to give to Tom and Peggy. Tom's mouth dropped open in amazement when Edgar Cayce told me to tell Tom about his intestinal trouble, the pain in his lower back, and the problems he was having with shaking and pain in his legs.

During the reading, I stayed totally energized and focused while I was receiving audio messages from spirit. I sat with my forearms and palms facing Peggy and Tom, who were sitting transfixed and becoming increasingly warm to the point of being hot. They felt that they were receiving healing light and energy from my angels, because they saw my aura as a dazzling white radiating healing to them which they were experiencing within themselves. They both had a sense of security knowing that they were getting the truth. Suddenly, Tom asked me if one of my spirit guides was standing on my left, and he described Ezekial. At the same time, Peggy also saw him.

As the reading was coming to a close, I could feel the angels shutting down. Then their energy force and presence just vanished. It was like they turned off the lights and went home." **Cynthia Kyle, Fountain Hills, Arizona**

Healing into death: "Alvaro Fuentes had been introduced to me close to his death. He had suffered from AIDS and had pursued allopathic as his choice of medicine. After exhausting all forms of medical treatment with little or no response, he went into a harsh chemotherapy program. When this failed, he decided to go off all drugs and allow his body to die. (He had a death wish before he became ill, but he had planned on living a bit longer.) I had offered him a chance to recover with the use of an underground treatment called electromedicine, but as he really did not want to be here and since the machines could reverse his illness, he refused.

Choosing death over life brought up many issues for me as a healer, which I needed to move through in order to assist him in his passing. Morphine is a compassionate way to allow someone to die without too much suffering as it shuts down the body functions slowly. Towards the end, he had an unusually high amount of morphine in his body and he was down to two respirations per minute. I did not know that the doctors expected him to die that night. I entered his room, which was full of family members, at 3:00 A.M. with the intention of making him a Reiki Master. I came not to help him physically, but to heal his emotional, mental and spiritual bodies so as to aid him in his transition.

With the aid of spirit guides and angels, I initiated him into all three levels of Reiki. Twice he opened his glazed eyes and looked at me when the energy levels of the initiations intensified and

189

then slowly closed them. Alvaro's hands had been ice cold before I started initiating him. That soon changed! When I finished, they were extremely hot and emitting very intense energy (top and bottom). I whispered in his unconscious ears, "Forgive every one. Use the attunement to release as much garbage as possible. Feel all the love the people here have for you. Take the love and the healing energy and ability to heal with you when you pass." To the amazement of the doctors, Alvaro did not die that night. They were confused as to how his body could stabilize at such a high morphine IV drip. In fact, his vital signs began to improve, his breathing became stronger, and he lived for five more days. It is my belief that his guides and angels had him stay here awhile longer to process the attunements." **Bevan Eisnor, Toronto, Ontario, Canada**

Healing nature: "Last night a widespread and powerful weather system passed through most of Scandinavia. In the middle of the night, I woke up, listening to the wind. I became very anxious when I thought of the barn. It came to me to use Reiki and Seichem healing. I said to myself, "I have to do my very best!" I lay in bed and began to work. Within a short time, the fury of the storm and the force of the wind decreased in strength. Soon it was quiet outside and so it remained.

I started to think of the spirits of nature as workers of the four elements, and the elements working within the sphere of the Ethereal - Prana (India), Qi (China), Mana (Polynesia), Pneuma (Greece) Aether or Od (Germany). My mind expanded as I thought of the elemental and nature spirits working under the guidance of the Hierarchy - Seraphim (Spirits of the Love), Cherubim (Spirits of the Harmony), Throne (Spirits of the Will), Kyriotetes (Spirits of the Wisdom), Dynameis (Spirits of the Motion), Exusiai or Elohim (Spirits of the Form), Archai (Spirits of the Times), Achangeloi (Archangels), and Angeloi (Guardian Angels). I fell asleep. In the morning I understood that it is possible for us to work with the ethereal in a conscious way, but we must maintain consciously high moral standards. Respect is essential! During long dark epochs of the evolutionary process, misuse of elemental and spiritual forces is nothing new. This misuse has brought about the downfall of great civilizations and powerful humans. We must now remember, God, Thy will be done!" **Ulf Herrstrom, Luled, Sweden**

Using a Buddhist approach to healing: "There has been many dramatic changes in my life this past year. I am no longer a Buddhist monk, although my connection to Kagyu Samye Ling and my faith in Buddhism have not altered. I am working more deeply with Tera-Mai™ Reiki, Seichem and the other rays that I have been initiated into. I have absolute faith in this energy that I am channeling. Through my own experience I know that as long as my motivation remains pure, healings will happen!

There is something that I would like to share with you and the rest of the Tera-Mai™ practitioners. It is a very simple and effective way of increasing the energy and healing at much deeper levels during a treatment:

!) Before every session, always focus the mind. Simple breathing meditation is very effective.

2) I will then ask the blessing power of my Root Guru, the Buddhas, Bodhisattvas and enlightened beings of the past, present and future to be present during the treatment. Tera-Mai™ practitioners can change this to suit their own personal beliefs. (For example, I ask that the blessing power of Jesus Christ be present during this healing.) I then ask that the treatment is protected from any negative energy and that I will be assisted and guided where needed.

3) Remind myself, why is it that I am doing this healing? What do I want to achieve? I do not limit the healing by only focusing at the beginning on the healee. I am open as a channel to facilitate healing on all levels of body, mind and spirit. I request that the energy that I am channeling may benefit all sentient beings without any exception. Now I focus my mind on the healee and begin the treatment. If my mind strays during a healing, I repeat step 3.

4) When the session has come to an end, I always dedicate any benefit and accumulation of merit for the enlightenment and healing of all sentient beings. This simple gesture will then make the power of the healing limitless.

Within Tibetan Buddhism we look at the practice as having three aspects. It is these same three aspects that I apply to all my healing sessions. First, we have the aspiration aspect, the attitude that we want to do the practice of healing for the benefit and enlightenment of all suffering beings. Second, while we are doing the healing, we remind ourselves that we are doing this healing for the benefit and enlightenment of all beings. Third, having done the treatment, it is crucial to dedicate the merit. Therefore, the practice should have a good beginning, middle and end.

If we are trying to hold onto the merit for ourselves, the accumulation of merit will be destroyed at that point like a piece of wood that is burned when we put it into fire. **Ven Khenpo Karthar Rinpoche**

191

I feel that any Tera-Mai™ practitioner who applies this to their practice will experience the purity of the Tera-Mai™ energy at a much greater and profound level. **Legden, Cornwall, England**

I was in awe of their gold and maroon robes when I met Kunsel and Legden for the first time in Ireland. More profoundly touching was their dedication to healing – both hands-on and in their Buddhist practices. I have had many individuals tell me that Legden's foreword to this book, which is on the back cover, is the best explanation of the connection between Reiki and Buddhism that they have ever read.

Sometimes, it is the family who is healed: One of my friends in Phoenix had told me about her sister, Sandy, who was originally diagnosed as having MS. Then the doctors found out that she actually had a congenital, previously undiagnosed case of water on the brain, which apparently worsened with her pregnancy two years ago. Sandy was told that she had to have surgery, and she was scared. As a 'born-again Christian', Sandy had previously admonished her sister for her interest in the paranormal and healing. Now that she faced surgery, she wanted to come to Arizona to see me. My friend told me that her sister was only hoping to release her fear so that she could face surgery. I asked my friend to tell her sister that I could offer her no guarantees as to how or if healing would transpire. My friend called me back and told me that Sandy was coming the next weekend, and would I set some time aside so that I could see her. I agreed. Both my friend and I received the message that Sandy needed to see me on Friday, Saturday and Sunday, and that message was given to Sandy.

Late Friday afternoon, my friend called me to say that her sister was exhausted from the plane flight and her physical state was not good. I told my friend to tell her sister that she was free to do as she wanted, but that now would be the best time for me to see her. I was surprised when my friend called me back and said that Sandy had agreed to see me.

Sandy was sitting on the couch in excruciating pain when I arrived. We were introduced, I asked her where the pain was, and began to lay my hands on her. When my friend, who is both clairvoyant and clairaudient, sat down to watch what was going on, she and Sandy found out that they were both seeing the identical colors and healing patterns that the angels were bringing in. My friend had told her sister about the psychic surgery that I had done on her, and Sandy asked me to do the same for her. Sandy was shocked to find that she could really feel that her aura was gone. The healing angels started with Sandy's head. Sandy could feel her head opening and the water draining. Sandy could see blackness in her head turning to light and light colors.

She could also feel fear coming off of her neck. When it was time to work on her spine, at the same time she told me that she felt as though her spine was fluid-like and undulating, I saw a murky red snake in her spine which the angels removed. Needless to say, I did not mention what I had seen to Sandy.

When the healing was through, Sandy stood up and walked without the aid of either her walker or her cane. She then went into the kitchen and ate heartily - something that she had not done for a long time. I noticed that she was not content unless she was either doing the talking or the conversation was about her. I also listened to the long series of illness, disasters and accidents that had plagued Sandy, even though I encouraged her to let the past go and talk about how good she was feeling now. I had a gut feeling that if this disease left, Sandy was going to miss all of the attention it brought to her. I didn't say anything!

On Saturday, Sandy was having a hard time because her rage and doubts were coming up. She told her sister that she did not want me to come to see her. Interestingly, both my friend and my friend's mother on Saturday were able to see the same character trait in Sandy that I had the night before. Sandy's mother commented on how Sandy truly enjoyed playing the role of the martyr and probably would not know what to do if her husband could stop waiting on her hand and foot. Unless Sandy has a change in attitude, I felt that she was going to bring about her own death. Her sister and her mother on Sunday both independently came to that same conclusion. I discovered this when my friend called me later during the week. I do not know if Sandy's negative thoughts and emotions recreated the same disease or something different. I do not know if Sandy kept any of the healing energy she received that Friday night for her transition at the time of her death. What I do know is that the healing angels were working on Sandy's sister and mother to help each of them that Friday evening, whether they were conscious of the fact or not. While they can still see Sandy's many positive qualities, their eyes were opened wide that weekend, and they both moved into a state of consciousness whereby they could allow Sandy the freedom to leave and not be devastated by her passing.

The angels are not boring. Every healing is different. Typically, the energy will be blocked completely if there is a karmic issue to be worked out. The block can be in the healee's body, or the healing energy can be blocked in the aura. In the former case, I can feel the healing energy stop flowing through me. In the latter case, I feel as though I am touching a solid wall in front of me as the energy builds up. The only thing that I can do at that point is send the wall of healing into the Earth Mother. The intended healee will feel this, and on some level, if not consciously,

193

s/he knows that physical healing will not transpire. Oftentimes, the healee will release the fear surrounding the situation or the karma may be eased.

If the intended healee will not look at his/her issues, the angels step back, too. The angels are not interested in superficial physical healings. In Sandy's case, I do not know why the angels went to such great effort to produce such a dramatic physical healing. Perhaps, the angels did not know themselves whether or not Sandy would face her mental and emotional issues, and they were giving her the best possible opportunity that they could give her. Maybe Sandy's healing was a demonstration to her mother and her sister.

"Our deepest fear is not that we are inadequate. Our deepest fear is that we are powerful beyond measure. It is our light, not our darkness that most frightens us. We ask ourselves, "Who am I to be brilliant, gorgeous, talented and fabulous?" Actually, who are you not to be? You are a child of God. Your playing small does not serve the world. There is nothing enlightened about shrinking so that other people won't feel insecure around you. We were born to make manifest the glory of God that is within us. It's within everyone! And as we let our own light shine, we unconsciously give other people permission to do the same. As we are liberated from our own fears, our presence automatically liberates others." **Nelson Mandela, Inaugural Speech, 1994**

The following affirmation has been used by members of the clergy for exorcisms and can be used by all of us to chase away unconscious thoughts and heavy emotions: *Begone infernal enemies, conquered by the line of the tribe of Judah, the root of David. Alleluia! Alleluia! Alleluia!* (Repeat 3 times, or 3 times 3 times or as many times as needed.)

Iridology and Herbs

Healing the Body With Herbs & the Iris as a Diagnostic Tool

THE INFORMATION HEREIN IS PRESENTED FOR ITS EDUCATIONAL VALUE AND IS NOT INTENDED TO BE A GUIDE TO MEDICAL PARCTICE OR TO REPLACE THE SERVICES OF A PHYSICIAN OR TO RECOMMEND THAT HERBS BE USED FOR MEDICINAL PURPOSES.

I was born with blue eyes. When I was nine months old, I came down with pneumonia, was hospitalized and given penicillin. Every year afterwards until I was an adult, I suffered from recurring pneumonia or severe bronchitis. I also had terrible ear infections. In each of these cases, I was given antibiotics. By the time I was 13, my blue eyes had turned brown. Even though both of my parents had blue eyes, nobody wondered why this had happened.

Several years ago, I went to a woman who had studied iridology (one who analyzes the iris of the eye) and she told me that my eyes were still blue. She told me that the brown color was toxicity, that I was eating too many acid-type foods and that I should give up coffee. Well, I changed my diet and gave up coffee, but that didn't turn my brown eyes blue.

In the summer of 1996, I met Zhenia Hc Heigh, who is originally from Tibet. She takes both a transcendental as well as a scientific approach to iridology. Zhenia utilizes exercise, diet modification and the nutritional qualities of herbs to stimulate the body's own self-healing capabilities. The underlying idea is that the body can heal itself with proper nutrition and care. Zhenia informed me that there was a brown film over the iris of my eye, which was an indication that my body needed to be detoxified. Herbs tend to work slowly in the body. After six months, by alternating combinations of various herbs, under close examination a circle of green could be seen on the outer edge of the iris of my eyes. By the summer of 1997, the circle of green extended farther inwards and was visible without a magnifying glass. By the winter of 1998, the brown film had decreased in size so that from a distance my eyes appeared hazel; close up, the circle of green could be clearly observed. As my internal tissues were cleansed, my skin became clearer and tighter.

The validity of the nutritional quality of herbs is neither recognized by modern allopathic medicine nor is it taught in modern American medical schools. Botany is not a course requirement in medical schools. I am obliged to state that iridology (the study of the iris and eye as a diagnostic tool) and the use of herbs is not a substitute for modern medicine and discernment should be exercised whenever anything is put into or on the body. In the past, the

FDA has made Chaparral illegal and unavailable in health food stores; recently, Chaparral has again become available on the market because the FDA could not back up its claims that Chaparral was harmful. A few years ago under the pressure of lobbying groups, Congress tried to make vitamins a prescription drug. Health food stores and other interested people collected so many signatures, that Congress was forced to back down.

Because of allopathic medicine's refusal to recognize traditional medicine, which has now become commonly referred to as alternative methods of healing, information that would have been taught only in the old medical schools is now available to the general public. This book is not all-inclusive; so, I have included titles of a few books on subjects that this chapter touches upon. I have only tried to weave a tapestry of understanding between the various schools of thought and methods in which herbs are utilized, which is based upon my personal research and classes that I have taken. Because of the increased interest in herbs, I was encouraged to expand this chapter in the second edition of this book. <u>Within these pages can be found information that I have discovered which works for me and other people that I have come in contact with.</u>

There are herbs such as Echinacea that should only be taken when the physical body is ill. Some people successfully take Echinacea ten days out of a month to help build up the immune system; Astragalus is a good substitute. In any case, herbs that are antiviral such as Echinacea, Usnea, Goldenseal and Larix (from the larch tree and available from Eclectic Institute) are best taken for only ten days. So, when I am ill, I might take Echinacea or a combination of Echinacea and Goldenseal for ten days and then switch to Usnea. Golden Seal should be avoided by anyone who has low bloodpressure; anyone with high bloodpressure should not take Licorice. Ephedra or Ma Wong can stimulate metabolism, but is too hard on the adrenal glands to take for more than four days in a row; it is best rotated (four days on - four days off). Herbologists believe that nature created plants to be full spectrum; that is, the parts are determined by the function of the whole. Pharmaceutical companies cannot patent a plant; they look for one element or one kind of molecule from a plant, isolate it, extract it and then increase its potency. Reductionistic thinking does not consider that the constituents of a plant need to be in balance in order for it to function as it did before. Fen Pen comes from Ephedra. Fen Pen is neither full spectrum nor was it prescribed to be rotated. Valum comes from the Valerian plant, and while Valerian is not recommended for either the elderly or children, nobody to my knowledge has ever committed suicide from taking Valerian. Allopathic medicine either overpowers a disease with a powerful drug or suppresses (masks) the symptoms, hopefully until the body recovers on its own. Undesirable side effects and toxicity can occur from pharmaceuticals. In a lecture that I heard by

Dr. Andrew Weil, he stated that in his practice, he would occasionally use pharmaceuticals on a temporary basis to get a patient through a crisis and then switch them over to botanicals.

I have found that the effectiveness of all herbs is increased when they are rotated. However, there are herbs, which some people have found are successfully taken on a regular basis; such as, Hawthorne for the heart and Triphala for the intestines. I typically take a combination of herbs for up to three weeks and then switch to another combination for three weeks. I take the herbs to strengthen my body in quantities of three capsules each twice a day - usually first thing in the morning and about two hours after lunch on an empty stomach. Busy people with busy schedules simply buy the herbs that they are going to take in bottles of 100 capsules. When the bottles are gone, they switch to another combination; the rotation time is just over two weeks. There are herbs such as Lobelia that can only be taken a few drops at a time. Sena and Cascara Sagarata stimulate the intestines, but if taken for too long a period, like any laxative, prevents the intestines from moving on their own. It is also prudent to work on a few issues at a time, go slowly and <u>not overload the body with too many herbs, or take excessive quantities of a particular herb</u>. When the body detoxes too fast, nausea, headaches, fatigue, constipation and other flu-like symptoms can occur; in this case, I take activated charcoal or bentonite clay with lots of water to help absorb the toxins and remove the poisons from the body. When the body is ill it is important to stop taking detoxing formulas and concentrate on herbs that will help the body relieve itself of the distress. My belief is that the physical body will heal itself if given the proper support. Herbs that are organic, just like organic fruits and vegetables, contain more beneficial properties.

In the order of their potency, herbs can be taken in the form of teas, capsules, freeze-dried capsules or liquid extracts. Teas are a nice way to introduce herbs to the body in order to determine compatibility. The dosage is 1 teaspoon of dried herbs or 1 tablespoon of fresh herbs per cup of hot water. Capsules are a convenient way to take herbs; they are dried herbs that have been ground and encapsulated. Freeze cried herbs are 3 to 4 times stronger than normal capsules. Extracts are often taken in a small amount of warm water and they are for acute problems and for those who cannot swallow pills. The typical dosage on the side of the bottle is 40 – 60 drops three times a day and is correct for a person weighing 150 pounds. People weighing 75 pounds take half that dosage, while small children, as a rule of thumb, take 5 drops per year of age. Eclectic Institute carries a line of non-alcohol extracts for children, some of which are mentioned at the end of this chapter.

There are several schools of thought, each one uniquely different that use herbs to heal the body. The Gaylan Principle whereby herbs are given as either a preventatives or to treat the ailment is used in the Western Hemisphere. Homeopathy works under the principle that 'like treats like' and was used in Atlantis and rediscovered by Dr. Hanneman. The mother tincture is reduced or successed in a systematic manner until only the memory of the herb is left; the more times it has been diluted, the stronger it is. For example, Alium Sepa, which is made from onions, causes the eyes to water; so, people take Homeopathic Alium Sepa if they have a cold and watery eyes. Homeopathic Coffea is prescribed to calm the nerves and induce sleep. Ayurveda, the science of life, is 5 to 6 thousand years old and works with combination remedies and 3 body types or doshas: Vata (air element), Pitta (fire element) and Kapha (water element). Chinese patent formulas have also been around for thousands of years and work with the underlying premise that there are 5 elements. All diseases are deficiencies and the patent formulas go to the primary cause to treat the symptoms. Flower Essences were rediscovered by Dr. Edward Bach in the 1800's. They work primarily on emotions and also mental blocks, which are the cause of all diseases. Aromatherapy heals with pure essential oils; if the oils are not pure, there is no medicinal value.

Homeopathy's approach is to stimulate the body's natural capacity to heal itself safely. The Homeopathic doctor would find the remedy that matched the symptom of the disease to bring it to crisis so that the body could heal itself. On a metaphysical level, a Homeopathic remedy stimulates the issues lying behind the disease or pain. There are, however, some individuals for whom Homeopathy does not work at all! It could be that the power of their mind to disbelieve is stronger than the remedy or that their vibration is too low or that the emotion behind the disease has to be specifically addressed first or that karma has not been worked out. Shirley once had a customer who had done everything to treat his cancer but nothing worked. His first treatment had been surgery. The surgeon had successfully cut away the entire cancerous tumor. It was not the surgeon's fault, but when he was lifting it out, the tumor burst open and spilled into the open body. The man then turned to alternative therapies, which in his case extended his life in a quality manner so that he was able to look within and release self-destructive patterns before he died. When the correct Homeopathic remedy has been determined, after the first dosage, 1 of 4 things commonly happens. One, the patient gets better. The remedy is not repeated while improvement is still occurring. Two, the symptoms get slightly worse which is a good sign, and the remedy is repeated after there is an improvement. Three, there is an improvement but it only lasts for a short time and then either the patient stops getting better or begins to slip back. In this case, the same remedy is repeated. Four, the symptoms remain but the patient is emotionally feeling better, which is a good sign. Before retaking the same remedy, wait for other improvements.   The sooner the Homeopathic is administered after an injury, the more effective it is.   There are documented miracle cures from Homeopathic Arnica and the flower essence combination, Rescue Remedy.   Homeopathic Causticum and Cantharis both work on burns; most people alternate them until they realize which one is working.

Ayurvedic medicine has been practiced in India for 5,000 years; most Westerners are familiar with it today because of Deepak Chopra. Ayurvedic physicians look at pulse, tongue, eyes and nails. The emphasis of Ayurvedic medicine is on the body, mind and spirit. Constitutions or body types are the key to Ayurvedic medicine; each dosha refers to the overall health and profile of the individual, including strengths and susceptibilities.   Doshas govern the creation, preservation and dissolution of specific bodily tissues.   Most people are a combination of dosha constitutions.   Among their many combination extract formulas, Gaia Herbs, Inc. offers a selection of Chinese Patent Formulas as well as elixirs for the 3 doshas.   Gaia Herbs does an excellent job of maintaining the quality of the herb. For example, there is only a 2-day period where milky white silica is present in oat seed. Gaia Herbs process oat seed within that period and their efforts can be visually seen in the liquid extract itself.

Vata (air) is motion that activates the physical system and allows the body to breathe and circulate blood. The seats of the Vata are the large intestine, pelvic cavity, bones, skin, ears and thighs. Vata primary characteristics are unpredictability and variability in size, shape, mood and action. Vata types have a quick metabolism and tend to be slender, with predominant features, joints and veins and have cool, dry skin. They are mostly enthusiastic, impulsive and prone to anxiety, insomnia and PMS. Can be nervous and restless. Vata constitutions require a greater sense of balance, calming the nervous system and to replenish the vital energies. Some individuals take Gaia's Vata Soothing Elixir to support the nerves, mind, induce sleep and bring greater flexibility to the joints. When I took this formula, I found that the tendons that were injured in 2 car accidents were healing and becoming more mobile. I could ride my horse and get off without pain. I take the formula for 3 weeks and then switch to another herbal combination.

The seat of Pitta is in the stomach and the primary cause of imbalance in Pitta types is digestive disturbances. Pitta is the metabolism process of food, air and water and is responsible for hundreds of enzymatic activity throughout the body. Pitta constitution is catabolic, fire energy. Pitta types are of medium build, strength and endurance. They are well proportioned and have a stable weight. They often have fair, red or blond hair, freckles and ruddy complexion. They are quick, articulate, intelligent and can have quick, explosive tempers. Pittas eat and sleep regularly, perspire heavily and are often thirsty. They suffer from acne, ulcers, and stomach ailments. Pitta types need to be careful not to overheat the body. Gaia's Pitta Balancing Elixir focuses on the organs of digestion and glands.

Everything about Kapha is SLOW - slow to anger, eat, act, etc. Kapha constitution has a tendency to be overweight, have a slow digestion, somewhat oily hair and cool, damp, pale skin. They like to sleep long and heavy. Kapha is prone to high cholesterol, obesity, allergies and sinus problems – they can have lots of mucus. The seat is in the lungs and the constitution is anabolic, nutritive energy. Kapha is the structure of bones, muscle and fat that holds the body together and offers nourishment and protection. The chest, lungs and spinal fluid surround the spinal cord are the seats of Kapha in the body. Gaia's Kapha Invigorating Elixir activates and restores strength to the metabolic system and enlivens the constitution.

Popular Ayurvedic herbs include Calamus, which rejuvenates the brain and nervous system. It also cleans the lungs and is in anti-smoking by Gaia – Lobelia/Calamus Supreme. Gotu Kola revitalizes nerves and brain cells, decreases senility and aging, and strengthens the adrenals. Shatavari (she who possesses 100 husbands) cleans the female reproductive organs and blood. It also is used for stomach ulcers.

Ayurveda: The Science of Self Healing by *Dr. Vasant Lad*
The Ayurvedic Cookbook by *Amadea Morningstar*
The Yoga of Herbs by *Dr. David Frawley* and *Dr. Vasent Lad*

The dosage is not always on the packaging, so people rely on Chinese Herbal Patent Formulas by Jake Fratkin. There are some people for whom these combinations work consistently. Pill Curing is primarily for the flu, but also works for food poisoning and a variety of other digestive disorders. Lung Tan Xie Gan Pill works on urinary tract infections. Xizo Yao Wan helps digestion, especially the liver. To flush the liver, first thing in the morning mix and drink 1 cup warm water, the juice of 1 lemon (or lime), 1 capsule or dropper full of ginger and 1 teaspoon of pure, cold pressed olive oil. A cooling tea to help cleanse the body of excess acid caused by diet, hot climate and street, after breakfast mix and drink 1 cup warm water, 1/8 teaspoon Cuman, 1/8 teaspoon Coriander and 1/8 teaspoon of ground fennel seed.

Flower remedies contain the vibrational energy or life force of a particular plant. They work on the underlying emotion that is causing the disease, not the symptoms like Homeopathy. For example, cancer-like the anger that is behind the cancer eats away the body until it kills the body. Dr. Edward Bach said that two fundamental errors were at the root of all disease. The first error is that the personality is no longer in accord with the soul and in stages the personality has separated from the soul. The second error occurs as a result of the first; that is, in acting contrary to the Higher Self, the soul has separated from God. When the personality forces its will, virtues become twisted and manifest as destructive moods. Each of the 38 Bach Flower Remedies represents an archetypal state. The flower remedy that is taken has the missing essence. For example, "Mimulus relates to the soul qualities of courage and confidence. In the negative Mimulus state, one has to learn to overcome one's fears." ••• "Taking Mimulus, one will find the way out of the confusion of fears and anxieties, back to one's own true nature." *Mechthild Scheffer*, Bach Flower Therapy: Theory and Practice.

Rescue Remedy is the most commonly known and used flower remedy combination. It is used internally or external creams (cream also has Crab Apple). The components are: Rock Rose (panic, terror), Star of Bethlehem (reaches into cellular memory and releases physical/emotional trauma), Cherry Plum (uncontrolled or irrational thoughts), Clematis (inattentive or absentmindedness) and Impatiens (impatience and irritability).

Flower remedy combination for addictions: Walnut (breaks cycle and attachment), Cherry Plum (out of control, impulsive behavior), Chestnut Bud (for those who do not learn from their experiences), Agrimony (suppressed anxieties), Crab Apple (for those who are stuck and lost in detail), Pine (guilt surrounding actions), and Star of Bethlehem (trauma from past).

Flower remedy combination for depression: Mustard (depression comes and goes for no reason), Gorse (hopelessness), Olive (exhausted to tears), Sweet Chestnut (anguish), Star of Bethlehem (grief, trauma) and Gentian (lack of faith).

Flower Essences are not traditional herbal therapy. Since Dr. Edward Bach, other individuals have done further study. Indian Paintbrush can stimulate creativity and Mugwort taken before bed can help recall dreams. "Although flower essences are typically chosen for specific emotional issues, profound soul growth can occur which goes beyond resolving the particular situation for which the essences were selected." *Patricia Kaminski* and *Richard Katz*, Flower Essence Repertory: A Comprehensive Guide to North American and English Flower Essences for Emotional and Spiritual Well-Being

"Aromatherapy is therapy using aromas. The aromas come from the plant kingdom - flowers, trees, bushes and herbs. The relevant part of the plant is put through a process of distillation, where the volatile odiferous substance is captured equaling essential oil." *Maggie Tisserand*, Aromatherapy for Women. Essential oils are potent because they are condensed; one drop of essential oil equals one 1 oz. Bottle of herbal extract. Essential oils cannot be used with Homeopathy because they work on opposite extremes of the spectrum and they cancel each other out.

Essential oils are used as preventatives because they protect from pollutants, bacteria and viruses. Our sense of smell is linked to our emotions; thus, essential oils are used for depression, relaxation, stimulants and aphrodisiacs. For example, Melissa is used for depression, Marjoram is an antidepressant and relaxant, Basil is a stimulant and Ylang Ylang is an aphrodisiac.

Essential oils are strong and can cause skin irritations if they are not diluted in a carrier oil (Apricot, Sweet Almond, Sesame or Olive - Jahoba is a wax, not an oil, but it is also used because it doesn't clog the skin). When mixing more than one Essential Oil in a carrier oil, mix the Essential Oils first and then add the carrier oil. There are two oils that can be applied in small amounts directly onto the skin; these exceptions are Lavender and Tea Tree. Lavender is used for scarring, insect bites, scratches and at the temples for headaches. Tea Tree is anti-fungal and anti-viral. Some people use a single drop of Peppermint in the hairline at the temples for headaches.

The typical dilution is as follows: 15 drops of Essential Oil to 1 oz. carrier oil for massage; 20-15 drops per 1 oz. carrier oil for localized massage. 3-4 drops of Essential Oil in near boiling water for inhalation therapy. 6 drops to 1/2 pint hot or cold water for compresses. 50 – 150 drops to 4 oz. distilled water for mists. For baths, 6 drops are mixed with milk or honey, which helps to disperse the oil in water. Be it mineral salts or Essential Oils, I set aside 1/2 hour to soak in the tub; it is when the water begins to cool down that is when the toxins are pulled out of my body. After about 20 minutes, I can scrub the dead skin off. I drip dry because a dry terrycloth towel can absorb my own body's oils and dry my skin out. For great skin I have discovered that keeping the colon clean, drinking lots of good water and detoxing the liver are essential. Motherlove Herbal Company has a tincture called Liver Lover (use for 3 weeks) that can be alternated with their Purif-1 (use for 3 weeks) which is a blood cleansing formula that also works on lymph and kidney elimination.

There are 12 inorganic materials of cells that are called Cell Salts. Cell Salts that are used in Biochemic Therapy are prepared in much the same manner as Homeopathic Medicine is prepared. Its premise is based on Virchow's "cell theory" which states that since the body is a collection of cells, treatment should be directed towards the individual cells. People take 2 tiny

Cell Salts tablets 3 times a day in order to replace specific depleted inorganic materials. <u>Biochemic Theory and Practice</u> by *J. B. Chapman, M.D.* and *Edward L. Perry, M.D.*

Mushroom extracts are used in many Chinese Patent Formulas. Cordyceps *(Cordyceps sinensis)* is a sexual enhancer for men and exercise enhancer for women. The Chinese name for Cordyceps is Dong Chong Xia Cao; common name is Caterpillar Fungus. Enokitake, its Japanese name, *(Flammulina velutipes)* is good for the immune system. The common name is Golden Needle Mushroom. Lion's Mane *(Hericium erinaceus)* encourages nerve endings to grow and has been used in the treatment of Alzheimer's. Maitake, its Japanese name, *(Grifola frondosa)* is anti-cancer and tumors regression. The common name is Hen of the Woods. Reishi, its Japanese name, *(Ganoderma ludicum)* is anti-viral, anti-inflammatory, athletic enhancer and modulator of the immune system. The Chinese name for Reishi is Ling Chi. Royal Sun Agaricus *(Agaricus blazei)* is used for breast cancer. The Japanese name is Himematsutake. Shitake *(Lentinula edodes)* is anti-tumor and lowers serium cholesterol. The Chinese name for Shitake is Xiang Gu. Yun Zhi, its Chinese name, *(Trametes versicolor)* is anti-tumor. The common name for Yun Zhi is Turkey Tail. Eclectic Mycomedcidinals™ (mushroom extracts) are made from organic mushrooms and like their herbal extracts, the Mycomedcidinals™ are preserved in organic grape alcohol. <u>Medicinal Mushrooms</u> by *Christopher Hobs*

Michael Gillroy Tifres of Holland combines herbs with crystals. For acne, Chamomile flowers, the rasp from the skin of a yellow citrus fruit and green green adventurine are soaked in water overnight. The next morning, an amethist is dipped into the water and applied to the acne. Within 2 to 3 weeks, the acne is gone. For parasites, harmful bacteria and to quit smoking, drink the water in which Herkimer diamonds and lapis were soaked for only two hours. For swollen eyes aquamarine and obsidian can be laid on the closed eyes; hematite for red eyes or eye infections; and red tiger eye for tired eyes.

History of Iridology

Where in the world did iridology come from? Believe it or not, iridology actually came from the scientific observations of a medical doctor! There are several books on iridology. Dr. Bernard Jensen, a nutritionist, along with two collaborators, Keith Wills and Michael Diogo, wrote <u>Iridology Simplified</u>, which contains comprehensive iris charts. The iridology books tell the story of how the young Ignatz von Peczely caught an owl. In the struggle with the owl, the bird's leg broke. At that precise instant, a black stripe appeared in the owl's eye. As the owl's leg healed, white, branch-like lines filled in the black stripe. When the young boy became Dr. von Peczely, he studied the eyes of hospital patients and documented the correlation between their physical diseases and traumas to the visible traits that could be found on the iris of their eyes. Dr. Ignatz von Prczely became convinced that the iris is a complex reflex organ; that is, specific nerves in the iris are connected to every system, gland, organ and tissue in the human body. When there is a problem in the body, it can be observed in a particular location in the iris. The eye is not only the window to the soul, but a map of the human body.

The iris reveals physical imbalances, and metaphysically the iris is an indicator of karmic issues that are brought in as challenges. In working through these challenges, we grow spiritually. Many of our struggles are inherited, and perhaps as much as 70% of our body physiology has a direct correlation with our ancestral line. Before each incarnation, we choose which issues we want to overcome. This is what Jesus meant when he said, "You must be reborn in the spirit." If we choose not to grow, we become stagnant and Universal Energy no longer flows into and through us. This is the reason why 'dark souls' who are lacking in Light are drawn to souls that radiate the Light. When enough evolved souls pay attention and say, "If you need to play your games, go ahead, but not here!", then the 'dark soul' is either forced to grow or stultify like petrified wood.

What I enjoyed most about Zhenia's reading of my eyes was that she did not just give me a long list of things that were wrong with my body. In reading the signs on the iris and using her intuition, she was able to explain issues that I had been able to work through from both my mother's side (reflected in my left eye) and father's side (reflected in my right eye). Then she gave me some realistic goals and a means whereby to work through the healing of my body. According to Zhenia's interpretation, the brown discoloration was actually raised above or on top of my iris, overcastting my blue-green iris and causing a color distortion. Brown discoloration represented toxicity in my body, which was self-created through exposure to chemicals, drugs or pharmaceutical drugs. In the human eye, the thicker and the darker the color, the longer the toxicity has been there. When the eye becomes continually dull and murky, there is an indication of large accumulations of toxicity in the body. It also reflects strong emotions and strong stress.

As I have never 'done drugs', worked in a chemical environment or been to war, that left the penicillin. It is not that the antibiotics did not save my life; as a matter of fact, I know that they did. My Aunt Kathryn told me many years ago that when she went to visit me in the hospital when I was 9 months old, I was in crisis and the medical staff was reviving me - she thought that I

204

had died and that they brought me back to life. What I started working on was to clear the effects of the antibiotics and the underlying cause behind the pneumonia and ear infections.

Just as the homeopathic doctors all learn the same basic principles and make the practice of medicine unique to their abilities and creativity, so, too, iridologists interpret the iris and recommend herbs differently. I took what I learned from Zhenia in the reading she did for me, the two classes I took from her (Iridology for the New Age and Advanced Iridology), information from Shirley at Natural Health, Darcy at the Herb Stop, information from Hanna Kroeger and other sources to create a nutritional, herbal program that I personally felt worked for me.

Each herb has its own special frequency vibration. Herbs are concentrated food that work on a nutritional level by adjusting the vibrational rate of the body so that the body can balance itself. Organically raised herbs offer the maximum benefits to the physical body. Using single herbs addresses specific issues; herbal combinations hit broad areas.

Two of the qualities of herbs are building and cleansing. When we cleanse and release toxins, we leave an empty space that is vulnerable (the Universe does not like a void). Thus, the herbal program I went on consisted of 2/3 building and 1/3 cleansing herbs. Thus, not only are more building herbs taken, but they are also taken in quantities of three capsules twice a day for a total of six capsules. Only four capsules of each cleansing herb are taken an hour before bedtime. Herbs that are antiparasite like Wormwood and Black Walnut are best taken on an empty stomach and just before the full moon, when they are most active. Some people do a deep cleanse whereby they are only taking herbs along with fresh, organic juices. This is very stressful on the body and is not recommended in hot summers or cold winters because in extreme cold the body loses calcium too fast. Spring and fall are the best times to detox; however, some individuals with cancer have chosen not to wait for a change in season. Some people have found the following herbs or herbal combinations to be successful in releasing cancer from their bodies: Astragalus, Scudder's Formula (a combination of Cordydalis Tubers, Fresh Black Alder Bark, Mayapple Root, Figwort Flowering and Yellow Dock from Gaia Herbs), Red Clover in GBE strength, Tumeric & Bromiline, Ojibwa Tea (Sheep Sorel, Burdock Root, Slippery Elm Bark and Indian Turkey Rhubarb), Chaparral and Red Clover, Scudder's Alterative and Pau d'Arco. Naturopathic Handbook of Herbal Formulas includes Mistletoe and/or fresh Thuja leaf and/or Venus' Flytrap and/or a combination of Turmeric Root and Bromelain in herbal combination therapies. It is highly recommended that one work with a Naturopathic Doctor.

When we choose to heal, we initiate a process, but we have to follow through. It is like when I go into a home or a business and do a Feng Shui` reading (Chinese art of altering the environment to bring about beneficial results); people who are sensitive to energy can feel the movement of the change. Sometimes a family member will look at me and ask, "What are you doing?" or "How are you doing that?" But if the physical changes are not implemented, the energy patterns falter and dissipate. This same phenomenon can also be witnessed in those wishing to be initiated into Universal healing rays; that is, the initiation begins before they go for the initiation. If there is no follow-through, the initiation does not take physical form. This also holds true for Feng Shui` readings (the Chinese art of placement). I experienced the winds of change moving through my body when Zhenia did my iridology reading. When Zhenia said, "If I were you, I would use these herbs to balance my nutritional needs", I knew in my gut that I needed to get the herbs.

We come from spirit into the physical. During pregnancy, the soul can attach to the fetus at any time (I am sure that in the case of abortions, the soul was intelligent enough to never attach to the fetus). While the foundation for the mental and emotional bodies are laid down in the womb, the soul does not enter the baby's body until the baby takes the first breath (the soul leaves the body with the last breath). There are a lot of unnecessarily guilty women because as Joseph Campbell says, "religions take away the religious experience", and modern religions do not teach basic fundamental spiritual knowledge. In herbology, the healing process works backwards; that is, initially, herbs work through the physical body and then outwards through the emotional (guilts, fears, anger), into the mental (control, distortions, worry) and lastly, into the spiritual.

Iridology

Each one of us is re born on Earth with our own issues to work through and karma can be 'good' or bad'. Many of the problem areas that are reflected in the eyes are ancestral in nature; that is, these are issues that were left unresolved by those who came before. For example, one of the biggest issues on this planet is money. Deepak Chopra says that the only ones who think more about money than the poor are the very rich. In either extreme, if we allow money to enslave us, we will not be free. We are all manifesters. Money is meant to flow. It has to flow or it will get stuck. The same is true for all personal relationships; if we try to control another individual by trying to live their lives for them, we create cement. When we get stuck anywhere, we step out of the flow of the circle of life. This creates an etheric blockage, which in turn creates pain and/or disease. If we refuse to face our issues and see the true meaning of life, we can become blind. When we are afraid to look at our issues and ourselves we create degenerative ailments. It is up to us to overcome self-fears. Herbs work on many levels, not just the physical, to help us get through our stuff. Herbs are not a pill that will hide real problems or create an illusion to seemingly make things go away.

The eye is the window to the soul. It is only with great humility that we can look into another's soul. The clock positions for different body parts on the iris are the positions that we see when we look into another person's eyes. If we look into a mirror at our own eyes, we need to make the necessary adjustment - this can be accomplished by using a large mirror and having a clock on the wall behind us. When we see our issues as "imbalances" rather than "problems", it is easier to bring ourselves back into alignment.

5 eliminative systems in body:

Lungs (+ bronchus); kidneys (+bladder); bowel (large + small intestines); skin and lymph

Iris - complex reflex organ, as is the colon. Iris and colon are both connected to every single cell, tissue, organ and gland of the body, which in itself is both mechanical and artistic. When using the iris as a diagnostic tool, it may not be advisable for the iridologist to read 100% of the eye's imbalances - it would be too overwhelming for most people. It is often more effective to look at those issues that are in need of immediate attention. Sometimes, treating the larger issues with herbs takes care of smaller imbalances. Rather than naming diseases, the iridologist will ask if there is a family tendency. If in reading the iris, the iridologist finds that there is overlapping, that is, a landmark could possibly be for two different body parts, the iridologist will typically treat both areas with herbs.

What the iridologist looks for in the eyes:

Lesions

Broken, expanded or separated tissue. Inherited.

1. <u>Acute</u> - White in color and raised above the surface of the eye (protrudes). Associated with nerves, sharp pain, or mucus.

2. <u>Subacute</u> - nerve and blood supply affected. Light gray in color and are below surface of the eye.

3. <u>Chronic</u> - 10 to 20-year involvement. Blood and nerve supply barely making it. Dark gray in color and further beneath the surface. Sometimes, whole eye appears dark gray which is an indication that the whole body is functioning between subacute and chronic levels.

4. <u>Degenerative</u> - Zero nerve and blood supply. Often there is no pain because the nerves are gone. Black in color and deep beneath the surface of the eye.

<u>Healing signs</u> - fibers regrowing and filling in the lesions look like white branches. Calcium is important in order for healing to take place.

<u>More lesions</u> - weaker the constitution.

<u>Open Lesion</u> - open at one or both ends. Loose, fibrous. Easier to heal.

<u>Closed Lesion</u> - lack of blood. Harder to heal.

<u>Butterfly lesions</u> - several closed lesions together - inherited tendencies are strong.

<u>Large petals</u> - emotional issues.

<u>Lesions that are found within Lymphatic Rosary, or Psoras, or Stress Ring</u> - weak area.

<u>Teardrop shape</u> - "sealed off". Can be signs of tumors. The smaller and the darker they are, the harder they are to clean up.

<u>Right eye</u> - what has been inherited from father.

<u>Left eye</u> - what has been inherited from mother.

Constitutional Strength

<u>Fibers</u>

Strongest constitution - fibers are close together (tight) and evenly distributed. Indication of better blood and nerve supply.

Looser fibers - a tendency for looser constitutional strength.

Daisy petal eyed - broken fibers. If petals are open, it is an indication that the individual is giving energy away and allowing other people's "stuff" to come in.

When an iridologist rates the constitutional strength, 10 is the strongest constitutional strength and 1 is the weakest.

Inherited constitution - up to 70% of body physiology has to do with ancestral line. We choose the issues we want to overcome before we are born. This is called karma.

Brown eyes - cannot read fibers. True brown eyes - fibers are very fine. Iridologist can read landmark (Autonomic Nerve Wreath), toxicity and spokes (Radii Solaris)

Biliary eyes (brown-blue combination) are read like blue eyes.

<u>Landmark</u> - Autonomic Nerve Wreath will be close to pupil if individual is tightly holding on.

<u>Pupil</u>

Center of life. Heart center.

Small Pupil - 8 out of 10 people have a strong constitution. In varying degrees, they are neither open to nor do they take into consideration other people's opinions. Many of these individuals are difficult to treat because of their own tenacity or stubbornness and a corresponding feeling of invincibility. They typically have constricted heart chakras. Hilda in "Stormsfury's Last Son" is an extreme example of an individual with a strong constitution.

Weak constitution - these people have to work to take care of themselves and overcome genetic patterns. Everyone has some kind of vulnerability.

Large pupil - emotional, mental, physical energy is being drained because they allow others to take their energy. Indecisive! Can indicate drugs, poison, trance state or long-term physical abuse. Look at the eyes of someone who is going through chemotherapy or radiation. What most doctors do not tell their patients who go through radiation is that modern medicine knows that after radiation treatments, they expect that the cancer will come back within ten years - sooner for some and later for others. For those who survive longer than ten years, the radiation will break down the tissue in the body. Unbleached almonds release X-rays from the body; Kelp cleanses radiation out of the body and Epsom Salt baths draw toxins out of the body.

After death, pupil expands to fill entire iris.

Irregular-shaped pupil - emotions are 'bent out of shape', or it is an indication of repressed, suppressed emotional patterns.

Pupil changes with emotional state.

Pulsating pupil - adrenals overworked or they are out. Can indicate nervous breakdown.

White light from pupil - tendency to get cataracts.

Green light from pupil - tendency to get glaucoma.

Color of Eye

Original color of eye?

Texture of brown eye is like Sahara Desert.

Most dominant color in iris now?

Red eye = stress.

Murky = precancer eye can be seen as murky. Everything is reversible; however, pattern has to be changed. Root cause of problem has to be addressed - usually suppressed anger or rage.

Alcoholism shows differently - ego body is overdeveloped and in control. Individual's true self can emerge as the large picture (in control) with work. Alcoholics, drug abusers lack joy (**DHA**). The flower essence Borage can bring joy back into life and the Shen (essence of who we really are) back to the heart.

Orange = pancreatic weaknesses can be seen as orange. In this case, the iridologist looks for lesions on the right eye in the area of the iris correlating to the pancreas.

The question is: *"Are there any diabetics in your family?"*

Orange also comes up above the surface of the eye and is toxic in nature.

Pancreas imbalance - suppressed resentment. Life has a lack of sweet flow; pancreas is not creating insulin.

"Soma" is a mantra that can create sweetness and a sense of feeling alive.

Some individuals have found relief from chiropractic spinal adjustments because when the vertebrae are out of alignment, they can pinch nerves and blood vessels that control and feed specific organs or glands. A poltice out of gingerroot put over the pancreas, or whatever gland is congested, can draw out congestion. Tomato poltice has been used for tumors. To draw out toxins, rub Cod Liver Oil over the area, cover with white linen and then cover with warm blankets or hot water bottle.

<u>Psora</u> = hyperpigmentation. Spots of color randomly distributed in iris. Toxicity! Typically, the closer to the pupil and the darker they are, the more serious.

Inherited, genetic tendencies, especially from mother. Psora spots can be passed down to children in same area of iris. Psoras reflect karmic pattern of family. Weak tissues - if someone has a psora on the iris which correlates to a particular organ, gland, etc., then recovery from surgery on that particular organ, gland, etc. is difficult and slow.

<u>Yellow</u> = can indicate urinary involvement. Flow of urinary tract. Lots of acid going through. Poison stuck in urinary tract. Blockage in flow! Trapped poisonous water in body causes puffiness. Acid is fire and burns calcium and nerves. The following three spices in warm water has been found by some to cool the body by releasing excess acid: Steep 1/8 teaspoon Coriander, 1/8 teaspoon Cumin and 1/8 teaspoon ground fennel seed for 5 minutes and then drink.

<u>White eye throughout iris</u> = can be an indication of mucus or acid (overacid body chemistry). Thick, swollen, white fibers - poor diet. Can indicate Rheumatism (joint pains) or an overabundance of parasites in bloodstream. When parasites eliminate their waste, they secrete toxins wherever they happen to be in the body - toxins make our bodies sick. Hanna Kroeger and Hulda Clark both say that wherever there is cancer in the body, you can also find flukes.

A straight allopathic doctor is not going to agree with much of any of this, and no iridologist or individual practicing the ancient art of hands-on healing is going to tell anyone to go off of their pharmaceutical prescriptions. Every individual has the right to decide for him/herself which course of action s/he will take. We are all different; we all have choices! Current studies show that 70% of Americans take vitamins and/or herbs and the majority of these people do not tell their doctors because they know the doctor will ridicule their course of action or has no knowledge of alternative supplements. **Herb Contraindications and Drug Interactions** by Francis Brinker, M.D.

Iris Sign - Autonomic Nerve Wreath

1/3 out and away from pupil.

Autonomic nerve system response. General nerve system. How well or how badly nerve system is working.

More broken the wreath - more likely to have nervous breakdown.

Where landmark is broken or not present, there is poor nerve supply to the corresponding part of the body. Where nerves are not supported, the problem is genetic.

Tighter the fibers of the Autonomic Nerve Wreath, the stronger the nerve supply.

<u>Condition and integrity of bowel.</u>

How we digest food shows how we digest life.

If we cannot eliminate properly, then we are not circulating life.

Darkness - holding onto.

Large intestine - is defined by the outside edge of the Autonomic Nerve Wreath, which shows the condition of the large intestine. Iris frill shows size, shape, continuity, and depth of colon by outlining the second ring in iris, which is the Autonomic Nerve Wreath. (*First ring from the pupil is the halo, and that shows the condition of the stomach.*)

<u>Ballooning</u> (outside of normal landmark) can indicate low-grade infections like colitis.

<u>Small, tight Autonomic Nerve Wreath</u> is an indication of chronic constipation.

<u>Tiny holes</u> in the Autonomic Nerve Wreath indicate bowel pockets that are toxic and nests for parasites.

<u>Opening at bottom of Wreath</u> - poor circulation in legs (6:00 in either eye). Kidney (5:45 right eye/6:15 left eye) & bladder involved, which would be an indication that there is lots of uric acid in the body.

<u>Darker from 11:00 to 1:00 </u>(in either eye) - complication in brain and thought process.

Irritations

White and raised - indication of toxicity, mucus, acidity, nerve pinching, or nerves overworked.

If whiteness appears from 11:00 to 1:00 on either eye (mental area), it can mean that there is mucus in sinuses. Also an indication of an unclear mind.

Mucus and gas can go anywhere in the body.

Thicker and whiter the iris, the more mucus.

Thick white lines are irritations. Fibers are swollen.

If body is too acidic, then it needs more alkaline.

Acute inflammation - discharge (body's way of clearing). Thick white lines.

Arcus Senilis

Brain anemia - lack of iron and oxygen.

11:00 to 1:00 almost outside of iris. Almond shaped. Usually light gray. Brain anemia. Lack of proper food and organic iron. **Gotu Kola and Ginkgo Biloba**.

If present in a younger person - overworked, analytical mind.

Absorption Ring

Between pupil and stomach area. Some can get so dark that it looks like part of the pupil.

Darker - less ability to absorb food.

If Absorption Ring cannot be seen - not absorbing nutrients well.

Flat - not too bad.

Raised - absorption is irritated.

Halo

White in halo - overacid stomach. Whiter than any other part of the iris. Could mean stomach ulcers. **Lysine** - alkaline.

Overacid body - whiteness in whole eye. Stop eating dairy (worst), sweets, and wheat. Strong constitutional people hold on; acid will not always show as brown or orange.

Dark halo - not enough hydrochloric acid. Cannot digest food well. **Celery** - high in organic sodium. (Celery also helps body to adjust to extremes in external temperatures.)

Large halo - large stomach.

Nerve Rings

Neurovascular cramping. Stress.

Whiter they are, the deeper the stress and the longer they have been there.

Closer together they are, deeper the stress.

More than 2 rings - stress in more than one lifetime.

Nerve Ring inside of halo - "sick to my stomach".

If Nerve Ring runs across lesion - area is in stress.

Look at solar plexus - 3:45 on Autonomic Nerve Wreath in left eye.

(The herbs herein are neither all-inclusive nor are they for everyone. The herbal program I describe works for my body weight and constitution. Professional consultation is recommended.)

Lymphatic Rosary

Lymphatic person - easily gains weight. Hard to lose weight. Congested.

Lymph is 5th eliminative system.

3 times more lymph than blood in the human body.

15 pints of blood/45 pints of lymph in average human body.

Collective consciousness is associated with lymph. Tailbone (which pumps the lymph) can go out with stress in environment such as nuclear testing or earthquakes.

Lymphatic Rosary starts on the outside of the iris and works its way inwards. If they are in Autonomic Nerve Wreath, death is at hand.

Below the lung is breast area - rosary beads often start there.

Body brush with a dry brush before taking a shower or bath. This is what I do: Move brush in small clockwise circles from the outer extremities to the descending colon. (Lymph as well as the blood dump toxins into the large intestines, not the heart.) Movement of lymph in right breast is counterclockwise. (Breasts - lymph moves from the sternum up and to the sides.) With feet, start at bottom of feet (hands - start with the palms), circling clockwise and brush up to descending colon. Do the backs of the hands and feet, circling up the extremities, and move lymph to descending colon. On right side of body, move across transverse colon and end at descending colon. For the back: Brush in strokes from spine slightly downward and to each side.

Trampoline is good for moving the lymph unless transverse colon is collapsed.

Scurf Rim

Dark shadows on outermost zone, which indicates health of the skin. Lack of circulation and silicon - **Oatstraw and Horsetail**.

Cholesterol or Sodium Ring

Cholesterol and heart.

Opaque color. Inside of iris. Can hide Scurf Rim. Walks from outside to inside.

Lecithin breaks down cholesterol.

Whey - organic sodium and organic calcium.

Anemia in Extremities

Outside of iris. Continuation of Arcus Senilis. **Spinach, chlorophyll and spirulina** - high in iron and other minerals.

Restricted blood flow - tissues scream. (Heart attack is like muscle cells screaming.)

Gangrene - lack of oxygen.

Venous Congestion

Anemia in extremities (hands and feet can turn blue)- indication of a lack of oxygen. Can also be purple in color.

Radius Solaris

9 out of 10 - Radius Solaris appears first in brain (between 11:00 and 1:00). Toxic thoughts create disease and toxins in the body.

Indication of complicated genetic patterns on mental level.

Ask about connections to parents.

Often in pairs opposite one another.

Shape of Eye

Left eye bent out of shape, especially near corner of eye, indication that female energy is suppressed. Lack of nurturing and nourishment.

Right eye bent out of shape, especially near corner of eye, indication that male energy suppressed.

Brown Eyes

Iridologist needs strong light in order to read the eyes, but cannot shine light in client's eyes for longer than a few seconds. (Crenton Light Bulb)

Cannot see lesions in brown eyes because fibers are too fine.

1. Find landmarks and read fibers inside of landmark. Landmark will tell you about nerve supply, shape of bowel, pockets in bowel, breaks, and toxicity. Toxicity can be heavy and raised above the surface of the eye. Some toxicity is so thick that the fibers inside of the landmark cannot be seen.

2. Can see Radii Solaris, Nerve Rings, Venous Congestion, Scurf Rim, Anemia in Extremities, Arcus Senilis, Absorption Ring and Light from Pupil.

3. Biliary Eyes, which are a combination of blue and brown eyes, are read like blue eyes.

4. Acute - light yellow color on iris

   Subacute - light gray

   Chronic - dark gray

   Degenerative - black

5. Yellow throughout eyes - can be an indication of an overacidic body.

6. Lungs & kidneys - easier to find signs, which are mucus and acid.

7. Spokes and bowel pockets - areas that need immediate attention.

Herbs & Things

'Modern' or allopathic medicine does not recognize herbs, Vitamins or mineral supplements (suggested usage on bottle) as being beneficial to the human body. It is up to the consumer to read and research. In part, because of the wide range of problems that even a single herb may address, books will take different approaches. <u>Naturopathic Handbook of Herbal Formulas</u> by Herbal Research Publications also gives contraindications; for example, there are many herbs that cannot be taken by pregnant women or nursing mothers, or small children.

Botanicals, in whatever form they are taken, bring to the surface issues and emotions for healing. So as not to become overwhelmed, it is advisable to work on one issue at a time. If the body detoxes too fast, the body can go into a healing crisis, which is characterized by headaches and nausea. When I have gone into a healing crisis, I immediately stop taking detoxing herbs and take the Bach Flower Remedy, Rescue Remedy. I drink water and take natural products to help absorb the toxins and flush them out of my body and run over to see my colon therapist. My grandfather was a pharmacist and whenever my mother got sick, she was given Milk of Magnesia to flush the germs out of the intestines. In Europe colonics are given to sick people in the hospital.

Slow and steady wins the race. Herbs are not a quick fix and the benefits are noted over time. Detoxing and supporting the body is what keeps it healthy and youthful. 95% of all ailments may be due to toxicity. Is it worth the effort to detox? Healthy body tissue is what youth is. Scientists talk about transplanting old heads onto youthful bodies. That would be the equivalent of putting new wine into old skins. Much easier and far less traumatic to detox the body and support the glands, organs and tissues with herbs and nutrients.

To detox, I use 2/3 building herbs to support the body and 1/3 cleansing herbs. The candida diet, which is basically rice and vegetables, is too stressful on the body unless supplemented with building herbs like kelp, alfalfa, etc. Many people take building herbs twice a day – once in the morning and then 1 to 1 1/2 hours after lunch. I take 3 capsules of each herb twice a day in this manner. I take the cleansing herbs (including the anti-parasitic herbs) before bed. Typically I take 4 capsules of each herb. Herbs are more effective when they are rotated, so that my body does not build up a tolerance to them. I take one combination of herbs for about 3 weeks, and then I switch to an alternate herbal program. For example, I switch back and forth from black walnut to herbal pumpkin as an evening cleanser (everyone and in particular anyone who works with animals might consider taking anti-parasitic herbs). In Taoism, organs have corresponding sense organs that they govern; for example, the liver governs the eyes. Thus, one possible herbal rotation might be to take herbs for the liver for three weeks, and then switch to herbs for the eyes if that is an issue. Another possible herbal rotation would be to take some herbs for the liver and eyes and then switch to a different combination of herbs for the liver and eyes. <u>Whenever in doubt, what I do is consult an herbologist and/or iridologist or I have</u>

somebody who knows how to muscle test (kinesiology) test me to see which herbs are best for me and when is the best time for me to take those herbs.

As a source for other possible herbal rotations: In Taoism, the lungs govern the skin and nose. Kidneys govern bones, reproductive organs and ears. Liver governs nerves, brain, tendons, facial hair and eyes. Heart governs blood, body hair and tongue. And spleen governs muscles, lymph glands, lips and gums.

The following is a list of some common herbal and natural products and some of their properties. It is by no means complete. It serves as food for thought:

Alfalfa - 25% cleanser/75% builder. Digestive stimulation. High in chlorophyll, Vitamins A, K & D, calcium, iron, potassium and enzymes. Blood purifier, for arthritis, diabetes, sinus problems, mental and physical fatigue, pituitary gland and kidney cleanser. Most people's bodies are too acidic, which among other things can cause nerve damage. Alfalfa is an alkaline which has been taken to bring the body back to a normal state. Black cherry juice is another high alkaline food. (Lemon turns alkaline in body.) Alfalfa is best taken with meals to avoid gas

Aloe Vera - Whole leaf with gel - powerful, bitter taste. 65% cleanser/35% builder. Internally and externally. Stomach ulcer - 1 oz. a few times a day on empty stomach. Gets rid of X-rays in environment. Used by pregnant women for a laxative. Calcium, Potassium (good for skin), Sodium. Used to treat hemorrhoids, radiation burns and scar tissue - inside and outside of body.

Angelica Root – Not during pregnancy or for diabetics. Diuretic, vascular builder, digestive tonic and promotes perspiration, so it aids skin in elimination.

Bee Pollen - 95% builder. Whole food - all minerals, all vitamins, amino acids (Bragg's Soy Sauce - free amino acids), 35% protein. B complex (reduces stress level). Lecithin - breaks down cholesterol. Slows down aging. Hormone system. Allergies. Energy. Hay fever. Longevity.

Most people who have allergies are highly toxic. One possible way to take bee pollen is to start with one granule of bee pollen the first day; second day, take two granules. Build up to 1/2 tsp. a day. Take 1/2 tsp. for a couple of months. Then build up to 1/2 tsp. twice a day for 3 to 6 months. Then begin building up to 1 tsp. twice a day. Mountain High Bee Pollen in Phoenix is one popular distributor.

Bentonite & Slippery Elm - Bentonite pulls 40 times its weight in toxins. 2-oz. bentonite two times a day in water when detoxing. Store liquid clay in refrigerator after opening bottle. Replace friendly bacteria after detoxing, colon therapy or severe diarrhea by taking acidophilus with water the first thing the following morning. (Drink a glass of distilled water first thing in the morning an hour before eating or drinking coffee to flush toxins out of the body.)

Black Cohosh, Dong Quai, & He-Shou-Wu - female hormone herbs. Chronic bronchitis. Hormone balance. Dong Quai is hotter, more heating - for emotional stress, high toxicity, and menopause. It is best to check with a Chinese herbologist before taking Chinese herbs.

Black Elder flower and berry - infections, inflammations, common cold virus, sinus and respiratory infections, and retroviruses. Eliminates toxins and promotes sweating.

Black Walnut - 85% cleanser/15% builder. Kills parasites and breaks up parasite nests. Most skin problems caused by candida or parasites. Full moon is time parasites become most active. Oxygenates blood! Organic iodine - important for thyroid! 98% of people have thyroid issues. Balances sugar level! Contains Vitamin B15, manganese and silica.

Blessed Thistle - taken in small doses increases urination and sweating to flush body of toxins. Stimulates menstruation and increases the flow of mother's milk. Combined with Red Raspberry leaves – stimulates gastric secretions.

Calcium - without Calcium, there is no healing. Calcium needs magnesium in order for it to be absorbed and zinc (trace amounts) to retain calcium in body. Copper (trace amounts) for proper skeletal development. Calcium, Magnesium and Potassium are key electrolytes in muscle contraction and relaxation. Hannah Kroeger believes that people who cannot hold a chiropractic adjustment need Calcium.

Capsicum (Cayenne Pepper) is a catalyst - enhances other herbs. Capsicum & Goldenseal - stomach ulcer. (Goldenseal is not given to people with low blood sugar.) Stops bleeding. For mucus - some people have taken 1 to 2 capsules in 1 ounce of water, 3 times a day. Capsicum neutralizes sugar; therefore, pancreas won't work as hard if Capsicum tablets are taken with sweets. Rebuilds lungs.

Cascara Sagrada + Psyllium Hulls (helps to pull away encrusted matter from bowel walls) - Cascara Sagrada causes bowel to move - take on an empty stomach. **Pumpkin Seed + Cascara Sagrada** kills parasites and aids in elimination.

Chamomile, Passionflower, Valerian, Skullcap, Hops - for nerves, nervousness, releasing stress and insomnia. Take one or more herbs or combination formula just before going to sleep at night.

Chaparral, Red Clover, Taheebo (Pau d'Arco) - anticancer, antiviral. Pau d'Arco is also for leukemia. **Chaparral + Echinacea** for lymph system and upper respiratory. Cancer is the physical expression of unexpressed anger or rage and typically strikes that part of the body that has been overly expressed or repressed. AIDS and homosexuality are both strongly karmic. Homosexuality is not a sin; it is the overexpression of the 1/3 masculine or feminine and repression of the corresponding 2/3 feminine or masculine. Typically, I have found in working with individuals who have extreme self-hatred of either the masculine or the feminine that this aspect of the self is completely or greatly suppressed. There are also complex karmic patterns at issue. We all have self-hatred issues – be it our nose or a past life or whatever. Correspondingly, abuse victims often have self-hatred issues. It is not the outward manifestation of our self-hatred that is a "sin", but rather the hatred itself. God is Love; hatred, any hatred, is the opposing force that prevents us from experiencing ourselves as a loving, interactive, creative being. Whatever our issue(s), we need to take responsibility so we can create wholeness and love.

Chaste Tree Berry – beneficial for female reproductive system. Taken premenstrually helps maintain a normal balance between estrogen and progesterone.

Comfrey - is called "the bone knitter" (powerful healing effects on bone, blood and tissue). For thousands of years it has been taken internal and as a poultice (strong drawing power). In some cases Comfrey has been toxic to the liver – whether this had to do with the dosage or toxicity of the liver, I do not know. High in calcium! **Fenugreek** with comfrey removes mucus.

Cornsilk - Urinary, bladder & kidney stones and ailments, bedwetting and also good for the heart. **Uva Ursi** - to flush out kidney stones and cysts and is good for diabetes. **Hydrangea** – helps prevent stones and gravel. In iridology, the kidney & bladder are often treated together just as liver & gallbladder are treated together.

Dandelion - cleanser for blood & blood circulation; builder of liver and gallbladder. Nutrients - Vitamins B & D and potassium. Helps liver assimilate iron. Safe diuretic *(herb that increases the flow of urine)*, used in treatment of congestive jaundice, water retention caused by heart problems, lowers blood pressure and for inflammation of liver and gallbladder.

Devil's Claw - gets rid of yeast, fungus and candida. Candida thrives on vinegar, fermented foods, and mushrooms. Peanuts are pure yeast; Almond butter is an alternative.

DHEA - antiaging. Vitality on subtle level! Good for entire glandular system.

Eyebright - cataracts. **Bilberry** - Eyes - disease & vision. Feeds capillaries. Often found in combination together.

Garlic - *Natural antibiotic.* Bless garlic before you eat it because garlic absorbs human stresses of farmer and shippers. Works like Goldenseal. Garlic good for blood & high blood pressure. Parasites + candida. **Garlic** & **Mullein** come in combination as ear drops.

Goldenseal - *Natural antibiotic.* Internal hemorrhage. Infections. Do not take on a regular basis; do not take for any longer than 10 days. May lower blood sugar - do not give it to low blood sugar people. Natural form of insulin. **Goldenseal** & **Capsicum** - stomach ulcer. **Capsicum** is an enhancer for other herbs.

Ginger - produces lots of heat. Use less in summer. For gas and bloating - 2 slices of ginger will eliminate bloating and gas. Cook with seafood to kill germs & fishy smell. (Cup of vinegar left out will absorb fish smells.) Herb enhancer.

Ginkgo & **Hawthorn** - 75% builder/25% cleanser. Low blood pressure, low blood sugar, enlarged heart, palpitations. Circulation + heart + arteries. **Ginkgo** & **Gotu Kola** - circulation & mental.

Ginseng - king of herbs. 3 different kinds. Korean Ginseng - too hot. Siberian Ginseng - most neutral. Supports adrenals. Wild American Ginseng - most cooling, most expensive.

For energy, senility and fatigue. High blood pressure (potassium). Heart + circulation. *While I am not a Chinese herbologist, I have been told that Ginseng is so yang (masculine) that the Chinese balance ginseng with 14 other herbs. Enhances everything, do not take when sick!*

Gotu Kola - Brain. Physical vitality. 75% builder. Prevents nervous breakdown. (Fo-Ti is also used for depression; however, its main use is as an anti-inflammatory, vasodilator, sexual tonic and rejuvenator.)

Green Tea – Anticarcinogenic, enhances immune system and breaks down cellulite.

Hyssop - regulates low or high blood pressure.

Horsetail – Astringent, urinary tonic, used for incontinence and inflamed prostate. **Horsetail + Oatstraw** - Silicon and selenium. (Only a few things contain selenium.) Works with Zinc. Skin, nails + hair. Blood cleanser.

Juniper Berry - herb for pancreas - high in natural insulin. Also for water retention. Do not use if there is kidney disease.

Kelp - number one for thyroid. Iodine + 30 different minerals. Glandular system in general and specifically for Pituitary (master gland)! Pulsation of pupil can be an indication that adrenals are stressed (leads to chronic fatigue symptom). Fingernails. Complexion.

Kola Nut – stimulant (contains caffeine) and diuretic; used for depression and migraines.

Licorice - happy herb. When blood sugar drops, take licorice. <u>Not given to high blood pressure person or diabetic</u> (increases blood sugar level) or <u>someone with colitis</u> (stimulates the bowel) or if pregnant. Adrenal support, natural laxative, hormone support for female organs, hypoglycemia, for drug withdrawal, gastric ulcers, expectorant and antispasmodic. Counteracts Goldenseal.

Ligustrum – Cleansing and rejuvenating tonic.

Lobelia - herb with its own intelligence! Works wonders. Works on whatever needs to be healed. Respiratory. Ear infections (2 drops in ear). Garlic & Mullein are also good for ears. Lobelia oil for sore throat – gargle and spit. Removes mucus and congestion in body, not just sinuses. Used for asthma and bronchitis. Nerves and nervousness. Too strong for most people - take only 1 or 2 drops. Overdosing can cause vomiting.

Mullein - natural painkiller. Allows mucus to loosen. Fresh Mullein flowers - warts. (Juice of fig also draws warts out of skin.) Dries out warts. Lymphatic system. Bronchitis.

Asthma.   Bleeding from lower bowel & lungs.   Sinus congestion.   For sinus polyps - Frankincense & Myrrh oils. Pau d' Arco (also good for Leukemia).

Myrrh - Natural antibiotic. Lung diseases. Stimulant - vitality and strength to digestive system. Mucus. Antiseptic for sores. Use a few drops of oil for thyroid.   Sore throat and mouthwash.

Oats - Nervine, safe tonic for impotence and strengthens heart.

Oregon Grape - bitter is good for liver and gallbladder.   Anticancer.   (The mineral Selenium - popular anticancer.) Yellow jaundice. Skin diseases. Psoriasis.

Pantetheine – coenzyme form of Pantothenic acid. Increases energy production, lowers serium cholesterol and immune system stimulator.

Papaya - food enzyme. Best part right next to skin. Facial mask - middle part with seeds.

Parsley + Garlic + Capsicum - bladder, kidney, urine retention, jaundice, gallstones, cancer preventative. Do not use parsley when pregnant because it could induce labor.

Peppermint – digestive and appetite aid. 2 drops of peppermint oil in warm water - takes away gas pain.

Sage - mental exhaustion, insanity, too much saliva and digestion.   Cleanses sinuses and bronchial tubes.

Sarsaparilla - hormone food for hormone balance. Increases circulation for rheumatic joints.   Stimulates metabolic rate.

Slippery Elm - neutralizes stomach acidity.   Gas. A little bit of Slippery Elm - stops diarrhea. A lot of Slippery Elm - causes diarrhea. Slippery Elm + Bentonite clay - pulls toxins out of body (refrigerate bentonite clay after opening bottle so that it stays sanitized).

Swedish Bitters - combination of Tumeric, Gentian, Calemus, Milk Thistle, Wild Yam, Cardamom, Fennel, Ginger, Gooseberry, Bitter Orange, Anise, Sea Vegetables and Marine Algae, which brings back good flora and is often added to Candida diets (basically rice and vegetables).

Thyme & **Fenugreek** work similarly for respiratory and lung congestion issues. They are antifungal and help eliminate skin parasites.

Tumeric (also known as Curcumin) – is an antioxidant *(Oxidation in the body casuses free radical to form. Free radicals damage heaalthy cells and form toxic cless, which can lead to disease. Antioxidant nutrients protect cells from free-radical damage.)* It is also anti-inflamatory and improves absorption. With Calimus root and Fennel – stimulates digestion.

White Oak Bark - varicose veins (inherited). Cellulite (inherited condition) - water toxins. Can make a paste and apply it to skin if there are varicose veins.   Good for circulation.

Wild Yam - glandular balance. Vitality. Fiber.

Wormwood – is an anthelmintic *(stimulating herb that works against parasitic worms that may be present in the digestive tract).*

Gland Body Types
Indicators of strengths and weaknesses in body

Adrenal - usually gets fat in stomach (beer belly). Aggravated, stubborn. Foods - steak, meat, potatoes, fats, salt, nuts, eggs. Apple shaped (solid), square, round head. Work habits - workaholic, steady energy. Health problems - lower back, high blood pressure, arthritis, seldom catches cold.

Pituitary - (controls water in the body) mental. Large rear end. Stress reaction, spacey, anxious, and worried. Food - dairy, starches sweets and fruit. Appearance - small chest, youthful, underchin pouch. Working habits - procrastinator, perfectionist, intellectual, idealistic, philosophizes. High energy in AM. Health problems - allergies, irritable bowel, migraine, low blood pressure, asthma, hypoglycemia, weak digestion, lactose intolerance.

Thyroid - (when tonsils are taken out, thyroid gets weaker) Usually gains weight in spare tire. Long arms and legs. Starches caffeine, sweets and fruit. Nervous and quick- tempered. Long limbs, long fingers and long neck. Working habits are intense. Enjoys changes. Unstable energy. Sinus problems, cold hands + feet. Hyperthyroid and Hypoglycemia.

Gonadal - (reproductive) gets fat in gut. Reproductive glands most dominant. Gains weight in rear end and thighs. Frustrated quickly and quick-tempered. Favorite foods are creamy, fatty food, chocolate. Working habits - energetic in later day. Likes to cook. Health problems - lumpy breasts, bladder, constipation and loses weight slowly.

Body Parts

AGAIN, IT IS HIGHLY RECOMMENDED THAT PEOPLE DO FURTHER READING AND CONSULTATION BEFORE TAKING HERBS. THERE ARE CONTRAINDICATIONS FOR HERBS AND MANY ARE NOT SUITABLE FOR CHILDREN OR PREGNANT OR NURSING MOTHERS.

Adrenal - has to do with self-preservation and they are the #2 kidneys in Chinese medicine. Works with kidneys. Adrenal or thyroid is out - two of the most common problems in people. Kelp. Licorice. Vitamin C and Gota Kola and B-5 (panothenic acid).

Animation Life - Life force. Twelve o'clock on iris. Spoke or lesion on Animation Life indication of lack of energy or mental deficiency. Appendix and tonsils are a part of the immune system and serve as radar for body. When there are parasites in the intestines the appendix secrets tiny droplets of oil that are antiparasitic. When there is a parasite infestation, the eggs can get into the appendix, which is why Hannah Kroeger believes appendixes are removed.

Blood – On iris, blood is the second ring from the periphery. Burdock is a blood purifier that stimulates the liver and kidneys. Yellow Dock is a builder and cleanser of the liver (also for spleen and skin). Chaparral is a liver cleanser. Any herb that cleanses the liver will have a positive effect on the blood (also the eyes). Echinacea is good for the blood as well as the lymph.

Anemia is the reduction in the amount of oxygen that the blood is able to carry which results in fatigue, dizziness and irritability. 20% of women have anemia. Iron makes hemoglobin, the component of the blood that carries oxygen. Nettles, Yellowdock, Dandelion and Alfalfa have been used to treat anemia.

Guggal is an Ayurvedic resin that increases the white blood cell count. It also clears lungs, helps heal skin and mucous membranes and fights cholesterol

Essential oils (external use) that have been used successfully are Hyssop as an adaptogen of high or low blood pressure, Carrot Seed for anemia and Geranium for varicose veins.

Bones - Burdock is used for calcification in joints. For arthritis - Devil's Claw (anti-inflammatory), Garlic and Dandelion. Comfrey is a healer that has been used externally and internally for hundreds of years. It is high in calcium and is often referred to as the boneknitter and is also used for arthritis. Devil's Claw has been used in place of cortisone. It is a painkiller and anti-inflammatory for arthritis and rheumatism. Yucca helps the body produce its own cortisone by helping our adrenals produce it for pain and inflammation. Sarsaparilla increases circulation for rheumatic joints, Aloe Vera Juice - rids joints of acid; Dandelion is a builder and used for joints and those suffering from arthritis. Lecithin –is used for breaks.

For arthritis - twice a day drink a combination of 8 ounces of calcium fortified orange juice, 1 packet of drinkable Know gelatin and 2 ounces of an essential mineral product (read directions for any variations). Externally – Arnica gel. In one ounce of distilled water combined 10 drops each of White Willow and Devil's Claw and rub into knuckles or arthritic joints. White Willow is an anodyne *(herb that has the action of pain relief)*. Caster oil packs.

Joell Wallich was a veterinarian before he became a medical doctor. He is an author, and in 1991 he was nominated for the Nobel Prize. He says that most doctors think that bone spurs are an indication that an individual is getting too much calcium. Dr. Wallich says that veterinarians and farmers know that in animals, bone spurs and kidney stones are indications that the animals are not getting enough calcium. Dr. Wallich says that the same is true for people.

Things like heel spurs can also result from bad digestion. Minerals, especially calcium, are not being digested or absorbed. Clean colon. (See stomach)

For calcium deposits in the joints, an herbal combination for long-time use is Alfalfa, Horsetail, Shavegrass, Oats, Dandelion and Ginger. Silica binds to calcium and removes deposits over time.

Can lubricate joints internally with essential fatty acids (don't do it if there is too much estrogen). Wobenzym enzymes for joints and also tendons, muscles and sinus infections.

Two minutes of hot water and 30 seconds of cold water can follow footbaths with Epsom Salts.

Essential Oils:

Sweet Birch - anti-inflammatory. Joints and arthritis.

Juniper 'Berry Oil - good for arthritis

Vetiver - anti-arthritic

Laventine - aches and pains.

Homeopathic First Aid Remedies:

Ruta Graveolens (Ruta) – for bruised bones and after chiropractic manipulations.

Symphytum – bone fractures and breaks and to relieve the pain.

Brain - 11:00 - 1:00 on both eyes.

Alfalfa is used for mental fatigue, Sage for mental exhaustion and insanity, Ginseng for senility and fatigue, Fo-Ti for depression, and Lecithin and Phosphatidyl Choline for memory. Periwinkle transports oxygen to brain (astringent and sedative). Herbs that support the veins and arteries will benefit the brain.

Ginkgo Biloba and Gotu Kola revitalizes nerves and helps oxygenate and thus feeds the brain by aiding cerebral circulation. Thus, it helps in focusing and increased mental stamina and decreases senility and aging. Helps prevent nervous breakdown. Rosemary can be taken with this combination. Prickle Ash stimulates the brain and is the push or driving herb in a lot of herbal combinations.

DMAE-H3 by Twinlab – I take 10 drops in water in the morning on an empty stomach. Shirley at Country Health feels that it wakes up her brain. To be honest, I am not entirely sure what DMAE-H3 does for me, but I know that whatever it is, it is good.

(See Nerves and Veins)

Colon - ballooned descending colon can be an indication of colitis or low-grade infection. For a prolapsed transverse colon, lie on slant board and massage transverse colon upwards. Spastic and strictured colons can be cause by emotional stress, which could be inherited. Thus, a person is taking on nerve pattern of parents. If colon is not working properly, the blood is dirty and lymph is overworked.

For parasites, alternate herbal Pumpkin with Black Walnut. Take 4 capsules just before going to sleep at night. If herbal Pumpkin is not available, eat 12 organic pumpkinseeds before going to bed. (3 weeks on Black Walnut and then 3 weeks on pumpkin seeds) Wormwood is anti-fungal and is another anti-parasitic herb. Some individuals have found that 2 drops of oil of Clove Bud and 2 drops of oil of Oregano in fresh lemon juice cleans the intestines and is anti-parasitic.

Triphala is an Ayurvedic formula containing 3 fruits - Amla, Haritaki and Bibhitaki. As Triphala balances all 3 body types, it is considered tri-doshic. Amla (Indian Goose Berry) is a fruit similar to pears, which is high in natural Vitamin C. Amla pulls water into the colon, which assists the other fruits in cleaning the colon. Haritaki pulls and carries disease and toxins out of the body. *Bibhitaki* is a rejuvenation herb. Ayurvedic doctors have said that Triphala will rebuild the entire digestive system if taken for one year; my colon therapist said that it has been her experience that Triphala does not work for everyone - specifically, people with a low vibration. The dosage is typically 3 capsules, 2 or 3 times a day with fiber. If the fiber contains apple pectins and grapefruit pectins, chemicals and heavy metals can also be pulled out of the body. Triphala, Kelp & Spiralina suppress the appetite. Indians take Triphala in a powder form under the tongue. In this way, it mixes with the saliva to ultimately remove fat deposits. For most Westerners, Triphala is too strong to be taken in this manner.
Psyllium Husks, Flaxseeds and Bentonite clay (refrigerate after opening) help to pull the crud off of the walls of the colon and absorb toxins. Drink lots of water when taking these products and follow the directions on the bottle. Bentonite clay that is purified will state on the bottle that it is for internal use. Bentonite clay works well with Slippery Elm.

Acidophilus - take 6 capsules first thing in morning if doing a bowel cleanse or colonics or after taking antibiotics.

Intestines require oil (cold pressed) to move digestion. There are also products like Natures Secret Ultimate Oil.

Irritable bowels, colitis, diaraticulitus or ulcers - Marshmallow, Slippery Elm are both mucilagenous, which means that they are gelatinous substance of essential oil and alcohols. Cayenne can be taken with Marshmallow and Slippery Elm for irritable bowels, colitis or diaraticulitus (fiber is also good for this symptom).
Mullein - for bleeding from lower bowel or lungs.

Lobelia Extract, Capsicum, Aloe Vera Juice, Vitamin C - breaks up mucus.

The Master Cleanse is a juice fast that pulls mucus and cleans the walls of the intestines. A juice fast means that only juice; water and herbs are consumed for a predetermined number of days. The Master Cleanse consists of fresh (organic) lemon juice, grade B maple syrup (minerals have not been refined out – it can be found at the health food store) and Capsicum. One of Shirley's customers at Country Health had been on the Master Cleanse for 3 days when she suddenly felt a strong urge to use the toilet. (She had used the Master Cleanse as a juice cleanse in the morning for over a week before using it as a fast.) So much old crusted fecal matter and black mucus came out of her that her gut feeling was to go off the fast for the time being and eat some chicken and rice soup. She told Shirley, "Now I know why I have been so sick." To this day, her health is very much improved.

Juice cleanses are best done on an empty stomach and followed by only water afterwards (for at least 1/2 hour after fruit juice and two hours after vegetable juice). There are a number of good juicing books on the market. Cranberry juice is very good for the kidneys; cucumber juice is good for the skin (anything that is good for the skin is good for the liver). When I returned from England in December 1998, for over a week, I was strongly impressed to go to Wild Oats after riding each day and order their freshly squeezed juice called Earth Goddess. Earth Goddess is a combination of spinach, parsley, carrots, celery, wheatgrass, beets and spirolena – a combination for people who have already done a good deal of detoxing and colon cleansing. About an hour before I went in for the colonic, along with my Earth Goddess drink I took an herbal combination called Livatone to detox the liver. During the colonic, my liver was dumping crud into my intestines - Rosemarie Siciliano told me that she could hear my liver squishing the toxins out. Because I was having a colonic while my liver was dumping the toxins were not given a chance to reabsorb into my body. I made the choice to continue with the Earth Goddess for another week and then come in for another appointment. Rosemarie showed me how to feel how soft my liver was on the right side and in the middle and how hard it was on the left side. During the colonic my liver continued to release "stuff" that was definitely not colon "stuff". When the colonic was finished the hard area to the left had softened by more than half. By this time, my eyes were more blue-green than brown. The brown toxic layer over the iris of each of my eyes was centered over the pupils and spiked out towards the periphery of each iris. Since I was on a roll I stayed with the Earth Goddess for yet a third week. As my liver was more than 90% cleansed, I took the liver tonic pills with my daily Earth Goddess drink. Before my colon therapy session, Rosemarie checked my liver and discovered that the juicing and detoxing herbs had cleaned out the remaining hard area in my liver. Because my large intestine is relatively clean after doing colonics for twenty years and I juice the day before going in for a treatment, it is sometimes easy to see in the glass tube what part of my body is releasing. For example, when my liver releases we see the yellow bile and the gritty material that is being flushed out. As I lay on the table, we watched as old, dark matter was flushed out through the glass tube and Rosemarie said, "That's from your small intestine." I asked her why my small intestine would be releasing when the water was only being pumped into my large intestine? She responded, "You have done this so often that your body knows what to do – it goes into automatic release."

Releasing on any level - be it emotional, mental, physical or in the aura - produces corresponding changes on all levels. So, I asked Ann Borrell to do the Tera-Mai™ Seichem psychic surgery on me. Her first impression of me was that I looked younger and very healthy; however, I could see by my face that something was ready to come up and out. When Ann cut open my aura, the 'stuff' that was ready to be released was exposed and it easily came off.

When I went in to have my teeth cleaned and examined, Dr. Thomas Wais told me that my gum tissue was the healthiest he had ever seen in his entire practice. He also looked under my lower eyelid and said that my entire body tissue was a reflection of everything that I was doing. Toxicity, malnutrition and dehydration are the things that age and kill us. I detox my body, eat organic foods and supplements, and drink pure water when I am thirsty. Anyone can do this. I also meditate and go to healers. In my particular case what I have found that works for me are chiropractors, colon therapists, massage therapists and hands-on healing from people who have demonstrated clearly that they are channeling healing energy.

Ears – detoxing the kidneys helps the ears. Most ear oils contain Hypericum (nerve pain), and Garlic and Mullein (antibacterial and antifungal). Lobelia is also used for ear infections (2 drops in ear). White Willow is a natural aspirin. Larix for chronic ear infections. Sage for excessive mucous (antiseptic and anti-inflammatory).

Bio-Flavonoids *(for assimilation of Vitamin C and other nutrients, and for building capillary strength and circulation to the extremities. Anti-inflammatory and anti-oxidant support.)* and Ginkgo Biloba for tinnitus.

Ear coning removes pressure in the ear, earwax and toxins. Directions on how to do ear coning frequently accompanies the beeswax cones.

Two home remedies for earaches: Cotton balls with a small amount of black pepper on them are put into the ear. A hairdryer melts the wax and relieves the pressure.

Endocrine System – ductless glands that help regulate all body activity through the blood. Can send messages to speed up or slow down body processes. Related to the nervous system. Bitter herbs are best to rejuvenate Endocrine System. Licorice can be used to flavor bitter herbs (Licorice is not for high blood pressure people.)

Eyes – detoxing the liver benefits the eyes. Eyebright is used to strengthen eyes and in the treatment of inflammations, cataracts and stinging or weeping eyes. Bilberry corrects eye problems and night blindness by improving blood supply and strengthening capillaries. Carrots are good for night vision. DHA.

Exercising the eyes by slowly circling them first to the right several times and then to the left, looking up and down several times and then from side to side are beneficial to the eyes. Eye problems can also be the result of a stiff or sore neck; so, slowly rotating the neck to the right several times and then to the left, front and back and then from side to side are exercises that are good for both the neck and the eyes.

Homeopathic First-Aid Remedies:

Aconite – scratched eyeball or pain form a foreign body in the eye.

Arnica Montana (Arnica) - black eyes and surgery around eyes.

Ledum – for black eyes after Arnica when all of the blood has not been absorbed.

Ruta Graveolens (Ruta) – injured or bruised eyes.

Symphytum – after eyeball has been hit with a blunt object.

Gallbladder - Hydrangea - gallstones. Parsley + Garlic + Capsicum - gallstones.

Another popular 'home remedy', which I have tried for gallstones and the gallbladder, involves drinking one gallon of apple juice a day (not apple cider) for three days in a row. No other food is eaten for these three days. On the third day just before going to bed at night, mix half a cup of olive oil with a tablespoon of either lemon juice or apple cider vinegar (I put the mixture in a clean glass jar and shake it). The mixture cannot be sipped; it has to be chugged down. My daughter, Jennifer, told me that sometimes at bars in the United States they have drinking contests – not to see who can drink the most alcohol but who can drink the most vile-looking thing. She has offered to enter me in such a contest and said that I would probably win with the olive oil/lemon juice mixture. Because no fat has been eaten for three days, the gallbladder empties bile into the stomach; because the apple juice has softened the bile duct, gallstones are released into the stomach and then out of the body through the colon.

When I was in Mexico, one of my traveling companions had a severe gallbladder attack. She ended up repeating the 3-day process three times, each time eliminating gallstones, and she still has her gallbladder. Ideally, it is recommended that the individual drink a glass of apple juice once a day for a month prior to doing the cleanse. I did this 1/2-hour before breakfast each morning. After the 3-day cleanse, I observed that I had eliminated what looked like 3 large, white marbles.

Glandular System - Horsetail + Oatstraw. Kelp. Sarsaparilla - hormone food, hormone balance. Wild Yam - glandular balance. Pipsissewa is used in the treatment of glandular disorders as an

227

alterative *(agents that gradually and favorably alter the condition of the body).* Multiminerals support glands - best taken at night on an empty stomach with water (also helps induce sleep). (Vitamins are best taken with food. New Chapter has created a line of vitamins from whole foods – 2 of their popular vitamin products include Every Man and Every Woman.) Pharmaceutical or 'magical' cures that are stopgap measures do not address real issue.

Hair – healthy hair essentially comes from a well-balanced diet. In order for nutrients to be absorbed into the body, the walls of the intestines must be clean.

Ayurvedic - Bhringraj oil rubbed into the bottom of the feet at night just before going to sleeep strengthens the hair and bones. In addition, it helps induce sleep.

Heart - emotional issues behind most heart problems are lack of forgiveness and failure to open the heart to love. The Chinese doctors refer to cardiovascular disorders as stuck Chi and they believe that all disease starts with digestion or stress. If digestion is impeded, circulation for the rest of the body suffers and eventually the heart suffers. In stress-related, anxiety attacks, the heart is like a knot in the middle of a rope. A red face denotes heat emanating from the heart; purplish lips indicate poor blood circulation. Louise Hay says that the heart is the center of love; and heart attacks are a signal that the joy has been squeezed out of life. In the iris the heart is located at 2:30 to 3:00 on left eye on Autonomic Nerve Wreath and Bronchials.

Hawthorne is the number one herb for the heart, which is used as a long-term tonic to strengthen the heart muscles. Hawthorn brings micronutrients to the heart, arteries and capillaries to restore the entire system. It is a natural regulator of both low and high blood pressure. Shen, the essence of who we are, sits in the heart. Chinese doctors believe that Hawthorn brings the Shen back. The flower essence, Borage, does the same thing – it is the bringer of happiness. Cornsilk, Ginkgo and Hawthorn for enlarged heart or palpitations.

Vitamin E is an anti-oxidant, destroys free radicals, blood thinner and speeds the assimilation of lecithin into the body. It strengthens immune system and heart muscle. Vitamin C (Alma is high in natural Vitamin C) aids in treating cardiovascular disease by strengthening veins and capillaries. Most people with high blood pressure lack adequate calcium in the body (calcium needs magnesium in order for it to be absorbed). Potassium, Chlorophyll and Ginseng support the heart. Lemon water restores PH balance and was what Hanna Kroeger recommended if someone were having a heart attack.

Linden (Melissa) prevents and reduces cholesterol, and lowers high blood pressure. Motherwort is used for heart palpitations. Gotu Kola relieves high blood pressure. Ginkgo nourishes the arteries. Bugleweed acts as a digitalis in calming the pulse and is an excellent choice for an irregular heartbeat. Alacin is the smelly part of garlic and it is what makes garlic work. Garlic is an anti-oxidant, which prevents the formation of the toxic derivatives of cholesterol. Arjuna (Ayurvedic) is used for the prevention and treatment of heart disorders. Typically, one capsule is taken twice a day as a preventative; four capsules twice daily in treatment. Co Q 10 is good for the gums, and anything this is good for the gums will also strengthen the heart.

Cayenne strengthens the heart and increases blood circulation to cold hands and feet. Before diabetics lose limbs to surgery, try Cayenne internally and externally. For shock, a small amount of Cayenne is put under the tongue or in the mouth. Like Ginger, it is a carrier herb, which increases the effectiveness of other herbs. Ten Essential Herbs by Lobitha

Kidney & bladder – regulates body's water content, filters and regulates salt and maintains PH balance. Problems are caused when there is an inability to circulate life. Louise Hay says that bladder problems are caused by anxiety, holding onto old ideas, fear of letting go or being "pissed off". Lesions in the eye are usually large.

Gravel Root breaks up kidney stones; Uva Ursi flushes out stones and cysts. Avoid red meats and acidic foods. Drink lots of water.

Pipsissewa stimulates waste removal as a diuretic and removes irritation and congestion of the urinary tract and kidneys.

For incontinence (lost tone of sphinxter muscle) use Horsetail; St. Johnswort if it is nerve related. Gais's Plantain Bucho Supreme strengthens urinary membranes and musculature.

Uva Ursi is an antiseptic and strengthens membranes. Cranberry and Uva Ursi cancel one another out. Cranberry acidifies the urine and in the process kills invading bacteria that cause infection. It may also prevent bacteria from sticking to the wall of the bladder. Usnea is an effective antibiotic which tragets respiratory and urinary systems. Parsley is a preventative herb and has a tonic effect on the entire urinary system. Alfalfa is a kidney cleanser. Chinese Lung Tan Xie Gan Pill is used for both scany urine and urinary tract infections.

Diuretics increase the flow of urine. Cornsilk is a safe diuretic for kids. Dandelion is a safe diuretic for heart patients and pregnant women. Buchu Leaves are a diuretic; it heals and soothes urinary membranes. Cleavers is also a diuretic and used for painful urination. Hydrangea has been used as a sedative in cases of painful urination and kidney stones.

Juniper Berries are strong and have been used in cases of urinary tract infections. If there is bleeding, add Marshmallow or Cornsilk (also good for inflamed prostate). If there is blood in the urine, heal with Strawgrass (astringent) which is high in silica and calcium. Also moves stones out.

In Aromatherapy, Juniper and Sandalwood are used to treat the urinary tract.

Homeopathic Cantharis is used to treat itching, burning urination.

Older men who have lower kidney problems (kidneys associated with reproductive organs) - often cannot have sex any longer; they blame it on their wives. Rather than cleaning out their kidneys, they look for younger and younger women. Lots of self-judgement when people hit 40.

Men tend to draw energy up through their feet; women tend to bring energy in from crown.

Liver – Anger is stuck qi in the liver. The liver aids in digestion and eleimination, and is also responsible for filtering potentially toxic waste from the blood. Every culture in the world used to have a practice of cleansing the liver at least once a year – traditionally spring or fall is the best time to clean the liver. Dandeloin, Milk Thistle, Yellow Dock, Oregon Grape – bitter is good for the liver and gallbladder. Chlorophyll and Kelp are good for all of the glands.

XAIO YAO WAM cleanses a full and overburdened liver. Eliminates chronic constipation and yellowish color. Frees the flow of bile. SHU GAN WAM aids circulation, digestion and mood. Removes jaundice resulting from stuck bile because they smooth qi circulation in the center. Also calms our emotions aiding in depression and anxiety. Aids chest pains caused by stuck qi.

Hepato-Pure from Planetary Formulas is an herbal combination of Bupleurum, Milk Thistle and Oregon Grape that can release stuck toxins that have accumulated in the liver. The healthy liver is reflected in people who have clear skin and sparkling eyes and who are energetic, creative and display an even temper.

Lungs and bronchi - how one filters life. Lungs - 9:00 - 10:00 on right eye/2:00 - 3:00 on left eye - Lesions common here. Myrrh and Mullein (loosens mucus, is good for bronchitis and asthma, and good for coughing up blood). Thyme and Fenugreek (removes mucus) – can also add Comfrey. One or two drops of Lobelia help removes mucus and congestion. Capsicum and Saw Palmetto- rebuild lungs. Marshmallow for scar tissue! Lemon Balm and Garlic are antibacterial and a decongestant. Rotate antivirals such as Usnea or Echinacea and Chaparral or Echinacea and Goldenseal or Olive Leaf or or Black Elder (flower and berry) or 500 mg of L-Lysine with water on empty stomach. Calamus cleans the lungs and rejuvenates the brain and nervous system, which is why it is used in formulas designed to help people quit smoking. (Gaia's Lobelia/Calamus)

Naturade's Herbal Expectorant contains the following herbs: Wild Cherry Bark, Horehound, Coccillana Bark, Euphorbia, Wild Lettuce, Senega Root, Rose Hips, Ginkgo Biloba, and Red Clover as well as Menthol and Honey. *(Expectorants are herbs that assist in expelling mucous from the lungs and throat.)*

Glyco-Thymoline Packs: Saturate 2 to 3 thicknesses of cotton cloth with warmed Glyco-Thymoline and apply cloth over affected areas. Then place a piece of plastic over the cloth to prevent soiling. Cover with a towel and then place a hot water bottle on top of towel for 20 to 30 minutes.

Lymph – removes toxins, prevents disease and aids immunity. The lymph, like the blood, dumps toxic waste into the large intestine. Lymph is not found in the nails, cuticles or hair. Lymphatic pump is in the tailbone and also next to the heart. Every single woman who has ever come to me for healing after her breast had been removed also had her tailbone out of allignment! On Iris, the lymph is the second ring from the periphery. Exercise and massage helps to move the lymph. Trampoline, except in the case of a prolapsed colon, to move the lymph. For a prolapsed colon, use a slant board and massage transverse colon upwards. Regular exercise, stretching, elevation of extremities, diaphragmatic breathing, lymphatic massage and drinking pure water help to improve lymphatic function.

Lymphatic Rosary - the darker the beads, the longer they have been there, the closer the beads are to the pupil, the more severe the condition. Body brush with dry brush before shower or bath to move lymph to descending colon.

It takes 6 to 9 months to recover from 5 days of antibiotics. It is easy to catch cold or flu again afterwards. If there are no blood vessels in whites of eyes, immune system is down.

Echinacea and Red Root combination is a blood and lymph cleanser. Mullein reduces inflammation and soothes sore tissues. Pau D'Arco has been used to treat leukemia (tailbone may also need to be adjusted). Grapes are antineoplastic *(herbs that have the specific action of inhibiting and combating the development of tumors)*. Ginger and Cinnamon oils are antifungal and antiviral. Pokeroot is usually used in combination with other antiseptic herbs to treat infections; it is especially indicated for conditions with hard, swollen lymph nodes. Pipsissewa acts to decongest lymphatic tissue.

An alterative is an herb which alters/changes the composition of blood and lymph through metabolism. Dr. John Scudder combined 5 herbs in equal proportions – Cordyalis Tubers, Black Alder Bark, Mayapple Root, Figwort and Yellow Dock. This alterative combination is a deep cleanser and replaces tissues of a disorganized nature. Scudder's is toxic to human tumor cells; it won't let cells become carcinogenic. It has been used for tumors, cysts and other growths. It can be used as a detoxic for 3 to 6 weeks in the fall or spring. It can be used at the end of the summer to remove excess heat. 40 drops are typically taken 3 times a day.

Retroviruses effect genetics of cells by reversing the process of genetic transcription. They attack and infect RNA found in normal DNA; RNA then acts as a virus secreting enzymes. The result being that the DNA then acts as an invading and moving virus. Retroviruses include HIV, herpes, mono, Epstein Barr and lymph cancers. To bring the body back to homeostasis, cellular intelligence has to be stimulated and awakened so that the body again knows right from wrong. Reishi/Bupleurum Supreme (Gaia) is a deep tonic. People usually take 40-60 drops, 3 times a day for 6 months. May add Bloodroot/Celandine – 15-20 drops 3 times a day for 3 weeks only. Then go off the Bloodroot/Celandine for 3 weeks and continue alternating – 3 weeks on then 3 weeks off.

Sea Vegetables have been used as a preventative to breast cancer. Sea Herbs (in particular the species of laminaria) have the ability to bind up radioactive isotopes of strontium, cadmium, barium and zinc as well as heavy metals and other toxins, and blocking their absorption. Once bound, the toxins are excreted from the body. Sea Herbs also provide essential trace minerals to support the body. Natural doctors have also recommended replacing hydrogenated fats and oils (including margarine) with cold pressed oils, replacing fillings containing mercury, maintaining healthy intestinal flora and eating whole foods that are rich in fiber.

The lymph system houses the immune system!

To Build Immune System

Defense Force (Michael Tiera's Planetary Formulas) for prevention and weakened immune system. Has been used for colds, flu, candida overgrowth and immune deficiency.

Echinacea - 10 days out of the month and Astragalus for the rest of the month. Cats Claw may be rotated with Astragalus.

Sore throat – gargle with lemon, salt and ginger.

Prana – Ayurvedic formula to strengthen lungs.

Vitamin C – enhances body's immune response and helps in eliminating toxins. Daily C Elixir contains Rose Hips, Gooseberry (Amla), Sea Vegetables, Orange Essence and Vegetable Glycerin – all natural forms of Vitamin C.

E-mergen-C contains Vitamins C and B, mineral ascorbates and 27 mineral complexes.

Siberian or American Ginseng – energy and stress adaptogen. (Stress can weaken immune system.) Ginseng enhances everything, so, do not take Ginseng when sick because it will enhance the infection.

Vita Biotic – freeze dried vitamin mineral herbal combination which contains Garlic, Myrrh, Ginger, Cayenne and Echinacea.

Wellness Formula – Propolis (used by bees as a sealant for the hive, the use of propolis as an antibacterial dates back to ancient Egypt and Greece), Echinacea, Garlic, Boneset, Isatis, Horehound, Astragalus, Angelica, Mullein, Goldenseal, Siberian Ginseng, Hawthorn Berry, Oregon Grape Root, Pau d' Arco, Cayenne and Vitamins and minerals.

As a cold prevention combine the following powdered herbs and put them into capsules: 1 part Cayenne, 3 parts Ginger and 3 parts Garlic. Take 3-4 capsules per day.

Flower Essences if emotionally stressed.

Formulas that contain a great number of herbs are going to have a wide range of effects upon the body and the quantity of each herb is going to be less than formulas that have fewer herbs. Many individuals like to experiment to see which products work for them or rotate products.

Homeopathic

Occillococium – triggers immune system by acting like a homeopathic flu shot. Can take once a week as a preventative or every six hours at the onset of symptoms.

Chinese

Astra 8 – is based on the Chinese herb formula called "The Four Gentlemen" that was used by ancient Chinese doctors to treat the condition called "Spleen Qi Deficiency". boost immune system. It is an immune enhancement and energy tonic that contains Ganoderma, Astragalus, Ligustrum, Codonopsis and Licorice to build the immune system. Eleutheroginseng and Schizandra enhance energy and mental activity, and protect the liver. Schizandra Berry enhances the regenerative capabilities of liver cells and protects against free-radical incuded tissue injury.

Conceptual Stage of a Flu or Cold

To create an incubator effect - take ginger (stimulant, warming and diaphoretic – *herb used to induce sweating*) and then soak in a hot tub with cool towel on head (keeps fever out of brain). Allows body to push infection out by sweating it out - elimination is through the skin rather than through mucous.

Flu – boil Ginger and Cinnamon, add honey and drink. Then soak in a hot Epsom Salt bath until you sweat. Keep a cool towel on head.

Cold & Flu Bath by Kiss My Face contains Aloe Vera Gel, Eucalyptus Oil, Fennel, Horehound and other extracts.

Just before going to sleep at night, pour carrier oil into the palm of hand and add a few drops of Ginger Essential Oil or Eucalyptus Essential Oil and rub on the soles of feet. Go to sleep! Herb goes up into the body through lymph.

Homeopathic

Aconite – after exposure to cold, dry wind where symptoms include runny nose and a raw, burning throat.

Natrum Muriaticum – for colds that start with sneezing, dry cracked lips and thirst.

Gelsemium - an early flu remedy where there is high temperature, chills, fatigue headache and bodyache.

Nux Vomica – early stages of flu where there is coughing, constipation and shivering.

Belladonna – for sudden, violent symptoms characterized by flushing, heat, redness and throbbing pain. For children with high fever! 6 or 30C every 1/2-hour.

Allium Cepa – relief of watery eyes and runny nose.

Ferrum Phos. – inflammation, fever with throbbing head, ear infections and nosebleeds

Chinese

GAN MAO LING – take every 4 hours at onset. If dosage is not on bottle, look it up in Chinese herb book.

YIN CHIAO – 5 - 6 pills every 2 –3 hours for the first nine hours. Then 2 – 3 pills every 4 – 5 hours as needed. Discontinue by third day. Taken at first onset or don't bother. Not for children!

ZHONG GAN LING – raises fever.

Mom was right! When the body is sick, rest and sleep are required so that the body can use the energy for healing.

Cold and Flu Have Set In

Echinacea/Goldenseal (astringent) – to dry up mucous tissues and membranes for 10 days at the maximum. Goldenseal is not for low blood sugar people. (Anticatarrhal – herbs that eliminate or counteract the formation of mucous.)

Lomatium is a deep antiviral for lingering cold or flu. Dosage is typically 30 – 40 drops four times a day for 3 – 4 days.

Goldenseal and Oregon Grape (berberines) for infections.

Echinacea and Eyebright – drying and healing to mucous membranes.

Linden – diaphoretic – cools body.

Oregon Grape and Barberry Root Bark acts against some bacteria, protozoa and fungi.

St. Johnswort - respiratory expectorant and is used in the treatment of the flu, Epstein Barr and HIV.

Usnea – antibiotic that targets the respiratory and urinary tracts.

Ephedra (Ma Huang) – antispasmodic that relaxes bronchials. Ephedra depletes adrenal glands - most people take licorice. Ma Huang also elevates the blood pressure.

Lobelia is very strong and can cause vomiting – dosage is only 2 or 3 drops. Respiratory relaxant! Helps body excrete mucous through coughing and liquefies phlegm.

Lungwort is high in mucilage and is indicated in respiratory conditions such as chronic bronchial cough and asthma.

Wild Cherry Bark to quite coughs.

Mullein is an expectorant and antispasmodic, and throat soother.

Horehound for the respiratory system and lining of lungs.

Elderberry Flower (Sambucol) – promotes sweating and reduces fevers.

Osha – used by Western Native Americans to ward off viral infections. Osho and Lomatium in combination is a deep respiratory and deep antiviral. Immune enhancer!

Red Root for swollen glands – stimulates circulation of lymphatic system and targets liver and spleen (largest lymph gland). Take 1 teaspoon every 1/2 -hour for up to 4 hours. Not for children!

Throat infections – take 2 full droppers of Echinacea/Goldenseal, gargle and swallow. Thirty minutes later take 1/2 dosage.

Spray with Thyme Oil (Thyme destroys microbial).

Tea Tree – 1 dropper full, gargle and spit.

Lemon Essential Oil and teaspoon of honey – gargle and swallow.

Cleavers (or Bedstraw) – tonsillitis and for a variety of lymph system problems.

Essential Oils

Camphor – one drop on each armpit.

Eucalyptus – 3 – 5 drops in boiling water. Remove from stove. Place towel over head, close eyes and take 5 deep breaths to clear sinuses.

Sage, Peppermint and Eucalyptus – antispasmodic

Thyme and Pine – soften phlem.

Bengelm, Cedarwood, Eucalyptus and Myrrh – expectorants.

Chinese Formulas

PING CHAUN PILL – bronchitis and emphysema.

SANG CHU – chest cold or upper repiratory. 4 pills 2 times a day.

Homeopathic

Arsenicum - for accute cold with symptoms of abundant, watery mucus, burning throat and dry eyes. Also used for hayfever that worsens with weather changes and diarrhea associated with bad food.

Pulsatilla - where mucus is yellow or yellow-green, chapped lips, chills and dry mouth.

Bryonia – body pain, especially in the chest.

Ipecac – constant nausea when vomiting produces no relief. Rattling, gaggin cough or bronchitis accompanied by nausea.

Mercurius – gum disease, toothaches with loose teeth, and swollen and inflamed glands. Excessive slavation with metallic taste!

Phosphorus – for relief of laryngitis, chest colds and tickling or dry coughs.

Sulphur – for lingering and relapsing ailments.

Medulla - Regulates heartbeat and breathing while sleeping. Becoming more active as we move into the Golden Age. Lots of people need hands-on healing at the back of their heads.

On iris - medulla/lung syndrome - can indicate major lung problems. Lung - 9:00 - 10:00 on right eye/2:00 - 3:00 on left eye. Brain - 11:00 - 1:00 on both eyes.

On iris - medulla/heart syndrome - heart problems (heart - 2:30 - 3:00 on left eye)

Mental - 11:00 - 1:00 on both eyes. If this area is toxic, then there will be problems reflected in the rest of the iris. Our body is created in our mind - health issues begin in the brain. Clean thoughts + positive attitude produces healthy body. For mental alertness use cleansing herbs + Ginkgo Biloba and Gotu Kola; Periwinkle for senility and Rosemary.

Muscles - L-Arginine and L-Ornithine (amino acids) taken with water (minerals can be taken at the same time because they naturally occur in water and are not food) before bed on an empty stomach (no food in stomach for 3 hours) to build muscle mass and reduce fat.

Externally – Arnica gel, Tiger Balm, Feng Shih, Caster oil packs, Eclectic's Muscle Gel and massage threapy. Soaking in the tub with a natural mineral product such as Batherapy for 1/2 hour can pull out strain. When the bathwater cools down, that is when the toxicity can be pulled out.

For gout people have taken Yucca, Burdock and Celery. Stay away from acidic foods – coffee, bread, pasta, red meat. White Willow is similar to aspirin with no stomach upset. Feverfew is a muscle relaxant and anti-inflamatory. Louise Hay says that gout results from the need to dominate, impatience and anger. Is it any wonder that Henry VIII suffered from gout?

Essential Oils:

Tarragon is used for muscles and is an antispasmodic.

Laventine for aches and pains.

Homeopathic remedies:

Arnica Montana – injuries to the soft tissues of the body. For soreness of muscles from overexertion, strain and sprains of joints. *(Also used for eye injuries, concussions, after childbirth, after tooth extraction or after any shock or injury. Helps the body to absorb extravasated blood – blood that has leaked out in the body from injury or a stroke.)*

Aconitum Napellus (Aconite) – used in injury, shock or trauma when the person is experiencing fright and restlessness. *(Also used before and after surgival and dental operations.)*

Nerves - Nervine *(herbs used to ease anxiety and stress and nourish the nerves)* tonics feed and strengthen nervous system, especially if there is excess stress, anxiety or insomnia. Oats are high in silica and minerals are great for shingles and recovering addicts. It increases the life force. Scullcap is also used for shingles and is a tonic for stress and helps seizures; it calms and tones the nervous and muscular systems. (Rescue Remedy Cream has been proven extremely helpful at the first signs of shingles.) Passionflower is used for stress, hysteria and high anxiety; it also benefits the brain and circulation. Passionflower in combination with Valerian is used for insomnia. Lemon Balm or Melissa is used for both nervous tension and insomnia, and for hyperactive children and those with attention deficit. Melatonin and also 5-HTP have been used to promote sleep. Gota Kola has anti-stress and anti-anxiety effects. Mugwort tones the nervous system. Kava Kava reduces anxiety by subtly working directly on the limbic system, addressing deep emotional imbalances. Wild Oats is used in chronic and acute anxiety states.

For headaches people have used Jamaican Dogwood, Feverfew and White Willow Bark. Saint Johnswort is used for nerve pain and as a sedative. Saint Johnswort contains hypericum and is anti-inflammatory and antispasmodic as well as an antidepressant. Saint Johnswort strengthens and feeds nerves, and raises the vibration; it is an antidepressant. People who are sensitive to St. Johnswort can develop a rash. Skullcap and Saint Johnswort in combination are used to treat shingles and herpies. Side effects of Prosac include anxiety, insomnia and change in kidney function; in 1992 there were 3,000 Prosac suicides. Prosac was designed to be used for a short time to get individuals through a crisis before other treatment began.

Herbs that inhibit MAO's are Saint Johnswort, Passionflower and Calimus Root.

Herbs that stimulate seratonin release are Gotu Kola, Siberian Ginseng and Schizandra.

Herbs that inhibit re-uptake of seretonin are Gotu Kola, Siberian Ginseng, Schizandra and Oats.

Herbs that are adaptogins help the body adapt to stress. Siberian and American Ginseng are stress adaptogins; Korean Ginseng is taken in specific instances when a lot of energy is needed (just before hiking, etc.) but it is too strong for some people.

For insomnia, some people take a combination of Passionflower and Valarian. (Valarian is neither for the very old or very young or depressed.) Other relaxants include Chamomile (mild sedative that children can use), Hops, Lavender, Linden and Motherwort. Homeopathic remedies include Calms Forte or Coffea.

Cold sores are stress related – Erapao, Tea Tree Oil and Myrrh. For canker sores, use Myrrh powder right away.

Essential oils that are used to treat the nervous system include: Neroli or Rose for emotional shock, Melissa for depression, Lavendar or Marjoram for insomnia and Rosemary as a mental stimulant.

In Chinese medicine, Peppermint Leaf stimulates the flow of Qi or energy in the body. It is said that to know all of the properties of Peppermint is to know the number of fish that swim in the ocean. In the nervous system, Peppermint is anti-stress and antispasmodic.

Homeopathic Remedies

Coffea - to calm the nerves and help induce sleep.

Chamomilla – for tension, irritability, PMS and teething pain.

Hypericum Perfoliatum (Hypericum) – primary action is on nerves; it relieves pain and promotes healing of the nerves. Hypericum is used when there is numbness or the pain from the injury tingles or radiates up the limb, severe concussions of the brain and spine (where pain is going up and down the spine). It is used for smashed fingertips and toes and injury to the tailbone. Homeopathic remedies are reduced to the vibrational essence; essential oils are a concentrated form of the plant. Thus, one would not want to use homeopathic Hypericum and an essential oil of St. Johnswort because they would cancel one another out.

Our nervous system is greatly affected by our emotions. Flower essences help bring us to a positive emotional and mental state so that a natural state of balance of homeostasis returns to the body. There is no disease when the body is in homeostasis. *"To find the herb that will help us find the object of life and understand the difficulties of our path, the difficulties we call faults, failings. Let us not mind them; they are proof that we are attaining bigger things and should be our encouragements."* Dr. Edward Bach

Flower essence combination can be made by filling a 1 ounce amber or blue bottle 3/4 way with spring water, adding 1 teaspoon of Brandy and then 3 to 5 drops of up to 7 flower essences (Rescue Remedy counts as one remedy). Take 1/2 dropper 4 times a day. Let one time be just as you are waking up and another be just before you go to sleep. Flower essences can be put into the baby's bathwater. There is no effect if the wrong remedy is taken and they can be taken with other medicines. Flower essences have been used successfully with animals. (Put a few drops in the animal's water dish or water bucket.) When choosing a remedy for an animal, I put myself in the animal's situation. If I am treating one of my animals with a remedy, I also take it myself as our pets reflect back to us our own issues. Oftentimes, when we heal ourselves, our pet's condition disappears. Rescue Remedy has been used as a sprits for plants.

Late one Thursday evening, my cat, Ziggy, began running an extremely high temperature. After I laid my hands on him for about ten minutes, his temperature went back to normal. The next morning, he was not able to use his left paw, as it curled under. During the course of the morning, he lost control over his limbs until by noon on Friday, he was unable to walk. One of his eyes was completely dilated. I took him to the veterinarian who ran $360 worth of tests and found nothing. Ziggy stayed at the animal hospital for the remainder of the afternoon where he *was given an I.V. I took him home that evening since there would not be anyone around to care for him at the hospital. When I got home, I started to give him drops of Lobelia. When I woke up Saturday morning, there was hardly any life left in his body and both eyes were completely dilated. I took him back to the animal hospital where he was put on another I.V. I didn't think that he was going to make it; however, when I picked him up, the veterinarian told me that there was good news. Ziggy had an automatic reflex reaction in one of his legs. I took him home and continued to give him Lobelia twice a day, as well as water, and force-fed him special food with a syringe that the doctor had given to me. That evening, he improved further. On Sunday, he began walking a little and by the afternoon, he was able to use his litterbox and his eyes were starting to return to normal. I continued to give him Lobelia and within two weeks, Ziggy had complete use of all of his limbs.*

On Saturday, I had called Kim Williamson, and together the two of us worked psychically to heal Ziggy. She and I both felt that he had eaten something, and I could feel a lump in my small intestine, which I felt was an awareness telling me that Ziggy had eaten something and where it was in his body. As we were working, I felt something move into my own ascending colon and at the same time, Kim told me that she saw the remains of whatever he had eaten move into his large intestine. We continued to drain the poison out of his body and at one point, Kim saw a pair of eyes in Ziggy's large intestine (not that there were undigested physical remains of eyes in Ziggy's intestine; rather, it was more like the astral body talking to Kim). The eyes said to Kim, "I didn't ask to be eaten." I responded, "I didn't invite you to come on my porch." We asked whoever it was we were talking to if it would like to go to the Light. It agreed and the angels took it there.

Occipital - can become a psychic junk-mailbox for other people's thoughts. Think cobalt blue and do Hosanna clearing (see symbol chapter).

Pancreas (Isle of Lagerhorn) – gland that produces insulin. Problems maybe indicated by an orange color in eye (also look for pancreas lesions). Alfalfa and Uva Ursi for diabetes. Juniper Berry is a natural form of insulin. Under the supervision of a Naturopathic Doctor, Essiac Combo helps people who want to get off of insulin. Devil's Club Root Bark is a blood sugar stabilizing agent and a natural alternative to insulin.

Ojibwa Tea consists of Burdock and Turkey Rhubarb for cleansing; Sheep Sorrel and Slippery Elm to nourish. Cleanses pancreas and rids accumulation of insulin.

A nurse I met at the Phoenix Holistic Expo took the following combination once a day when she noticed the onset of diabetes: Chromium Picolinate, Vanadium Sulphate, Spirulina and Fiber.

Parathyroid - regulates calcium and phosphorus.

Pineal - higher consciousness, nervous system, spirituality and sexual urges. Gotu Kola.

Pituitary - controls water level of body, is responsible for growth, it is the master gland, normalizes hormones and balances and control the immune system. Alfalfa good for pituitary (crown chakra) and Pineal gland (third eye). Vitex for the Pituitary - Kelp and minerals support all of the glands.

Reproductive organs – *(Men)* problems can occur with desires or fears to create life. Saw Palmetto for prostate function; Pumpkin seeds to break up parasite nests. Pygeum Bark for inflammation of the prostate. For impotence Yohimba can be taken with caution and absolutely no dairy can be consumed while taking Yohimba. Male hormonals include Damiana, Ginseng, Oats, Sarsaparilla and Suma. DHEA is beneficial to reproductive organs.

(Women) Dong Quai is an herbal tonic for the female reproductive system. Licorice is a woman's herb. It is important for women to do liver cleanses to clear excess estrogen. Iron should be taken after giving birth or menstruation or any blood loss. Herbs that clean and support the kidneys will benefit the reproductive organs. A clean colon benefits the reproductive organs.

Uterine Tonics which tone and strengthen tissues of reproductive organs include: Black Cohosh has estrogen-like properties that balances estrogen and progesterone. It is a muscle relaxant and has been used for PMS, menopause and during the last few weeks of pregnancy. Blue Cohosh is an antispasmodic, which relieves cramps and eases childbirth. As a Uterine stimulant, it encourages a high blood flow to pelvic area. It balances estrogen and lowers emotional and nervous tension. Vitex (Chase Tree Berry) works through the pituitary to balances estrogen and progesterone to restore normal ovulation and menstruation, and strengthens female organs. False Unicorn (Helnoid) prevents miscarriages and restores health and muscle tone to uterus. Motherwort is taken during the first stages of labor because of its calming effect. It is also used for night sweats and delayed menstruation. Raspberry Leaf is high in minerals and strengthens uterus wall. Can be taken throughout pregnancy and after giving birth. Squaw Vine is a hormone balancer and is specific for infertility. Alone or with raspberry, Squaw Vine can also induce labor during pregnancy. Crampbark is good for excessive bleeding and cramping. Valerian and Black Haw are antispasmodic. Ginger is used for morning sickness. To increase milk production, Anise, Fennel and Carroway have been used. Wild Yam is a progesterone herb that also works with estrogen and regulates hormone production. Marshmallow has been used for vaginitis (caused by bacteria, yeast infection, Vitamin B deficiency or parasites). Dong Quai and Vitex have been used for endometriosis. Rosemary stimulates blood flow to uterus and flushes out 'bad stuff'. For uterine fibroids, it is taken in small amounts (10 drops for 1 or 2 weeks). Vitamins E and C along with Evening Primrose have also been used for fibroids. Fraxinus/Ceanotheus and Scudders Alterative have been used for fibroids (end result of endometriosis) and ovarian cysts. Louise Hay says that endometrioisis is caused by insecurity, disappointment and frustration resulting in self-blame and replacing self with sugar. Again, the emotional and mental issues behind any disease, dysfunction or pain have to be addressed.

Chinese combinations that women have used are Two Immortals for menopausal symptoms, Cramp Bark Plus for cramping (cinnamon is frequently found in herbal formulas for women) and Zhi Bai Bo Wei Wan for hot flashes.

Shatavari or "she who possesses 100 husbands" is an Ayurvedic herb used to treat female reproductive organs. Cleanses blood and reproductive organs.

Homeopathics remedies include Sepia for PMS and Mayphos for cramping. Pulsatilla for irregular menstruation!

Essential Oils women have used include Clary Sage for PMS and hormone balancing, and Geranium for heavy menstruation. As an antifungal, one drop of Tea Tree oil is put into a douche or on a tampon.

Herbal Healing for Women by Rosemary Gladstar
Today's Herbal Health for Women by Louise Tenney
The Complete Women's Herbal by Anne McIntyre
Aromatherapy for Women by Maggies Tisserand

Sinus - Mullein for sinus congestion. For sinus polyps - Frankincense & Myrrh oils. Pau d' Arco. Freeze Dried Nettles by Eclectic Institute for hayfever. Liquid Goldenseal is used as an antibiotic; Eyebright, Bayberry and Horseradish for allergies and sinus problems. Sinus problems can be an indication of parasites – in this case Black Walnut can be used to kill the parasites.

Ear coning can get energy in sinuses moving. Sue Szymanski R.N. told me she noticed that candida came out before the excess earwax.

Olive Leaf extract is both anti-viral and anti-candida

Aromatherapy – Breathe Free to open breathing passages. Marshmallow is muscelagenous. Tumeric is good for swelling. If there is an infection, Echinacea or Usnea are both antiviral and can be alternated.

Homeopathic – Yeast Clear.

Ayurvedic – gargling and swishing cold pressed Safflower oil for five minutes the first thing in the morning breaks up mucus in the mouth and throat and pulls toxins out of the sinuses. It is highly recommended to spit in the toilet.

Irrigation of the sinuses with warm salt water washes mucus crusts and other debris from the nose. It decongests by pulling fluid out of the swollen membranes and shrinking them. Recipe: Fill thoroughly cleaned quart glass jar with bottled water. Add 2 – 3 heaping teaspoons of sea salt (not table salt because it contains additives). Add 1 teaspoon Arm & Hammer Baking Soda. Mix together and store at room temperature. Discard after one week. Instructions: Pour water into a small, clean *bowl (it may be warmed first but NOT HOT)*. Use a water pik with irrigation tip, bulb/ear syringe or large medical syringe. *(DO NOT put syringe into the quart jar because it will contaminate the solution.)* Stand over the sink or while in the shower or bathtub, squirt the solution into each side of the nose aiming the stream toward the back of the head NOT the top of the head. In this way, salt water can be spit out of the mouth. *(When using a nasal steroid product, use the salt water first.)*

Cynthia Kyle is a spiritual medium *(communicates with personalities who have made their final transition)* who sometimes consults with Edgar Cayce. When my sinuses were raw, Edgar Cayce suggested that I use Cayenne to irrigate my sinuses. Because the herb is strong, I began by putting only a few granuals in the salt salution. The Cayenne did heal the sore tissue.

Chinese formula PE MIN KAU WAN for allergies, runny nose and eyes.

Skin - celery. Potassium is good for wrinkles. Advisable to release toxins from underlying musculature and avoid carbonate beverages, coffee, tobacco, drugs and alcohol. Horsetail and Oatstraw are good for hair and nails. Yellow Dock and Milk Thistle are good for the liver – cleanse the liver and the skin improves. Aloe Vera - radiation burns, scar tissue on skin or inside of body. Silica (mineral supplement). Louise Hay says that the skin protects our individuality.

Largest eliminative organ. Dry brush for both skin and lymph. Much of the dust in our homes is dried, flaked-off skin. Ultimate Oil by Nature's Secret is taken internally and is good for the hair and skin. Chlorophyll helps maintain the color in the hair and the skin smooth.

Warts – are caused by a belief in ugliness. Women who get warts in their first-time pregnancy are not sure about the baby. They don't think that they look beautiful. In children, warts are stress-induced and commonly appear when children learn to write and especially when children switch from printing to cursive writing. Fresh Mullein flowers - dries out warts. Fig juice also draws warts out of skin. Black Walnut - externally and internally, Thuja Oil (infused) or Tea Tree Oil, also homeopathic Thuja. Apply liquid from stem of Dandelion flower.

Wrinkles – White Sage and Elder Flower Cream by Eclectic Institute. Alpha hydroxy liquid used at night before going to bed. Camomile is good for both the hair and skin.

Acne – purify with blood and liver cleansers. Chinese – Margarite Acne Pills. Tea Tree essential oil can be put directly on acne. Aromatheraphy – Lemongrass, Geranium, Lavender and Cleary Sage. Mild Streak from Tiahuanaco Guardians is a gentle liver and kidney cleanser. The people who make these extracts use their healing energy and work with the herbs in the way that the shaman would. For example, Mild Streak provides support and nurturing. Clear by Tiahuanaco Guardians is an acne formula, which works on balancing the hormones and endocrine system, improves circulation and builds the immune system. The metaphysical effects of Clear can be a calmer approach to life. Organic herbs will root out the cause behind diseases, pain and fear-based reality. When a healer energizes herbs and the herbs are respected and loved, they become stronger and more purposeful. How supplements and food is prepared makes a big difference. Meals that are cooked with love warm the stomach; if the chef is angry, the whole restaurant could have stomach pains of one sort or another. A meatpacking house was built over the execution site in London where thousands of people lost their heads. Is it any wonder that mad cow disease started in England? Turning vegetarian animals into carnivores and cannibals is against Natural Law and at some point would produce drastic repercussions. Opera is not the only one who has either stopped eating beef or turned to range-free, grain-fed cattle. Planetary Formulas, regardless of whether or not it is intentional, seem to bring up the underlying issues for healing. Products by Planetary Formulas and the other manufacturers I have mentioned and have not mentioned can be found in most health food stores. For a list of products by Tiahuanaco Guardians write to: *Tiahuanaco Guardians, 5803 North 7th Street, Phoenix, Arizone 85014*

Bites or stings – homeopathic Apis Mellifica (Apis) where there is stinging, itching and redness.

Boils – Red Clover (internally and externally), Myrrh and Burdock Root.

Bruises – homeopathic Arnica.

Burns - homeopathic Cantharus or Causticum. Causticum is repeated every couple of minutes until the pain significantly diminishes, and then repeated whenever the pain returns. Cantharus is used when Causticum does not provide relief or when burned area becomes inflamed. While Causticum is indicated in the largest percentage of burn cases, people will often alternate every 10 minutes between Cantharus and Causticum to find out which one is working. Also for burns - Lavender, and Rescue Remedy. Calendula Tincture (diluted) has been used as a dressing for burns, wounds, contusions and scrapes; it promotes the growth of skin and inhibits the browth of germs.

Dermatitis – Comfrey Salve, Red Clover, flower essences, and liver cleansing formulas.

Eczema - Honeyrush, Calendula, Oregon Grape Root and Red Clover.

Erruptions – homeopathic sulphur.

243

Psoriasis - Goldenseal, Sarsaparilla. Aromatherapy – Carrot Seed, Palmarosa, Cleary Sage and Lavender.

Shingles – Rescue Remedy cream, St. Johnswort, Lavender essential oil. Benedictine Oil's major ingredient is St. Johnswort, on other levels it promotes spiritual opening, strength, clarity and grounding.

Hives – Coptis Perge Fire, Margarite.

Topical use of natural products:

Aloe – promotes wound healing.

Arnica – anodyne, anti-inflammatory and wound healing for sprains and bruises, inflamed joints and trauma.

Calendula – for wounds, sores, boils and bruises. Prevents the formation of pus, and prevents scarring from burns or lesions.

Chickweed – where there is swelling, skin irritations, bruising and old, painless ulcers.

Comfrey – healing, regenerative and pain relief qualities. Do not apply to broken skin.

Coneflower – wound healing and anti-inflammatory.

Elder Flower – used topically when there are crusts forming from discharge, burns, old ulcers and poison ivy.

Ginger Root Oil – stimulates circulation.

Goldenseal – antiseptic and antifungal for wounds, skin diseases, sores and ringworm.

Juniper Oil – for gout, arthritis and soreness.

Myrrh – antiseptic wash for sores and wounds.

Propolis – antimicrobial and anti-inflammatory used for treatment of wounds, burns, boils and herpes.

St. John's Wort –analgestic for treatment of wounds, bruises, inflammations, back injury, nerve injury or trauma.

Thuja Leaf Oil - antimicrobial commonly used for warts.

White Sage – astringent and antiseptic wash. Applied to abrasions, bruises, chafing and inflamed skin.

Witch Hazel – astringent for muscle pain, bruises and soreness.

Small Intestine – has a lot to do with the blood. Old fecal matter can also become trapped here. Take 2 to 3 tablets of Triphala twice a day with fiber between meals. The East Indians take Triphala as a powder. They put it under their tongue so as to mix it with saliva before swallowing it. Most Westerners including myself are unable to do this. Planetary Formulas has a product called Triphala Internal Cleanser in tablet form. What I have personally found with any of the Planetary Formulas is that they work on the issues as well as on the physical body.

Bananas + green colon cleanser from health food store helps clean the small intestine. Bentonite Clay has also been used by individuals to clean out the small intestine.

Spleen – cleanser and a filter for bloodstream and storehouse for blood cells. Bone marrow produces white blood cells and antibodies. Blood toxemia - give blood cleanser, builder, purifier and circulator. Yellow Dock.

Stamina - Krebs' cycle acids when complexed with minerals fight fatigue by assisting the conversion of fats,carbohydrates and proteins into chemical energy. Reduces lactic acid.

Stomach - digests - also how one digests life. Small Intestine - assimilates. Large Intestine - eliminates. Aloe Vera - stomach ulcers. Sage - too much saliva, aids digestion. Peppermint - digestion. Slippery Elm - neutralizes stomach acidity. Marshmallow - coats stomach and colon. Shatavari is used for stomach ulcers. Garcinia Cambogia is an appetite suppressant; Gentian and Rhubarb are appetite stimulants.

Ayurvedic herbs that are used include Shatavari for stomach ulcers, Cardamom as a digestive stimulant (added to milk it neutralizes mucous-forming properties of milk and detoxifies caffeine in coffee), Cloves are a stimulant for stomach and lungs (antiparasitic and good for colds because it is warming), Coriander for digestive and urinary tracts (treats cystitis) and Cumin aids digestion and absorption of food and is an antidote for hot, pungent foods.

Chinese Herbal Patent Formulas

PILL CURING – digestive disturbances. Primarily used for the flu but also food poisoning.

PING WEI – "Peaceful Stomach Pills". Soothes gastric imbalances and is a simple formula for maintaining digestive function.

SHU BAN WAN – for gas, hiccups, belching and poor digestion.

XIZO YAO WAN – for PMS or digestive headaches. It is an all around digestive panacea for indigestion, bloating, hiccups, food allergies and hypoglycemia. It is a blend of warming and cooling digestive berbs that treats stagnant liver chi.

Homeopathic Remedies

Carbo Veg – for nausia, overeating and burning stomach or if acid backs up into the esophagus.

Lycopodium – for heartburn or full feelilng.

Nux Vomica – too much rich food or alcohol or coffee leading to nausea and acidity.

Tendons and Cartilage - Grape Seed (PCO) Extract, Germanium and Glucosamine Chondroitin Complex. Silica or silicon which is a trace mineral. Lecitin. Hawthorn protects connective tissue from the degenerative effects of stress. Wild Oats for weakened connective tissue (Wild Oats is an anti-fungal).

Arthritis – Devil's Claw, Garlic and Dandelion. Biovlavonoids.

Homeopathic First-Aid Remedies:

Rhus Toxicodendron (Rhus Tox) – sprains to the joints and tendons, and injuries that leave the part still. *(Also used immediately after exposure to poison oak.)*

Ruta Graveolens (Ruta) – torn and wrenched tendons, split ligaments and sprains (after Arnica). *(Also used for bruised bones and to heal the periosteum – the bone covering. Also used for the eyes, rectum and dry socket after tooth extraction.)*

Throat – 1/2 Mullen flowers and 1/2 Mullen leaves reduces inflammation and soothes tissues. YIN CHAIO if taken at the first signs of a cold or flu. Echinacea/Goldenseal gargle or throat spray – after gargling, swallow. 1 teaspoon honey and 1 drop of lemon essential oil.

Thymus - protection. Part of immune system (but not according to 'modern' medicine) and central organ of lymph. It wasn't that long ago when 'modern medicine' advocated X-raying the thymus to destroy it because they didn't think it was necessary. To build immune system some people take Echinacea the first 7 days of every month and Astragalus for the rest of the month.

Thyroid - all emotions pass through thyroid, which is one reason why fear usually clutches our throat. Healthy thyroid - in control of life and temperament. When tonsils are taken out, thyroid gets weaker. Bulging eyes indicate thyroid problems. Thyroid is responsible for metabolism; if the thyroid is overactive, the heart feels like it is in the throat. If you take your temperature before getting out of bed in the morning and it is below 98.6, the thyroid is down.

Kelp is #1 for thyroid (speeds up metabolism); it is high in minerals. Other seaweed and ocean herbs such as Dulse and Bladderwrack. Sarsaparilla stimulates the metabolic rate. Support glands with potassium, iron and mineral supplements. Again, detox the body and clean the colon.

Thyroid & L-Tyrosine Complex by Enzymatic Therapy, which also contains vitamins and minerals essential for proper thyroid function.

Whenever I do a juice fast, I also take herbs to keep my metabolic rate up. I typically do not stay on a juice fast for longer than 3 days. I found that some natural substances such as Psyllium Husks, amino acids, minerals, DHEA, and herbs can also be taken.

Uterus & Ovaries - Black Cohosh, Dong Quai, He-Shou-Wu, Evening Primrose, False Unicorn, Licorice and Suma for female hormonal. Clean colon, detox body and glands, and support adrenals and other glands. Periwinkle for excessive menses. Red Raspberry (builder + good for nausea during pregnancy). Soybeans are rich in estrogen. Dandelion, Kelp and Alfalfa - prevent birth defects (Dr. Louise Tenney). Some women have used Mexican Wild Yam combined with touching the points for the reproductive organs (p. 166) during meditation as birth control. *(see reproductive organs)*

Urinary - Juniper berry for water retention. If there is yellow in the iris, it may be an indication that there is toxic urine in the body. Horsetail and Oatstraw support urinary system. Gravelroot to break up stones and then Uva Ursi to flush out kidneys. *(Antilithic - herbs with ability to remove or prevent the formation of stones or gravel in the urinary system.)* For constant, burning urine - Organic Cranberry juice to kill bacteria, STOP Cranberry, and then take Uva Ursi. Uva Ursi and Cranberry cancel one another out! Cleavers and Parsley - support urinary system. Sandalwood - for bladder inflammation. Saw Palmetto and Yarrow - diuretic.

Veins & Arteries - Dandelion for hardening of arteries. Pau d' Arco is used in treatment of leukemia. Ginkgo and Gotu Kola are used to improve circulation. White Oak Bark is used in the treatment of varicose veins (as a paste it can be applied directly to the skin). Lecithin breaks down cholesterol because it enables fats to be dispersed in water so that they can be removed from the body. Essential fatty acids prevent the hardening of arteries and balance cholesterol. Hernias (opening or hole in the diaphragm muscles through which the stomach pushes - symptoms are heartburn and belching) and prolapsed organs can be helped with Lecithin which is good for connective tissue.

Arteriosclerosis involves the buildup of calcium deposits on the inside of artery walls, which causes thickening and hardening of the arteries. Cayenne, Ginkgo and Hawthorn. Butchers Broom is used for hemorrhoids. Fargelin (Chinese) is used internally and externally in the treatment of hemorrhoids. Butchers Broom tones the internal surface of veins and constricts blood vessels while increasing efficiency of each heartbeat. For "heavy leg" syndrome in elderly. Horsechestnut is an astringent *(constricting or binding effect)* that strengthens and tones veins. Butaio (Chinese) is a blood tonic that is useful in treating blood deficiencies with stagnation. Dong Quai is also a good blood tonic (do not take during menstruation).

Stone Root by Herb Pharm is a liquid extract from the leaves and flowers. It is an herbal tonic specific to the veins and mucus membranes. Stone Root is also used for hemorrhoids and after rectal surgery, strengthens and tones uterus, heart tonic and alterative to the urinary tract. It is used for chronic laryngitis, middle ear inflammation, bronchitis and hoarseness due to excess use of the voice. Again, this illustrates the numerous uses of a single herb and hints at the potential, dynamic interrelationship between the individual constituents of an herb. By chemically reducing an herb to a single molecule and then enhancing it, any supporting or safety influence by other agents is lost.

Personally, I prefer to use herbal products from small, independent companies, such as the ones I have mentioned throughout this chapter, who have always had my best interest in mind. Again, organic plants retain their nutrients, minerals, etc. Products that are toxic to insects and weeds would have to affect anything that is living.

For Kids: Eclectic Institue has a variety of 22 herbal compounds and single herbs in alcohol-free herbal extracts; most of which are fruit flavored. These include Echinacea & Goldenseal + Vitamin C or Echinacea + Vitamin C. Singles include Ginger, Lemon Balm, St. John's Wort, Elder Berry, Hyssop and Valerian.

Compound Herbal Biotic + Vitamin C contains Rosehips, Wild Cherry, Licorice Root, Echinacea Root & Seed, Peppermint, Red Clover, Astragalus, Osha, Lomatium, Elder Flower, Calendula flower, Lemon Balm and Myrrh.

Herbal Cough Elixir + Vitamin C contains Licorice, Elecampane root, Red Clover, Wild Cherry, Horehound, Bumweed, Lobelia, Fennel, Lomatium, White Pine and Poplar.

Neutralizing Cordial contains Turkey Rhubarb, Cinnamon, Goldenseal and Potassium Bicarbonate.

Chamomile-Catnip also contains Elder Flower, Lemon Balm, Hyssop and Peppermint.

Pau d' Arco-Usnea also contains black Walnut, Yerba Mansa and White Pond Lily.

Nettles-Eyebright also contains Mullein and Ephedra.

Valerian-Passion Flower also contains Chamomile, Hops and Anise.

MotherLove is another herbal company with an excellent line of herbal products for children.

Colonics are not for everyone: Some people are physically unable to go through colon therapy. Personally, I feel it is the best way to clean out my large intestine - even after going through an herbal cleanse (strict herbal and juice cleanses are best done in the spring or fall when body is naturally releasing). If there is a buildup of old debris on the walls of the large intestine, then vitamins and minerals are less likely to be absorbed into the body. The old debris provides a home for parasites that take the nutrients and excrete their own toxic waste, and parasites do not confine themselves to the intestines. A week before a colonic, at night I rub cold-pressed linseed oil onto my belly. The day before, if not 2 or 3 days before, I go on a juice fast (Hanna Kroeger has specific cleanses for specific issues or body parts in Good Health Through Special Diets). After a colonic, I drink lemon water and replace the acidophilus the following morning before eating.

Some Suggested Reading:

For those interested in pursuing iridology, Zhenia Hc Heigh and other iridologists offer classes. There are numerous books on iridology for comprehensive eye charts and the landmarks of the iris.

Ayurveda: The Science of self Healing by Vasant Lad

The Alchemist's Handbook to Homeopathy by Rev. Mary Hardy, B.A., Ph.D. and Dotty Nonman, Ph.D.

The Bach Flower Remedies - Step by Step by Judy Howard

Bach Flower Therapy: Theory and Practice by Mechthild Scheffer

Cleanse and Purify Thyself, by Richard Anderson, M.D. (information concerning colonics)

The Complete Book of Chinese Health and Healing by Daniel Reed

The Complete Herbal Handbook for Farm and Stable by Juliette de Bairacli-Levy

Drug-Free Remedies Using Vitamins, Minerals, Herbs & Food Supplements by James F. Balch, M.D. and Phyllis A. Balch, C.N.C.

Earl Mindell's Herb Bible by Earl Mindell, R.Ph., Ph.D.

Earthway by Mary Summer Rain (contains "the Earth Mother's Pharmacy")

Herbal Medicine: The Natural Way to Get Well and Stay Well by Dian Dincin Buchman, Ph.D.

Materia Medica with Repertory by William Boericke, M.D. (homeopathy)

Mind, Food and Smart Pills by Ross Pelton P. Ph., Ph. D.

The New Age Herbalist by Richard Mabey

Original Writings of Edward Bach by Judy Howard and John Ramsell

Prescription for Nutritional Healing, subtitled A Practical A-Z Reference to Drug-Free Remedies Using Vitamins, Minerals, Herbs & Food Supplements by James F. Balch M.D. and Phyllis A Balch C.N.C.

Questions and Answers – The Bach Flower Remedies by John Ramsell

Seven Herbs - Plants As Teaches by Matthew Wood, talks about using herbs for spiritual growth

Smart Drugs & Nutrients by Ward Dean, M. D. & John Morgenthaler

Thirty Plants That Can Save Your Life by Douglas Schar, with practical ways to take herbs, formulas for ointments and tonics, when to collect herbs or places to order them from.

The Yoga of Herbs: An Ayurvedic Guide to Herbal Medicine by Dr. David Frawley and Dr. Vasant Lad

For Hanna Kroeger's classes, which are now being taught by her former students, and her books write to: New Age Foods, 1122 Pearl, Boulder, Co 8030

Herbs for Horses

For your information only!

Aloe – first aid cream for skin injuries and cracked heals.

Apple Cider Vinegar with the mother (vinegar with the mother is PH balanced; without the mother it is acidic) – 1/4 cup on horse's hay once a day to control flies and helps with fungus. Can transfer the mother to ordinary vinegar and let it sit for 9 days.

Cabbage – poultice for joint pain and swelling.

Calendula – internally – liver and digestive problems. Externally – antifungal and antibacterial.

Chamomile – mild sedative and eases digestive troubles.

Comfrey – poultice for wounds; ointment for bones, tendons and joints.

Dandeloin – blood cleanser and , liver and kidney tonic. Juice from stem can be applied to warts.

Garlic – insect repellent and for parasit infestation. For lung and circulatory disorders. Strengthens immune system. For infections – can be taken internally or applied externally.

Dried Ginger – stimulates digestion and circulation, and releives conjection in the lungs.

Dyn-o-Mite Contact Insecticide made from ground foscils begins killing flies from the minute the y land on it by destroying their internal organs including their reproductive organs, which means that they are unable to reproduce in the 3 days before they die. This white powder is completely safe for animals and humans. Frank Sarno spread this around Santa Rita Stables where flies landed and in 3 days the results were dramatic. *Port Chemical Corp., 1664 Cypress Pointe Drive, Coral Springs, FL 33071*

Horseradish root - poltice for strains and sprains.

Marigold flower – digestive and liver disorders. Externally – antibacterial and antifungal.

Fresh Mint – appetite stimulant. Antifungal.

Orange peal extract (d-Limonene) – kills flies! I do not spray it on my horses; I spray it on the flies that are around my horses and it kills them. If the spray gets on my horse, I rinse the spray off with water. It is nontoxic to my horses!

Fresh Parsley – lungs, kidneys and digestion.

Raspberry leaves - strengthens uterus and increases milk production after birth.

Red Clover – internally cleans blood and used for bronchitis.

Rose Hips – High in Vitamin C. Good for liver.

Slippery Elm – coats digestive track.

Stinging Nettle – spring tonic. Rich in vitamins and minerals. Increases excretion of uric acid.

Organic produce and herbs retain nutrients and other active ingredients! Herbicides, pesticides and chemical fertilizers can and do affect active agents in plants.

Moving Qi

With Movement, Sound & Visualization

Lao Tzu, a Chinese philosopher of the sixth century B. C., wrote the Tao Te Ching. In R. L. Wing's The Tao of Power: Lao Tzu's Classic Guide to Leadership, Influence, and Excellence, he begins by stating that *Tao*, which is traditionally translated as "the Way", is more accurately translated as "the Way the universe works". Physicists who have read it find that it is in allignment with 'modern' theories. *Te* has been translated as "virtue", thus, suggesting righteousness • • • "but in fact *Te* is a term that refers to the potential energy that comes from being in the right place and in the right frame of mind at the right time. • • • Not until the widespread popularity of Confucian ideals centuries later, did *Te* begin to take on the meaning of socially imposed moral conduct. • • • I have returned the meaning of *Te* to its original concept, Power."

The Tao of Power: Lao Tzu's Classic Guide to Leadership, Influence, and Excellence is not only an excellent translation of Lao Tzu's work, but R. L. Wing provides additional food for thought apart from the translation. In their attempts to admonish and then impeach President Clinton, what both politicians and the news media did was to discredit themselves in the public's eye. Everyday, more and more people came to their own conclusions, they began to think for themselves rather than letting somebody else do it for them. When Americans were told by the media and society's leaders that a recession was at hand, most Americans did not buy into that either with the result being that the United States remained prospering. That is the power of individual thought and that is what the Tao Te Ching encourages individuals to do. "What Lao Tzu tells leaders is essentially this: Discover who you are. Learn to sense the world around you directly, and contemplate your impressions deeply. Do not rely on ideologies, because to do so will rob your life of meaning and make you unfit to lead. Cultivate and make trustworthy your intuition, because a leader who is not intuitive cannot predict change. Build up your personal power *(Te)* through your awareness and knowledge of the physical laws as they operate both in the universe and in the minds of others *(Tao)* - then use that power to direct events, without resorting to force. • • • "

In China there evolved those individuals who could bring about change for others. The Feng Shui Masters could move energy in the environment; the Chi Kung Masters could move energy within the human body. What follows are two exercises that move Qi. They are self-cultivating and have been practiced for over a thousand years.

251

Healing Sounds for the Body

Organ	Sound	Visualize and Feel	Body Movement
Lungs	"hsss"	Cool and white Element is metal Planet is Venus Spirit animal is white tiger	Look up! Push hands above head with thumbs up with knees apart
Kidneys	silent "wh" wind	Cold, blue and wet Element is water Planet is Mercury Spirit animal is blue deer	Scoop hands together and clasp in front of knees. Open scapula. Pull up! Look out!
Liver	"shhh"	Green, warm and moist Element is wood Planet is Jupiter Spirit animal is green dragon	Fingers interlocked. Palms up. Lift above head andpress with right hand.
Heart	"haaw"	Hot and dry Element is fire Planet is Mars Spirit animal is red pheasant	Fingers interlocked. Palms up. Lift above head and press with left hand.
Spleen	"wh" What	Yellow, warm & cool Element is earth Planet is Saturn Spirit animal is golden phoenix	Scoop hands in front Back of hands together Press finger into solar plexis. Thumbs up

---

Triple Burner	"hsss" flat tongue	Lie down! Breathe into abdoman, then stomach and then the lungs *(beginning at the bottom and lastly filling the upper portion of the lungs)*. Exhale in reverse *(from the top of the lungs)* – like squeezing out a tube of toothpaste. Vocalize "hsss"	

Transforms	Organ Governs	Organ Governs Sence Organ	Taste
Sadness and Grief into Righteousness and courage	Skin	Nose	Pungent Spicy
Fear into Gentleness	Bone Sperm & Egg	Ears	Salty
Hatred and Disrespect Into Love & Joy	Blood & Body hair	Tongue	Bitter
Anger into Kindness	Nerves Brain Tendons Facial hair	Eyes	Sour
Worry & Vulnerability Into Self-worth	Muscles Lymph Glands	Lips & Gums	Sweet

---

Purges heat & balances Triple Warmer	Triple Warmer consists of Kidneys & Bladder, Liver & Stomach and Heart & Lungs	North Star is the the first gate to heaven

The Hammer of Thor (page 280) symbolizes the Big Dipper revolving around the North Star. Cosmic energy is golden and comes into the body through the third eye.

Universal energy is both the purple from the North Star and red from the Big Dipper and comes into the body through the crown. Earth energy is blue and comes into the body through the root chakra.

Cultivating QI

1) Give thanks and gratitude. (Traditionally, bow 3 times before an altar or other sacred place.) Ask for blessings. Tongue on roof of mouth. Feet shoulder width apart and parallel to one another – not pigeon toed or Charlie Chapman.

2) Focus on a point. (Traditionally, look straight ahead; if you look up at a 20 degree angle while keeping the head straight ahead, you will begin to see an indigo circle.) Keep eyes still and do not blink. Tongue on roof of mouth throughout.

3) To keep heaven's gate or palm chakras open: Elbows at shoulder height, palms facing each other. Up on toes. As you bring heals down, clap hands together and say "Haaa!" Sound should come from the diaphragm. Do this 3 times. Keep staring at single point.

4) Moving and cultivating Qi: Drop arms and hands to your side – not in front or in back of legs. Bring arms and hands up above the head with elbows straight as though you were making angel wings in the snow and clap hands together above head. Hold hands tightly together with fingertips and thumbs together. Keep staring at single point.

5) Keep hands in tight prayer position and move them to below the chin. Relax shoulders and arms. Arms and hands about one inch from chest. Keep staring at single point. Open eyes wider if you feel like blinking. Hold! Try not to blink! Mentally calming! Center on third eye point. Smile! Work up to holding this position for 15 minutes.

6) Bring hand and arms down to sides. Palms parallel to floor. Keep staring at point for a few minutes. Close eyes and hold position. Work up to 15 minutes. You are integrating heaven & earth. Healing position! Palms will start breathing. Smile!

7) With as little movement as possible, keep eyes closed and sit on floor. Sit in Yoga position if you can. Do the best you can and knees will slowly come down. Concentrate on third eye point and palms of hands. Smile! Hold position and work up to 15 minutes. Visualize, feel or imagine that you are floating on a cloud. Healing position!

8) Move excess energy to a place about 2 inches below belly button.

9) Utilizing Qi for self-healing:
- Rub hands together vigorously in front of bellybutton – you are moving Qi into hands. Then with cupped hands, place them over the eyes. Do this 3 times.
- Rub hands together vigorously in front of bellybutton! Then with cupped hands, place them over the nose. Do this 3 times.
- Rub hands together vigorously in front of bellybutton! Then with cupped hands, place them over the ears. Do this 3 times.
- Massage meridians of ears!
- Rub hands together vigorously in front of bellybutton! Then with cupped hands, place them over an area of the body that needs healing. Do this 3 times.
- Rub hands and pat body – arms, torso and legs.

Hands in prayer position. Give thanks and gratitude. Bow 3 times.

Exercising

Tai Chi, Martial Arts and body building all work on the similar premise that exercises that are natural body movements tone muscles; movements that are not natural body movements strain muscles, tendons and joints, which will at some point cause soreness or injury. For example, the movement whereby weights are pulled down in front of the chest is a natural movement; pulling the same weights behind the head and neck is an unnatural movement. Many back and spinal injuries are caused when an individual twists and ten bends over to pick up an object.

Locking the elbow or knee joints in Tai Chi or martial arts creates vulnerability. When the arms or legs are extended to a locked position when lifting weights, this position strains or damages the small muscles around the joints. Whether it is skiing or horseback riding, the athlete is more effective when the knee, ankle and elbow joints are slightly bent and the spine is supple.

When using the machines to lift weights rather than dumbbells it is important to be mindful that the weights are being pulled evenly by each side of the body. For example, if one arm is pulling more weight than the other arm, the body is torked and the muscles on one side are lengthened and shortened on the other. **Robin Hormann, The Netherlands**

Building Stamina & Muscle Strength

FOR YOUR INFORMATION ONLY, HEREIN IS ADDITIONAL INFORMATION NOT INCLUDED IN THE FOLLOWING CHAPTER ON HERBS. ALSO, TRACE MINERALS MEANS MINIMAL DOSAGE!

Antioxidants (Vitamins C, E, Beta Carotene and Selenium) can help extend endurance and promote cardiovascular efficiency and help to protect cells against oxygen-induced damage. Athletes exercising in urgan polluted environments require greater amounts of antioxidant nutrients, which protect their lungs.

B-Complex Vitamins: **B-1** (thiamine) is crucial to the breakdown of carbohydrates and the release of energy. **B-2** (riboflavin) aids in the utilization of energy. **B-3** (miacin) aids in the utilization of energy. **B-6** (pyridoxine) facilitates the conversion of stored liver and muscle glycogen into energy and helps body utilize amino acids and protein. **B-12** (cobalamin) for maintance of nerve tissue and normal blood formation!

Biotin helps to increase glucose production from lactic acid.

Boron naturally raises steroid hormone synthesis and plays an important role in the hardening of bones.

Branched Chain Amino Acids (BCAA's) act as a direct source of energy for muscles and promote muscle growth.

Choline is important in membrane structure and assists in clear brain functioning.

Chromium and insulin is required for the uptake of glucose (blood sugar, which is a major source of energy for working muscles) by muscles.

High Carbohydrate Diets allow athletes to perform longer at peak levels.

Inositol deficiency leads to a fatty liver and increased fat deposits in other tissues.

Iodine benefits the thyroid and is necessary for the synthesis of thyroxin, the hormone that accelerate the rate of energy metabolism in cells.

Iron is a crucial constituent of oxygen-carrying hemoglobin.

L-Carnitine is a natural fat burner.

Lipoic Acid functions to increase glucose burning for short, high-energy activities. Antioxidant!

Manganese helps to heal bone, cartilage, tendon and ligament injuries. Essential for sugar and carbohydrate metabolism!

Peptide-Bonded Amino Acids are handled more efficiently in the colon and have been clinically tested to be superior to crystaline free-form amino acid mixtures for muscle development.

Phosphorus is an essential component of high-energy compounds, which supply the energy for biologic work. Phosphorus also combines with substances in the blood and acts to buffer the acid and products of energy metabolism.

Vitamin D aids in the absorption of calcium essential for building strong teeth and bones.

Tera-Mai™ Seichem II

Using All Four Elemental Healing Rays to Energize Symbols

In this chapter, there are only a few of the symbols that I included in <u>Reiki & Other Rays of Touch Healing</u>. This was done purposefully in order to emphasize that symbols themselves do not bring empowerment. Just like computers, symbols are tools. Computers become assets when the individual who is working with one is knowledgeable; symbols are effective healing techniques when the individual working with them is channeling healing energy. When an individual has been attuned to healing or has been born with healing, Holy Spirit (angels, guides, etc.) is able to work through the healer in order to bring about transformation in the physical, mental, emotional and other spiritual bodies of the healee. Symbols that are used as a part of an initiation process are not 'stuffed' into the initiate's aura or healing channels; rather, they are imprinted into the aura and healing channels of the initiate by Higher Forces, who are the ones who are doing the actual initiation. This imprinting finely tunes the initiate to healing rays that emanate from Mother-Father God. Just as we do not use just any thick liquid to lubricate our automobiles, so too, not all symbols are equipped to function as symbols of initiation. Symbols that are used in initiation raise the frequency of the healing vibration within the healer. Because there are symbols that only work or only work effectively in higher vibrations, a true initiation into healing will increase the healer's ability to facilitate both hands-on healing and distant healing with or without the use of symbols. Thus, the healer does not necessarily have to be attuned to every symbol in order for them to work.

The proof of an initiation is evidenced by the healing work that the healer is able to do afterwards. It is not airy-fairy, pie in the sky, maybe something happened! Healing is a reality that is experienced physically, mentally, emotionally and spiritually. Healing comes from Mother-Father God, and God chooses to work through His/Her Creation in order to bring about change; that is, God works through each one of us, angels, spirit guides, herbs, crystals, animals, trees, etc.

The ancient art of hands-on healing has been practiced throughout time. What I have done in this chapter and the following chapter, "Symbols", is to energize the symbols so that my readers could have firsthand experiences. I did this in my last book, and I have received interesting feedback. One woman wrote to me, saying, *"I was lying on my left side on my bed and reading your book. When I got to the part where you said that you had energized the symbols, I touched*

Harth, but I wasn't really expecting anything to happen. Suddenly, my right leg shot into the air and started to shake. I could neither stop it from shaking nor move it back down. Rather than taking my hand off of the symbol, I relaxed and felt heaviness leaving my leg as it shook itself out. When the heaviness was gone, my leg returned to normal. The next day I was again lying on my bed and reading your book. This time I was lying on my right side. I turned the pages of your book and looked at Harth. I touched Harth but I knew that it couldn't happen again. This time, my left leg shot up into the air and shook itself until the heaviness in that leg was gone. Both of my legs are fine. I have no idea what it was that I released, but I know that it was something.

The prerequisite for this class is Tera-Mai™ Seichem I. The same procedure will be used for the second-degree initiation; however, the initiation points are the crown, palms of both hands and the soles of both feet. The second-degree initiation further opens the crown chakra so that more elemental healing energy flows into the crown. The initiation at the feet opens the chakra located at the soles of the feet so that blue electromagnetic energy from earth can be drawn into the healer. Opening of the chakras at the soles of the feet also serves to ground the elemental healing rays.

Like the first initiation, the second initiation also initiates a 21-day cleansing cycle that begins at the root chakra. The second day, it moves up to the second or creative chakra, by the seventh day it is at the crown chakra. Thus, the initiate experiences three cleansings of the seven major chakras.

After the initiation, everyone will be given the opportunity to share his or her experiences. This helps the left brain to remember what the right brain just experienced - it is like writing dreams down immediately upon awakening. Not sharing is also a legitimate option. Class members may want to keep a journal during the class or make additional notes on the handout.

Everything comes from Father-Mother God - healing, symbols, angels, animals, people - everything! When we become open channels for healing, we work directly with the elemental healing energy that emanates from God. We can also work indirectly through nature, angels or symbols that are also channels for elemental healing energy. As we all have spirit guides and angels, and given that the initiation imprints healing symbols into the healer's aura and healing channels, working with Holy Spirit and symbols can be done at a subconscious level. In this class, however, we will consciously work with symbols.

Symbols can be drawn directly on the body or in the aura of the healee with his/her permission. Now, the reason why we can send healing and healing symbols to individuals without asking their permission is because the symbols are not drawn directly on the individual; thus, giving the person the opportunity to either accept or reject the healing. (Yes, there are people who do not want to, or are not ready to be healed. That is their freewill option.) If the absentee healing is rejected, the healing energy is multiplied a hundredfold and sent back to the healer(s). However, if the intended healee rejects the healing, we cannot continue to send healing or healing symbols. People should not have to keep fighting off healing. If the intended healee only takes some of the healing that is sent, then we must tune in before sending the healing a second time.

Everyone will have opportunities during the class to put a name into the circle for healing. Yes, you can mention an entire family unit; however, this type of group healing has a "shotgun approach". That is, the healing is dispersed. If one member of the group is particularly strong, or has a powerful spirit helper, there is the possibility that s/he may pull more healing energy towards him/her. Thus, absentee healing is more effective when we focus our concentration on one individual at a time. This does not mean that there won't be times when we will be asked to send healing to a group. For example, many people were impressed to send healing to the victims of the TWA jet that was shot down over Long Island, as well as to their families and friends.

Usually, if a name pops into the healer's mind, it means that that individual is asking for healing. So, I would suggest that when it is your turn to put a name into the circle, go with the first name that comes to you. The effectiveness of the absentee healing works under the same set of conditions as hands-on healing; that is, healing techniques and symbols are only as effective as the amount and quality of healing energy that the healer is channeling. If an individual is requesting healing by coming into the mind of the healer, this usually means that s/he is willing to release the issues behind his/her pain or disease. Just as in hands-on healing, each healee is going to go through his/her own unique healing process during a session.

Healers can set up a specific time with an individual who has requested absentee healing. At the appointed time, the healee gets into a meditative and receptive state. The healer draws and empowers the symbols with Cho Ku Rays, and then watches with the mind's inner eye as the symbols leave to see what happens. The idea is to hold the image of the symbol in the mind's inner eye and then observe what happens. The outcome is never manipulated or the healer runs the risk of losing his/her healing energy. As in hands-on healing, the healer communicates with spirit guides and angels to ask what needs to be done. Many really good psychics use their hands when they are describing psychic impressions. Likewise, in absentee healing, the healer can use his/her hands to pull off "negativity", drain the pus-like residue and fill the space with healing energy. The key to all of healing is watching and asking Holy Spirit, "What needs to be done?" Then the healer observes. Initially, the healer may only feel energy leaving his/her hands or see colors. This is fine! This works! With practice, more is possible.

Immediately after an accident, the aura is shattered. The "negative" energy patterns will not become ingrained (established) for 3 days. The absentee healing technique can be sent to victims of accidents. The healer sends healing and healing symbols, drains misqualified energy, and visualizes correct energy patterns being reestablished by the angels.

Likewise, after a healing, while the aura has not been shattered, the "positive" energy patterns will not become ingrained (established) for 3 days. This is the reason why healees who leave the healing session and talk about their old pains and how they used to feel actually release the healing and reconnect their "negative" energy patterns. This is also why it is advisable for the healee (absentee or hands-on) to rest and drink plenty of water (coffee, soda, juice are not water - the only liquid that is water is water). In like manner, people who deny healing initiations after they receive them, out of arrogance or ignorance, cancel their own initiation.

To increase the effectiveness of healing symbols, they should be empowered. We will go through this empowerment procedure step by step during the class so that healers can experience firsthand how each adjustment increases the energy of the symbol. Techniques for empowerment:

1. Speak the name of the symbol three times out loud while you draw. (Symbol is drawn once.) "In the beginning was the word." God did not dream it, write it or visualize it. He/She spoke it! Each symbol has a series of sounds, which we call a word that works to vibrate the symbol. Three is the number of creation. The healer is working with Holy Spirit and healing rays to create a tool for the purpose of bringing about a transformation in the physical, mental, emotional and/or other spiritual bodies.

2. Using only the index finger to draw symbols means that only the chakra of that fingertip is being used. If we draw with our palms, only the palm chakra is being used. However, if we cone our fingers and draw the symbols in the air in front of us, we are using the chakras of five fingers as well as the palm chakra. We can observe this for ourselves by looking in a mirror while we draw with our hands.

3. Cho Ku Rays are energy notes that come from Mother-Father God and they empower all other symbols. Cho Ku Rays are like the electric company; the other symbols are like your appliances. Counterclockwise spirals connect with the earth; clockwise spirals connect to the heavens. Together, they produce a balanced energy.

In this class, we will be sending healing and healing symbols to people, places and events. We will be experimenting with several techniques using our hands. After the symbols have been drawn:

1. Healer holds hands in front of his/her body with his/her palms facing outwards; thus, radiating energy to the healee wherever s/he is.

2. Same as one, but the healer psychically invites the healee to stand in front of him/her. Some healers feel or see the presence of the astral body of the healee. Given that time and space are an illusion of this 3-dimensional world, a healer can feel that s/he and the healee are somehow together and the sensation is somewhat like being displaced in time and space.

3. Healer places his/her hands on his/her own body where the symptoms are manifesting in the healee.

4. Healer holds his/hers hands so that the palms are facing one another, and visualizes the healee between his/her hands.

5. Same as four, but the healer visualizes or feels the blockage that is in the healee as being between his/her hands. Slowly, the healer brings his/her hands together. When the palms touch, the "negativity" has been transformed, or whatever was ready to be released has been transformed. In using this technique, it is important for the healer to ask to feel the "negativity" and not the energy that radiates from his/her hands. *(Technique from Steven Bogdan)*

6. Like the magician in the tarot, healer raises his/her left hand to bring in the energy of the symbols that were drawn, and grounds the energy with the palm of the right hand facing down towards the earth.

7. Symbols are not drawn directly on the healee unless the healer asks permission to do so.

8. Likewise, photographs or articles of clothing are not used in absentee healing unless the healer has the healee's permission to send healing. Parents can ask for their children and owners of pets can ask for their animals.

I have not included all of the symbols from <u>Reiki & Other Rays of Touch Healing</u>. What I have done herein is to give additional information and techniques on using a few of them. Again, symbols can be useful but are not an end in and of themselves. Since the publication of <u>Reiki & Other Rays of Touch Healing</u> there has been a mad pursuit of symbols by some individuals. There is even one Reiki offshoot system from India that has 1,500 symbols for Reiki I alone. All of the symbols herein have been energized so that the reader may have the opportunity if s/he wishes to experience the healing power that is possible from certain symbols.

Say Hay Key

Mental healing. Since emotions are strong thoughts with feelings attached to them, it is possible to use Say Hay Key on the emotional body as well. Trauma that is held in the body is also a thought form. Universal symbols have a consciousness, they come from God; they know how to go about and do their work.

When we clean up our thoughts, the physical, emotional and other spiritual bodies follow suit. When we change our ideas, we change our whole lives as well.

Line 1) is Say, 2) is Hay and 3) is Key. If we draw it once in this manner and then repeat "Say Hay Key" 2 more times, we will have said the name of the symbol 3 times.

When we use all ten of our coned fingers to draw a symbol, the energy becomes stronger. We can feel the difference for ourselves by drawing and empowering Say Hay Key first with the index finger of one hand only. Feel the energy and then we send it to the earth. Now we draw Say Hay

Key with the coned fingers of one hand. Feel the energy and then send it to the earth. Finally, with the coned fingers of both hands, draw Say Hay Key; feel the energy and then send it to the earth. By sending the healing energy into Mother Earth after we have experienced it, we are clearing the field in front of us rather than building up the energy in the field. If we continue to build the energy in the field, of course, the energy will become stronger. Thus, by sending the energy out after energizing symbols, we always begin with a clean etheric chalkboard.

Cho Ku Ray

Spirals are found in all indigenous cultures! The Kahunas of Hawaii rapidly drew spirals with their hands and arms in the aura of the healee. This is movement by a healer is particularly helpful after an injury. Cho Ku Rays are spiraled symbols that work together to energize other symbols, be they Reiki, Egyptian or Runes. Other symbols should be checked out and cleared, if necessary, before they are energized and used. Some people prefer to check out any symbol before it is energized and used.

Together, the Cho Ku Rays that spiral in focuses on specific aspects of an issue.

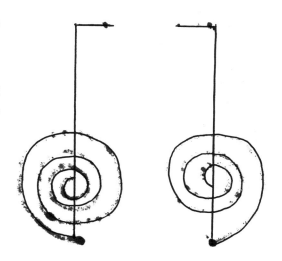

Symbols can bring up negativity for us to work through. However, if the symbol is twisted, the energy produced from that symbol will be twisted as well. The best rule of thumb to follow is, "When in doubt, don't!"

Line 1) is Cho, line 2) is Ku and the spiraling line 3) is Ray. The healer can punch these symbols in the center after drawing them to further empower them.

In class I want my students to experience the difference for themselves between not using Cho Ku Rays to empower a symbol and then using only one Cho Ku Ray at a time and then using both Cho Ku Rays to empower Say Hay Key. Then we practice sending Say Hay Key and both Cho Ku Rays to individuals in need of mental healing.

Cho Ku Ray

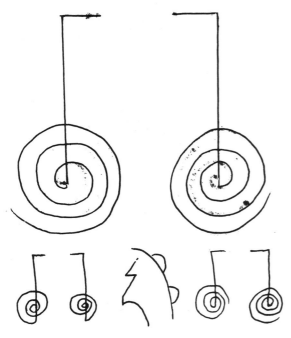

Together the Cho Ku Rays that spiral outwards looks at the big picture or all sides of an issue.

We then empower Say Hay Key with these Cho Ku Rays only so that the class can feel the difference for themselves.

We then empower Say Hay Key with all 4 Cho Ku Rays by sandwiching Say Hay Key in between the Cho Ku Rays that get smaller and the Cho Ku Rays that get bigger.

Afterwards, we send mental healing to the same people who accepted absentee healing when we energized Say Hay Key with only 2 Cho Ku Rays so that the class might see the difference for themselves. During this process, students are learning not only how easy it is to send healing, but also how to do readings as well because after we send healing to an individual, everyone has the opportunity to share what they saw, felt or heard. The individual who put the name into the circle goes last so that s/he can confirm or add comments to what his/her fellow class member received intuitively.

These additional Cho Ku Rays were a part of the knowledge that Takata received from the Japanese energy masters. I know this to be true because I met one individual who was close in lineage who had received all four Cho Ku Rays. Just as in Reiki, these Seichem Cho Ku Rays are more powerful when the individual has been initiated into Tera-Mai™ Seichem. Original Seichem does not use all four Cho Ku Rays as part of the initiation procedure; the original Seichem only uses the Cho Ku Ray that spirals larger in a clockwise motion.

There are sequences of Cho Ku Rays that energize and produce a harmonic flow of energy (I have drawn them on pages 264 and 273). Perhaps Takata knew that the wrong combination of Cho Ku Rays will produce static, not healing, and that is why she withheld the information. For those individuals who experiment with other patterns and find that they do not like what they created, ask with your heart that the energy be taken to the Light for clearing and then grab hold of the misqualified energy and slowly send it up to the Light.

Hon Sha Za Sho Nen

There are at least 16 different variations of Hon Sha Za Sho Nen that Takata gave out. George Matsui watched a friend go into an altered state and draw this one.

Harth

Harth is a symbol for the heart and it is from the heart. It is from the heart where we are supposed to listen to God and to our own higher self. Our brain is a library resource reference center. Thus, this symbol could be used in combination with Say Hay Key to open one's heart so that the Truth can be heard and one can be true to oneself. *"You gain strength, courage and confidence by every experience in which you really stop to look fear in the face. . . You must do the thing you think you cannot do."* Eleanor Roosevelt
Say Hay Key and Harth can help connect heart + brain.

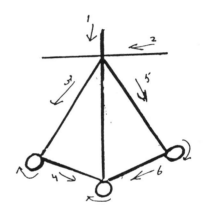

Mara

Mara is a part of the initiation in the second degree of both Tera-Mai™ Reiki and Tera-Mai™ Seichem. It opens the chakras that are located at the soles of the feet and attunes the initiate to the electromagnetic, cobalt blue healing energy of Mother Earth. When this blue ray comes up through the initiate, it combines with the golden ray of Reiki to form a third, green healing ray.

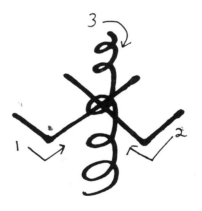

This symbol vibrates strongly to the intonation "Mara". Both the blue and the green healing rays that are brought about during this initiation are particularly important in Seichem, because these colors cool down the healer's body so that s/he can safely channel fire energy. Intoning this symbol as "Rama" does not produce the same effect! While "Rama" may or may not be a more powerful intonation than "Mara", "Rama" is not the vibration that creates the green healing ray.

265

This symbol vibrates strongly to the intonation "Mara". Both the blue and the green healing rays that are brought about during this initiation are particularly important in Seichem, because these colors cool down the healer's body so that s/he can safely channel fire energy. Intoning this symbol as "Rama" does not produce the same effect! While "Rama" may or may not be a more powerful intonation than "Mara", "Rama" is not the vibration that creates the green healing ray. Ulf Herrstrom had been initiated with the symbol Mara intoned as Rama at his feet. When I reinitiated him, he felt the chakras at the soles of his feet open further.

Mara can be used in ceremonies to ground magic. Mara is a symbol for the healing of the physical body. However, if there is not a corresponding attitude change on the part of the healee, the healing will not hold.

I wonder if the reason why our bodies tend to sag with time is because we are no longer connected to the heart of the Goddess. We are out of balance! Is it possible that it is our connection to and honoring of Mother, which is the energy of Mara, that counteracts or balances gravity within our bodies?

There is a story of how Buddha was once tempted by the demon Mara. This symbol is not the work of the devil. First of all, Buddha's later followers changed his teachings just like the Roman Catholic Church altered Jesus' true teachings. R. L. Wing in The Tao of Power provides convincing evidence that men even Lao-Tzu's Tao Te Ching (I Ching) has been incorrectly translated in parts. "Individuals who do not feel personal power feel fear. They fear the unknown because they do not identify with the world outside of themselves; . . . Tyrants do not feel power, they feel frustration and impotency. They wield force, but it is a form of aggression, not authority." Secondly, nowhere in any version of any bible is any demon credited with healing anyone. Prosperity and healing do not serve the devil's interest. "Ye shall know them by their works!" is just as true now as when Jesus spoke these words 2,000 years ago.

Just as Christianity was birthed from Judaism, Buddhism is the child of Hinduism. Thousands of years ago, India pursued metaphysics with the same great vigor that the present world seeks technological advancement. What follows is The Epic Ramayana which is found in The Great Epics of India as written by Valmiki after a change in his life: There was once a young man named Valmiki, who felt that he was responsible for feeding his mother, father, wife, children and himself. In order to do this, he was a hunter as well as a highwayman. One day, Valmiki met Sage Narada in the forest. Sage Narada asked Valmiki, "Why are you killing and stealing?"

Valmiki explained that he had many mouths to feed. Sage Narada then asked, "Is your family also willing to share your karma with you?" He answered, "Of course!" Sage Narada then said, "That's your answer! Now go home and ask them." Valmiki, who had plans to rob the sage, said, "No, you will run away." The sage answered, "Tie me to a tree and go home and ask them." Valmiki did as the sage requested. When he reached his home, he asked his parents if they would share in his karma. They answered, "No! It is your duty to feed us. How you are going to feed us is up to you, and it is your karma." Valmiki then went to his wife and asked her the same question. She also gave him the same reply. Valmiki was disillusioned and returned to Sage Narada, told him what happened and then asked, "What am I to do?" Sage then initiated him into the mantra "Rama"; however, because of all of his karma, Valmiki could not say "Rama". So, Sage Narada asked him to chant "Mara", which then turned into "Rama". With the chanting of Mara, all of his sins were burned up and he was purified to the point that when he saw a hunter killing a swan he said, "You have no right to take a life if you cannot give it life." When Valmiki spoke those words, he could feel the power of his words. The Creator, Brahman, asked Valmiki, to write a story on the mantra "Mara" or "Rama" so that others would be able to read and know the story. This was the beginning of The Epic Ramayana. (The other epics were written later by Veda Vyasa.)

It is extremely difficult for me to believe that Buddha, who honored everyone's path, would insult Hindus by saying that a demon named Mara tempted him. Just as the Roman Catholic Church invented Satan in the Dark Ages to frighten people into giving their money and remaining loyal to the Church, I believe that Buddha's later followers invented this story in an attempt to sway Hindus into converting to Buddhism. Neither Buddha nor Jesus came to establish dogmas or religious fanaticism. They both preached that we are all Buddhas, we are all children of God and that each one of us has our own particular road to follow. Jesus NEVER said that unbaptised children would not go to heaven; Gregory the Great said "Unbaptised babies went straight to hell." Both Innocent I and Gelasiu I added that unless babies also received communion that they too would suffer the same fate as the unbaptised. Later, this was changed by the Council of Trent!

Affirmations can change our thought patterns. When we change our thought patterns, we change our lives. However, if there is a part of us on any level that does not "buy into" the affirmation, then either change is not complete, or the change may not happen at all.

Invocations come from the heart, which is our connection to both our own higher self and to Mother-Father God. So, when we say, "From the Lord God of my being, to the Lord God of the Universe", we create an affirmation that is accepted on all levels of consciousness. It is best to release the old programming before reprogramming. For example, "From the Lord God of my repeat the affirmations after us. In asking for blessings or gifts, it is best to be specific without confining the Universe. For example, if we need a car (vehicle), we ask for a car (vehicle) and allow the Universe to determine the best possible one for us. This is also called leaving matters in Divine Order and for the highest good of all concerned.

Johre

Iris Ishikuro

From the 100-year-old Japanese calligraphy which is also called Johre or White Light. The American Johre Society received it from a Japanese gentleman visiting the United States.

It is an important symbol, which is why I am mentioning it again. Johre works well on releasing blockages. Maria Rawlins of Ireland uses it to open closed chakras. Connects us to the guardians or ancient ones. Thus, it works well for those who have been initiated into the Order of Melchizedek.

To empower a symbol, I say its name 3 times (the number of creation). In instances such as this where a symbol has 6 characters, I find myself saying the name Johre each time I draw a character for a total of 6 times (a multiple of 3).

Other Ways to Experience Healing Symbols

Place a glass of water in the center of the circle. One person thinks of somebody who needs healing. Everyone draws and sends symbols towards the glass of water. The individual, who knows the healee, then drinks the water and the healee, if open, will receive the healing. (Robert Wachsberger - Beachwood, Ohio)

Each person in the circle picks a symbol they want sent to them and everyone else sends it.

Draw a triangle on a piece of paper (red ink on yellow paper is powerful, grounding and lucky). In the lower left-hand corner, write the individual's name (or your own name). In the lower right-hand corner, write the situation. At the top of the triangle, write the desired outcome and add the words, "this or something better". If the desired outcome is unknown, write, "in Divine Order and for the highest good of all concerned." Then empower the triangle with symbols (could be drawn with red ink). The class members can take their triangles home and work with them, or collect them in a basket. Whenever you meditate, hold a class or meet with a group, place the basket in the center of the circle so that the triangles will automatically be energized. Every so often, you may wish to have a ceremony and burn them, perhaps on a new or full moon. (Joyce Morris)

The following is a variation of a healing with Archangel Raphael from Brian Johnson: Get into a meditative state and call upon Raphael (3 times) holding the sound of each vowel. See yourself clearly in your mind's eye. See yourself touching the healee. Ask Raphael to surround the healee with pale, mint green color. Watch as the color slowly changes to emerald green. Ask if there is anything you need to do. Close the healing session.

Symbols can be drawn on candles as part of candle magic. Dr. Usui may have burned candles while he was performing the ancient art of hands-on healing.

Symbols can be drawn by the healer on him/herself for self-healing. Then the healer goes into a meditative state and lays his/her hands on his/her body.

Symbols can be drawn over food before eating it and water before drinking it.

Symbols can be drawn on the palms of the healer's hands before sending or giving healing.

Symbols can be sent to the gas in automobiles for the purpose of increasing gas mileage and making cars cleaner and more fuel-efficient. These are just some of the possibilities.

There are languages of healing symbols, like Ama Deus and the Ascension symbols on the print, Babaji & the Eight Ascension Symbols, where it is considered impure to mix in other symbols, even Cho Ku Rays, when using them. It would be like speaking 2 languages in the same sentence; there would be no clarity in either language.

Symbols have the ability to get to the core issues. For example, some people (particularly those in government) are too quick to blame the Columbine High School murders on violent movies, videos, etc. and completely ignore the fact that the arts and other programs have been cut from many school curriculums and there is enormous stress on families because of the financial burdens that are created by high taxes. Then nightly we all hear on the news how citizens' tax dollars are wasted and the influences of big interests on government at the expense of everybody else. The anti-trust laws really have not been enforced since Jimmy Carter was in office, so, monstrously huge, multi-diverged corporations eliminate thousands of jobs, which means that those remaining are forced to do the work formerly done by many people. This adds more stress to the family situation. It also it the reason why kids are told in school that there will be few if any good jobs available by the time they graduate from college and if they would be lucky enough to find one, the pay would not come up to their expectations. Morality is taught by example and not through legislation or by lectures from the pulpit. Yet, people are aware that many government elected officials and agents are corrupt. There is even a children's board game that is based on the corruption in the state government of Louisiana. In a physical reality, we can all take the time to vote for real people (how about retired accountants and senior citizens?) and encouraging ethical people who are not career politicians to run for office. In a metaphysical reality, we can energize symbols and place them in appropriate Feng Shui areas of the home. For example, Say Hay Key or Halu would be appropriate for the *Knowledge and Self-Cultivation* corner. Harth would work well on either the *Health and Family* wall or the *Inspiration and Children* wall. For *Fame and Fortune, Career* or the *Money* corner, Mara can help manifest the abundance of the Absolute. How about Johre in the in the *Marriage and Partnership* corner to break up old patterns and blockages or Protection in the *Helpful People and Travel* corner.

Feng Shui is the Chinese art of placement whereby cleaning the home frees blockages and using crystals, mirrors, specific colors, etc. in specific corners or walls energies positive qualities. Of the two schools, location and compass, I personally prefer the original system, which is the location school. There are numerous books out on Feng Shui and like everything else, some are better than others are. Major businesses and top executives have successfully utilized Feng Shui. Feng Shui and other metaphysics are used to improve life situations because Feng Shui and white magic work!

Symbols

Abstract Vehicles for Practical Means

We as humans are only just beginning to reidentify and reclaim our ability to serve as channels for healing. Our capacity for holding healing energy became a rarity rather than the norm when the Goddess aspect of Divinity was trampled underfoot by the patriarchal, out-of-control warrior. Many thousands of years ago, Divinity was represented solely by the feminine. When these matriarchies became too extreme and the qualities of masculinity were suppressed (teacher, consoler, and the protective warrior), the real Mother-Father God stepped in and changed the "spirit of the times". With a change in emphasis, the Universe now supported left-brained knowledge and technological human endeavors. Mayans could foresee these shifts in the movement of the stars in our galaxy, and conceptualized these cycles in cosmic calendars. Mayan, Incan, Egyptian and even the Australian Aboriginal calendars are all coming to completion now, and all of them within 30 or so years of one another. Given the thousands of years that the patriarchy has thrived on Mother Earth, this is no coincidence.

Rather than moving back into another matriarchy, we are now moving into a time of balance where both Mother-God and Father-God are recognized, actualized, respected and loved. It is the Golden Age of the Return of the Angels, which is probably why so much attention is now being given to angels. In order to go into this Golden Age, the balance of male-female has to be restored within us, which may be why attention is focused on healing the inner child and men want to develop their nurturing, creative side. The Spirit of the Times is reflected in some television advertisements; it was unheard-of 20 years ago to see a strong male presence changing a baby's diaper or cooking in the kitchen with an apron on. This movement is reflected in women feeling good about themselves and contributing in other ways besides being sexy and bearing children. It is not that being sexy or bearing children is wrong or 'out of fashion'; rather, it is the allowing of women to successfully use their talents in government and business. I remember when I was in grade school and the teacher asked each of us to stand up and tell the class what we wanted to be when we grew up. The boys all gave a wide variety of answers; most of the girls said that they wanted to be either nurses or teachers. When it was my turn, I announced that I wanted to be a veterinarian. The whole class laughed at me and the teacher scowled. She must have told my mother about the incident, because a few days later my mother took me aside to explain to me that I should and would be a secretary when I grew up so that I would have health insurance and a pension when I retired. The possibility of this scenario happening to my daughter is nonexistent.

As we reconnect with our healing, nurturing and creative abilities, we are opening to our feminine qualities and the Goddess. Each one of us has a 2/3 - 1/3 balance of feminine/masculine or masculine/feminine energies. Our twin flame holds the other half of the formula. This split-away aspect of ourselves is more than likely our guardian angel, who watches out for us from the world of spirit. Murry Hope in The Way of Cartouche presents this concept when she discusses the Egyptian symbol, The Twins, where the goddess Sekhmet sits opposite her counterpart. We find this balance in Hindu gods and goddesses; such as, Shiva (Father-God) and Shakti (Mother-God), who symbolize aspects of the Divine which are also qualities found within each of us.

Roman gods and goddesses are an example of an expression of the lower nature of mankind. The outward turmoil and jealousy shown by these beings is a mirror image of the Roman society as a whole, and of the inward conflict within the majority of Roman citizens. Our thoughts truly do create the world in which we live as well as the symbology we use.

It was Constantine who conquered Rome and merged the Catholic Church with the Roman government; thus, the Roman Catholic Church. Church officials desiring riches and power were afraid that the wise women, like Joan of Arc who was burned at Rouen as a witch in 1431, would interfere with their schemes of world domination through fear. So, in 1232, Pope Gregory IX created the not so Holy Inquisition, which in modern times is being blamed on the Spanish. Pope Innocent IV in his Bull, *Ad extirpanda*, like the Nazi SS, allowed the Inquisition to use torture. Of the 11,000,000 people the Roman Catholic Church burned to death in a period of 500 years, 9,000,000 of them were women and most historians would agree that these figures are probably too low. To crush dissent and spread religious intolerance, Jews, whole towns (Beziers) and even children were burned. The guilty were presumed guilty and were not allowed to ask questions or even know who was charging him/her of what. Defense witnesses and counsel were denied to the accused. Heresy and corruption by the Roman Catholic Church and popes, along with the defilement of women, is well documented in Vicars of Christ, The Dark Side of The Papacy by Peter De Rosa, a former priest who served in the Vatican library. Church officials and Christian fanatics now argue that infallibility and impeccability are two different things. However, most of us would agree that if one claims to be infallible, then it would have to follow that s/he would also be impeccable. If only one pope was not infallible than none of them were.

The symbol the Church assigned to Mary was a closed M drawn like this ᙢ . It is representative of the confined role of womanhood. In the Middle Ages, women artists had to paint under their father's name, or under the protection of another man.

Mary or **Maria** is open, and there is a loop of power in the beginning of the symbol. It is drawn from left to right with the same freedom of movement and flowing line as the letter $\mathcal{M}$ is written. Mary or Maria connects us to the feminine qualities of healing, nurturing, love and creativity. This symbol can be used alone or in combination with **Christ Light**.

Christ Light: While a dark star draws light into itself, the symbol Christ Light pulls in the darkness of unconsciousness and misqualified energy for transformation. Using the coned fingers of both hands, first draw the vertical line. Secondly, simultaneously draw > with your left hand and < with your right hand. Christ Light is like the warrior who protects the kingdom. Using both Christ Light and Mary or Maria together resonates to a high vibration, helps release misqualified energy and restores a balance of the masculine and feminine.

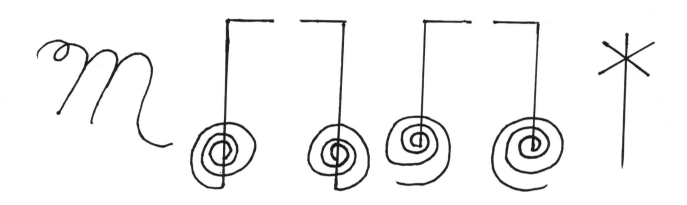

Before Babaji died in the late 1980's, he said publicly, "real evil does exist". Evil is multidimensional. Evil seeks to lure us away from living, loving and joyfully being in the moment. As Carol Bridges says in The Medicine Woman Inner Guidebook, "'Devil' is 'lived' spelled backwards. It is living and looking to only what has been." Evil perpetuates with our denial to look within for the problem, or our refusal to pursue a different course of action. Evil takes our attention away from Mother-Father God by limiting the Almighty to a single artifact or individual. Evil divides mankind through slavery, sexism or racism. Evil abhors nature. Evil begins when we forget to give thanks to God and be grateful for what we have. Evil begins when we make excuses and do not pay attention. Evil brings about its own destruction. For example, there are now and have been in Atlantis ultimate weapons that one army can use to completely destroy its 'enemy'; however, their implementation brings about total annihilation for everyone.

King Arthur was the 13th and last of the Druid kings. <u>Camelot</u> is the story of the remembrance of the last Golden Age on Mother Earth. Within this tale are the aspects of balance. The king is the guardian of the people. He is neither a weakling who allows outside forces to subdue and enslave his people, nor is he a blind tyrant. The knights, who protect the kingdom, are neither self-destructive, nor are they bullies. The magician works with the forces of nature and is open to learning from events and people around her. She is neither the know-nothing nor the know-it-all. Personal relationships in Golden Ages reflect the consciousness of society. Lovers respect one another's autonomy, are supportive of one another and enjoy their time together. Individuals are neither sexless, nor do they abuse sex. When the balance fell apart, Camelot and healthy relationships went with it.

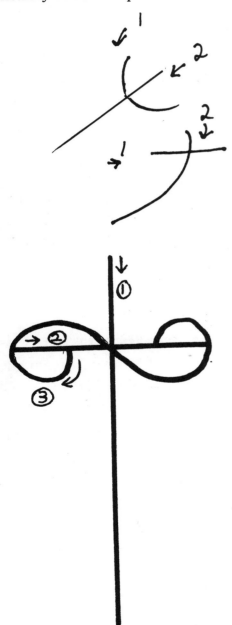

Saint Michael's Sword for the cutting away of ties and cords that keep us in the torture chambers of our own mind and prevent us from moving into the Golden Age. Saint Michael's Sword is energized with Cho Ku Rays, which seem to set up a special field for the Sword to do the work. The Sword always turns a brilliant, illuminating white while doing the work, and the light turns off when the work is completed. This symbol is drastically different each time it is used, and it is very powerful. It is possible to use it alone or in combination with the Hosanna symbols. Or use Saint Michael's Sword with Say Hay Key to specifically cut away mental 'garbage'. Experiment and see what works best for you, or your clients (if you are a therapist), or your friends in different situations. **Penny Cantley, Scottsdale, Arizona**

Saint Michael's Sword is like the second character in Hon Sha Za Sho Nen, and may be the power behind that particular symbol. A second version of Saint Michael's Sword is to draw the hilt of the sword as a horizontal line and curve the blade.

A third version is also attributed to Saint Michael. This symbol gives us the courage to be our true selves (self-realization) and to express our personal truth to the world.

274

The third version of Saint Michael's Sword also works well drawn down the spine and across the shoulders for all fears and anxieties. It is a gentler version of the other two versions of Saint Michael's Sword. **Tamisha Sabrin, England**

"When Kathleen asked me to work on her horse, the first Cho Ku Ray opened his upper neck at the 2nd vertebra (Kathleen told me later that he had been injured there). The Sword illuminated and electrical-like healing rays flowed into the spine. As the horse exhaled, fear came out of his mouth (Kathleen confirmed that this was her horse's way of releasing 'hot emotions'.). Closing Cho Ku Ray collected waste and sent it to the Light. White Light filled the void.

A friend of mine was about to give birth prematurely to her baby (24 weeks). The first Cho Ku Ray went into the mother's body and created a cradle-like support for the womb. The Sword illuminated and sent electrical-like healing rays to the baby and also the mother. The closing Cho Ku Ray energized more support for the baby so it could have the opportunity to develop further before being born. White Light filled the void. The baby was born at 34 weeks in good condition.

My son asked me to send him absentee healing. The first Cho Ku Ray opened up his spine. The Sword illuminated and pulled rope-like 'gray gunk' out of his spine. As the 'gray gunk' was pulled out of the spine, it was dumped in the Sword hilt and was then taken up to the Light for transformation. Closing Cho Ku Ray then closed up the spine. White Light filled the void." **Penny Cantley, Scottsdale, Arizona**

Try this in meditation: See yourself clearly in your mind's eye. Draw Saint Michael's Sword and energize it with Cho Ku Rays with your physical hands and at the same time see yourself drawing the symbols. Send them to Archangel Michael, and then ask him to cut away from you that which is holding you back. Or try touching the symbol. As in Reiki & Other Rays of Touch Healing, I have energized all of the symbols herein so that you could experience the energy firsthand if you so choose. Symbols come from God just like we do, so when the healing is completed, it is important to give gratitude to Archangel Michael, any other spirit helpers or angels, and the symbol(s). The strongest force in this entire Universe is that of love, and close on its heels is that of gratitude. When we forget to give thanks, the cycle is broken. When we remember to give thanks, we complete the cycle so that more can be given to us.

Symbol for healing self. Penny Cantley received this symbol when she asked for a symbol to heal herself. Cho Ku Rays energizes it. Then the symbol and Cho Ku Rays are blown into the open palms. The palms face self and reflect the power back to self. Like Saint Michael's Sword, the effects of this self-healing symbol have been different every time it is used. Unlike Saint Michael's Sword, the energies of this symbol are soft and gentle.

Symbols from the Yaqui of South America: Just as there is a connection between the Mayans and the Tibetans and the Hawaiians and the Hindus, there is also a link between the Yaqui of South America and the Mongolians. Yaqui shaman listens and talks to plants, and knows the qualities of each spiritual plant by the nature of its leaves and flowers. They know when each plant blooms and where, as well as the time of the moon when each plant opens up to communicate. In addition, there is a belief called The Doctrine of Signatures whereby each plant has been "signed" by the Creator in order to give us information as to the plant's use. Eyebright looks like an eye. Yellow Dock's color is like the liver's bile. Thus, having an awareness of plants and also how animals use herbs provides additional knowledge.

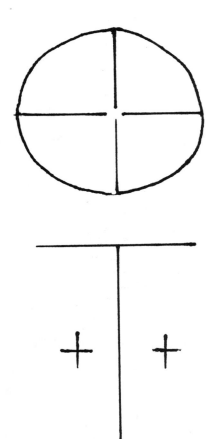

Yaqui shaman also read the iris to determine the disease. For spiritual healing, the Yaqui people fast and meditate to cleanse the body and make it become more sensitive to the herbs as well as the spirit. Without spirit helpers or angels, who restore the balance, there is no healing. Yaqui shaman works in the Otherworld as well as hands-on. The 4 directions and 4 elements are drawn out with the hand or a stick in the dirt to connect with these forces before journeywork, healing or magic. Just as in personal relationships, there is no true connection without love and respect. The second symbol on this page can be meditated upon to help restore the connection between heaven and Earth. **TEZLCAZI GUTIMEA, Yaqui shaman**

276

Iava: In 1991, Catherine Mills Bellamont of Ireland received this symbol after she had prayed for a symbol to help her country. Her angels had told her that it was to be used by fully initiated Reiki Masters <u>for the purpose of planetary or earth healing only</u>! If you wish to send this symbol to Earth or a particular place, the angels have safely empowered Iava so that you can help with the healing of Mother Earth. Simply get into a meditative state, visualize this symbol (you may also touch it) and watch to see what happens. Iava power symbol is drawn in two continuous lines. First, inscribe the cosmic wave crest from top to bottom saying "Iava" (ee-a-va) three times. Secondly, touch the top half of the wave crest, come down and then draw the four loops saying, "Earth, Water, Wind and Fire". **Catherine Mills Bellamont, Ireland**

OM BENZA SATTO HUNG is the mantra of Vajrasattva the Bodhisattvas. Mantras become a powerful vibration when they are repeated in a monotone rather than in a singsong voice or a melody. The main use of OM BENZA SATTO HUNG is for purification of negatives. A simple meditation might be to look at OM BENZA SATTO HUNG for one minute, then close the eyes and go into meditation and repeat the mantra silently. As negative thoughts and negative emotions surface, the can be breathed into the Light or fire for transformation. If a pain comes up in the body, the mantra can be repeated into the pain. If the mediator finds that they are no longer repeating the mantra and it feels comfortable to do so, s/he can go back to repeating the mantra. In Tera-Mai™ Reiki and Tera-Mai™ Seichem it is used in the first and second initiation. When the initiator lifts on the occipital ridge after breathing the symbols of initiation into the crown of the initiate and grounding the energy, s/he visualizes this symbol and repeats the mantra for the symbol three times. OM BENZA SATTO HUNG does clean out any humanly contrived

initiations. The mantra can also be pronounced OM VAJRA (VAJRA is pronounced BENZA in either mantra) SATTVA HUM. The circle on top of the half circle denotes that this as a sacred symbol and this character is also above both the Tibetan OM and Sanscrit OM. The first symbol of OM BENZA SATTO HUNG or OM VAJRA SATTVA HUM is the Tibetan OM and it dissolves systematically into the other syllables. In Tibetan Buddhism, OM represents the body, AH the speech and HUNG the mind, which is at the heart center. On a grander scale, the Tibetan OM represents the body of all Buddhas and the wisdom of equanimity. HUNG purifies the veil that covers knowledge.

Healing the Heart: The first two symbols in this series were sent to me by **Dr. S. G. Sadiq, Pakistan**. He felt that they could help mend broken hearts, especially after a broken love affair. He also asked me what I picked up concerning the symbols. I saw a third symbol in the series and felt that they could work at deep levels of betrayal and abandonment. Like the other symbols in this book, they have been energized. If you wish, get into a meditative state, place your hand on the symbols, allow heartaches to come up and breathe them out to the violet flame for transformation. Then breathe in love from the Absolute, feel your heart opening and allow love to begin flowing through you. Keep turning the love inward and love yourself without conditions. I believe that there is a right partner for everyone. However, we are always given free will choice. If one individual opts out, God/Goddess will heal the broken heart and bring in another. For the one who would throw love that was intended for him/her away, I do not know if God/Goddess would create another true love before deep-seated mental and emotional issues were addressed.

Protection: by extending safety, provides structure and is a place for heart-centered meditation. It is an interesting fact that if we change our outlook, we change our whole lives as well. By altering the perspective of this symbol, it changes from a square to a diamond. If this symbol were to be graphically portrayed on a floor or carpet, the lines should be painted or woven or tiled in pink. **Sophia Lucia, England** sent me this symbol and **Susan Fereday, Australia** provided information concerning it.

Kathryn O'Connell told me that of late, she and other Irish psychics were finding themselves meditating on the ancient Celtic symbol of the **Triple Spiral**. On one level, it is symbolic of the Otherworlds of the Land, the Sea and the Sky revolving around the Fire. The Celts honored nature as a reflection of the Creator and believed that women were equal to men and had similar rights. Among other ideas, this symbol could be meditated upon before journeywork. For additional information on Celtic spiritualism, read North Star Road subtitled Shamanism, Witchcraft & the Otherworld Journey by Kenneth Johnson and The Serpent and the Goddess subtitled Women, Religion, and Power in Celtic Ireland by Mary Condren. Something new is birthing; old paradigms are breaking up and there is a new reality in the offing. Any fear-based religion that is guilt-producing is not spiritual in nature; governments that support a few multinational companies do so at the expense of nature and everybody else. We need to look at this reality without focusing on it, because if we see only half of the truth, we are also halfblind. When we release our own fear, rage, guilt, etc., we help to heal the mass consciousness. When we change the way we think, we change what comes into our lives. In seeing only a glimmer of the future, we help to create the reality of the wonder and beauty of the Golden Age. It is like the future is sending us a lifeline, which we can use to pull ourselves forward. In the year 2012, the I Ching calendar drops into 'no time'.

Angels use this symbol for **cellular restructuring**. The symbol reminds me of angels that children draw in the snow with their bodies. This symbol works well with crystals. **Jeremiah Brod, Lake Tomahawk, Wisconsin**

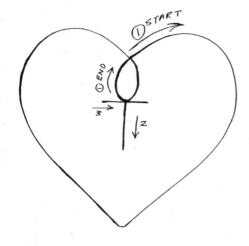

When I was a little girl, I knew that I would never get old. I thought that it was because I would die young. That wasn't it! Our physical bodies are supposed to be vibrant, youthful, whole and healthy throughout our entire lives, and this is how we are going to enter the Golden Age. Age is a dream; the dream is changing. Eternity is who we are.

Harmony Through Conflict is drawn in three strokes and visualized in gold. When drawing first stroke say, "Harmony". With second stroke say, "Through". With third stroke say, "Conflict". **Gabriel River, San Anselo, California** Gabriel said that it was the first of seven symbols (one for each Soul Ray) to help align with Soul Ray qualities. The phrase "Harmony through conflict" is the keynote of the Fourth Ray, the spiritual warrior, whose forte is <u>conflict resolution</u>.

Harmony Through Conflict can be used with any adversary. It can be drawn over the heart and empowered with double Cho Ku Rays. If the individual will not accept the symbol, simply visualize Harmony Through Conflict in meditation. It can also be used when we become overwhelmed by our perception of the world. Gabriel said he has witnessed other people as well as himself suddenly becoming reasonable and peaceful after using this symbol, and higher good prevailing.

Star of David before it comes together. It can be meditated upon to bring into form conceptualized ideas. Or it can be used to send prayers to heaven. As always, if we let go and let God, the best happens. If we do not allow Divine Order to prevail, we create garbage, frustration, pain and fear.

Hammer of Thor symbolizes the Big Dipper revolving around the North Star. Just because black magicians misuse the pentagram and the Nazis misused symbols from

280

the Runes, it does not follow that these powerful symbols cannot be used for good. In meditation bring the red and the purple from the universe into the crown. *(See meditation chapter.)*

The next four symbols I give to my students who have taken Sakara II, Sophi-El II and the second levels of Angeliclight. Some people have gotten a hold of these symbols and sold them as part of a package they call Sakara Mastership or some other impressive sounding name. When their students find out where the symbols came from and contact me, their complaints are that the symbols do not work. First of all, the instructors who will be teaching at the school that the angels have asked me to establish will not have to pay to learn how to do initiations into Sakara, Sophi-El and Angeliclight; rather, they will be paid for the work that they do! Secondly, manmade initiations fail to connect the initiate to healing rays emanating from the Absolute. There are healing and metaphysical systems that people paid large sums of money to learn or be initiated into ten years ago that are no longer around because they failed to produce their claims. Thirdly, the symbols herein do work! In order to use them, an individual has to be vibrating at a high level because they are high vibrational symbols. Kodoish heals the feminine aspect and Samaran heals the male aspect. Used together they help to open and integrate the personality, and heal deep seated emotional issues from childhood or past lives. In the manner in which Kodoish and Samaran are drawn, like the Yin/Yang symbol, a splash of the masculine remains in the feminine and a splash of the feminine remains in the masculine.

Trikaya is used for healing the aura. Each chakra is associated with a layer of the aura. The first chakra or root chakra has a relationship to the astral body. The astral body looks very much like our physical body and reflects the condition of the soul. The second or creative chakra is related to the first emotional body. The third chakra or solar plexus has a relationship to the first mental body even though the solar plexus on the physical body is a touch point for emotional issues. The heart chakra is the fulcrum between the lower and upper chakras, and I would like to add that all of the chakras are important. The throat chakra has a relationship to the physical body. The third eye is a high love center. The crown chakra connects to our own higher self, high vibrational spirit guides and celestial angels. However, there is a relationship between all of the chakras and layers of the aura. For example, our crown and root chakras are one chakra with us in between. Therefore, in order to manifest heaven on earth, we have to have an open mind - oftentimes, we only allow ourselves to process information that supports our own beliefs and that limits us and prevents us from perceiving upcoming changes. We also have to resolve our root chakra issues concerning sex, money and power – otherwise, our dreams and thoughts pass through garbage as they pass through the root chakra and are grounded into

Mother Earth. Again, meditate and touch Trikaya alone to experience a general healing of the aura, or Trikaya and Mara to heal the physical, Trikaya and Harth for emotional healing, or Trikaya and Halu for mental healing. Abba Nartoomid also creates a body of energy. If you wish to manifest the secret desires of your heart and it feels right to do so, touch Abba Nartoomid and meditate.

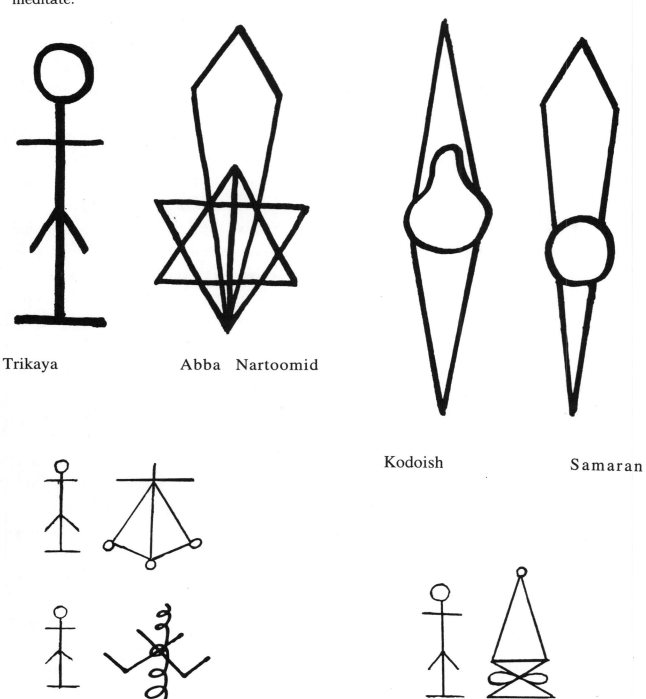

Trikaya   Abba Nartoomid

Kodoish   Samaran

Initiation

All Healing Energy Comes From Mother-Father God

It is not necessary to be initiated into the vast majority of symbols in order for them to work. The effectiveness of a symbol, like all healing techniques, depends upon how much healing energy the healer is able to facilitate. There are some symbols that work only at a higher vibration, which is why the initiate needs to be channeling a lot of healing energy in order to work with them. There are only a few symbols that are symbols of initiation. Some clairvoyants see Reiki Masters who have symbols packed into their aura through man-made initiations and these symbols are actually blocking their healing channels. This is the equivalent of pouring gold dust down the drain; yes, it is valuable, but it will also clog the drain.

Ama Deus is a collection of symbols, which express a language of healing. Hebrew and the English alphabet are also a collection of symbols, which express a language of knowledge. Mathematics has its own symbols, which express relationships between figures and form, and quantities. We cannot throw just any old symbol into a language and still expect that language to make sense. Scott Robinson of Woodstock Georgia asked Spirit why symbols could be used in healing. His answer was that symbols have a subtle energy, and when the healer draws healing symbols in the subtle aura the healer's body movements and the consciousness of the symbols have the capability of facilitating changes.

Also, an initiation is much more than just a symbol. For example, in the movie, The Fifth Element, Bruce Willis needed intention, but he also needed the stones with the symbols, the fifth element and the knowledge of how to do the procedure. Anyone can take symbols from a book, a video or another source and think up an initiation procedure; whether it connects an individual to a healing ray or aspect of healing is another question. Some individuals believe that they can alter Reiki initiations without consequences and that all Reiki initiations work. In elementary physics we learned that if we changed the source of a wave, then we inexorably the wave itself is altered. Likewise, if an individual alters a healing initiation, then the initiation itself has to be changed. In addition, not all initiations involve symbols. There are no symbols of initiation into either the Order of Melchizedek or Angeliclight.

I was initiated into and taught the initiation into the Order of Melchizedek by one of my students who had been ordained and knew how to do the initiation. This individual was holding the energy of this initiation prior to the initiation because the clergy, with the exception of a few individuals does not practice facilitating healing. The initiation into the Order of Melchizedek is supposed to establish a foundation for and ground all other healing work. It opens the initiate's healing channels (healing energy is carried through the physical body via the nerves). It also connects the initiate to the ascended masters as well as the Divine Plan for earth. Hardly a minor initiation, yet the easiest one to give. Like other healing energies, in order to pass the energy down, the initiator has to be carrying the energy of the initiation and must also be able to hold enough healing energy so that s/he can hold ceremony, as shaman do. The initiator is able to hold ceremony with his/her second chakra. This chakra radiates energy so that the higher beings who are doing the initiation (or ceremony) are able to step in and do the work that is asked of them.

I received the Enochian Magic initiations from another individual who was initiated by a former member of the clergy. Again, this former member of the clergy had to have been carrying the energy before he was initiated. The Enochian Magic initiations I talk about in Reiki & Other Rays of Touch Healing have nothing at all to do with any of the books I have seen on the subject of Enochian Magic. I personally cannot recommend any of the books I have seen on Enochian Magic because I could not read them myself. The books I have looked at are all based on the Enochian Magic channeled by John Dee and Edward Kelley during the reign of Elizabeth I and later practiced by the Golden Dawn; not on the Enochian Magic practiced by Christ and his followers.

The first clue that the Enochian Magic channeled by Dee and Kelley comes from a lower vibration is this statement given to Dee and Kelley by their angels: *As a punishment (to mankind) God sent false and deceiving angels to teach what is presently known as black magic. In this way, God allowed humankind to be the instrument of its own destruction.* In the first place, God does not punish; we punish ourselves through guilt, worry, hate and fear when the Natural Laws of the Absolute are forgotten. Secondly, a vengeful, punishing, judgmental God sounds more like the devil than a benevolent Being. Within the Enochian Magic of Dee and Kelley can be found some truth or else it wouldn't work at all. For example, there is reference to the 4 elements and directions, the power of 3 and the Ancient Ones (Guardians of the Watchtowers). Using Dee's and Kelley's Enochian Magic, a small group of Freemasons formed a secret society known as the Golden Dawn. Aleister Crowley, who worked with both black and white magic, was a member of the Golden Dawn. His tarot deck gives insightful glimpses into the mingling of truth and confusion. For example, Aleister Crowley refers to the Queen of Pentacles as being the water element of earth. Would that be mud?

The initiations that I have received from Higher Beings and that I pass down only open the healer's channels so that more of the elemental energy rays that the initiate is already attuned to can **easily** come into the initiate. In books on what is referred to as high magic, it is stated that an enormous force of the magician's own will is required in order to summon the elemental forces (earth, air, fire, water), which is the energy behind the magic and the healing. If an individual is channeling elemental healing rays and working in Divine Order and for the highest good of all concerned, this intense feat of will power is totally unnecessary. There are symbols for the Enochian Magic initiation; however, in order to be able to initiate another individual, the initiator must be holding the fire energy (Sakara) because much of the initiation itself is done in the aura. Again, the initiator must also be able to hold ceremony so that the celestial angels and beings of Light who are doing the initiations can step in and have a stage as it were to operate from.

In general, even though these initiations are supposedly given to the clergy, the Catholic Church treats those who are healing as a public embarrassment. It has gotten to the point that modern priests are discouraged from doing exorcisms. In their day, the saints who were gifted with healing were hidden away in monasteries. Jesus taught ignorant fishermen how to heal and sent them out to heal and to instruct others how to heal. If the Pope is the successor to Jesus then why aren't the faithful taught to do the same things Jesus did? If the Church claims to be carrying on the work of Jesus and those later changes in his teachings by popes were advancements, then why isn't the clergy doing advanced healing or any kind of healing for that matter? Darkness and light serve each other well in that they contrast one another so that they clearly define the other. The evils of popes Julius II and Leo X were a contrast to Leonardo, Michelangelo, Raphael and the Italian Renaissance. Through forged documents and the rewriting of the New Testament, by the Middle Ages, the Catholic Church had become a dogmatic, materialistic institution that was in complete contrast to the spiritual teachings of Jesus. When Jesus spoke of "the gifts of the Spirit", he talked, taught and practiced "spiritualism" – healing, prophesying, telekinesis, etc. Yet, to this day, fanatical religious zealots claim that the devil is working through modern-day healers even though nowhere in any bible is the devil credited with healing anyone.

In my first book, I discuss how the elemental healing rays were brought back to this earth by Dr. Usui and how a Japanese-American woman named Takata brought the empowerment back to America and taught 22 Reiki Masters. For a long time, each of these 22 Reiki Masters thought that they all had the same knowledge and empowerment. Why? Because Takata spoke of the universal quality of the Reiki Mastership initiation (something she learned from her Japanese teachers), and the books on Reiki also relate this universal quality of an initiation into Reiki.

When we look up the word 'universal' in the dictionary, it means 'one'. There is only one initiation that fully opens the initiate to the healing Reiki (elemental earth) ray. As all healing comes from God, that Universal initiation connects the initiate to the One. Each of the other elemental healing rays - Sakara (fire), Sophi-El (water) and Angeliclight (air) - also have one initiation that fully opens the initiate to the full expanse of that particular healing ray. Because our physical bodies and our consciousness cannot accept the full energy at once, there are steps that the initiate takes before the final initiation. These preparatory steps in Reiki are the first and second-degree initiations. These initiations are similar to, but not the same as the third and final initiation. This is true for all of the elemental healing rays.

When an initiator takes it upon him/herself to change the initiation and not tell the students, s/he alters the vibrational quality of the connection to the healing ray. (They do not alter the vibrational quality of the ray itself - only God can do that!) How does an initiation occur? After the initiator calls in the higher forces (celestial angels, saints, masters, etc.) who are the ones who actually bring in and do the initiation, the initiator then goes through the initiation procedure. The higher forces are able to bring the initiation through the crown chakra of the initiator, who resonates to the energy because s/he is attuned to it, and the initiation is then smoothly passed on to the initiate. If the initiation is altered, the result is static or the energy comes in at sharp, cutting angles. It is like this: If the piano wire that connects to the piano key that is called middle C is tuned to middle C, when we strike that particular key, we hear the musical note middle C. If we 'mess around' with the piano wire, we will hear something other than middle C when we strike the key known as middle C. The more the wire has been altered, the more wretched the sound. As none of the 22 Reiki Masters Takata initiated were able to do the same healings as Takata did or even come close to what Dr. Usui did, we can rightly assume that not only did Takata change the initiations, but her Master, Chujiro Hayashi, did as well.

What I have found is that the most common reason an initiator changes the initiations and does not tell his/her students is because the initiator is afraid that the student will surpass him/her. Reasons closely following are ego ("I will do initiations my way!") and greed. When the initiator changes the procedure, the altered initiation is also brought into the initiator before it is transferred to the initiate. After the initiation, the initiator also goes through a cleansing cycle of sorts. In this way, the initiator is held accountable for any alterations. These are reasons why some Reiki Masters are losing the healing energy they were channeling and their connection to the Reiki (earth) ray. Intention positively or adversely affects any initiation! Initiations involve more than intention! If I was in York and I really, really wanted to go to London and I headed north, with all of the best intentions in the world, I would still end up in Scotland.

Spirit is a real force that is aware, creative and potential. Part of our lesson here in a 3-dimensional world is to watch the forces of creation at work, to learn to be respectful of these forces and to understand fully that all our actions and thoughts have consequences proportionate in magnitude to what is sent out. Our conscious thoughts and good deeds come back to us a hundredfold as good karma. So, too, the opposite is true, and this is our own higher self bringing our lessons home to us. I have students, who are physically challenged, and Spirit intervenes to help with the initiations, and their students are fully initiated. However, playing with earth initiations may cause our sandcastles to crumble and fall about us; playing with fire initiations could produce spontaneous combustion at some point in time. Kim Williamson and other psychics have been shown visions of not just the temples, but whole civilizations being destroyed because of individuals 'messing around' with fire energy and fire initiations.

Man-made initiations into healing rays either do not pass down the full expanse of the healing energy, do not last the test of time, do not work at all, or in some cases, actually pass down negative energy. In addition, multiple, dissimilar initiations into a single ray of healing produces disharmony; the energy is like scrambled eggs. Trying to initiate Tera-Mai™ and other types of Reiki initiations is like trying to play more than one radio station at the same time- the language is reduced to static. This practice actually closes the crown chakra. Dowsing the crown chakra of both the initiator and initiate can prove that it is closed. My words are also proven by the supposed healings that fail to occur. It is not the number of initiations that authenticates the teacher; rather, it is the quality of the healings of his/her healing practice! Reiki is much more than a warm comforting touch. I personally believe that it behooves us to check out the teacher (and even his/her students) before receiving Reiki or any other initiation, by asking to witness demonstrations. It is in this way that each one of us chooses for him/herself, which initiation is the universal initiation, and then if we want to, we go for it.

I was in Holland in December of 1996. One evening, I was lying down on the massage table in Jane Rijgersberg's apartment while Toby and Marcelle, two of my students, worked on me. The intercom buzzed and Jane answered it. Einar had arrived from Germany to take my Shamanic Workshop. As Jane walked by me to get the door, I blurted out "Don't let him touch me." Jane told me later that she thought that that was a pretty rude thing for me to say. After Einar entered the apartment, I was aware of their conversation. When I got off of the table and walked around to greet Einar, his eyes told me that he was barely present in his body. The left corner of his mouth was drawn up tightly to his cheekbone in a permanent smile and he was unable to blink his right eye. When I dowsed his crown chakra, it was closed so tightly that the pendulum swung up to the height of my fingers. Jane had seen a black aura when he walked into her apartment and

Marcelle saw negative entities. Einar had taken and was giving many different Reiki initiations, as well as any number of other man-made initiations. We worked on him that night and when he asked, I told him what I thought was going on. During the course of the weekend, other healers that were taking the Shamanic Workshop worked on Einar and told him the same thing. Once, I overheard Einar say that he liked the power that he was feeling from these different initiations. Robin Hormann responded, "I have walked away from power." Jane told Einar that the dark forces can produce a lot of power but it cannot be used for healing and there are consequences to be paid.

The clairvoyants in the Shamanic Workshop could see that not only did Einar not receive the seven rays or any of the other initiations that were given, but he was no longer channeling the Reiki or any of the other elemental healing rays. During the first day of the class, Einar was draining a lot of energy from the other participants. So at one point, I had everyone in the class work on Einar at the same time, but Einar refused to let go and surrender to God. During the break, I could hear him still trying to sell people on a variety of different Reiki initiations. Saturday evening, the angels asked that I do a clearing for the other class participants and that Einar be bound in a way that he could not harm himself or others, something like the movie, The Craft. Sunday was a better day for everyone but Einar! He left Holland Sunday night (his face was still distorted and crown closed) to teach some kind of a Reiki class in Austria.

Some people think that the initiation is the final resting stop; rather, it is an open door to the beginning of a new journey. Like life, it is the journey that produces experiences and the experiences are the goal. If we pray for something and then turn our back on the experience or the teacher when they come into our life, we fail to manifest our wish. "Until concept becomes experience, all there is is speculation." Conversations with God, Book 1 by Neale Donald Walsch

The initiation sets off a 21-day cleansing cycle of the seven major chakras that begins with the root chakra. By the seventh day, it is at the crown and on the eighth day, it is at the root chakra. Thus, three cleansing cycles of the seven major chakras. Jane Rijgersberg of Holland found that during this period the initiate is wide open. It is a wonderful opportunity to release 'stuff'. However, if the initiate chooses to hold onto this 'stuff', s/he will attract more negative energy to him/herself and the energy of the initiation will either be diminished or be taken away entirely. It is the Creator's way of saying that this energy will not be misused in the Golden Age. Even if the initiate successfully goes through the 21-day cleansing cycle, if s/he gets caught up later in greed or delusions of grandeur, or fails to use discernment and discrimination before going through other initiations, the energy will be taken away from him/her. Clairvoyants see angels unweaving the connection between the initiate and the Reiki (earth) ray. They see a different process when the angels remove the other rays. In this 3-dimensional reality, it is our physical bodies (earth) that hold the other elements. In aura, it is the Sakara (fire) that is the vessel that holds the Angeliclight (air), Sophi-El (water) and Reiki (earth). The Sakara initiation is in the aura. Clairvoyants observe that as the angels remove the Sakara from the aura it is like watching a car being dismantled. When the vehicle is gone then the Sophi-El and Angeliclight leave as well.

The Teachings of the Inner Christ has a broad definition of channeling and I apologize to my readers if there was any confusion in my first book. In the third edition of Reiki & Other Rays of Touch Healing, I make it very clear that my experience in the Siddha ashram in Los Angeles was a consciousness-raising experience. As I said in the first edition, the walls and ceiling of this small, one-story home suddenly became cathedral-size. The Higher Being who appeared made only a small addition to the three degrees of Reiki initiations that Iris Ishikuru had learned from Takata and the healings that the Reiki initiates were able to do were increasingly profound and occurred in a shorter period of time and more often. The consciousness-raising experience was so totally out of the ordinary and produced such profoundly beneficial results that I risked all and went for it. Since that time, Spirit has on a few occasions added onto the initiations. When they do this, I am consciously and fully participating in another reality; it is what the Native Americans refer to as a vision quest. Peak experiences can be found in the modern world. For example, there are football players who suddenly find themselves playing ball in a field that has been slowed down in time. In this heightened state of awareness, they are fully knowing what action is going to occur and at the same time fully participating and consciously observing. Personally, I tend to get very upset with the angels when they have made additions and afterwards and I usually ask, "How am I going to explain this one?" They reply, "You asked to heal in the manner that Jesus did, didn't you?" Jane Rijgersberg and other psychics feel that the initiation procedure that the man in the golden robes brought in and then added to is not absolutely identical in structure to that which Dr. Usui used, but the healing energy is exactly the same. It is up to each one of us to ask for the Truth and witness healing demonstrations in order to discern the Truth. *"Ye shall know them by their works."*

I feel that my students paid me once for Reiki or Seichem Mastership and that they should not have to keep paying to become a Reiki or Seichem Master. So, within the newsletters that I send out to my students, periodically there will be a symbol that has been energized by the celestial angels with the higher initiation transmission. Spirit asks each student to meditate, touch the symbol and pull in the higher vibration. If the initiate is clear, then they receive it. Some who are not clear will call me and I will do it over the telephone for them. Any of us can get off the path!

Donald Bates of Australia had the following experience with one of the 'angel letters': *"I followed your directions and meditated and touched the Symbol. I felt energy climbing both sides of my hand and meeting at the crown chakra. It felt like a volcano was coming out of the top of my head. The crown chakra was pulsating (vibrating). I then felt the top of my head and it was extremely hot. Up to this point of my letter to you, the feeling and pulsating is easing off, so I can assume that I got it and I will use it from now on in."*

Margaret K. Felling of Missouri had the following experience meditating with the energized HUNG symbol I sent out in my October 3, 1996 newsletter: *"Laying my left hand on the symbol a great heat and a numbing-like energy radiated out to cover my entire left hand. Then I placed my right hand on the symbol. The experience was not as intense as with the left hand, but I felt the expanded energy. While this was taking place I noticed an expansion in my crown. I consciously began to chant the mantra and visualize this symbol going into my crown. Finally, I laid the symbol on my crown chakra and continued to chant. A very intense energy expanded out encompassing my whole head and I began to feel this energy throughout my entire body and sensed my auric body being filled with this heightened energy."*

The reason why I put up with Spirit making alterations and the reason why my students put up with me is because every time Spirit makes these changes, the healing energy that is facilitated by the healer goes up and s/he is able to do more. In this process, I acknowledge that I have had help from my students; such as, Roxanne Polsley of Long Island, Nora O'Neill and Kathryn O'Connell of Ireland. However, when people personalize the initiations and do their own thing, the Universal quality of the initiation, which includes the power to facilitate healing is lost. If the individual is working with a Higher Being, then the healings should increase rather than decrease. Many initiates, in going through the consciousness-raising experience of an initiation, see masters making gestures, colors or symbols during the initiation process. Sometimes, some individuals within a group will have similar experiences; more often, everyone has their own feeling, seeing, hearing or knowing that is unique to them. It does not follow that these experiences should be added into the initiation process. If everyone did this, it would not be long before it would take hours or days to do an initiation. When I was speaking at the Midwest Reiki Conference in the fall of 1998, I learned that there was a Reiki system from India that had 1,500 symbols for the first degree alone. A Reiki lineage that is given to the initiate at the time of his/her initiation is a legal contract stating that what is being given is that which has come before.

What clairvoyants see happening with the Tera-Mai™ initiations is that the initiation is held within perfectly formed triangles that reach up to the Creator. The base of the triangle is within the initiate. If part of the initiation procedure is left out, there is a space left for anything else to come in. If additional symbols are put into the initiation, the triangles break and the energy comes in jagged. *"Too much is less than just enough."* Chinese adage

When I became a Seichem Master, I learned that the symbols for the Seichem (fire) initiations were, for the most part, identical to those in the original Reiki initiations. It is impossible to do the Seichem initiations without also doing Reiki initiations at the same time. I understood that fire energy had to be grounded with the earth element (Reiki). What I didn't understand was the length of time that was required to do the Seichem initiations. I had a deep feeling that fire had its own vocabulary of symbols and within this structure could be found symbols and more importantly, a safe process by which to initiate fire energy. Jesus transferred fire energy to his apostles on the Pentecost.

When Spirit told me that Seichem Mastership was equivalent in energy to the first degree of Sakara (fire), I was never impressed or guided to do the lengthy, original Seichem initiations. Before I moved to Arizona, I woke up one morning to find that I was only half in my body. (This had happened to me a couple of times before and when I asked, I found several other people who have had similar experiences.) The experience was unlike being either here on earth or 'up there'. When I opened my physical eyes, it was like looking out into a world through cut glass. All I wanted to do was close my eyes and go back to sleep again, but Spirit insisted that they had something to show me and that they needed to do it then and there. What they revealed to me in this state were the three Tera-Mai™ Seichem initiations. Spirit added two additional symbols to the Tera-Mai™ Reiki initiations, as well as two additional colors; thus, the Tera-Mai™ Seichem initiations pass down the three levels of Tera-Mai™ Reiki as well as the first levels of Sakara (fire), Sophi-El (water) and Angeliclight (air). Because the initiations came from Spirit, the triangles became larger in order to hold the additional energy, and the initiations work. In order to pass these initiations on, the initiator has to be channeling the full extent of the initiation and know how to do these initiations. There are many teachers throughout this world who are healing and are teaching and initiating others into the four elemental healing rays of Tera-Mai™ Seichem. Because the initiations are standardized people do not have to come to me to be initiated.

"As a Tera-Mai™ Reiki/Seichem Master, I am passing the attunements in the way you have laid down and not only do they work, they are powerful and balanced. I am blessed with an ability to 'see' people on a vibrational level - this enables me to 'know' how they respond to attunements. Tera-Mai™ attunements have a very profound resonance." **David Driver, England**

My preferred way to teach these classes is to begin with Seichem I, then go on and teach Seichem II, followed by Reiki Mastership and lastly Seichem Mastership. I understand that there are people who prefer to take things slowly, so I still do teach Reiki I and II. When people come to me from other states or countries, it is not feasible or affordable for them to keep coming back to me after each 21-day cleansing cycle. In these cases, Spirit will stack the initiations. I found that if I date the certificates 21 days apart, they would know when the next initiation would be coming in. My students who are initiating Tera-Mai™ Reiki and Tera-Mai™ Seichem have had the same experience with their students. The process works because Spirit designed it; however, we are expected to let go and let God. One of my students from England wrote to me saying, *"I did not tell you when you initiated me, but I asked Spirit that if it were possible, could I integrate two levels of Sophi-El at once. I hardly made it through the cleansing cycle that I went through. When it came time to bring in the next initiation, I sat exhausted waiting for it to come in. When it didn't, I asked my guides what happened. They told me that I wasn't ready for it because I needed to heal from the cleansing cycle. About 21 days later Spirit brought in the next level of initiation. What did I do wrong?"* I answered that she hadn't done anything wrong; she had just forgotten to ask all of the questions. Yes, it was possible for Spirit to bring in two levels of an initiation for her to process, but she forgot to ask if it was in her highest and best interest to do so. She learned a valuable lesson and has a deep respect for initiations, healing energy and Holy Spirit which she passes down to her students.

Einar had taken the initiations about the same time and I also received a letter from him. *"I do not understand this, Kathleen. The second initiation came in just as you said that it would. When it came time to bring in the third initiation, I decided that I would wait and bring it in the following weekend because I was going to a sacred site. I was shopping in the grocery store on the day it was supposed to come in. The initiation came in while I was shopping. This was very disturbing to me. I hardly made it out of the store. What happened?"* I told Einar that neither he nor I were in charge of the initiation process and that Spirit was trying to get that message through to him. As Spirit was bringing in the initiations, if he had asked Spirit, they might very well have waited.

I leave it entirely up to my students how much they charge and how they teach. There are as many ways to teach, as there are teachers who are teaching. So, what instructors do beyond giving and teaching Tera-Mai™ Reiki and Tera-Mai™ Seichem initiations is entirely up to them. Mother-Father God expects all of us to act professionally and be personally responsible with this energy; otherwise, the healing energy will be taken away by Holy Spirit.

One day, I found a FAX in my machine from David, who was a student of one of my students whom I shall call Tony. David stated, "A most powerful channeling took place during the seminar through me which had a significant effect on the initiation procedures that your student was exercising. It turned out that I, who was supposed to be a participant in the seminar, did the initiation procedures in a different or more precisely to say - a modified manner. (He then gave a flowery description of a symbol that he received.) While being initiated into the YOD, I received additional steps on the procedure to be done during the initiation. ••• I would like to add one more thing. It is about the Wand and I received it while being in the initiation to Melchizedek Order - The wand should be drawn on the new Priest/Priestess before placing the hands on their shoulders. I also received much more information that was not known to my teacher." I wrote David back saying that changes in Universal initiations did not come through in simple channeling sessions or in meditation. If everybody who saw a color, symbol or master gesturing added it into the initiations, soon the initiations would be 24 hours long, but all of the energy would be lost. (Too much is less than just enough.) I also told him that the biggest clue for me that he was not clear about these changes that he wanted to instill was the fact that there are no symbols for the initiation into the Order of Melchizedek. As David had performed these initiations on his teacher as well as the other students in the class, I also stated that I felt that they were already losing their healing energy, and if they wanted to be cleared, that they should call me.

David wrote back to me asking me to help him write his book and 'get it out into the world'. He added that perhaps he might have been wrong about the symbol for the Order of Melchizedek. I responded, "I did not have an established individual help me get started. People wanted the initiations that the Higher Being brought in during my consciousness-raising experience because of the healings that my students and I were able to facilitate. Spirit helped me because I put my ego aside and I didn't try to make things happen." I added that the reason he was able to heal after being initiated was because he had been initiated, not because of what he had seen. "You said that you now think that you were premature with the symbol of initiation you received in your channeling session for the Order of Melchizedek - don't you think that quite possibly you were premature with the additions and simplifications to the other initiations as well? ? ?"

293

My student, Tony, asked me to call him and clear him because he said that he had done a great deal of work and spent a large sum of money to promote my book and Tera-Mai™, which was the system of Reiki and Seichem that he was teaching. We could not connect. When I sent a symbol of clearing to him absentee, I got the feeling that Tony still felt that he might have something and had asked for the clearing just to 'hedge his bet'. The clearing for Tony did not take place.

David insisted that he was fine; however, over the next week or so, they both lost their healing energy. When they found out that they had, they both contacted me again. Tony had exactly the same complaints and he added that it was not fair that I was taking initiations away from him. I told him that he had done this to himself and that Spirit would allow him to keep the Reiki. Spirit added that if he acted responsibly, they would allow another Tera-Mai™ Seichem Master to reinitiate him at a future date. Spirit also told him that he could not play on both sides of the fence any longer, that he had to make a decision and that he knew what they were talking about. David, on the other hand, sent me a third letter apologizing and saying that he was putting his ego aside and asking for the angels to clear him through me so that he could do the healing work for people. God listened to David's request and the angels cleared him and brought back his initiations.

When I went to England in the winter of 1999, I met Ann Watters. Ann had been in the class with David that Tony had taught. She told me that while the class was practicing using symbols in healing David refused to participate because he said that he knew it all. That should have been a clue to everyone! David then proceeded to dominate the class with the result being confusion.

Before Nagalakshmy left her son's home and returned to India, she called me and asked, "Why couldn't you see Prabha for who she truly was? Why did you initiate her and teach her Tera-Mai™ Seichem?" While I did not see Tony's involvement with the forces of Pandu (ignorance) immediately, I could see the dark thoughts behind Prabha's eyes and feel the heaviness of her aura when she got off of the plane, and I told that to Nagalakshmy. I went on to tell Nagalakshmy that I do not want to be the judge of anyone, and that I had told that to God after I became a Reiki Master and found out that other people wanted me to teach them. It is my personal belief that Tera-Mai™ Reiki and Tera-Mai™ Seichem initiations should be made available to everyone. The perception that 'we can get away with things on a 3-dimensional reality' is an illusion. We are all held accountable for our thoughts and actions. The first initiation into Reiki or Seichem can jar people back into consciousness. Kathryn O'Connell and many of my other students agree with me on this. If the initiate chooses not to let go of his/her core issues, then the healing energy will not be processed in the 21-day cleansing cycle; if the individual makes unconscious decisions at a later date, Holy Spirit will come in and remove the initiations. My students can always come back and be reinitiated on a donations-are-accepted basis. Many of my students offer the same to their students. However, if there is not a change in attitude, or if the motivation is other than healing oneself or others, then the reinitiation will not even go into the initiate's crown. In addition, if the individual has not processed the first initiation, higher initiations are not possible. Higher Forces have put lots of safeguards into this initiation procedure.

When I am initiating a person, my whole attention is on that individual. I occasionally have Otherworld experiences, like the time Buddha appeared full-dimensionally and in living color when I was initiating Dorothy Bell in England. Sometimes, initiates have experiences that go way beyond seeing symbols. When I was in Holland, Hissy Moonen-Nagtagoal experienced both of us as horses. *"I am writing in my best English to explain to you what happened when you initiated me into Enochian Magic. When you came in front of me, there was a white light, and I felt a nice breeze. Then I saw the head of a white mustang come in front of your right shoulder. On my left shoulder, there was a white Arabian horse. The two horses put their noses together and breathed softly and then they whispered something that I could not catch. When you left to go on to the next person, the horses whinnied. Throughout the initiation, sometimes I saw the horses, other times we became the horses."*

The more Universal healing energy that a teacher is holding, initiating and teaching, the more Spirit demands from the teacher. Just before Einar arrived in Holland, I had had a class in which I initiated eleven or so Tera-Mai™ Seichem Masters into the second and third levels of Sakara, Sophi-El and Angeliclight. Six of these students had paid for and thought that they were going to do the first level of Cahokia the following day. Cahokia is the combined force of elemental rays used in healing and magic, and the initiations are very different from the elemental initiations. Quite literally, Spirit weaves the elemental initiations like yarn into brightly colored designs. Since these initiates hadn't even integrated the second initiation, let alone brought in the third, there was not enough yarn, so to speak, for weaving. I looked at the six individuals, apologized and told them that they were going to be given back their money. Immediately after I reinitiated Einar into Seichem so that he might heal through the 21-day cleansing cycle, I knew that if I had taken those people's money knowing at that time that I could not initiate them into Cahokia, Marcelle would not have seen the entity at the back of Einar's head and by my own actions, I would have left the door open for the entity to enter into my own solar plexus. A chill went through my body at the thought. When I told this to Jane and some other Dutch psychics, they received chills of confirmation as they listened to my words.

The elementary rays of healing must be firmly and accurately in place before the healing patters of Cahokia can be woven; otherwise it is like trying to weave a tapestry with only fragments of thread rather than balls of yarn. The fact that the full expression of the 4 elemental healing rays are in place is clearly demonstrated by the common occurrence of healing miracles that Spirit is able to facilitate through the healer. I have received feedback from individuals who have done Cahokia initiations. Level I - broad expansion of the aspects of healing. Level II – healing can be easily and dramatically focused at the cellular level. Level III – the ability to step back and objectively look at all sides of an issue without judgment. To see the big picture! To access, process and pull in the truth so that it can be expressed in a new way!

Cahokia is an expansion of the mind and an integration of left and right-brained thinking. Why is this important? It is not only how much healing energy an individual is channeling, but also the power of the mind that determines the quality and ease of the healing experience. The expansion of the mind creates a bigger playing field not only for the possibilities of healing but also in the expression of how one experiences life. An open mind is not demonstrated by vast quantities of factual information. Greed, fear or hate closes the mind because the individual involved will look at and process only that information which supports his or her belief system of greed, fear or hate. People with closed minds are so locked into their egos that they lack the ability to perceive changes coming. As a young boy, when Monty Roberts explained to his father his new idea for taming horses, it was so outside of and contrary to the father's belief system that the father took a length of metal chain and beat his son so badly that Monty had to be hospitalized.

Most students taking a class put aside their judgements and allow themselves to be open to new ideas or techniques. Students also have the responsibility to use their own intuition and inner knowing, whether they are in a class or lecture or reading a book. Teachers are responsible for what is being presented, as well as for their students, during the class. Teachers have the responsibility to teach the material as the agenda or promotional materials have described the class. If initiations are given in the class and they have been altered, it is the teacher's responsibility to tell his/her students. Both the students and the teacher are expected to use discrimination. Spirit is insistent that the second and third levels of Sakara, Sophi-El and Angeliclight and Cahokia be initiated and taught from a central school by qualified instructors only. It is only my responsibility to see that the school is established. Two of the people whom I would trust to teach the fire initiations both told me that they did not want the responsibility. They said that they were perfectly happy being able to use the energy. They were my confirmation from Spirit that I was doing as Spirit requested. I simply tell people who want to do the second and third levels that their primary motivation should be healing, not to make money from doing initiations. Even though I charge far less for these initiations than most people charge for Reiki Mastership, many people, upon hearing my words, are not interested. Other people are perfectly happy with the healings that they are doing at the level that they are at. If we do the work we love, the money will follow.

I was guided by Spirit to trademark Tera-Mai™ as a first step to the establishment of the school and to set standards for the initiations so that the empowerment would be kept pure. I have many wonderful students as well as wonderful students of my students who are doing an excellent job of initiating and teaching under the trademark Tera-Mai™. It is also beneficial for people who wish to receive Tera-Mai™ Reiki or Tea-Mai™ Seichem to know that they do not have to come to me to be initiated; they can trust another Tera-Mai™ master to give them the same energy transfer. Consistently, if I reinitiate one of my student's student one of two things will happen. If my student has changed the initiation, their student whom I am reinitiating will feel an increase in energy and facilitate more healing energy. If my student has kept the initiations according to the Tera-Mai™ standards, their student whom I am reinitiating will feel no difference – the healing energy is the same and the healings that are facilitated remain within the same range of possibilities.

If people want to personalize Universal initiations by changing them, then they would have to teach and initiate under their own name or establish their own trademark. Unfortunately, just because a professional has a college degree hanging on his/her office wall, it does not necessarily mean that s/he is ethical or well-versed in his/her subject matter; it follows that just because a metaphysical teacher has a Tera-Mai™ or other healing arts certificate in his/her resume, it does not necessarily mean that s/he is honest or holding the energy. No matter whom we are dealing with in whatever capacity, we are always expected to use discernment and check out the validity of their statements and in this case, ask to witness healing demonstrations. I ask people to do the same with me. I have no desire to become anybody's guru. I would prefer that people meditate on my words, see what works for them, and if they feel comfortable, use it. Just because something is in print does not necessarily mean that it is Truth. Just because even 95% of a book or a speaker is in Truth does not necessarily mean that that holds true for the other 5%. It is imperative that we stop depending upon other people or the church or government to do our thinking for us. In this manner, we all discover that the guru, Buddha or Christ is within us and we come to a place of peace. When we are at peace with ourselves, we are at peace with other people and the whole world as well. It is here that we can discover who we are and our own unique path. It is in this state of consciousness that we live in the moment and become co-creators with Mother-Father God. It is really just this simple; we are the ones who make it either difficult or easy. We are the ones who must create balance in our lives.

As the Earth's vibration is moving up, we are being offered the opportunity by the Absolute to work through karma and our issues very quickly. The fact that the Earth's vibration is moving up is measurable. In 1986 Hertz increased from a constant of 7.8 to 8.23 – one scientist recently measured it at 9. It is probably on its way to 12. + or 13. 13 is the next Fibonacci number after 8. The Fibonacci numbers are an unending mathematical sequence whereby each term is defined as the sum of its two predecessors. It is the Golden Mean by which painters can establish order in their paintings; it is the way in which nature reproduces itself. Russian and German scientists openly discuss this. This fact is observable in the rapid quantum leaps that are being made in the computer industry and also in the metaphysical knowledge that is being made available.

The other interesting phenomenon that is going on is that the electromagnetic energy of Earth now measures 0.4 – in the span of a few years, it has dropped from a constant of 4.0 and we are headed towards zero. In outer space when the astronauts are at zero electromagnetic, they are stripped of superficial thoughts and blockages. They are left with their true feelings and no excuses. The Kivas also have a low electromagnetic measurement. Shaman would go into the Kiva to be free of extraneous matters so s/he could connect with his/her true self and spiritual connection. As the electromagnetic energy of this planet goes down, each one of us is left exposed and without excuses – our true motives and our intentions in being connected to others and the groups we belong to is revealed.

There are at least two obvious and observable physical changes that are a result of the change in these two constants. First, our physical bodies are increasingly reflecting out inward thoughts and emotions. The Absolute is the Great Revealer as well as the Great Equalizer. Secondly, our so-called modern technology is based upon a constant Hertz of 7.8 and a constant 4.0 measurement of the electromagnetic field. As these readings change, our technology will likewise have to change; that is a given. We actually know how to run engines on hydrogen from water and the byproduct is oxygen. This and other technology will soon be made available to the masses. The politics of power motivated by the doctrines of greed through the influences of corruption are completely out of date. The evil that used to work on this planet is failing to produce the same results. The Great Equalizer is moving Earth into balance. The Golden Age of the Return of the Angels is at hand. These angels are the advanced races from other galaxies commonly referred to as the Galactic Confederation, not "the greys"! Millions of people have sited spaced ships including thousands here in Phoenix on a clear night in 1997.

Meditation

A Means of Creating Health & Developing Psychic Abilities

Meditation takes us to an altered state of consciousness whereby we are able to access greater creativity and knowledge, and receive impressions beyond the physical environment where our consciousness usually resides. These images, feelings, aromas, sounds and auditory messages can come from a wide range of sources: Our own higher self, our guides or guardian angel, psychics who are sending messages, or unconscious, earthbound spirits. In a normal state of consciousness, our brains receive information from these same sources. The clearer our brains, the clearer the information we receive. It is when we stop playing the same old, bad recordings in our heads and take the time to listen with our hearts that we become open to streams of awareness. Worrying manifests the very thing we fear because it is like a negative prayer moaning out into the ethers. Worries and fears bring into being our worst nightmares; love manifests our highest good.

It is like Deepak Chopra says; we are conscious of the thoughts in our heads, but we can never find the thinker behind those thoughts. So in that sense, we are all receivers. Our brains are both a computer, as well as a radio receiver. We do not take action on all of the thoughts that come into our conscious mind. We are expected to use discernment because some thoughts we pick up are inappropriate, incorrect, or belong to somebody else. Otherworld ideas can fall into the realm of inspiration which when acted upon, meaningfully change our lives forever. We use discrimination, then we question dogmas and in this state of consciousness, we are able to search out the Truth for ourselves. This is the Fool in the tarot, whose name belies his clarity of mind and willingness to seek out What Is.

Sometimes we go from the "I know nothing" state of consciousness to the other extreme, which is "I know it all". The middle road is to be willing to learn from others, yet, at the same time, not to simply 'buy into' what we read, hear and see. This is not easy! There are speakers and writers who will warn their listeners and readers about something specific and then turn around and promote that very thing. Politicians do this all the time!

The same holds true in an altered state of consciousness; that is, we need to question the validity of the psychic impressions that we receive. Mother-Father God has always given us the ability to know the Truth. All we have to do is to ask. When we see spirits or hear messages from other

299

dimensions, we can ask three times if the messenger and message is in Divine Truth, or has come in the name of Jesus, or has come in the name of any of the thousand-and-one names of Mother-Father God. It is important to check out messengers and messages from the beginning. If not checked out, each time an earthbound spirit comes through an individual, they can weave their strands of influence like cords on a marionette. At this point, saying, "If you have come in the name of my Lord Jesus Christ, stay, otherwise go!", simply is not going to work. Like the little girl who unconsciously played with a spirit through an Ouija board in The Exorcist, what is needed is an exorcism. The board was not the cause of her possession; the cause was not asking the intentions of the spirit who came through. When I use an Ouija board or table tip, I keep demanding from the spirit who has come in if they have come in the name of Jesus Christ. If I get conflicting answers or answers that do not make sense, I do clearings and demand for Divine Truth until I am absolutely certain that the spirit is of the Light.

There is a **major** difference between being consciously aware of other dimensions so as to be able to receive visual impressions and auditory messages from Holy Spirit, and possession. When an individual is possessed, earthbound spirits continually chatter and are in control. I know one woman who won't even open her own mail unless her guides tell her to. We all have a code of ethics by which we consciously make choices in our lives. In cases of possession, freewill choice is gone. Higher forces will always leave if asked and never impose their will.

I neither see nor hear spirits all of the time, and I would not want to. The idea is to be conscious and joyfully participating in our lives, and yet be able to receive information from our guides, angels and higher self so as to make our lives the best possible. When I hear spirit, it is between my temple bones. For example, when I called my friend, Nancy Moore, the last time I was in New York, she told me, "I have some bad news." Immediately, it was like a tape went into my right temple and I heard the words spoken inside my head, "Tybia is dead." Then Nancy continued by telling me how she had died. Most of the time, my angels, spirit guides and higher self communicate with me through my inner knowing. It is like a whole sentence, paragraph or chapter is dropped into the top of my head and I know the complete idea. For the most part, this is how I have written this book. When I see spirit, it is usually with both of my inner vision centers at the forehead and between the eyebrows. The forms I see using both centers of the third eye are typically more colorful and dimensional than that in physical reality. Holy Spirit has brought these visions to me as a warning or an indication that something important is in the offing. Sometimes, I see the astral body of the individual that I am working on in order to reveal the Truth of What Is to me. For example, I was shown the astral body of my attorney, Ralph, who played a role in the first chapter of this book. The look on his face was sneaky and his astral body had a slimy appearance that is difficult to put into words. If there are wonders and signs, this was a sign something was not right.

Meditation helps to reduce stress, release negative thought forms and bring us to self-realization (our own life's plan which we helped to design before we were born). The greatest prayer we can ask for ourselves is to be self-realized. Meditation also opens our psychic centers. The skill behind meditation is to focus within and quiet the logical left brain so that the creative right brain can get through to our conscious minds. The point of focus can be anywhere within - at the third eye, behind the physical eyes, the heart, etc. The focus of attention can shift during meditation, and this can be done by suggestion. For example, the meditator can concentrate on a place in nature and may see him/herself there. The awareness of this space is then felt within. The awareness of this space is then felt without. The meditator feels him/herself infused with the space; that is, the meditator becomes the space. The meditator then witnesses him/herself infusing with the space. The awareness of the space can be felt within the heart. There are times in meditation and especially in journeywork when the individual can suddenly experience any one of these sensations. The meditator or the shaman who is journeying into other dimensions of thought is able to come out of this state of consciousness at any time. However, rather than immediately coming back to consciousness, the shaman views this as an opportunity to explore realms that lie beyond the veil of consciousness and to bring about positive transformation, which could also be called magic.

Yoga postures are of benefit to the spine by strengthening it and making it more flexible. A flexible, strong spine helps to keep us young. For example, horses who are trained to work off of their hind legs develop a strong spine and back, and are healthier and younger looking in their teens than their swaybacked horse friends who were not trained to work on the bit. Yoga postures also prepare the individual for meditation. The idea is to focus without overdoing; for example, an ice skater who overconcentrates will 'pop the jump'; a successful performance is one where the athlete allows his/her body to do what it was trained to do. A meditator, who tries to force his/her third eye to see or attempts to force future events to their will, will close their third eye. The best use of the third eye is to visualize oneself or ask the angels questions and watch to see what happens. Modern medicine uses meditation in the form of biofeedback machines, hypnosis as opposed to anesthetics in operations and past life regressions.

The insights and creative ideas gained in meditation and journeywork can expand our daily lives and remove us from limiting thoughts, but only if we take what we learn and put it into practical application. I personally believe that the problems that India faces today are the results of too many years spent on too much concentration on the Otherworlds and not enough rigorous, passionate living. It is up to mankind to manifest both the potential and the enlightenment of the Otherworlds on Earth. *"Insofar as the mystic chooses to talk about his experience • • • he has to follow the rules governing the domain of the ordinary, that is, he has to be reasonable, logical and clear."* David Bohm

I am including the script for my meditation tape, Journey to Sacred Mountain, which you are free to record for your own personal use. You will want to pause frequently, slow your speech and allow the spiritual quality of your voice to come through. It would also be advisable to tape your voice in a quite place to avoid outside noises. You will notice the short sentences and fragments of sentences, which are intentional. The idea is to quiet the left brain, not give it complex sentences with which to ponder. My meditation tapes are also available through your favorite bookstore or there is an order form in the back of this book; people often find that the vibration of my voice carries healing energy. In Shaman's Drumbeat the quality of the overtone did come through when I was beating the drum. Journey to Sacred Mountain works with many aspects of the spiritual world and ends with the meditator circulating Qi, prana or energy through his/her own spiritual channels. When we open our channels and release our blockages on a deep level of consciousness, the physical, mental and emotional have to follow. It is impossible to heal the spiritual without some kind of physical manifestation - a fundamental law of the universe is as above, so below. Granted, there are individuals who might still be working out karma with physical challenges, but it cannot hold true for everyone who comes for a healing. Healing is a reality!

Journey to Sacred Mountain
Kathleen Milner
Copyright © 1990 & 1996

Close your eyes. Relax your body. Allow all of the tension to drain from you, out your fingertips and through the soles of your feet. Take in a deep, healing breath and exhale the stress of the day. Watch your breath. Watch your breath as it slows. With every breath that you take, breathe in light and exhale darkness, breathe in love and exhale anger, breathe in joy and exhale sorrow. With every breath that you take, with every beat of your heart, you go deeper and deeper, deeper and deeper within. Feel yourself immersed in a pond of white, watery light. The light supports, heals and protects you. As thoughts come in, see them bubble up and out like so many champagne bubbles. Be the magic of the moment. Be the breath.

I stand in the timeless darkness between two worlds. I feel the energy of Creation all around me. I hold open the doorway and invite higher forces to come in to assist with healing and ceremony.

I call upon the Tibetan Masters. I call on all who have been Reiki before me and who will come after me - Dr. Usui, Takata. I invoke and call forth the core and the essence of Healing Elemental Universal Rays. I call upon the Lords of Light and the Ascended Masters. I call forth and invoke the great archangels - Michael, Gabriel, Uriel, Raphael, Metatron, Melchizedek, Mytraya, Jophiel, Zadkiel, Chamuel, Kamuel, Ashma the Transformed. I call upon the blessed angels, the celestial beings of love, light, joy, radiance, peace, healing, illumination, abundance. I call forth the Great White Brotherhood from the Great White Lodge - Jesus, Moses, Mohammed, Wa-Bin-Gau-Won-Nong, Blue Star, Buddha, Thoth, Krishna, Sai Baba, Babaji, Senat Kumara, Serapis Bey, El Moray, Tamarasha, So Se Gung, Muktananda, Master Mary, Mary Magdalen of the Veil, the Black Madonna, White Buffalo Calf Woman, Quanyen, Locksheme, Kali, Amagee, Athena, Isis, Asatarte, Hagati, Demitra, Diana, Inarna.

I call upon the saints - Joseph, Jude, Christoper, Lucy - help us to see clearly; Theresa, Patrick, Shella, Bridget, David, Elijah, Martin - help us with our psychic development; Dorothy, Clare, Francis - bring in the power of the animals. And the lightworkers, Kathryn Cullman, Edgar Cayce, Thomas Alva Edison, Einstein, Tesla, Mozart, Beethoven, Dr. Bach, Mendel, Jim Gore, Chief Black Hawk, Chief Sitting Bull, Eleanor Moore, Audrey Hepburn, Michael Landon, Anne Frank, Elizabeth Ann Seton, Jackie Kennedy, White Horse.

I call forth and invoke the elemental forces - Earth, Air, Fire, Water - gnomes, sylphs, salamanders and undines. I call upon the four directions and the four winds - dazzling wind of the East - bring energies of fire; fiery wind of the South - bring energies of water; buoyant wind of the West - bring energies of earth; and blustery wind of the North - bring energies of air. I call forth and invoke powers of Mother Earth herself - her great lapis blue heart, her fiery core, her great mountains and her deep, blue oceans. I summon the power of the sun and the moon and the planets, the Great Star Nation and the Galactic Confederation - Sonanda, Hilarian.

Omatochawasi, all my relations, I call upon stone people, mineral, quartz, crystal and gem kingdoms. Plant kingdom and blessed herbs. I summon the winged - eagle - help us to create heaven on earth; hawk - bring messages from Holy Spirit; raven, crow, hummingbird, swan, pheasant, grouse, loon, owl, wren, robin, sparrow, Quetzal, Cockatoo. I invoke four-legged - horse, antelope, bear, buffalo, beaver, otter, lynx, mountain lion, white tiger, elephant, snow leopard, wolf, dog, fox, coyote, jaguar, ram - bring your striking force. And six-legged -

grasshopper, cricket, dragonfly, butterfly, scarab - bring transformation, honeybee - bring the sweetness of life. Eight-legged - spider. I call forth the finned creatures - whale, dolphin - help us to communicate on higher levels. Shark - clean up the garbage we have created. And creepers and crawlers - dreamtime of lizard, magical healing qualities of snake, turtle, who honors Mother Earth and the creative source within us all, and the protection and regeneration of salamander. Crocodile - bite through the cords and chains and ties that bind and constrict us. Ingest them and transmute them in your solar plexus. I cry out to Great Spirit, Great Mystery, "Aid me in my journey." All whom I have summoned who wish to be here to participate in this ceremony, please be here and present now!

See yourself in your mind's eye standing upon your Good Red Road, which is your path of life. Look around you. What does the foliage look like? Smell. Take a leaf in your hand. What is the texture like? Inhale deeply and smell its fragrance. • • • Are there animals or birds about? Look up. What is the color of the sky?

Take your attention to the bottom of your feet. Grip the earth between your toes. Allow your heels to sink deeply into the earth. Even the sides of your feet are planted firmly on the ground. Take all of your attention to the soles of your feet. Be at your feet. Feel the particles of earth against your skin. • • • Now slip into the earth and spiral down counterclockwise. Deeply, deeply, down, down, down • • • until you come to the great lapis blue heart of Mother Earth. Every time her heart beats, she utters an Om of thanks and gratitude to All There Is. • • • She invites you to lie upon this great heart of hers. The vibrations of color blue and sound of Om and the slow movement heals and connects you to the earth. Be with the heart of Mother Earth.

Come back into your body. As you do so, bring back a blue ray from Mother Earth. Move this creative, nurturing energy in through the soles of your feet and up into the root chakra. Feel blue energy from Mother Earth's own heart healing your emotional, mental, physical and other spiritual bodies. • • • Feel this energy activate your right brain and the left side of your body. • • • Now take the energy of Mother Earth to the center of your being, at a place between your navel and the small of the back, and allow the energies of Mother Earth to spiral and mingle there.

Now take your entire consciousness to the top of your head at your crown chakra. Feel a slight breeze blowing through your hair. Take your whole attention to the top of your head. Be totally at the top of your head. Now step up and out, above your head. Spiral upwards clockwise. Up, up, up, further and further up and out. Be at one with All There Is.

As you come into your body, bring blue, red and purple back with you from Father Sky. Breathe in the energies of teacher, consoler, warrior that protects all you have created. Feel this energy healing the physical and on through the subtle bodies. ••• Feel this energy activate your left brain and the right side of your body. ••• Now take the energy of Father Sky to the center of your being, at a place between your navel and the small of the back, and allow the energies of Father Sky and Mother Earth to spiral and mingle.

Pause for a moment. Be aware. Feel your connections to both heaven and earth. Feel that you are perfectly balanced between right and left sides of your body; balanced between left and right sides of your brain. Feel the integration of your brain - the ability to think intuitively and logically at the same time. Open fully to both your feminine and masculine aspects. As you do so, you are becoming a fully integrated personality. ••• Now, look around! How has your Good Red Road changed? How is it the same? ••• Begin walking on this road of yours. Feel your legs carrying you forwards from your hips. Feel your feet touching the ground. Walk on and on, on and on. Take in a healing breath. Breathe in love and joy. Exhale stress and worries. ••• Off the side of the road you see the Waters of Life. You may stop and refresh yourself. Go in if you so wish. Feel the water washing through your emotional bodies. Feel and release any negative emotional patterns. Feel the persistence of the water. Be in the Universal Flow of Love, Joy, Peace and Abundance.

Take one last drink of the Waters of Life before you leave. Walk back onto your Good Red Road. How has it changed? ••• Begin walking forwards. As you walk, be aware. ••• walk on and on, on and on. On your journey, you meet one of Mother Earth's creatures. Is it a 4-legged, 6-legged, 8-legged, winged, finned or creeper or crawler? Ask, "What is your name?" ••• Ask, "What is the animal medicine you wish to share with me?" ••• Ask any other questions you so wish.

Look around. Be aware. What does your Good Red Road look like? Inhale and smell. Touch something near to you. Begin walking. Feel your legs carrying you forwards from your hips. Feel your feet touching the ground as you walk. Your journey has brought you to Sacred Mountain, the place within you where you are connected to both your higher self and to Great Spirit, Great Mystery. Start up the side of the mountain. ••• The way is much easier, easier that you ever thought it would be

When you reach the top of the mountain, you find a great medicine wheel. Feel the energy of the stones. Step into the wheel. Face the South. This is the place of innocence, the place of unconditional Love and Trust. Breathe in energies of the South. Feel the Love from the great beings all around you. Feel your heart opening like a beautiful red tulip to the sun. Allow Love to pour into and compassion to flow from you. At this moment, feel and release any unforgiveness towards yourself and others. • • • From your heart chakra, connect upwards through the vertical energy line that runs through you. Up through the throat, through the head, out through the crown chakra. Up to the soul star, a chakra about 6 inches above your head, and up to the soul. Draw in the abundant Universal flow of Love and Joy into the soul. • • • Move this energy down to the soul star, to the crown chakra, and down through the head and throat to the heart. Feel compassion welling up in your heart. • • • Center at your heart and feel your connection to Great Spirit, Great Mystery. • • • Messages you can trust come down the vertical energy line and into your heart.

Now take the energy of the South to the center of your being at a place between your navel and the small of your back! Allow energies of the South to mingle and spiral with energies of Father Sky and Mother Earth.

Turn and face the West. This is the place of grounding, abundance, introspection and prayer. Breathe in energies of the West. • • • Feel energies of prosperity all around you. Breathe it into the consciousness of all of the cells in your body. Breathe out any thoughts of lack or limitation. This is an abundant universe. We are all the beloved children of a Father-Mother God that loves us dearly. Our God wishes abundance in all its wondrous forms for each and every one of us. Inhale deeply, breathing in prosperity and joy. Become conscious of your ability to draw abundance into you, • • • and of abundance flowing from you. • • • Now look within and ask, "What is my will? What is my destiny?" • • • Send a heartfelt prayer to God asking that your destiny be fulfilled. • • • Behind your solar plexus is your will center. Be at your solar plexus. Take your entire consciousness to your will center. Now connect to the vertical energy line behind your solar plexus - your higher self knows where it is. • • • Now move upwards through your vertical energy line. Move up to the third eye. You have a second will center behind your third eye. Connect to this center. Move up through the top of the head to the soul star - which is about 6 inches above your head. Move up to your soul. Connect with your soul's purpose and will for this lifetime. Bring your soul's purpose and intention down your vertical energy line and into your consciousness. • • • Ground your soul's intention in the will center behind your third eye. Move your soul's intention down to the will center behind your solar plexus and ground the energy. Move your soul's purpose down through the vertical energy line, out the root chakra and into the earth. Firmly ground your soul's purpose. Be self-realized.

Now take the energy of the West to the center of your being at a place between your navel and the small of your back and allow energies of the West to spiral and mingle with energies of the South, Father Sky and Mother Earth.

Now face the North. This is the place of wisdom and this is the place of gratitude. Breathe energies of the North into you. Feel a sunshine yellow light washing through your mental body and your brain. At this moment, release any judgements on yourself or others. Simply let them go.

If you are playing any old, worn-out negative programs and attitudes about yourself, breathe them away. See them leaving like old, crinkled, bent audiotapes. • • • If you are playing any old, bad movies in your head, scenes from the past, breathe them away! See them leaving like old, dented movie reels. • • • If there are any thoughts that you have been told in this or any other lifetime that are outside of Universal Truth, breathe them away. It really is this easy. See them leaving like old, dusty library books. Feel the knowing of Universal Truth in every cell of your being. You are a cosmic human. • • • Now with a heartfelt prayer of gratitude to All There Is, give thanks for all you have been given. The strongest force in all this universe is that of love. Close on its heels is that of gratitude. When you remember to give thanks, you complete the cycle so that more can be given to you. • • • Now take the energies of the North to the center of your being at a place between your navel and the small of your back and allow the energies of the North to spiral and mingle with energies of the West, South, Father Sky and Mother Earth.

Turn and face the East. This is the golden door to spiritual awareness. Knock on the door. • • • The door opens. • • • Standing before you is a great golden angel of the Lord. • • • This angel has a gift for you. Take your gift from the angel. Remove the bow, the ribbon and the wrappings. Take off the lid and look inside. What has the angel given you? • • • Ask any questions that you so wish. • • • Thank the angel for your gift. Now take the energies of the East to the center of your being at a place between your navel and the small of your back and allow the energies of the East to spiral and mingle with the energies of the North, West, South, Father Sky and Mother Earth.

Feel this ball of energy that you have created. • • • Move this energy into your navel. Psychic debris can become entrapped there. Watch as your Chi ball or energy ball releases and transmutes any and all misqualified energy. Feel lifeforce energy flowing into you through your navel once again. • • • Now take your energy ball and move it into the small of your back, or the door of life. Again, be aware that your Chi ball easily breaks up and transforms entrapped psychic debris. Feel Universal energy flowing into you, supporting you. • • • Now take the energy ball and move it into the center of your spinal column, into the nerve bundles themselves. Move the energy ball down to the root chakra at the base of the spine. Again, feel the blockages to your own power broken up, transformed and released down to the central fire. Your root chakra is freed to spiral outwards and downwards in a clockwise direction. Color red of the root chakra becomes clear, beautiful shades of red. • • • Lapis blue energy from Mother Earth flows up easily into the root chakra. • • • Move the Chi ball of energy and the blue energy of Mother Earth up your spine, through the nerve bundles. Up to the door of life, to the back heart chakra, to the back throat chakra, and into the head. Look, there is a beautiful light show going on in your head. Feel a release at your crown.

At your crown, draw in more red and purple energy from Father Sky. • • • At your third eye, draw in golden energy from the Cosmic Star. Move gold, red, purple, blue and the Chi ball of energy down the front of you. Down to the front throat chakra, the front heart chakra, navel and root chakra. Feel a release at your root chakra.

At the root chakra, draw in more blue energy from Mother Earth. Move the energy into the sacrum or tailbone. The sacrum acts as a second heart, pumping energy into the spinal column. Move the blue, gold, red, purple and the Chi ball of energy up to the door of life, to the heart, to the neck and into the head. Feel a release at your crown.

At your crown, more red and purple from Father Sky comes in. More golden energy from the Cosmic Star comes into the third eye. And the energy moves down the front of you. Down to the throat, down to the heart, down to the navel and down to the root chakra. Feel a release at your root chakra.

At the root chakra draw in more blue energy from Mother Earth. The energy moves into the sacrum. The sacrum pumps the energy into the spinal column. Up to the door of life, to the heart, to the neck and into the head. Feel a release at your crown.

At your crown, draw in more red and purple energy from Father Sky. Draw in more golden energy from the Cosmic Star into your third eye. And the energy moves down the front of you and up the back of you. A continuous flow of energy connecting you to Great Spirit, Great Mystery. Energy flow moving up your spine and down the front of you. See yourself clearly in your mind's eye. In all parts of the circle within you there is Light. See, know that you are a part of the greater Circle of Life. Be in peace. Be in love. Be in joy. Be in harmony with All There Is. May Mother-Father God bless you and be with you always.

Tera-Mai™

It is my personal belief that we are given freewill choice so that we can learn our lessons within a certain framework, which we describe here on planet Earth as the third dimension. In our learning process, Mother-Father God is like the good schoolteacher or good government; that is, one who has only a few rules, but those rules are purposeful and designed with the intention that they are for the common good of all. We refer to God's rules as sacred law. I believe that the Reiki initiations retrieved by Dr. Usui fit into the definition of sacred law. Madam Takata was probably well intentioned *(aren't we all?)* when she decided to charge $10,000 for the Reiki Mastership initiation and alter the Reiki initiations. I know this to be true because I have reinitiated and spoken with Reiki Masters who are one step away from the source. For whatever their reasons, they share the Reiki initiations that they have received and are teaching.   I personally believe that Madam Takata's decision laid the foundation for the confusion in Reiki today. I also believe that, for whatever the reason, this did have a higher purpose.

It is my personal belief that the highly-evolved being who appeared initially as brown-skinned, dressed in orange, and wearing an Afro hairstyle had found the same Universal empowerment, Universal symbols and Universal knowledge that Dr. Usui had when he made his consciousness raising journey into the inner planes. I also believe that the Reiki lineage (showing Dr. Usui's name and the names of the other Reiki Masters who came before) that is given to Reiki Masters at the time of their initiation, is actually a legal contract. The initiations I give and teach have been expanded upon by what I believe to be higher spiritual forces. Thus, if my name appeared on a Reiki lineage, one would believe that the empowerment and knowledge of the three Reiki initiations that one was being given was the same as those that I describe in my videos, lectures and this book, <u>Reiki & Other Rays of Touch Healing</u>.

To aid individuals in their search for either another Reiki system or the one I describe herein, I have trademarked the name Tera-Mai™. Tera-Mai™ Reiki and Tera-Mai™ Seichem are used by teachers only when they have been initiated into Tera-Mai™ by a Tera-Mai™ master who is holding the energy, and are initiating individuals and teaching the initiations in a specific manner. Tera-Mai™ Reiki initiations are described on a video along with the Reiki class structure that I developed. Tera-Mai ™ is the name, which my angels and spirit guides call the golden elemental earth ray of healing energy. I believe that all elemental healing rays come from Source or Mother-Father God, and to give healing energy any human being's name is actually very limiting. Healing rays are Universal; for as a sign that this is Truth, Spirit reveals their knowledge to me in visions of old texts which are bound in crow feathers.

Guidance for Prospective Metaphysical Students

1. Ask to witness healing demonstrations by the teacher. Just because there is energy does not necessarily mean it can be used for healing.
2. Speak to former students and witness demonstrations.
3. Ask for a general description of what is covered in class. "How is this applicable in my life?" and "What can I expect after initiations?"
4. Read and then question. Are names of real people given that can be check and verified? If evidence has been found, ask, "Where has it been?" or "Why is it just coming to light now?" Claims and good stories should be backed by healing miracles.
5. Look beyond marketing and convenience to find right system and teacher for you.
6. Meditate and go within to find guidance. A good question is, "Would this be of benefit to me?"
7. Go with what feels right.

Tera-Mai™ Vision

Tera-Mai™ is a healing system with standardized initiations so as to insure the quality of the energy transfer, and are not intended to be mixed into a marketing program whereby many different Seichem and/or Reiki initiations are given. The reason being that it has been shown time and again that altering the Tera-Mai™ initiations or mixing the energy with other initiations halts the healing energies and the miracles stop. Sakara, Sophi-El Angeliclight and Cahocia as described in the above books, will be taught from a central school by qualified instructors only. Tera-Mai™ initiates are connected to healing rays emanating from Source which raises their vibration for their own healing and enlightenment as well as others and this planet.

Videos

<u>$35 each.</u> Available in PAL (European or Australian system) or VHS (U.S. and Canada). Check or money order in U.S. dollars payable to Kathleen Milner includes handling and postage via surface (not airmail). Your favorite retail store may order most of these videotapes for you at the same price.

Symbols in Healing, subtitled **Reiki II** . . . Review in August 1994 **Body Mind Spirit** magazine by Jane Kuhn: "In this video, Kathleen Milner draws and explains the symbols most people are given in Reiki II initiation and goes beyond to explore additional symbols that work to heal. The first symbols that Satya Sai Baba gave her for the purpose of releasing karma and past life issues is shown. Each symbol presented is for a different purpose and for healing a different part of the body. She encourages us to heal the past and create a beautiful life for ourselves in the present."

Healing Hands, subtitled **Reiki I** . . . Review in August 1994 **Body Mind Spirit** magazine by Jane Kuhn: "Kathleen Milner works from the knowledge that all healing comes from God/Goddess and that we are all capable of channeling, healing and experiencing self-healing. She demonstrates working with touch points on the body to get to the root cause behind pain and disease. Angels and spirit guides are actively engaged in the healing process. She encourages participation of the healees as they share what they are experiencing in their minds and bodies as the healing occurs. Visualization and problem-solving techniques that have been used by great scientists and inventors including Thomas Edison and Albert Einstein are discussed. <u>The video and the healing experience are quite impactful. I experienced them first-hand.</u>"

Healing Animals . . . Native Americans say that the white man has only 3 directions; that is, sunrise, high noon and sunset. "Modern man" has also lost the knowledge of the power of animal medicine. Only by opening the heart to God's creatures and healing the wounds can mankind reconnect to the gifts that the animals bring. All animals (not just monkeys), be they 4-legged or winged, have the same bones and muscles that humans have; shortened or lengthened, combined or at a different angle. This video uses horses, a dog and the author to demonstrate some comparative anatomy, corresponding healing touch points and other healing techniques, dowsing and moving color through the chakras, the effects of initiations on the crown chakra, emergency technique and a short riding lesson.

Tera-Mai™ Reiki Mastership and **Tera-Mai™ Seichem Mastership** demonstrate clearly the standardized Tera-Mai™ initiations of Reiki, Seichem, YOD, Violet Flame and Order or Melchizedek. The video is available and useful to those individuals who have taken the class or those who have questions concerning the standardized initiations. $35 each.

Audio Tapes

$11 each Your favorite retail store may order most of these audio tapes for you at the same price.

Candle Meditation Meditator guided into the "gap" between thought and breath through spiritual techniques taught in ancient mystery schools. Some meditators can hear and experience the qualities of Angeliclight. Crystal Cave on side 2 is an inward journey to places of healing and self-empowerment.

Journey to Sacred Mountain Incorporates the 4 directions, 4 elements, and Mother-Father God into our own heart centers which is where sacred mountain lies. Ancient Symbology on side 2 works with Universal archetypal energies found within Egyptian hieroglyphs.

When the Angels Came Healing journey with angels to the vortexes and power places on Mother Earth. Passageways, music only by Richard Bennett on side 2.

Past Life Regression Begins with a healing meditation for the physical body and concludes with a healing for the past life that was experienced. Shaman's Journey on side 2 is a meditation with colors, symbols and the shaman's drum.

Atlantian Heart Chakra Meditation Group meditation using candles and combined consciousness to explore other realities and to bring back healing for the members of the group and for Mother Earth. From a meditation called Synergy that was channeled to William Buehler, a priest in the Church of Antioch. Atlantis, music by Paul Lincoln on side 2.

Prints of Illustrations by Kathleen Milner

Check or money order in U.S. dollars payable to Kathleen Milner includes handling and postage.

Babaji & Eight Ascension Symbols full-color, 8 1/2 X 11 inch print - $11
The symbols were given to me by Diane Schoolman and have a direct relationship to the seven major chakras and the new chakra (aquamarine in color) that is opening at the thymus. As we stood on the shores of Lake Superior looking out towards the Apostle Islands, Diane and I witnessed the ancient ones returning to Mother Earth. One higher being left me this message: The 11•11 is not two numbers. The 11•11 portrays two double beams of light on either side of an interdimensional doorway that is shaped like a diamond. Thus, the circle in the middle of the 11 ◊ 11 is a diamond. When these symbols are used in purity, that is, without other outside symbols, and combined with the geometry of a pyramid, they resonate to and awaken the ancient codings that were a reality within us before the fall, when mankind was cosmic human. This picture can be framed and hung on the wall, or laminated so that the meditator can touch the symbols with the fingers of the left hand and the pyramid with the fingers of the right hand.

La Voix - The Voice Reproduction of charcoal drawing of the head of the coming Christ. Individually signed, limited edition of 500, 21 X 30 inches - $150
In 1986 a psychic called me to say that she had received a message. Her angels had asked her to bring me a picture of the Shroud of Turin. She told me that it had something to do with my artwork. After she left, I sat down and started to sketch from the picture, but I felt like I was missing something. So, I sat down to meditate and held the picture next to my heart with my left hand. When I came out of meditation, I found that I could not move my left hand. Rather than panicking, I went to my easel and drew the image that came to me. When the archbishop of Milwaukee heard my story, he told me that he would like to have one of the prints.

Reiki & Other Rays of Touch Healing

November/December 1994 **The Inner Voice** by Nancy Rajala: "Cover art is a watercolor painted by the author. . . . A comprehensive manual on healing. The author gives concrete examples in both the use of symbols and a variety of healing techniques interwoven in her own healing process (following two automobile accidents) and her subsequent work on the inner planes with Sai Baba and other teachers. The book explains techniques that can be utilized to develop psychic abilities and how to achieve deeper levels of meditation, and then ties this in with the healing process and different mysticisms.

Kathleen offers her readers a fresh, meaningful understanding of the history of Reiki combined with Jesus' teachings and related aspects of other spiritualisms. There are chapters dealing with the use of healing energy in ceremonial work and Feng Shui, the Chinese art of altering life circumstances by altering one's environment. There's also a chapter devoted to healing animals, including a story of how a horse was healed of blindness in two weeks.

Kathleen believes that all healing energy comes from the Creative, Loving Force behind this universe, and the final chapter explains the dynamics of initiation into rays of healing. If you are a healer, or you're involved in a healing process, it is a source you may find yourself often referring to."

About the author

In 1988 after just finding a gallery in Chicago to represent her artwork, Kathleen Milner was involved in two car accidents, which left her career and her life at a standstill. When traditional medicine threw in the towel, Kathleen turned to alternative methods. Kathleen has been a speaker and workshop facilitator at natural health expos. She has taught people all over the world how to tune into their healing and psychic abilities. On October 28, 1993 she appeared on CBS's Connie Chung's **Eye to Eye** within a segment on angels doing actual healing work. **Reiki & Other Rays of Touch Healing**, Kathleen's first book, has been a popular selling book since the first printing in 1994.

On the opposite page is the pen & ink version of the watercolor/pen & ink cover of **Reiki & Other Rays of Touch Healing**.